"A Secret to Be Burried"

A Bur Oak Original

"A Secret to Be Burried"

THE DIARY AND LIFE OF EMILY HAWLEY GILLESPIE, 1858 – 1888

Judy Nolte Lensink

University of Iowa Press
Iowa City

University of Iowa Press, Iowa City 52242
Printed in the United States of America
First edition, 1989

Design by Sandra Strother Hudson
Typesetting by G&S Typesetters, Austin, Texas
Printing and binding by Edwards Brothers, Ann Arbor, Michigan

Library of Congress Cataloging-in-Publication Data

Gillespie, Emily Hawley, 1838–1888.
   A secret to be burried: the diary and life of Emily Hawley
Gillespie, 1858–1888 / by Judy Nolte Lensink.—1st ed.
      p.   cm.—(A Bur oak original)
   Bibliography: p.
   Includes index.
   ISBN 0-87745-229-6, ISBN 0-87745-237-7 (pbk.)
      1. Country life—Iowa—History—19th century.   2. Iowa—
Social life and customs.   3. Gillespie, Emily Hawley, 1838–
1888—Diaries.   4. Iowa—Biography.   5. Women—Iowa—
History—19th century.   I. Lensink, Judy Nolte, 1948–
II. Title.   III. Series.
F621.G48   1989   88-38514
977.7'02'0924—dc19   CIP

*Overleaf: Portraits of James and Emily Gillespie taken on their second
anniversary, September 1864.*

Contents

Acknowledgments

I wish to thank Joyce Giaquinta, past manuscripts librarian at the Iowa State Historical Society, for first showing me the Gillespie diary. The late David Kinnett of the society continued to care for the Gillespie Papers and was invaluable in gaining permission from the Iowa State Historical Society for use of the diary in this study. Mary Bennett in Manuscripts continues the legacy of cooperation and enthusiasm for research into the Gillespie diary. Assistance in historical research about Michigan came from LeRoy Barnett, reference archivist at the Michigan Historical Division, East Lansing, and Bernard A. Margolis of the Monroe County Library System.

Much thanks goes to Linda K. Kerber, Robert A. McCown, and Albert E. Stone, members of my University of Iowa thesis committee.

Special thanks to Wilma and Elmer Kehrli of Manchester, Iowa, who kindly took in a young scholar asking about the Gillespie family. George Goldsmith and Jean Hughes of Tucson tirelessly proofread the diary transcript with me. Friends and colleagues who have supported me in this long endeavor deserve recognition: Karen Anderson, Tina Kirkham, Stephen C. Lensink, Trudy Mills, Margaret A. Neale, Gregory B. Northcraft, Malcolm J. Rohrbough, Stephen West, and Martha (Marrie) Williams.

This book is dedicated to my parents, Venice and Vernon Nolte, who were raised on Nebraska farms and left them for the city. But they made sure their children had long summer visits to Aunt Martha's farm, where a young girl learned to dream of the past.

Introduction:
The Diary as Living History

Ah; am writing in my memoranda, sitting in the same chair, in
the same room and place that I did one year ago. What strange
thoughts pass through my mind.

Emily Hawley, April 11, 1859

while I have done my regular routine of work & writing in my
Diary, am holding baby. . . . he is not much help to me in
writing. but may he grow to be a kind man and worthy the name
which his father gave him.

Emily Gillespie, December 4, 1863

Tis now three o'clock and here I am writing once more in my
journal, the only confident I ever had, and *thou* dear journal,
dost not know *every* secret. Nay! Nay!!

Emily Gillespie, August 20, 1874

I was speaking . . . to James this evening—when he said in one
of his tones, which means he does not like to hear a word said,
"It seems to me your voice has a peculiar *whang* to night." I
asked him why? he did not reply. Dear old journal, none but you
greet me a welcome. . . . it is not very pleasant, to always keep
still & only listen.

Emily Gillespie, January 17, 1884

If we kill off the *sound* of our ancestors, the major portion of us,
all that is past, is history, is human being, is lost and we become
historically and spiritually thin, a mere shadow of who we were,
on the earth.

Alice Walker[1]

T he sound of nineteenth-century women, once thought lost to us, is alive because ordinary women like Emily Hawley Gillespie gave voice to their thoughts in their diaries. For years these books, intended for private use, lay buried in family storage places. At the turn of the century historian Henry Adams unwittingly lamented, "The woman who is known only through a man is known wrong, and excepting one or two . . . no woman has pictured herself. . . . and all this is pure loss to history, for the American woman of the nineteenth century was much better company than the American man."[2] The pictures that women created of themselves lay buried in their diaries. Now over a century later we are finally ready to appreciate them.[3] "Women's unpublished collections constitute gifts from the Fates," historian Carroll Smith-Rosenberg observes, "precious for having been preserved despite their very anonymity and supposed insignificance."[4]

The Victorian era has been called the apogee of diary writing. The rising rate of female literacy in the nineteenth century gave women access to this private form of expression. While seventeenth-century diarists had been primarily concerned with the "useful Exercise" of methodically tracing their daily relationship to God, by the mid-eighteenth century the emergence of secular self-consciousness meant some diarists were recording events they wanted to remember rather than those they needed to.[5] The combination of discipline and indulgence involved in daily self-examination could be appealing to nineteenth-century women: "Here I may review my feelings, mourn over my numerous imperfections. . . . Veiled from the world I vent my feelings on paper for I do find relief in recording the exercises of my mind," Sophronia Grout wrote in her 1823 journal.[6] Emily Hawley Gillespie fondly called her journal her "only confident."

Even the diaries of men enshrined in traditional history like John Quincy Adams and William Byrd tell us far more about personal life, with its myriad moods, occurrences, and interactions, than about the public events and achievements for which they are noted. Robert Fothergill read a multitude of British diaries and noted their effect on our conception of history:

One's sense of the substance of history is turned inside out. Where one habitually thought of "ordinary lives" forming a vast background to historical "events", now one's vision is of the great events dimly passing behind the immediate realities that comprise an individual's experience. In diary after diary events like the Old Pretender's rebellion in 1715, or the battle of Waterloo a century later, float by like rumours. Indeed, the very notion of an historical "event" becomes obscure and begins to seem like an abstraction, a fantasy. In the foreground is the individual consciousness, absolutely resisting the insistence of future historians that it should experience itself as peripheral. [7]

Ordinary women who would never have considered writing for the public record left volumes of journals that further challenge our perception of history. They provide authentic viewpoints that Joseph Wilder finds missing in traditional history: "The antinomy of life and thought, felt as a gap in our knowledge of ourselves and others, means that history is a conceptual reconstruction, never an intact resurrection of lived experience. History, then, is oriented toward impersonal, collective development, at the loss of the individual, affective climate of the experience being rethought. It is this orientation which allows the historical voice—the interpretation of the historian—to evade the plurality of perspectives which persists at the level of individuals." [8] Women's voices, no longer peripheral "secrets to be buried," challenge the dominant voice of the scholar and present female perspectives in texts that require innovative ways of reading and interdisciplinary methodology so that we may begin to rewrite history.

A long diary like the one Emily Hawley Gillespie kept for thirty years is an extensive and intensive life history which turns our sense of Victorian womanhood inside out. No longer a figure frozen in sepia portraits of the past, the diarist becomes a living being immersed in the now. Emily Gillespie felt the power within her journal, which she called "the history of my life," as she reread passages written a decade earlier: "have been writing off some more of my old Diary, it seems almost like living my life over again." Diaries contain both life and history, as James Boswell sensed when he wrote in his diary, "My wife, who does not like journalizing, said it was leaving myself embowelled to posterity—a good strong figure. But I think it is rather leaving myself embalmed. It is certainly preserving myself." [9]

If, as anthropologist Franz Boas argued, each person is the locus of culture, the crucible of interaction between the individual and social ideology, then the diary of an ordinary woman like Emily Hawley Gillespie, kept without literary or historical pretense, is an ideal ethnographical record. It provides the breadth of a thirty-year-long account (a "longitudinal study") with the depth of a single cultural informant's perspective. Her journal points "both outward to the world of recorded experience and inward to the reflective consciousness," maintaining in its immediacy the "tension between the individual text and social context" that Albert Stone finds in the best autobiographical writing.[10]

When anthropologists elicit a life history, they listen for the informant's interpretation as well as recall, knowing that interpretation changes the substance of a story. Boas questioned the empirical usefulness of such personal documents: "They are valuable rather as useful material for a study of the perversion of truth brought about by the play of memory with the past."[11] The liberties that the informant uses in telling a life history are the creative elements that interest literary critics of autobiography, and these will be addressed in the Conclusion. The diary form minimizes this play of memory upon experience because of its immediacy.

Diaries are not, however, direct records of real life. Each diarist has motives for undertaking her writing and is selective in creating the account of her days. These drives change over time and are often not explicit, although scholars have tried to classify them. Robert Fothergill, for example, categorizes diarists' rationales as profit (self-improvement), pleasure, egotism, compensation, and communication.[12] Nineteen-year-old Michigan farm girl Emily Hawley began her journal in 1858 without a statement of her intent:

March 29   Monday: Breakfast at 7. help Mother wash. at ten Mr. Barnum (the Presbyterian preacher) came along from Medina. I rode with him as far as the church then went on foot to Mr. Farsts, made Harriet a visit; after tea Cal Acker came there. I stayed with sister Edna at Charles Blanchards all night. Cyrus & Lowell Baldwin call to see their nephew (Orphas baby-boy).[13]

We know what she did on the day and whom she encountered, but not what she felt or thought. Only gradually did Emily Hawley, stimulated by experience, begin to write a commentary on the day's events and characters, letting her ego and voice emerge in her book.

Emily Hawley Gillespie set down her life story in her own words, without the prompting or influence of an ethnographer. But a century separates the diarist and her readers. We are faced with the difficult effort of trying to understand Gillespie across the gulfs created by both time and culture. From the onset of life history collection, anthropologists have been aware of the necessity to know the subject in context and to avoid as much as possible the ethnographer's own world view.[14] While no scholar intervened between Emily Hawley Gillespie and her private book, there is no live interaction in which we can further question Gillespie on certain points, clarify issues, be corrected and informed by her. We are left with her journal, our self-conscious subjectivity, and a responsibility to understand Emily Hawley Gillespie within the now-lost world she describes.

What we earn from the effort is insight into how women themselves defined the contexts of their daily lives. Diaries document and confirm the findings of feminist scholarship in several disciplines. Women have what Smith-Rosenberg calls "sociological otherness."[15] Scholars working with a wide variety of diaries have noted the different worlds of women and men. John Faragher's content analysis of 169 overland trail diaries demonstrated that while two-thirds of the topics in journals were the same for both genders, one-third differed. Women wrote about their families, their homes, and other women, while men's distinctive focus was on violence, aggressive feelings, and competition.[16] Faragher's findings are similar to Robert Fothergill's conclusions from reading English diaries: ordinary women showed less "self-assertion and ego" than their male contemporaries in the nineteenth century.[17] My study of a small sample of midwestern diaries showed that men perceived of themselves as individuals, while women wrote about themselves *and* their families.[18] Lillian Schlissel's methodical analysis of women's diaries in the context of life stage shows differences between the worlds of young and older women. Future comparative studies of women in various ethnic groups and classes will no doubt further illuminate the diversity among women's perceptions.[19]

An overall contextual pattern emerges from private journals and life histories that defines women's perceptions of their world. In a review of life histories Susan Geiger concludes, "Regardless of differences in culture, class, race, ethnicity, or religion, women seem to share a condition of familial 'embeddedness' that is central to the way we, as women, experience and construct the social world."[20] Emily Hawley Gillespie indeed most often defined herself within family relationships as a daughter, wife, and mother. In 600 B.C. Confucius noted that woman's status was derived from her affiliation with a triad of men (her father, her husband, and, finally, her son), and Gillespie's language acknowledges this power of men in her life; she writes about her father's house, her husband's farm. Instructed by feminist history, we also study her relationships with women, for Gillespie was deeply attached to her mother and her daughter, and thus we find the emotionally rich context that informed her life and diary.

We can begin to understand Emily Gillespie because for the past two decades women's historians have suggested a variety of useful theoretical perspectives for studying women's experiences.[21] Very few women in American history fit into the political/military model of human existence. Women have inhabited a separate sphere, a concept that has characterized Western thought about sexual difference. Linda K. Kerber says, "Much of the history of relations between the sexes in modern times can be written in terms of a continuing struggle to maintain or redefine the boundaries of women's sphere." In a historiographical analysis, Kerber suggests this rhetorical concept of separate spheres has both aided historians studying women and confined the creativity of historical inquiry.[22]

Research into Victorian prescriptive literature in the 1960s, for example, found an ideology that promoted a "cult of True Womanhood" for correct female behavior in the private sphere of the home. This historical view generally assumed that ideology unilaterally acted upon women who internalized ideals that entrapped them in purity, piety, domesticity, and submissiveness. However, a second view into separate spheres that relied on women's private writings suggested that they were creative actors who helped define domestic roles to empower their lives. In *The Bonds of Womanhood*, Nancy F. Cott concluded, "The more historians have relied on women's personal documents the more positively they have evaluated woman's sphere." Diarists like Emily Gillespie defined themselves in a variety of ways—pure and unappreciated daughter, anxious young wife, moral guide of children—that reflected the multiplicity of their roles and the limitations of the notion of "a" woman's sphere. Kerber suggests, "The ideology of separate spheres could be both instrumental and prescriptive; it is this double character that has made it so difficult for historians to work with."[23]

Indeed, once feminist historians entered the private literature by women, they uncovered complex networks of support and emotion, a "female world of love and ritual." This research, pioneered by Carroll Smith-Rosenberg, focused on women's desire to be autonomous actors rather than on the embeddedness of their lives lived amidst families dominated by fathers, husbands, and male children. Marilyn Ferris Motz's recent study of Michigan women's correspondence shows both the functional role of the "female family" and the ongoing struggle and negotiation involved in maintaining such networks.[24]

The far more difficult and dynamic history of women we are now writing describes them in fuller context and includes their complex relationships with men. Questions of how much actual power women had within the domestic sphere, of the economic as well as emotional sources of woman's agency, have been central to the best recent women's history. Attention to women's personal documents enables us to now see the nineteenth century from the female actors' point of view. This history of gender interaction suggests "an ongoing struggle between women and men actors for control of the script, a struggle that ultimately transforms the play, the players— even the theater itself," Smith-Rosenberg notes.[25]

The script of Emily Hawley Gillespie's life is recorded in her diary and illuminates this dynamic of a woman enacting Victorian ideology while using, questioning, and stretching its boundaries. Gillespie was not a victim of this ideology, although she read conventional sentimental novels about the roles of the sexes. Nor was she a heroine who aggressively defended women's rights. (She could not even imagine getting the horse and wagon herself in order to attend a Susan B. Anthony lecture in town.) She was simply a woman who described her daily encounters with expectations that came not only from her family and community but from her own aspirations. We witness the ongoing internalization of cultural values that formed Emily Gillespie and women like her into dutiful daughters and diligent mothers of the nineteenth century who attended church, supported community organizations, raised their children, and were buried as "wife of." "Simply because they failed in resisting dominant social currents does not mean they lacked character or courage," historian Altina Waller writes in her study of Elizabeth Tilton. Waller was impressed by "the intense pressures that had to be exerted before Elizabeth Tilton, Eunice Beecher, and others like them were 'domesticated.' "[26] Gillespie's diary reflects these pressures.

The work of several feminist historians has provided models for telling this complex story of the tension between nineteenth-century ideals and the reality women faced.[27] A particularly rich theater in which gender ideology and dynamics are enacted is marriage. Barbara Sicherman notes, "The disparities between expectations and reality, between stereotypes and actual behavior, are often highlighted in the emotional context of marriage."[28] While intriguing work has been done on the strains facing notable nineteenth-century women with supportive husbands, the bold face of gender ideology is to be found in studying traditional marriages. In Emily Hawley Gillespie's case, the relative isolation of farm life in pioneer Iowa further magnified the importance of her husband as a working partner and put particular pressures on the marital roles of lover and companion. As we learn more about the experiences of individual women and form theories that account for historical moment, class, and ethnicity, we will be able to judge how typical the graphically depicted ruptures within the Gillespie family were.

It was this mixture of typicality and atypicality that first attracted me to Emily Hawley Gillespie and her diary. Gillespie shared many characteristics and experiences with her midwestern contemporaries, making her a sort of rural Everywoman. She came to Iowa from the old Northwest Territory, she married at age twenty-four (the high end of the acceptable average), and she bore three children. Gillespie was active in community and agricultural affairs and was concerned about moral reform issues that interested many women.

But other traits emerged from the Gillespie diary that distinguished her from her peers and hinted at her questioning nature. She had youthful aspirations to be a painter or writer and showed some artistic talent. She was a Universalist and liberal in her ideas about the individual's power and natural dignity before God. A close reading between the lines of the diary showed that her small family was not accidental. She read *Woodhull and Claflin's Weekly*, a radical women's rights journal. Yet like all people who wish to get along, Gillespie inwardly suffered for the gulf she saw between what should have been her ideal performances as daughter, mother, and wife and what was. Perhaps it was the memory of some misdeed—a deed so bad she could not even confess it to her private journal—that plagued her to the end: "I have written *many* things in my journal. but the worst is a secret to be burried when I shall cease to be."

This diary reveals the private thoughts of a woman who lived a "dual life," like Edna in Kate Chopin's *The Awakening*: "that outward existence which conforms, the inward life which questions."[29] Gillespie's diary is the result of a Faustian bargain she seems to have made for survival—she would try to conform if she could express her rebellious questions in her private journal. And as many a woman diarist learns, according to Thomas Mallon, "the cultivated inner life can be a much more powerful and dangerous weapon. . . . It may be in her diary that she discovers how to keep part of herself back, and to take revenge on those who have wounded what part of her has been exposed."[30] Thus Gillespie's book is both her reaction to her daily role as a woman and her subversive action of questioning the script. The task of constructing a readable one-volume edition of Emily Hawley Gillespie's lifework, of uncovering the sound of her voice, is my welcome responsibility.

The Text

Emily Hawley began her diary in 1858 at age nineteen and wrote in it until a month before her death in 1888. The ten volumes of her journal contain approximately 2,500 handwritten pages. They were given to the Iowa State Historical Society of Iowa City in 1952 by Gillespie's daughter, Sarah Gillespie Huftalen, along with several other boxes of family papers. Huftalen sent the diary to the archives to serve a "historical purpose" and to be a memorial to her mother: "She was a martyr to her two children. . . . God bless her dear memory; her life full and fleeting filled with toil and sacrifice."[31]

The diary volumes exist in three states of composition. The first five books (March 29, 1858, to January 3, 1874) are Huftalen's holograph copy of her mother's early journals. The original unbound foolscap versions were given to a nephew in Michigan and efforts to validate the accuracy of Huftalen's copies are continuing. The remainder of the diary is in Gillespie's hand. She noted at the start of volume 6 (1874) that she was copying it over in July 1887. Gillespie mentioned several times as early as 1860 that she was "copying over" her old diaries. This concern with writing a good copy in higher quality bound books is evidence of Gillespie's growing desire to create a more permanent record of her life. The last volume, covering the final three years of Gillespie's life, is probably an original diary, as its profuse marginalia and deteriorating handwriting indicate.

The ten volumes of Emily Hawley Gillespie's journal form a *serial auto-biography*, to use Robert Fothergill's term. In the final chapter of this study I argue that conscious and unconscious artistry has gone into the creation of this ordinary woman's extraordinary autobiography in diary form. For an intertextual study of how the earliest diaries were changed, if at all, when Emily Gillespie and Sarah Huftalen copied them over, a comparison with the original Michigan journal fragments would be invaluable, but this is beyond the scope of this study. Certain unflattering details and uninten-tional ironies in the copied diaries have convinced me that Gillespie and Huftalen were faithful to their task of copying the original books. So we must take Gillespie at her "last word" in the copied diary record as she wished to leave it.

Editing and Entering the Text

This edition of Emily Hawley Gillespie's diary represents approximately one-tenth of the manuscript document. I have divided the diary into three chronological sections following Gillespie's life cycle and self-perception: unmarried woman, wife and mother, Woman. In the short essays that introduce each section I describe external circumstances to provide the setting of Gillespie's life in order to give the reader an orienta-tion into the world she depicts in her diary. However, I have purposefully avoided "giving away" Gillespie's story by foreshadowing events, for her diary *is* itself and I have chosen not to recast it as history or biography. Nor have I undermined Gillespie's diary by adding contradictory information from other sources. The Conclusion of this study examines Gillespie's con-struction of her autobiographical narrative compared to external informa-tion about her life. As editor, then, I have tried to preserve the experiential narrative flow of the diary, with all its frustrations—sketchy characteriza-tions, repetition, unrelenting one-sidedness—and its startling immediacy. I have not interwoven texts as C. Vann Woodward did with Mary Chesnut's diary, nor have I reorganized the diary to provide a more readable design, as Daniel Aaron did with the seventeen million–word Arthur Inman text.[32] Conventional history and biography describe individual lives in more accessible retrospective narrative form. Diaries like Emily Gillespie's provide an organic insider's view of what it was like to be *living* in the nineteenth century.

The annotative endnotes I have included for each chapter of the diary are explanatory rather than interpretive, intended to describe a term or process no longer familiar to twentieth-century readers. Biographical endnotes about the people mentioned in Gillespie's diary are sketchy because as an "ordinary" person she mostly encountered other ordinary people who left few records about themselves. Their place in the taxonomy and geography of Gillespie's world has been explained where possible in my notes; their role in Gillespie's emotional world is described in her journal. Again, I have not foretold the fates of characters in the diary in the annotations. What remains, then, is an edited volume that reads like the original document in its essential dailiness—its lack of perspective, Gillespie's merciful lack of foreknowledge as she recorded the events that comprised her life.

In selecting passages from the Gillespie diary I have constructed a distilled version of her story, deciding which leitmotifs to follow and which to abridge. Gillespie was an excellent journalist who recorded agricultural processes and details of nineteenth-century material culture as well as her inner life. Given this rich document, other scholars could create a different version of Emily Gillespie's journal.

The focus of my study is the daily interaction between an individual woman and prescriptive gender ideology. Throughout the reading and editing process I have asked the following questions: What does Gillespie think she should be doing? How does this conform with what she indeed does? How does she reconcile prescription and performance? I have focused on the messages Gillespie received about being a woman in Victorian America and her interpretation of this gender script. Using a phenomenological perspective, I have tried to use Gillespie's 2,500-page movable description of social realities to discover the social essences of her life. With this goal in mind, I have made several topics in the eclectic diary my priorities. First, I have traced the development of Gillespie's personal definition of ideal womanhood through her opinions about what it meant to be a good woman. For example, young Emily Hawley's desire to remain pure conflicted with her romantic impulses and the inclinations of her suitors. What emerges in the diary through a variety of such encounters is a complex Emily Hawley Gillespie (or, more accurately, the persona Emily) who is a mixture of the woman she wanted herself to be and the woman whose real-life actions she depicts.

I have also included descriptions of gender ideology being acted out in the performance or definition of familial duties. In Gillespie's diary family is paramount and I have preserved her emphasis, for her definition of ideal womanhood was most often tied to her family. She desired to be a good daughter and sister, later a good wife, and then a good mother. But the ideal Family was affected by many factors that are recorded in the diary: economic stress, distance, and varying reciprocity by each family member in his or her role as parent, sibling, husband, or child. The narrative reflects the vicissitudes of gender relationships in courtship, love, marriage, sexuality, and parenting.

In her encounters with other women Emily Gillespie also defined appropriate womanly behavior. For example, in middle age Gillespie compared her daughter's character to that of other young women; by inverting her comments about their shortcomings we arrive at her ideas about what true womanhood should be. In Gillespie's comparison of her own actions to those of her peers, her ideas of what a woman of her stature should properly do reveal her class aspirations.

Emily Gillespie's conception of womanhood was also enacted on the more public stage. Her ideas about what role women should play on the family farm form a solid definition and rationale for the sexual division of labor. On the community level, Gillespie was involved in female-defined activities involving education and rural improvement such as the county fair. I have also preserved Gillespie's opinions on political issues, including those defined as woman's domain (equal suffrage, temperance, local education), for her ideas about the male realms of war and justice reflect her values of caring and mercy.

The various platforms upon which Gillespie built her personal/public definitions of womanhood are not separate "chapters" in the diary. Rather, they form an interrelated network, arising from daily events as diverse as attending a childbirth or signing a petition that both defined and helped to mold one woman's ideas about female behavior. It is in the organic context of personal reflection, interpersonal relations, and public activities that Emily Gillespie's definitions of womanhood evolved.

While gender ideology interests modern readers, the underpinning of Gillespie's life and diary is the never-ending round of daily routine, the "usual work" that is the major motif of the journal. Recurring patterns of familial, community, and seasonal work formed the framework of Gillespie's world each day, but for reasons of space I have underrepresented that portion of her diary given to describing the maintenance of daily life. In each life stage section I have included a complete one-month transcription of the diary as a sample of that matrix of routine and to show Gillespie's priorities in her diary on her own terms.

Brackets in the diary passages indicate the editor's explanation, while parentheses indicate the diarist's. The insertion [*sic*] is used to correct the spelling of proper names or to clarify an error in the diary. Otherwise, Emily Hawley Gillespie's spellings and usage are retained. Editorial ellipses within the diary entries have been indicated in two ways. If words within a sentence or additional sentences continue in the same thematic vein, I have marked them with spaced periods. If the material omitted deals with a different subject, I have indicated this with three asterisks. In this way the reader will be able to tell when the diarist goes on with a subject and when she moves to a different topic.

Emily Gillespie's terms, her usage and spelling, will at first sound a bit quaint to those of us out of touch with nineteenth-century voices. I have not standardized Gillespie's spelling or punctuation, for they reflect how she probably would have pronounced and paced her words, how she actually spoke. When one reads several nineteenth-century diaries of people without literary pretense, many of the same terms recur and we can begin to reconstruct the lexicon of ordinary speech. The Alice Walker quotation that opens this chapter was her explanation for why she chose to use black rural dialect in *The Color Purple*. Walker explained that capturing the sound of colloquial speech was her way of "finding Celie's voice." Women's voices in the nineteenth century were often considered inappropriate for the lectern, the pulpit, or the statehouse and so were buried in silence. But some women resorted to private books in which they preserved the sound of their unique language. This diary edition is my effort to recover one such voice.

The edited diary, with its introductory essays and annotations, attempts to know Emily Hawley Gillespie in the context of her world. The next step toward understanding her is to study her life in comparison to what recent historical scholarship tells us about other nineteenth-century women. In the analytical essays that follow each section I have created a dialogue between current historiography of Victorian women and the individual Gillespie text. I not only examine whether Gillespie's experiences agree with what we know about other women but test the basis of the theories themselves. As Susan Geiger concludes in her review essay, "The personal contextualization of women's lives found in life histories makes them invaluable for deepening cross-cultural comparisons, preventing generalizations, and evaluating theories about women's experience or women's oppression."[33]

For example, Emily Gillespie shows less emotional attachment to the female world than Carroll Smith-Rosenberg found in her ground-breaking 1975 study. In the essay that concludes Part III, I examine both Gillespie and the theory to identify a variety of factors that could account for this discrepancy. By examining many of the parameters of Gillespie's life against data and theories, we better understand not only the individual diarist but the diversity in nineteenth-century women's experiences. Gillespie was not passive in life, nor is she passively measured against feminist theory. The analytical essays form a dialectic between what we think we know and what Gillespie experienced in order to deepen our understanding of both the individual and of women's history. The goal of this methodology was eloquently stated in *Interpreting Life Histories*: "The result of dialectical questioning is that, while we never totally abandon our preunderstandings, we come to enlarge the meaning of the text, integrating it into the framework of our present but changed understanding."[34]

My "preunderstandings" of Emily Gillespie and her text have changed during the eight years of our relationship. Stimulated by my reading in recent women's history scholarship, I went to the Iowa State Historical Division in Iowa City in 1978 and asked if they had any original pioneer women's diaries. I sensed the emotional intensity in Emily Hawley Gillespie's diary but only had time to read the first four years of the text. When I taught a course called Pioneer Women in fall 1979 at the University of Iowa, I asked each of my students to read two years of the Gillespie diary and to prepare a material culture data sheet as well as an oral report. The evening class set aside for reconstructing the diary extended to over three hours as we excitedly pieced together Gillespie's story. Given the youthful enthusiasm of the students and their instructor, the romantic tone of other class readings such as *O Pioneers!*, and our feminist historical/cultural groundings, Emily Gillespie emerged that night as an Iowa heroine misunderstood by her family and community. Two students and I wrote an essay about Gillespie and her diary for the *Annals of Iowa*. In checking the quotations gathered by the class against the original document, I saw that many of Gillespie's laments, so appealing to modern women, arose from encounters too complex for our short study.[35] We were curious to learn the other side of the story and made a rather unsuccessful field trip to Manchester, Iowa, to look for second-generation informants. We were left only with Gillespie's word.

When I decided to study Emily Gillespie's diary for my doctoral research, I read the entire manuscript on microfilm and in those darkened sessions encountered a far more interactive story of relationships that challenged my bias—my "feminist fallacy," as biographer Bell Gale Chevigny calls it.[36] I had held a heroic, distorted view of Gillespie due to my engagement with feminist theory and my anger over past misuse of women. In purposefully avoiding the traditional academic method of distancing oneself from the "subject," I had formed a link of affinity with Emily Gillespie, seeing in her the sort of person I imagined I would have been a hundred years ago: solid midwesterner, outward conformist, subversive diarist.

My initial reaction to the less flattering story that came from reading the full diary was disappointment, for Gillespie's point of view was too coherent, "like a paranoid's delusion or a swindler's story."[37] Instead of simply unearthing a lost woman, I was faced with the task of understanding a real person who had doubts, frustrations, inconsistencies, and irksome habits like the rest of us. I had individually traveled the route of recent women's historiography, seeing Gillespie first as a lone victim of history, finally as a woman actively immersed in cloudy private and public relationships. This discovery of the story behind Gillespie's diary led to a deeper understanding of the artistry that went into creating her serial autobiography, the only surviving narrative of a troubled life.

After my initial disappointment, I engaged the complexities of Gillespie's life and diary and rediscovered an interesting woman. Gillespie was not an oppressed victim of a bad marriage or a flawless heroine, as I had once hoped. Nor was she simply a querulous and alienated woman, as I had feared. Rather, grounded in her own historical-cultural-personal moment, this diarist recorded the details of her life so religiously that we can now disinter the patterns that connect her with many women and that Gillespie herself, enmeshed within that life, probably could not understand.

I came to explore the wreck.
The words are purposes.
The words are maps.
I came to see the damage that was done
and the treasures that prevail.
. . . .
the thing I came for:
the wreck and not the story of the wreck
the thing itself and not the myth.[38]

PART ONE

"Untill the Right One": Emily Hawley, Unmarried Woman

Overleaf: Emily Elizabeth Hawley at twenty.

CHAPTER ONE

"A Home at Father's": 1858–1860

Emily Elizabeth Hawley was born in a log house located on the bank of Bean Creek in Lenawee County, south-central Michigan, on April 11, 1838. She was the oldest of four children born to Sarah Baker Hawley and Hial Newton Hawley. A genealogical chart appears at the end of this introduction.[1]

Her mother, Sarah Baker, had been brought to Michigan Territory in 1823 at age seven from western New York state by her parents, Jacob Baker and Emily Garlick Baker. The Garlick and Baker families arrived before the county was organized and were considered pioneer settlers of the area. Baker family folklore includes a tale about the Pottawatamie Indians, displaced by the settlers, who still returned annually to the area for some years to hunt. A friendly brave, jokingly encouraged by Sarah's father, once chased Sarah into the house, claiming that he wanted her for his bride.

Hial Newton Hawley, Emily's father, came to the same Medina Township area of Lenawee County from Victor, New York. Settlers were attracted to southern Michigan's rich farmlands, making this desirable area the most densely populated part of the state.[2]

In 1836 Sarah Baker married Hial Hawley on the day following her twentieth birthday. Sarah announced that as the eldest daughter in the Baker family of eleven children, she was tired of caring for babies and doing big washings. Twenty-six months later she gave birth to her first daughter, Emily. Sarah Hawley was later characterized by her granddaughter as having a "resonant voice" and smoking a little clay pipe "for the toothache."

The Hawley family claimed some status because on both sides they could trace their ancestry to seventeenth-century New Englanders and their kin had founded the "Baker Settlement" section of the township, but they had little material wealth. Hial Hawley may have been a partner in his father-

in-law's sawmill, and the family lived on a thirty-acre farm. Over half the
landowners in the county owned fifty acres of land or more. The 1860 census lists Hial Hawley's real estate value as $1,000, while most of the fami-
lies living in the vicinity or mentioned in his daughter's diary recorded
values two or three times greater.[3]

By the time Emily Hawley began her diary, both she and her younger
sister Edna had worked as hired girls, usually within the familial network
of the Garlick-Baker-Hawley households in the area. Emily had taught
school in 1855 and also sewed for hire. In the family history, her daughter
later wrote that Emily Hawley was forced to drop out of the local Oak Grove
Academy in 1859 "due to financial embarrassment."

GENEALOGY OF EMILY ELIZABETH HAWLEY

Jacob Baker-Emily Garlick   Thomas Hawley-Elizabeth Terry
            | |
    Sarah Baker (b. 1816)-Hial Newton Hawley (b. 1807)
                          |
              Emily (b. 1838)
              Edna (b. 1840)
              Henry (b. 1842)
              Harriet (b. 1845)

Diary—which may compose reminiscences of the life, from day to day, of

Miss. Emmie E. Hawley.
A.D. 1858
Medina. Lenawee County. Michigan.

APRIL 1858

11th.   Sunday. This I find to be my birthday. Arose this morning
               at six o'clock; set emptyings at 1/2 past six; sponged my
               bread at eight; had it baked by one; at ten Father was read-
               ing his Bible & Mother the newspaper. It is now two o'clock;
               it has been raining all the morning & is cold enough to
               snow. Mother says, "Here you are twenty years old & not
               married yet." "I think I feel as happy today as I should with
               a man and half a dozen children to bother me," I replied.
               Thus passes the first day of my twentieth year.

14th.   Wednesday: Went to Uncle Benjamin Osborns, make a head
               dress [ornament for the head or an arrangement of the hair]
               for Aunt Mary & sunbonnet for Frances.[4] Aunt let me have
               2-1/4 yds. of belt ribbon for it (.45)   rain.

18th.   Sunday: Pleasant only the wind blows, & is cold. Mrs. Cul-
               ver borrow some soda.[5] * * * Hiram Crane called awhile.
               Mother says he comes to see me.—too old.[6]

20th.   Tuesday: * * * Last Christmas & New Years I attended
               Cotillion parties at Canandaigua with Sylvenus Hamlin.[7]
               Lizzie [Hamlin] wants him pretty badly, she can have him if
               he will marry her. *I* do *not* want him for a companion, no! no!
               not but that I like him. I do *very* much as a *friend*, our dis-
               positions are too much alike & though they are Cousins she
               worships him. I do not nor any one else. I'm thankful. * * *

MAY 1858

Sun.
2.

I go with Father & Mother to a Spiritual meeting at Medina.[8] *not* very good. pleasant.

Wed.
5.

Help Mother & sow some flower seeds. Fanny [Brower] call awhile; she has great stories to tell about her beau.[9] Pleasant.

Fri.
7.

* * * Mother & I get dinner for 18 besides our own family. . . . Three years ago today I commenced teaching school for the first time; the wind blew, rained & snowed & was very cold. . . .

Sun.
9.

Edna & I walk out over the garden & fields; the weather is pleasant but I am sad; how hard it is to be poor. but let us be content & look forward to brighter days. I sit me down in my bedroom alone and find relief in tears. at home.

Wed.
12.

knit on collar & do the housework. write Libbie Hamlin a letter. Am all alone. * * * I am writing & meditating. I do hope Sylvanus (Hamlin) will marry his cousin Libbie (Hamlin) and *not* ask me for any company any more because I do not want to trifle with him; he is too dear a friend & *I* can not marry him. I do not love him as a wife *should* love a companion. tis pleasant to be at home alone.

Sat.
15.

I stay at home. sew &c. crochet as usual. This evening Fanny Brower, Edna & I go to singing school. * * *

Tues.
18.

Knit, sew & visit. . . . stop at Mrs. Simms to rest; stay to tea. While we were eating Fred came home; he asked me to wait until he did the chores & he would accompany me home—but I did not want him to go. so when he was out I came away: He said he wished to talk with me and ask me a question requiring a final answer of yes or no, That was enough. I too well know what he would say & desire not to trifle with the affections of any one. I can never be the wife of an intemperate man. No! no! never![10] pleasant.

Tues. 25.	knit, sew &c. Aunt Emily & Uncle Jonas Acker are at Uncles. I am going home with them. Well tis now evening, I am at Aunt Emilys.[11] All day rain.
Wed. 26	Cut and partly make a dress for Aunt. I do think her children are awful noisy; seems as though I never was. Rain.
Mon. 31.	Sew, knit and help Mother wash & do housework; am glad to be at home. * * *

JUNE 1858

Sat. 12.	Help Mother work. work on hairflowers all day.[12] Last evening went to the Literary Society; there were but few present. . . . I think it will be the last Society. We have had a general good time. rain! rain!! rain!!! all the time, rain.
Sat. 19.	Finish my dress; have sixteen yards of ruffling on it; put it on and go over to Mrs. Culvers & Mrs. Browers,—they said it was real nice (for me). rain, shower.
Sun. 20.	Have been writing; will put it away & get some strawberries for a short-cake. Well, I got two quarts. Uncle Harvey Baker is here; he is always on hand when there's something good to eat.[13] pleasant
Tues. 22.	Tuck my dress; am going to wear short dresses. Mother laughs & calls them Bloomers.[14] pleasant.
Fri. 25.	Help Mother. work on wreath. well, there is a [Literary] Society this evening; am just home; not many in atten-

dance. . . . I was chosen Editress & Augusta Stone assistant for next society to be held four weeks from this evening. a frost last night so Father planted over his corn today   pleasant.

JULY 1858

Thurs.
1st.

Finish Aunt's sewing, help grain in mahogany & maple, tis indeed beautiful work. came home this evening. pleasant.

Monday
5.

I helped Mother wash this forenoon. Mrs. Brower sent for me to go to Morenci with them.[15] after we got there they went to Mr. Mosiers (her bro.) to tea. I went too. — they promised to come home early but there was to be an Independence Ball at Mosiers so they must stay. I did not like to. however there seemed to be no other resort, so I made the best of it & enjoyed it very well. I danced a number of times with Granville Corbin (by the way he was the first one that ever asked me for my company & was accepted). we did not get home untill near daylight. pleasant.

Wed.
7.

* * * Uncle Horace Baker came for Edna to work for them; she was gone so I thought I would go, so I laid away my flowers & went.[16]

Sun.
11.

Aunt Ann wants me to wash. I shall *not*. I am no servant & she may do her own work. All day, rain.

Mon.
12.

Just after we had a barrel & tub full of dirty clothes soaked & water hot ready to wash, Uncle Jacob came & I went home (to Fathers) with him on horse back.[17] Uncle Horace paid me a part. I do not know what Ann will do nor do I care. I am indeed glad to get home. * * *

Mon.
19.

Franc [Brower] & I went whortleberrying; did not get many, so we filled our pails with leaves & cheated our Mammas with them. my tooth aches. pleas.

Wed.
21.

Crochet & sew * * * Horace Jones ask me to attend a party with him. I refuse him again,—tis at least the 20th. time. * * *

Sun.
25.

Go to Medina to Quarterly meeting; the church very much crowded,—many could not get in. Libbie Hamlin & I were among those out of doors,—we went in the cemetery & sat down neath a shade tree. We had been there only a short time when Sylvanus came & visited with us. Ah me, I verily know we can never forget the past. I almost dread to be near him; he seems to be lured away into thought. Also I wish him well for Lizzie loves him, pleasant.

Sat.
31.

* * *   How oft do I wonder where we
             At the end of another year may be.

AUGUST 1858

Sun.
1st.

Help Mother. crochet, & knit. yesterday Truman & Henry Colegrove brought Edna home,—four weeks hard work has given her $4.00   Alas! Alas!! Rain.

Fri.
6.

Father has his wheat threshed, 60 bushels. for $5.00. I help Mother do the work,—four to breakfast & four to dinner. * * *

Sun.
8.

read & write some. looks like rain all day. Hiram Crane call after tea. * * * If Hiram was not such an old bachelor; he is very kind however, & my folks all like him,—'twill do no good for him to come to see me though. Rain.

Wed.
11.

Went to Medina. . . . Royal Hamlin came for me to go to their house to stay a week,—what a nice Dapple gray horse & carriage. Roancy Gowing was there, too. I wished her much joy as Luther's [Hamlin] wife; for we had heard dame rumor say she was married. she blushed & I *believe* they are. Royal, Roancy, Luther, Sylvanus, Lizzie & I have a grand visit and I like their Father & mother as well. I have knit some. tis late we are just ready to retire. How bright & happy is youth. Rain

Sabbath
15.

Libbie & I arose at six, breakfast at seven. Venus went to Hudson. Libbie so loves him she [*sic*] that she really appears ill at ease & jealous if we even speak together; it makes it quite unpleasant & I avoid his company as much as possible,—think I will go home this evening. after the morning's work was done Libbie & I lie on the bed and read a story, "The Doomed Sisters." Libbie half & I remainder. After we had finished reading that delightful story; we lay there awhile and talked,—talked of Luther's marriage. I felt sorry for her,—she wept. 'Tis evening, I am at home, again, after tea Royal brought me. I kissed them all goodbye & we parted. It seems to me to meet no more, In friendships chain as in days of yore,—Not that we are not friends,—Ah no! but there is to be a change. Very Pleasant

Thurs.
26.

We (all but Father) attended a celebration at Canandaigua. Edna was not at home; it looked cloudy in the morning but cleared off & then everybody started,—one hundred teams passed through Medina. After the Oration was commenced & the tables were being filled with a most bountiful supply of nice things, it began to rain; the rain fell in torrents & such a time.—some did one thing & some another while many hungry ones took all they could conveniently get & ate, & finally all dispersed for home wet,—wet all we could be. Rain

Fri.
27.

Had to wash my clothes today on account of yesterday's drenching. went & mixed Mrs. Culver's bread,—she has the ague. Rain

Tues.
31.

Try experiments coloring [dyeing], have good luck. Mother spinning. Pleasant.

SEPTEMBER 1858

Frid.
3.

Edna has fever since yesterday is quite sick. I went to Mr. Negus' this morning for Brass kettle to color. in afternoon colored two run of cochineal & one of purple,—beautiful colors, then I went over to Mrs. Culvers & did her ironing.[18] . . . * * *

Satur.
4.

* * * Edna is very sick,—we got quite afraid,—oh has such sinking spells & sent Harriet for Mrs. Brower. Henry went to get Dr Chappell, he was gone, & Dr. Weed can not come until tomorrow, Mr. & Mrs. Brower will stay all night P.S. I went to Mrs. Converse & got some brandy. Warm.

Mon.
6.

Mother says if I will take care of Edna, she will do the work. knit some &c. The Doctor here this evening   Edna's fever went off this evening. * * *

Thurs.
16.

* * * A Mr. Thirsting was killed today while going up in a balloon, or rather was carried off in it. He was holding it for Banister to take to pieces to carry back to Adrian; they had just made an ascension and were about ten miles from where they started,—no one can tell where he is yet all know he must be dead. at home. Pleasant

Tues.
21.

I got Mr. Culver's horse & Edna & I went to Hudson; take my picture frame for Mr. Armstrong to grain.[19] I stayed there to dinner. . . . called in the shop to see Mr. Armstrong's paintings how beautiful they are,—he said he would teach me how & give me my board while learning if I would give him the first picture I painted. * * *

Fri.
24.

Albert [Hawley] took Lucina & me to Ottikee to be examined in our studies &c. all got [teaching] Certificates.[20] . . .

Tues.
28.

Knit, sew &c. am going to see how Aunt Mary is & stay all night. Cold.

Thurs,
30.

Roderick, Charley & Hattie Hill came for Edna & me to attend the fair. I take my [hair] flowers, tidy & collar, buy family ticket,—there is a nice show of things   we are to stay with Fanny Brower at Morenci tonight   Rainy

OCTOBER 1858

Friday
1.

Edna & I help Fanny do her work so she could go with us to the fair ground,—it is the last day. I rode in the swing with Lyman Kennedy a long time,—until I was disgusted with his *goodness*. I suppose he thinks riches wins the hand,—it may but not the heart. All our folks came to the fair today. I get the *first premium* on all my things. * * *

Sun.
3.

Am at home alone. * * * There comes Harvey Warn, tis bed time, our folks have all got home & Harvey has gone.[21] why is it? I ask myself that every young man one meets with must begin to talk of love & marriage the first thing, I often wonder if they talk to every girl they associate with,—surely I am not a beauty nor an heiress and what is more do not desire to have anything to do with matrimony, though Mother says, 'I will sometime take a broken stick,' yet as friends I respect most of my associates. Pleas.

Tues. 5.	Went to sew for Mrs. Culver. Mother sent for me, that Maria Dawes & Eola Dod wanted to learn to make hairflowers. I came home & learned them. * * *
Sun. 10.	Edna has been sick all the week, is worse so Father called in the Dr. Mr. Armstrong called to see my flowers & to see if I could go to New York with them to learn to be an artist; he will pay my expenses there & hire me to paint for him enough to pay him when we get there. O, I would like so much to go but Mother says so much against it I will stay at home yet awhile,—though am sure I will regret. Rain.
Mon. 11.	Have been sewing for Mrs. Culver all day, this evening Royal Hamlin came for me on horseback I rode home with him,—he asked me to attend Libbie's wedding with him. I promise to go although I would not if I had not told Sylvenus I would attend his wedding the last time I went with him. Yes, Old Journal, I promised if I could not marry him that I would not refuse to see him married to my dear friend Libbie providing he ever made up his mind to make her his wife & he has. Rain
Tuesd, 12.	Mother did the washing. I helped some & got ready to go to the wedding. Royal came after me about two P.M. in a splendid covered carriage. we had baked chicken for dinner. we went on a ride & did not arrive at Mr. Hamlins 'till near five,—they all came out to meet us, except Sylvenus,—such a pleasant meeting. Venus & Libbie took our horse & carriage & went on a short ride after we got there, when they came back Mr. Pack was there & all the guest had assembled. I went with Libbie to her room; helped her arrange her collar and put a wreath of flowers on her hair and she was ready. "Oh! Emmie," she said & began to cry. I said I was sorry to see her weep when she should rejoice but did not ask her why,—we both knew too well. Then I left her after bidding her a kind adieu: we were all arranged

around the room and Sylvenus led his trembling bride to the altar. After the usual ceremony Br. Pack pronounced them man & wife just half past six. —then as is the custom we all went to kiss & wish much joy etc, the newly married pair. indeed I was almost as sad as happy for all through the ceremony Venus stood as one spellbound & looked at me, Oh! if I only could have left the room but, no,—I must cheer them with the rest, then, too, he did not first kiss his bride, I hope she may never know his feelings when he took my hand and gave me his first kiss instead of her, not that I love him (for I think I can not love any one) but I respect them both and sympathize with his past devotion,—may all end well. We had such a splendid supper,—every thing that heart could wish; were all to take a ride but could not because it rained,—had to sleep with Lucinda [Hamlin] first night. Rain.

Monday
18.

Have been to Morenci to see about getting the school. came to stay with Lucina (Hawley) all night, Cold.

Sun,
24.

At Father's alone in my room writing, Book best company. * * *

NOVEMBER 1858

Fri,
5.

Am writing. Help mother & knit, she has been spinning all the week. I helped her dip three dozen candles. Rain.

Fri.
19.

* * * I commenced my woolen dress. I went to get what Mrs. Culver owes me on sewing. could not, only the promise of it. Pleas

Thurs.
25.

Sew & help Mother. Aunt Mary [Osborn] came here; she has not spoken loud in fourteen weeks. I gave her a teaspoon of

"*Chamberlains Relief*" & in about half an hour she talked aloud;—she was so pleased that she cried. * * *

DECEMBER 1858

Mon.
6.

Jerome [Hawley] brought cloth & soles for him & me some shoes if I would make his. I cut & partly made them today. pleasant.

Tues.
7.

Sew on shoes & knit. Edna & I went with Francis Brower to visit Ann Converse. Fanny [Brower] is getting ready to be married to George Randolph. I do not know, yet I think she will be sadly disappointed   Rain & mud.

Thurs.
9.

finish Jerome's gaiters. This afternoon & evening have been visiting at Mrs. Browers; they are in ecstasy about George & Fanny; indeed 'tis amusing to hear them talk. Ah! 'There's many a slip Twixt the cup & the lip.' Pleasant.

Frid.
24.

At Uncle Marcus' [Hawley] today.—help Lucina and Aunt get ready for the dance. knit some, Cold.

Sat.
25.

Christmas,—there were about thirty couple at Uncles last evening. * * * Mother and Harriet are at Mr. Browers.— they invite us all there this evening. Pleasant.

Sun.
26.

Read & write. John Culver call. Hiram Crane has been here this evening,—he still persists in coming,—what nice stories he tells,—how good he is going to be to his wife;—says the children shall always mind their ma. I am like the lady that told the preacher, "My children shall never be *yours*." Pleasant.

Fri.
31.

Well, Diary, my cold is much better. Edna & I are ready to go to the Ball at Maces [hotel] at Morenci. Mother says curls look real nice. Hiram Randolph is just coming after us with Black Ponies & covered carriage. Father is plowing, 'tis muddy. Warm.

JANUARY 1859.

Satur.
1.

We had a very pleasant time at the party, there were eighty-three couple; we stayed until after breakfast then went to Mowry's on a ride,—several carriages of us. After dinner we came home. Father & Mother did not like it because we stayed so long,—seven this evening—perhaps we did stay too late but I guess it will not hurt us. Edna says Hiram Randolph fell in love with me,—he is a fine young man but too young. Colder

Sun.
2.

At home; think I got more cold yesterday—am quite hoarse. * * *

Wed.
5.

knit on my stocking and do some of the housework. Harriet & Mother went to Uncle Bens. * * * Mother brought home four shirts to make   Cold

Fri.
7.

Finish one shirt & commence another. Snow.

Mon.
10.

Sew in forenoon, then Charley Blanchard called to warm. I went with him to Peg-town to take a sleighride   This evening Jacob [?] (Uncle) . . . asked us to attend his infair to be at Uncle Bens. Edna got my journal & wrote in it, "Remember that Edna is your friend forever." Cold.

Sat.
15.

knit & sew some. We had a very pleasant time at the party last evening, only my cold is so bad. I sometimes think I will never get well of a cough. Nelly Baldwin came home with me,—he is another young beau. I accept his company just because he is a good boy.[22] Sammy Bothwell Edna's escort. Pleasant

Thurs. 27.

Sew all day on waist,—this evening finds me sitting by the table writing. Mother is sewing; Henry reading; Edna & Harriet are ciphering. Father is at Uncle Harveys sawing logs,—it is half past six.—I wonder where we will all be one year from today. no one knoweth. Pleasant.

Sun. 30.

Have been at home all day. Hiram Randolph came here this afternoon,—tis now evening. eight o'clock,—am writing. Hiram wants me to attend a party on the 22nd, with him. Mother said so much against me going with him I told him I could not go though I was sorry already because he so wanted me to go that he wept, but Mother does not like me to go with him, only because he is *not* rich; hope I can do as I please sometime. Pleas, but Cold.

FEBRUARY 1859.

Sat. 19.

'Tis evening,—have sewed some & done the work. Harriet is real sick with scarlet fever. Mrs. Wiley's little girl died with it last night. Robert Sims brought Mother home,—they are most all sick with scarlet fever, too. * * *

MARCH 1859.

Sat. 5,

knit as usual &c. Mr. Thirsting (Ira) [the balloonist] was found today about ten miles from where he started, in Seneca.—his watch & papers were the only things by which to identify him, he was crushed almost to atoms. * * *

Tues. 8.

Help do housework &c. . . . . not hardly a day but we hear of a death. sometimes more. There were five funerals in

Morenci last Sunday. our time, too, approaches nearer every day. Pleasant.

Fri.
11.

Commence some embroidery. Harriet go with me to see if Mrs. Rosa wants some sewing done. She will let me know in two or three days. Rain.

Sun.
13.

Attend the funeral of Mrs. Wiley's little boy   Mr. Crabb preached the sermon, now all their children are dead. sad, sad. * * * when I got home, found Harvey Warn waiting for me. he stayed to tea; did not want his company in the evening,—so Harriet & I call on Mrs. Culver.

Would not leave Harvey so
But that he drinks & chews we know,
Two habits quite dispensable. * * *

Tues.
15.

This evening finds me writing in my memoranda   help Mother some &c. Tis now evening,—am at Mr. Rosas sewing.—he came for me this afternoon. * * *

Thurs.
17.

Sew all day,—like Mrs. Roosa very well.—their oldest boy, Waterman, is eighteen today—their other is Milford. Rain.

Fri.
18.

Sew all day again, Waterman taught me to play a tune (Lilly Dale) on his dulcimer. Oh! yes I must not fail to note that Hiram Crane called to see me Wednesday   he has about given up hopes of my being his wife. Well, he has wisely concluded,—he is too old—yet I respect him for he is a very kind man and as I think 'his love is mine' I hope he may do well to marry Mandy Wood as he says he must if not me, because he needs some one to help him on his farm, Why, oh why can I not have a friend   But that they want me for a wife

Thurs.
24.

Am at home, it is late. * * * Waterman [Roosa] came home with me. Mother did not like it,—she says he is poor. What harm is that! only accepted his company however, because he wanted to come & 'tis his first attempt to go in society. We are poor, too, financially. I would feel bad indeed if that made any difference. I think it is the person, not the purse. Well! well! Hiram is at last married to Miss Amanda, he being 41 years old & she is 33 years old. 8 years is not quite as much as 20 is! They share in my good wishes,— they were married last Sunday. Pleas.

Tues.
29!!!²³

Commence broidery. Am at Julias [Blanchard] today & night.²⁴ Unpleasant.

APRIL 1859.

Wed.
6.

Work some on broidery. Tis evening I am writing in my memoranda. Marshall [Blanchard] says, "write down how many times he has kissed me since I have been here." *not once.* Julia & I trade again.—I get a silk waist for a skirt & am to make her a small bouquet of hair flowers. I think I have best bargain. . . .

Sun.
10.

'Tis a rainy, lonesome day,—spend the time reading. Uncle Harvey call. Rain.

Mon,
11.

Help do housework & piece on quilt. Edna has gone to Julias. 'Tis evening of my twenty-first birthday; am now of age,—some say 'can do as you please.' Ah; am writing in my memoranda, sitting in the same chair, in the same room and place that I did one year ago. What strange thoughts pass through my mind,—wonder where I'll be a year hence,—perhaps not here; maybe dead. Away with sad reverie, all is well. I got Mrs. Wiley's horse to ride to Morenci   Fanny Brower & Mother have *had a time* giving me a birthday whipping. Pleasant.

Tues.
12.

To night am at Aunt Amandas [Hawley]; have rode near twenty miles. (Mrs. Beach let me take her sidesaddle).[25] have been to Mr. Ferris' to engage their school,—he will let me have it if they have any school. * * *

Sat.
23.

Carry map to Julia & piece some blocks,—she is to furnish calico & thread for two quilts if I piece one for her and one for self. at Julias to night. Pleasant

MAY 1859

Sun.
1.

'Tis near the wee sma hours. Ephraim French is Edna's beau, he came this morning. I went with them to take a walk 'tis a beautiful day. I am about to retire. Edna is entertaining her beau. I do not believe in sparking of nights. Pleasant.

Mon.
2.

We all wash; then Mother, Edna, Henry, Harriet and I build a shanty to cook in. I commence to make me a hat, got straw at Mr. Browers, sow flower seeds, too. Pleasant.

Fri.
13.

Am at Uncle Marks [Hawley] to night. . . . help Aunt Sarah some & knit tatting. Sarah Coddington & I went to Uncle Lewis' (Baker) store & were weighed: Sarah 113-1/2 lbs; self 124.—11 lbs less than a year ago. Uncle gave me a fan.[26] Pleas.

Sat.
21.

Sewed until five o'clock, then came home. Ah! me, this having to work everyway to earn an honest penny. Father let Uncle Garlick have his oxen today to apply $100.00 on place. * * *

Tues.
24.

Do not feel very well.—sew on quilt however, Mother finish braid for my hat, I have a big boil. Pleas.

JUNE 1859.

Tues.
21.

Sew for Julia in forenoon, in afternoon make overhauls for Delos Walker. Pleas.

Sat.
25.

Sew all day again; she [Julia Blanchard] let me have a lawn dress & a rode [*sic*] dress for sewing all the week. Pleas.

Mon.
27.

came home,—am to make 2 shirts, 1 frock & a pair of over-hauls for Walker, commence sewing on them today & help Mother. Pleas.

Wed.
29.

Sew all day on fine shirt. Dr Chappell called,—he is an excellent good man. I like him because he has saved me from the grave, and more because he loves me. yet I cannot return his love only in respect & pure friendship, Ah, yes he is too old for me and too, knows not but he may die any time from the effects of cutting his hand with a lance when he was dissecting a person.[27] 'tis evening now. may all end well at last. I must retire, so good night, Old Journal. Pleasant.

Thur.
30.!!!

Help Mother & sew. Hard is the lot of those who are poor. Yet let us be brave, as chaste and pure as a little child, kind Providence will give us all a resting place. Pleasant.

JULY 1859.

Mon.
4.

have spent the 4th. at home; bind dress; put pockets in two; trace broidery for handkerchief; finish coat for Henry & commence *illusion* bonnet for Harriet. Independence was declared July 4, 1776; George Washington was elected first President of the United States in 1789. Edna has gone with Walter Jones to Morenci to the dance I prefer to stay at home than go with Jones, Pleasant.

Sun,
10.

Tis evening, am at home. . . . Ah, me, I must not write here what Uncle Lewis said. no! no!! 'tis the first time ever insulting words, words that would lead from virtue, were spoken to me, and by an Uncle, too, and may it be the *last*. what did I tell him: that I [*sic*] rather die than not to be virtuous, and, indeed I would. Walker came after his clothes; he brought two for me to make for Marshal. Pleasant.

Sat.
23.

Help Mother &c. went to Mr. Dawes to get some wire; Maria let me have 42 cts. worth, guess tis all I get for teaching her to make flowers.[28] * * *

AUGUST 1859.

Tues.
2.

Sew on Harriet's dress. John Culver here to tea, he is sick   Dr. Chappell call & stay a couple of hours, tell stories, and we visit, was standing in the door sewing when he came & put his hand on my shoulder, "May I kiss you, Emmie, dear girl I have watched you since you were only a little child, and yet you will not let me claim you my own, but I will wait for I know you will sometime." I did not reply for I knew not what to say,   Ah, meditating thoughts. Pleas

Wed.
3.

Sew on dress; work in the garden about two hours this forenoon;—driving potato bugs off of beets. they are like an army; they travel like so many sheep. Rain.

Sat.
13.

Help Mother all day. picked about half a pint of berries,—all gone; we had 111 bu. of wheat. Harriet & I, after tea, went after Mrs. Beach's papers to read. this evening have been reading 'Rosamond'; here is a part of it: "Darling Rosamond, say that you love me; let me hear that assurance once & I shall be almost willing to die." and this is her very appropriate answer: "Ladies do not often confess an attach-

ment untill sure it is retained." Let *us* ourselves profit by
the above, and not believe we are loved by everyone that
may talk; let actions and doings speak as well as words.
Pleasant

Tues.
16.

* * * I went berrying,—got 3 qts. there are two Immediate
Relief peddlers here to stay all night.—Davis & Chappell
are their names. Pleas.

Wed.
17.

Sew all day. peddlers went away this morning   I sold them
my old watch for a cameo pin bought some needles &
wintergreen essence they left 12 bottles of the Relief. Pleas.

Wed.
31.

broider on skirt. visit school this afternoon   Mr. Hodge,
teacher, am to stay with Hattie Hill all night, they want me
to come to school, would really like to go & will if I can find
a place to board,   Pleasant.

SEPTEMBER 1859.

Thur.
1.

Have made up my mind to attend school the remainder of
this term; am to board with Mrs. Thompson; she said she
would not ask anything only to bring provisions; that my
company would pay for trouble.[29] Broider some. came home
to night . . . my folks had got a letter for me; it was from
James Chappell (the peddler.) he acknowledges 'love at first
sight etc.' Mother says 'tis great for a stranger to write, and
he can't be much, though he be a stranger I shall answer
his letter; 'twill but be doing as one would be done by.
Pleasant

Mon.
5.

Mother did the washing. I help do the work & get ready to
go to school. . . . am to study Algebra viz. Ray's 2nd. part;
higher Arithmetic; physiology, Grammar, reading, write &
spell, pleasant.

Wed. 7,	have been to school today. this evening Ella (Mrs. Thompson's girl) & I attend temperance meeting. Lessons well learned. Pleasant.
Thur. 8.	Good lessons today.—help Elmira some do her work. * * * last night after I had retired Philip Stair came for me to sit up with him to watch with corpse (Mrs. Godfreys) little girl. Dr. Stocum & Hester Ann Jones were there, too. Pleasant.
Mon. 12.	knit some & visit. * * * Mrs. Thompson has gone away to stay a week, so Ella & I are to stay alone, we have been to the shows this evening, 'twas beautiful indeed,—done with gas. there was no school today. Pleas.
Fri. 30.	Attend school, am enjoying it, perhaps, too well, am getting along very fast in Algebra 'tis my *favorite study* though I like all the rest. Rain.

OCTOBER 1859.

Sat. 8.	'tis quite late, have been to school, good lessons. * * * Charley [Baker, a classmate] came & stayed with me untill the girls got home. we read Shakespeare & visit in general; he is good company though young. we are learning a play, Charley is to take the part of Romeo and I of Juliette; other pupils the rest. Pleas.
Tues. 11.	Went to school & got good lessons. Sammy Southworth asked me to go with him this evening to dancing school; because Johnny Fuller could not leave the store early enough. Johnny came home with me however, am to attend the rest of the term,—Johnny to be my partner[30] Pleasant.
Wed. 12.	Have been to school. Ella is not going any more, this evening Mrs. Thompson & I visit for the last time here,—she

is going away, I carried my things to Mrs. Hawses (next door) to board till school closes,   Some say Mrs. T—— is going to elope with a Mr. Lewis,   She says she is going to Chicago. Rain.

NOVEMBER 1859.

Wed.
2.

Today school closed; Charley says he is sorry because I cannot visit with him so much, as a friend I like him well, he, too, is but nineteen; says he 'will write the true sentiments of his heart in my Algebra'—here are the two lines:
"Emmie thou art my only treasure
For in others I find no pleasure."
                    Charley.
Ah, Charley, thou art like all the rest of admirers,—all are but friends. Pleasant.

Fri.
4.

Sew some for Mrs. Hawes. . . . Am sorry school is out, would like to go to school untill I could be master of a *good* education—Graduate—vain hope, dancing school closes this evening. Pleas.

Tues.
8.

Am at Mrs. Hawes this forenoon, write in my journal. Our exhibition was last evening,—got home too late to note it down. it was indeed good, Miss Jones & I read an excellent paper. Romeo & Juliette was nice & all the rest a success,—house crowded. Charley asked me to come & talk with him. I did not refuse. I gave him his ring though he did not want it; I told him he was only a boy, he would see someone to love better suited to him than I, and may he. Dr. Chappell was at the exhibition; he talked, Oh, so much I will not write it to night. perhaps never. * * *

Fri.
11.

'Tis nearly one o'clock; have just got home (At Mrs. Hawes) from the dance; it was a dancing school closing party.

Johnny & I had a really pleasant visit, he asked me to attend with him the next term of dancing school—but I cannot—*though* would like to. * * *

Sun.
13.

Uncle Lewis brought me to Uncle Harveys [?] this evening,—have spent a pleasant term of school, and had an excellent place to board,—would that I might ever enjoy life as well. Cold. Cold.

Thur.
17.!

Sew for Aunt,—she let me have a nice gold ring (cost $1.25) for pay. Pleasant.

Sun.
20.

We are all at home, I have been gone 9 weeks, Edna worked 23 weeks for Garlick for $24.00 * * * glad to be at home again, our folks are all well. Cold. Cold.

DECEMBER 1859.

Thurs.
1.

Winter has at last arrived, broider as usual. Cold. Rain.

Fri.
2.

All [Edna, Henry, and Harriet] at school. work on broidery. Today Brown is to be hung in Virginia for meddling with that which is none of his business about Kansas matters.[31] Snow.

Wed.
14,

Sew all day again, Edna & I are going to N. C. Lowes this evening to a surprise party.[32] Pleasant.

Thur.
15.

There were about thirty at Nathan's last night, a general good time, though I do not like these kissing parties, sew all day. Pleasant.

Sat.
17.

make overhauls for Father; commence to make a pair of muffers. Snow all day.—the largest flakes I *ever saw.* our first sleighing. Snow. Cold.

Sun. 25.	Christmas at home. Edna & I alone. Father, Mother, Henry & Harriet at Aunt Mary's. Lester Culver & Harvey Warn call a few minutes however; this evening Royal & Lucinda Hamlin have been here. Pleas.

JANUARY 1860

Wed. 4.	We all work as usual.—have just got home from Writing school. George Wilber says if I will attend the rest of the term he will pay my tuition, and would like to be my escort sometimes. I told him would like the writing school but did not want to make the other promise,—he said it would be all right anyway.—he is another old bachelor, yet guess I will go. Pleasant.
Sat. 7.	Churn & help Mother as usual. Children at school. . . . Father sold one of my sheep,—he gave me one dollar & kept rest. Thaw
Sat. 14.	Uncle Harvey's folks here visiting. I sew on shirt. Henry went to Morenci; he brought me another letter from J. C. Chappell,—'tis a good letter, too. Mother does not approve of letters from strangers perhaps a stranger is as good as some acquaintances.[33]
Thurs. 19.	Sew & knit. Uncle Jacob has come for Edna & me to attend a Ball at Mr. Schutts in Morenci. Pleasant, cold.
Fri. 20.	Tis evening. Edna & I went to writing school this evening. * * * We had a very good party, over 40 couple by the way, George Kellogg was there; is their adopted son,— he asked me to be his partner in the dance. I accepted, we had a long talk though I will not write it here his words of entreating love, yet I admire his candor & think him worthy a good wife and as I told him I hoped he might find his ideal of fancy one younger than himself that I'm nearly two years

older; he replied he thought that difference in age could not hinder me from returning his love, had I not some other greater cause. I hardly knew what to reply,—could only say to him let us be but friends at present and in time I may think different. and now that my folks are all asleep but me 'tis the time for reflection and thought.—and of George,— he has an impediment in his speech,—'tis his only fault. were I his wife I could but pity him all my life. no! no! if I can read my own heart I believe I am incapable of loving any one, at least untill the *right one*, and now I will retire. Cold.

Sun.
22.

We have all been at home all day. Mr. Separson Lewis came to visit with me this afternoon; he attends the writing school. I promised to attend a party with him at Mr. Heaths tomorrow evening.—he has just gone home, Father & Mother think he is just *the one*, Mother says he is rich, suppose he is worth ten or fifteen thousand. The clock chimes nine. good night.

Tues.
24.

Mr. Lewis came about six last evening with a *beautiful* horse & carriage,—he went by way of his farm,—said he had farm, barn, cattle, sheep, horses and indeed everything except a wife, told him *that* was bad, and I would introduce him to a lady I knew if she chanced to be at our party: and she was there,—Miss Carrie Drown, Mr. Lewis! and he asked her hand in the next dance;—a nicely matched couple, both of them little less or more than six feet tall. Well, when we came home Mr. Lewis asked me to accept him for my company and escort, and to go with him to visit Mr. Garrisons relatives of his that I was not yet acquainted with him; told him Miss Drown undoubtedly would marry him if he asked her and far as I know she is a nice girl, "there, Miss Emmie, he said if you *really refuse* me, I will take your word as truth, and call on Carrie, yet once more if you will you shall have the best wedding trousseau that has ever been worn in this place." "no, I cannot." and he bade me a 'good night, Emmie, my love is yours,' and he went back alone. 'tis true his beautiful horse is a temptation, the green silk wedding suit, too would be very fine, but, ah me, I rather Carrie would have them.

Commence to get signers to send to N.Y. for books. Aunt Mary sends for two. Pleasant.

Wed. 25.	Got Mrs. Beach's saddle, went to Richard Osborns; he sends for one book ($1.65), Mrs. Osborn one ($1.15); Janet Weed two ($2.30). Mr. Osborn said he complimented me to Mr. Lewis to go & spark for a wife; he is rich you know and will be a great catch, you will do well to get him &c. but I select for myself, think I know best who suits my ideal or fancy. Pleasant

FEBRUARY 1860

Mon. 6!	Mr. Willson came after me to stay with Mrs. Wilson a couple of weeks while he goes to New York for goods. 'tis now evening; have helped to do the work, they live in a very nice house in Morenci, am in my room,—the front room up stairs;—it contains a bed, stand, mirror, chairs & carpet.—and my trunk. Snow.
Tues. 7.	Help do housework & sew,—this evening have been to Harvey Hills to see about sending for my books, went to P.O. got a catalogue; have made out and written a form to send. . . . I am to get a book and prize for getting up the Club. I made my first jelly cake today, it was really good. Well, I must stop writing & go to bed. Pleasant.
Wed. 8.	Mrs. Wilson & I did the washing, and work; have been to the church to Donation this evening. George Kellogg came

back with me. we thought Mr. Wilson didn't live half far enough away from the meeting house. Pleasant

Mon.
13.

Do what little housework there was to do. have a sore finger. Mrs. Wilson is sick. Dr. Chappell called to see her this afternoon, he was astonished to see me there, Ah, I can never forget how he looked at me when he went away,—he only said 'How do you do, Emmie.' and 'good bye.' Yes, am now in my room alone. all is still and I am meditating on the past. Aye, that look of disappointment reminds me of these words he uttered the evening of our exhibition.—"My dear, dear girl," he said "I do love you, I would not harm one hair of your head, I have watched you when you have been sick and have waited until you are old enough to answer for yourself to ask you to be my wife. Oh, Emmie, *will* you, will you, if you only will say yes it shall be to night, now, in less than two hours." I told him I couldn't think of such a thing so soon but he seemed to be so very earnest in his entreaties that he was blind to any such thing as reason. "Yes, dear girl, you can think now let it be now or never." "never, then," I said. and that was most too much, he did not for a little while say another word. indeed I was sorry to see Doc shed tears, "O it is too bad, Emmie, after I have waited so long for you, ever since you were but a little girl only nine or ten years old, and now you refuse, but it may be all right." indeed I do think he is truly my best friend, had it not been for him, I without doubt, would have been in my grave long ere this, yet as much as I respect him and thank him for my life I do not feel as if I could accept his offer because he knows not but he may die any time from the effects of cutting his hand with a lance, and, too, he is eighteen years my senior: *two* great *reasons*, though my friendship is greater for him by far than any other one, he was hasty. perhaps I was, may we put our trust in Him who doeth all things well, to guide us aright. May we thank him for our lives, for all blessings bestowed upon us,—His will, not ours, be done. 'tis about eleven. I must to sleep. raining

Fri.
17.

do part of ironing. Uncle Garlick came to see if I could go and stay with them [in Morenci] a few days. Aunt Olive is sick. . . .[34]

Sat.
18.

Read & cook dinner for Uncle & me. they have *not anything* hardly to do—there were a number of callers. Snow.

Thur.
23.

Do *small* washing, Aunt is better, can go home in few days. Snow.

MARCH. 1860

Thur.
1

Work some on broidery. the gentleman that is [boarding] here is teaching people to cut coats & vests by model,—he taught me how to cut them today & let me have a set of models,—he is to stay all night again. Father in house all day reading. Children go to school, Mother & I do the work. * * *

Fri.
2.

Tis evening.—have been working on broidery all day. Children at school, Father shingling house, Mother done the housework. Mr. Quenlisque [the boarder] went away this morning about eleven o'clock. while Mother was out of the room making beds he (Mr. Quenlisque) said he had tarried so long for a favorable opportunity to tell me it was for *my* sake he stayed,—not for the rain & mud, "will you forgive me for telling you I *love* you *with all my heart.* and may I *hope* you will return my love:" Indeed I was surprised though I was sensitive of that some sort of mysterious feeling which tells us one is surely thinking of us. I told him he had done nothing for which to be forgiven; that I would not trifle with his affection; whether real or fancy that he must not hope "Then I know you must be plighted to another, I sincerely thank you, and though I must go I would rather stay. May I kiss you just once as *the* only one I ever loved for it *is the truth.*" he kissed me adieu. Though he was a stranger those tears plainly told he was in earnest. I must not tell Mother, however.—she would not approve. bed time. Pleasant.

Thur.
8.!

do not feel very well. am writing. we finished cleaning the house today. John Osborn brought six shirts for me to make   John Culver brought overhauls for me to make. * * *

Mon.
26.

Finish my embroidered night gown, tis very pretty indeed,—almost too nice to sleep in. sew, sew, sew all the time. at home. Very Pleasant.

Thurs.
29.

Harriet, Mother & I work out doors most all day. I laid down on the floor in kitchen; was so tired, Mother said I slept most two hours. Carlo (our Newfoundland) lay near me; they said he would not let any one come near; he is a nice fellow.[35] * * *

APRIL 1860

Sun.
8.

* * * Royal and Lucinda Hamlin have come for me to go home with them.—am going to stay a day or two. Pleasant.

Tues.
10.

Sinda [Hamlin] & I came to Hudson this morning with Luther on a load of corn to visit Sylvenus and Libbie, they live in a real cozy little house. after dinner we go down town. help Libbie sew. we are to stay all night. we are to go visiting this evening.[36] Rain.

Wed.
11.

Sinda & I went to the store this morning, got me a new dress & sew on it, croched some. we help Libbie do the work too. * * * we had a very good visit, only that Venus can scarcely give up the old affection at least not enough I fear but that Libbie might be jealous if I stayed very long. therefore I will not stay only another night for he is her own husband now, and her idol. if his whole love was hers, how I would enjoy staying with them; it must not be. 'tis getting late, Sinda is asleep and I must retire. Pleas.

Thur. 12.	Learn & help Libbie make some hair flowers. after dinner Royal came for us. Libbie came too; we are at her Fathers to night. she is now Libbie of old,—she & I are in the same old room to sleep as when we went to school. Rain
Sun. 15.	tis afternoon, have had *such a good visit*. Royal is going to take me home this evening. Pleasant.

MAY 1860

Wed. 2.	Mother & I went to Aunt Mary Osborns this morning to sewing society. Uncle Ben brought us home. Aunt set the table for thirty-two. We talked on Religion & Mrs. Culver got mad. Pleasant.
Fri. 4.	Make a box to put my flowers in. at home all day. heard to day the [*sic*] *Separson Lewis* is married to *Carrie Drown* but did not learn the particulars. I hope he may ever make a good and kind husband and their union may ever be blessed with happiness. They have my best wishes. I suppose the suit of wedding attire had much to lend enchantment to love's charm. Henry has gone fishing. Pleasant.
Tues. 8.	Have got ready to go to Mr. Turners, Tis now evening, Commenced to learn and help Mrs. Gallup. and Cornelia to make hair-flowers. am to stay with Cornelia to night. . . .
Thurs. 10.	Came home after dinner, am real tired. Mother has gone to Uncle Jonas Ackers. Cornelia paid me seventy-five cents. Father owed Mr. T——— [Turner] sixty cents,—so I only got

fifteen cents money. Why is it not my lot to be fortunate. I most certainly am morally,—though not financially. Ah let my motto be,—Although my luck be poor may I ever prove holy & pure. Mother came home this evening. Pleasant.

Fri.
11.

Am completely discouraged. I know not hardly what to do yet I can help Mother & stay at home. I have used the most of the money I got for teaching school—when that is gone I will trust to Providence to get more. I taught 6 weeks the summer of 1855 for $9.00—and the winter of 1856—13 weeks, $26.00—and the summer of 1856—for 13 weeks, $26.00, do not do much of anything to day, our teacher Augusta Stone is boarding here. Rain.

Mon.

Am at Mrs. Wileys this evening, she is sick with consumption. Oh, that horrid disease, Dr. Chappell came to see her this afternoon. Warm.

Sun.
20.

Am at Mrs. Wiley's this evening. she does not seem in her right mind.—she wants me to read to her all the time, poor woman, I do pity her, she took my hand & said, "your hand will be like mine sometime; mine was once like yours." . . . Wiley gone for a hired girl. tis near midnight and they not come yet, and I alone with one almost dying, as it were, a hard thunder shower of Rain.

Wed.
30.

At Julias [Blanchard] to night, she is a good woman. We called on Mrs. Wiley. I read a book, "The Angel of the Household." [37] Rain.

JUNE 1860

Sun
3.

[Entry begins in different handwriting.] to day Emmie & myself went over to see Mrs Wiley, come home & found Harvey

& Nancy here, Mother comes in the bedroom & tells me
that Emmies beau is coming. O how glad I was. I shook
hands with him. Edna

Well, as Edna has commenced writing for today I'll finish. . . . we all went over in the field to get strawberrys to
eat. after all had gone, George (it was George Griffith Edna
said was my beau) and I went to take a walk; we went perhaps forty rods from the house and sat on a log beneath a
beautiful shade tree and talked,—well, never mind what
about. I can only think & wonder what the future may bring
forth and trust in Providence that all may ever be well.
George *is* indeed a kind, intelligent & virtuous young man,
graceful, too, yet he *has one bad habit*; that is, he likes &
drinks intoxicating drink. although he says he is sorry and
weeps about it,—promises to never taste it again—yet I
fear. Though I *do* hope he may get a good wife as he says
he wants one, and that he may keep, to her his promise to
me. I have vowed to never marry the best man that lives if
he is addicted to strong drink, & with the help of God may
I keep that promise. 'tis now near eleven o'clock and I must
retire. Warm & pleasant.

Fri.
8.

Stay with Mrs. Wiley all day, finish pair of overhauls for
her.—last evening when she & I were alone she told me
what Mr. Wiley's brother told her. about his loving me etc.
I have often heard of the request of a dying person being
sacred   it may be, yet I think one is not under obligations
to grant it—if it concerns their own future happiness. am at
home, came this evening. Cold.

Tues.
26.

Go to Mrs. Culvers this morning, commence embroidery for
her; I with Sarah Ortt & Oscar Wiley sat up with Mrs. Wiley
to night. warm.

Sat.
30.

Broider some, finish Father's pants & do ironing. Mother is
sick, she works too hard. * * *

JULY 1860.

[This is the first full transcription of a month of Emily Hawley's diary to give the reader an idea of how the diary has been edited and how Hawley described each day.]

Sunday
1.

quite cool this morning. I am just going to write some letters to Lizzie Hamlin & Uncle Henry Baker. Edna & I went to meeting, called at Mrs. Wileys. she is no better. I with Mrs. Converse, Mrs. Evans and Mrs. Culver sit up with her to night, how sick she is,—she cannot live long. Pleasant

Mon.
2.

came home about noon. work on broidery all day. Mother bought Edna & I *each a work basket*. Jno. Culver here, he is not well, looks very pale. Pleas.

Tues.
3.

Work all day for Mother, 'tis evening. I am sad, because Henry said "I better go to Morenci & see what they say about me" he did not say what only "nothing good." but I will not mind anything about it for I have a clear conscience that my character is unblemished & what they say can harm me not, 'tis the first word I ever knew any one to speak ill of me. John Osborn here to night, may all be well at last though our hearts be grieved. Warm rain.

Wed.
4.

Henry & John Osborn went to Adrian on the [railroad] cars. Jane & Erbin Wetherbee call yesterday to wait for it to stop raining; they were going to Hudson, Erbin & Caroline are to be married today. *we work*. all at home all day. I made a mistake. Jane was married yesterday to Wm. Welch. Today is Pleasant.

Thur.
5.

Edna & I, Harriet Sutherland, Adison and Augusta Stone & Maria Dawes sit up to night with the corpse, Mrs. Wiley died this morning about 4. I help Mother & embroider some. rain.

Fri. 6.	The Dr's. came this morning to dissect Mrs. Wiley, her heart & lungs were grown *fast*. right *lung all gone* & left one except a part about the size of a hickory nut. Edna & I went home about eleven. I embroider & help Mother do the work. we go to the funeral at one. the consumption is an awful disease. Pleasant.
Sat. 7.	Edna & I went whortleberrying. it rains this evening. we are tired, got about 16 qts. of berries. Warm.
Sun 8.	Uncle Harvey [Baker] & Aunt Nancy here. Aunt Nancy told me there was a bad story about me. May I not care for God knows my heart I have a clear conscience, of ever doing or thinking an evil or unvirtuous act. all will be well, for a lie cannot be true. I'll fear not but trust in Providence *that wrong story* may do me no harm. Rain
Mon. 9.	I finished Mrs. Culver's embroidery, carried it to her, & help do housework. Mother & Edna wash. Father commence harvest. warm.
Tues. 10.	Make myself a white skirt. & help Mother, try not to be sad. rain.
Wed 11.	Father, Mother & Edna went to Hudson. Henry, Harriet & I at home. Pleasant. we do the work.
Thur. 12.	Commence my gown. at home. Pleasant
Fri. 13.	Sew on dress all day. Warm.

Sat.
14.

Edna & I go huckleberrying. the swamp full of people. I finished my new dress, looks nice. Warm.

Sun.
15.

Edna & I went to meeting. when we got home Mother said Fred & George had been here. Edna is O so vain; she is almost ashamed to go with me on acct. of my clothes, though I *try not* to care. I can not keep back the unbidden tears & sigh will it always be, ah no. Pleasant.

Mon.
16.

Get water & help Mother wash. finish Father's overhauls. * * * Mr. Beach here for hired girl. Mr. Wiley wanted me to work for him, too. I rather have less & stay at home & help Mother. I do most all of her sewing. Pleasant

Tues.
17.

Sew on Father's shirt. Mrs. Hall, Hattie and Caroline, Anna & Ola Brower call after tea. Cal. & I go to see John. Edna is to help Mrs. Culver a week. Warm.

Wed.
18.

Finish Father's shirt, make a sheet & pair of pillow casings. Harvey Warn call a few minutes. rain.

Thur.
19.

Make sheet & 3 pillow casings. after tea call at Mrs. halls. Cloudy.

[Five pages of personal financial accounts follow to end volume 1.]

Fri.
20.

Mr Beach here 2/3 day with team drawing wheat. I churned this morning & helped do housework. made one pillow case. Called to see John Culver.

Sat.
21.

made five pillow casings. Rain some   made 3 pillow casings. Edna came home this evening to stay. Mrs. Culver, Let & Emma, too, Harriet Hall here all night. I was at home all day.

Sun. 22.	Edna & me went to forenoon meeting. Text Isaiah 5, 1st & 7th inclusive. Nichols the minister. After I went to Mr. Culvers I wrote Mrs. C—— a letter. After I got back from that, Edna, Harriet & Mother had gone to Halls. I went over to Mr. Browers. Pleasant.
Mon. 23.	Ma done the washing. I got water, worked on Aunt Mary's hair flowers. Mr. Beach here drawing wheat for Pa this morning. Pleasant at home.
Tues. 24.	Edna gone whortleberrying, got 14 qts. did get back all most 4. Ma gone to Uncle Ben Osborns, Hattie to school, so I am at home alone, making hair flowers. John Culver here about an hour. Ma got home about sundown; brought, for me to make, a shirt, & dress for Ida, sent for pay 2 yards of ribbon $.50
Wed. 25.	Edna, Harriet & me went blackberrying this forenoon, got about 6 quarts, all of us. this afternoon nearly made John Osborn's shirt. Pleasant. why sad & lone?
Thur. 26.	finished shirt. Partly made Ida Osborn's dress. this afternoon Ann Converse & Frank Brower here. Edna & me went as far as George Browers with them (Frank worked there). Called on Fanny's Ma. Pleasant.
Fri. 27.	finished Ida's dress. Edna & Harriet went to Uncle Ben Osborns this afternoon. Ma & me went to Mrs. Culvers, carried home their ~~flower~~ flour. I got up the cows. I read some,—a paper, made some fun of one of the pieces. Ma said I acted simple; felt real bad about it. we met Aunt Mary & Uncle Ben; they had called at our house to leave some more hair. Henry went to Medina to see the Dr. today, he has sprained his hip, puts a blister on to night. Guess he will make some fuss when it draws? didn't.

Sat.
28.

Went blackberrying this forenoon. Emma Culver went with me. Ironed some after noon. Pa work for Beach today. Ma went to Culvers to get some salts. Henry better. Harriet came home. rain in the evening & night. showery. warm

Sunday,
29.

Mr. Hall here this morning. Eat an apple (each of us one) off from a tree in *our* orchard. Uncle Harvey & Aunt Nancy brought Edna home. Anna Salsbury came, too. John Colegrove here for a hired girl; didn't get.

Mon.
30.

sewed on factory this forenoon. Opha Blanchard here visiting Charley got back to dinner. worked on Aunt Mary's flowers in the afternoon. Mrs. Converse (Hattie's mother) called here, evening. very pleasant. at home. for yesterday, when Uncle went home, went as far as Culvers with them. borrowed a paper. Mrs. C. & Emma came home with me. John was here when we came. Let C.—Harvey Warn called to see Henry.

Tues.
31.

Mr. Beach helping Pa draw hay today. Ma called the Dr. when he went by and got some medicine for Henry. Pleasant.

C.E.C.

E.E.H.

[This ends the full transcription of one month.]

AUGUST 1860.

Sun.
5.

went over to meeting this forenoon. . . . * * * I commenced reading a book, entitled Tempest and Sunshine.[38] Ah, I have at last found out where that story started from,—from Caroline Hall but may I put my trust in God that I am innocent, yes indeed & may I ever be.

Tues.
7.

worked a little at this & that today, nothing in particular, cried because Pa scolded. very exceeding warm, what a foolish girl,—cried 3 times before I went to sleep. at home all day. * * *

Sat.
11.

work on flowers this forenoon. we went to Morenci this afternoon. called at Uncle H. Garlicks. when we went back stopped to Rob. Simms stayed to tea; saw Lucy Ann's baby. she has 3 children; the eldest only 2 years & 8 months old.[39] at July's [Julia Blanchard's] tonight.

Tues.
14.

am going to piece Julia a quilt for calicoes enough for me one; commenced cutting the blocks & piece one. 81 blocks, make 1 block. pleasant. at July's.

Sun.
19.

Edna & Harriet went to forenoon meeting. * * * at home all day. Harvey Warn, Let & John Culver here. Edna & me are in our bedroom; came in here on purpose because they— Hs—darn fools were here, need not think they can run here every Sunday; if they do they will not see Edna & me they can set their hearts at rest on that *thats so*! well we have got tired staying in the bedroom so we will get out of the window and go up in the woods and sit on a log teeter,—yes here we are sitting on the log,—there comes Osker Wiley, he says there are some gentlemen at our house, "we know it." "they look very wishfull," I guess they will look awhile. Edna reads aloud in Tempest and Sunshine, well, I declare if we haven't stayed here till Osker has come back. he asks us to take a ride. we accept the offer; had a nice ride of 6 miles, didn't get home till after dark. heigh ho. at home.

Thurs.
30.

got on a quilt & quilted some. rain in the evening, the sun's rays looked beautiful through the heavy clouds; thunder and lightning. at Julias all night.

SEPTEMBER 1860.

Sun.
9th

Edna went to the Presbyterian meeting. Harriet & me went to the Spiritual meeting at Medina afoot. * * * Mrs. Thompson of Toledo the principal speaker. * * *

Fri.
21.

Embroidery some. went to Mr. Shepherdsons to get harness & reed to loom, called on Mrs. Culver, stayed there (at Mrs. C's.) all night. * * *

Sat.
22.

Mrs. Culver here. I at home most all day helped us color [dye] red. rain in the evening, at home.

Mon.
24.

this morning went over in the woods to get some bark to color. Ma, Harriet & me colored green. * * *

OCTOBER. 1860.

Monday,
1st.

rainy all forenoon, this morning Henry & Mother brought me down to Aunt Amanda Hawleys. I am going to weave our cloth here (to Aunts), commence spooling, spooled 7 skeins.

Tues.
2nd.

this forenoon starched 9 run of cotton. spooled 7 skeins. this afternoon, Darwin [Hawley], Visena & me went to Morenci to the fair, saw Edna there & a good many that I was happy to meet with. Dr. Chappell, Lonny Griffith (George's brother) too; had quite a chat. he has been sick, I am sad in spirits today. I know not why. at Aunts.

Thurs.
4th

spooled 22 skeins of yarn & warped about 1/3 of my cloth. Aunt showed me how, pleasant, at Aunts tonight

Sat.
20.

rainy today, wove one yard, done some quilling.[40] Mr. Nivers folks here today & night too, this evening Mrs. Nivers

& me are in the room by ourselves, alone, she is the greatest talker I ever saw. well, I do not know but I might as well know all the events of the day. while I was weaving I cried, well *I* know what I cried for, guess I can remember if I don't write it here, sorrow, little anger & grief.

Monday
22.

wove about 3 yards at Aunts, rainy all day, sober, rather down hearted.

Sat.
27.

Father & Harriet come for me, we got home about 4. rainy. they told me of John Culver's death died yesterday afternoon funeral tomorrow. *at home to night.* * * *

NOVEMBER, 1860

Tues
6.

this morning the ground white with snow Election today. went over & sewed on Mrs. C's—— dress till about 3 (5?). came home to night. * * * quilt. pleasant only a few minutes rain. Douglas for Democrat; Lincoln for Republican was elected majority. heigh ho! hurrah! hurrah! hurrah![41]

Tues.
20.

knit on hood. cut Harriets dress. a peddler here, I bought me a dress (7 yds) borrowed $.75 of Pa. $1.10 of Henry to cost me $3.50   Pa killed a pig. Snow most all day, at home

Sat.
24.

very cold. blustery. at Uncles all day. make some tatting for Aunt Nancy [Baker]. . . . Uncle & me were talking about working, he said so much I cried.

DECEMBER. 1860.

Sat.
1st.

* * * Ma & me went over to Mrs. Smiths to warp a piece. Mrs. Smith warped for me (18 yards).[42] I called on Mrs. Culver. cold. cold.

Tues.
4.
had to take piece out of the harness & put it in another, O dear am about discouraged, snow. at home,

Sat.
8.
Henry went to Morenci, carried some chickens to pay postage $1.00 on our books, got them. Mas was Three Judsons [*sic*], prize gold locket $3.50. mine was D(ora) Dean [*sic*], prize gold sleeve buttons, $3.00. * * * Edna & me at home, we read in my book.[43] pleasant. at home.

Mon.
17.
Ma washed. I finished weaving had 17 yards. * * *

Tues.
25.
Christmas at home all day. read some knit some. Uncle Harvey [Baker] came for Ma. she stayed all night.

Thes.
27.
Samuel Bothwell came for me. I went to Mrs. Converses. there are 4 sick ones. pleasant.

JANUARY, 1861.

Tues.
1st.
at Mrs. Converses. read a book most through tis night. "The head but not the heart." ha! ha! New Years, this evening went over to James Converses with Oliver, a visiting party, pleasant. * * * Mrs. Dawes & me set up all night. they got a new girl this evening.

Thurs,
17.
sewed all day. Marvin Wood came to ask me to go to a dance tomorrow eve, snow some. pleasant. agreed to go.

Fri.
18.
Peddler here. * * * Marvin came for me (with horse & cutter) about 6 o'clock. we arrived at Mr. [*sic*] near or about 7. they had a very good party indeed. I had the pleasure of receiving an introduction to quite a number of the company

& one Arthur Bovee. heigh ho! we had quite a talk but never mind what we talked about, can remember. he is a good dancer. *shouldn't wonder if I went with him.* party broke up about 4 some time. Bade them good night hoping to meet again, pleasant but cold!! cold.

Mon.
21.

Ma & me done the washing. sewed on Henry's shirt, a peddler here. at home. Pa at work in the saw mill (has been since the 9th. of this month. he pays 25 dollars & is to have half the mill earns)

FEBRUARY. 1861.

Tues.
19.

crocheted my braid. Edna is done work today at Marshalls, has been there 15 weeks. they owe her $4.82. She is gone to Ransaler Bakers to work. * * *

MARCH, 1861.

Mon.
4.

today President Lincoln takes his seat   Mother, Hattie & me done the washing. I finished me pair of drawers &c. quilt skirt. pleasant. at home, snow in the night.

Thurs.
14.

piece on quilt, have 28 blocks done   this afternoon Edna & me went over to Ettas quilting. Mrs. Culver & Mrs. Beach came to our house to visit Ma. * * *

APRIL. 1861.

Monday.
1st.

rain this morning, not very pleasant for town meeting. couldn't be worse day as far as the going is concerned. Mr.

Russell came to see if I would work there. finished pair of cotton hose.

Wed.
3.

work in dooryard all day. Harriet Harriet, [*sic*] Ma & me. when we had done tea, Mr. Russell came for me. went, pleasant, tired.

Sat.
6.

cooking most of time, rain, like to stay here better than thought I should.

MAY. 1861.

Fri.
3.

done work. sewed some. Arthur Bovee called here, rain this afternoon   at Mrs. Russells, this evenig finds me writing here

Sun.
5.

this morning got up, built fire, got breakfast & killed two chickens before any of the rest were up. at Mrs. Russells, read some. this afternoon rain. heigh ho, a compliment from Arthur when the hired man came back.

Sat.
11.

today Harriet came to see me. I went home with her tonight. was glad to see my folks. pleasant.

Sun.
12.

at home all day. this morning was in the bedroom, looked out of the window   who should I see but Uncle Henry & Susan Baker from Iowa. Uncle Horace Garlick brought them here, mother & him did not know each other; has not been here in eighteen years, he is so deaf he can hardly hear a word. pleasant, started up to Russels about two. * * * Edna came most two miles with me   ah, that I cannot always have a home at Fathers, why, because my Father will not live always.[44]

Wed. 15.	sewed some on dress, done the rest of work. rain quite a shower. at Mrs. Russels six weeks today.
Tues. 21.	got my work done & dinner. went over to Cornelia Fermans'. her, Lucy & me went fishing. came back about 7 o'clock. found Mrs. Russel real sick. I named the baby Ellie Isadore, Miss. Jillet & Mrs. Ferman watched here tonight. tired very.
Thurs. 30.	done the ironing Mother came to see me; she was here to dinner. I went over to town with her. * * * Mrs. Russel is now sitting up, is some better. pleasant.
Friday. 31st.	Mr. Russell paid me $4.50 I went to the store, traded $4.32 got two dresses, one lawn, the other calico, a shaker [bonnet] & a parasol, got my goods of Mr. Bennet. at Mrs. Russels. pleasant.

JUNE 1861.

Sun. 9.	at home. last Monday Mr. Douglass (Stephen A) died. Alas another great man has left this world of trouble just the time when he is most needed. perhaps 'tis better though that he should die but see on History's page will sound the name of another Hero one who has so long helped to make our laws. he has lived only to see the commencement of this Civil War where hundreds of thousands are being killed.[45] Uncle Henry's folks here to tea. Edna & me went up the road walking. O the comfort we can take; more now than we can ever again. pleasant
Wed. 12.	this morning Edna & me went to Mrs. Russels. he paid me $3.18. this afternoon we went to Canandaigua to Mrs.

Rices. I trimmed my shaker, we went to the store. Edna got her a new parasol & a pair of mitts. I lent her $.38. * * *

Fri.
14.

at home. finished making over my silk waist. . . . I read the last of Ida Norman, a good story indeed.[46] * * *

Sat.
15.

Edna borrowed of me $1.25.   I ironed   sent six pence to pay postage on something sent from Washington   got it, a something that gentlemen wear on their coats & some trimming off from some ones uniform, don't know whose it was though,—guess Horace Jones sent them, sewed some, turned lawn skirt bottom side up   pleasant. Pa went to Morenci got the paper, news of war, death of Colonel Elmer Ellsworth died 24th. of May. born April 11, 1838. just my age exactly. & death of Honorable Stephen A. Douglas the greatest statesman of our country 11 minutes past 9 June 3rd. age   years. the last words of Col. Ellsworth were "My God."[47] pleasant. at home.

Wed.
19.

sew some & read in a book ("The Lamp Lighter")[48]   Mr. Beach brought me another letter from Washington, there goes 5 cents more for postage, pleasant. at home. Edna gone to Morenci stayed all night. Father up to Osborns, have made up my mind. my letters from Washington are from Horace Jones

Wed.
26.

today & tonight am at home perhaps for the last time for I am (if no preventing providence) going to start for Iowa. Uncle Henry & Susan are at our house today. Uncle Benjamin & Aunt Mary brought them. Mother went with them to Morenci with the intention of staying all night but she came back, said she would not stay away if I was going. if I did go she never would see me again, but I have made up my mind to go, think I am doing perfectly right in so doing. indeed I would not go if I had the first thought of it being wrong. perhaps 'tis as Mother says, we may never while on earth, meet again. if not I trust we will meet in a far happier home than this, yes, where parting is not known & sin & sorrow do not come. tonight at my Fathers home. Edna has the tooth ache all night. Mother as is her wont to do, comes in our room to bid us good night. ah, yes, I have a good Mother, one I love & a kind Father   he has ever been to me a true friend such as I can never find elsewhere. indeed 'tis a sad parting, the parting of Father, Mother, brother & sisters. I can hardly realize it. we had a nice time eating some strawberrys. have made up my mind to go home with Uncle Henry. my folks feel bad to have me go. we are all at home tonight. Mrs. Culver & Emmie and Addie Stone came to bid me good bye.

CHAPTER TWO

"We Cannot Always Live at Home": 1861—1862

T he decision that Emily Hawley should leave her parents' home for the "Far West" of Iowa was not as sudden as the diary indicates. (For a discussion of foreknowledge and disclosure in the text, see the Conclusion on the diary as autobiography.) As early as 1857, eighteen-year-old Emily had shown interest in the prospect of going to eastern Iowa to visit her Uncle Henry and Aunt Elizabeth Baker at their large inn. She wrote, "I wish you and Aunt would come out here this spring, I would go home with you if I could get father and mother to let me, which I think they would."[1] After his wife's death in 1859, widower Baker was eager to have one of his Hawley nieces come to board at the inn and keep house, although family correspondence suggests that his sister Sarah Baker Hawley was not as enthusiastic over the idea. Henry Baker was frank about one of his reasons for wanting to hire a niece: "I admit that I did not materely [sic] consult my intrest [sic] . . . for I could hire girls for less money but I thought it would seem better to have a relative and look better perhaps in the sight of the world."[2] By mid-1861, the idea of Emily going to Iowa seemed more appealing to her parents; factors that may have led to their and her decision are discussed at the end of Part I.

The train trip to Iowa from Michigan, seen through a young woman's eyes, opens the next section of the diary. Although it may have seemed the Far West to Emily Hawley, eastern Iowa was not a frontier by 1861. Iowa had been a state for fifteen years and had 674,913 residents at the time of the 1860 census, the majority of whom lived in the easternmost ten counties.[3] A third of the settlers had come from the old Northwest Territory states (Ohio, Indiana, and Michigan), so Emily Hawley was following a well-traveled pattern in her move west.[4] Her destination, the village of Manchester about forty miles west of the Mississippi River in Delaware County, could be reached by rail and boasted over seven hundred citizens.[5]

Henry Baker's inn was approximately three miles west of Manchester and was the showcase of his six hundred-acre farmstead. Still an impressive structure today, the three-story brick building must have awed his niece. The inn was built in 1856 on the Dubuque-Manchester-Independence stagecoach route by Baker and his father-in-law, Clement J. Coffin. Although the new railroad had decreased stagecoach travel, Emily recounted cooking for dozens of persons who either boarded at the inn or stopped for meals.

Emily Hawley made a drawing of the inn and sent it home to Michigan, asking that it be placed in her letter box. The inn contained approximately 3,400 square feet, excluding porches. On the main floor there were parlors, an office, a bedroom, a large dining room, and a kitchen with large pantry attached. There was a great open hearth in the kitchen as well as a free-standing wood stove for cooking. Two other fireplaces were in the front parlors. Upstairs were five bedrooms on the second floor and two on the third floor under the eaves. A large ballroom (14 feet by 28 feet) dominated the second floor of the inn. It served as a meeting place and as a courtroom when Henry Baker performed his duties as justice of the peace.[6]

Henry Baker, forty-seven, was a prominent figure in Delaware County. He had moved there in a covered wagon from Lenawee County, Michigan, in 1841 with his new bride, Elizabeth Coffin, to join her parents in Iowa Territory. Clement Coffin was the first settler of the area which eventually bore his name, Coffins Grove. Together Coffin and Baker built the first frame barn in the township (raised on the Fourth of July, 1845) and the large inn. Elizabeth Coffin Baker bore four children, three of whom died young. Elizabeth died in 1859, leaving Henry Baker to raise their only surviving child, sixteen-year-old Susan. To help him with this task and to work as a hired girl at the inn, Baker brought his niece Emily Hawley to Iowa, an arrangement that was attractive to both.

27th.   Thursday, this morning Edna & Henry carry me to Morenci. I leave home half past six. I had my likeness taken for Edna and she gave me hers. ($.38 apiece) Henry gave me cord & slide and Ma gave me her locket. Alas 'tis hard to leave home and friends, but the words "we cannot always live at home" are too true. I bid Pa, Ma & Hattie good bye at home.

Henry Baker's inn near Coffins Grove, Iowa. Top photo is from
the inn's dilapidated period. Below is a photo of the restored
building, now a private home.

Edna, Henry & me are perhaps taking our last ride, but we
will trust if we meet not on earth we may all meet in heaven
at last. now I take the stage, bid Edna good bye, I leave her
crying, I could weep, too, if it would do any good. the last
of all good bye to Henry, arrived at Clayton half past ten
now my first ride on the cars, tis indeed a pleasure to travel,
one could hardly believe there is so much to be seen all
in one day: such beautiful prairies, and flowers of almost
every color but I am far away from home in a land among
strangers, will have to form new acquaintances & associates, yes we may find as true friends among strangers those
we have never seen, as we have at home; how pleasant 'tis
to listen to the conversation of one that is well educated and
can talk on any subject, I quite strangely met with just such
a person, however he was an entire stranger, yes, his conversation was so interesting I was sorry that we could not
have longer time to converse the last Pa said to me was, "be
careful, Emily and not get your cape in that buggy wheel."
tonight finds me in one of the Hotels in Chicago, we arrived
here about six, after tea, Susan, Uncle & me went out walking, went in the Observatory of the Court House (about 80
feet high) where we could see all over the City of Chicago
and behold the ships sailing on Lake Michigan, beautiful
place indeed. here comes Uncle to bid Susan and me good
night so to night I sleep far away from home: my last
thoughts are of those that are near and dear to me. pleasant.

28th.   Friday. this morning arose at five o'clock   wrote a letter
home before breakfast. Uncle Susan and me went walking,
we saw a great many splendid buildings, Uncle bought us
some cherries, berries & oranges. I bought this book $.25.
we were standing on a swing bridge, it swung around while
we were on it, to let a steam boat pass by. we went in the
Depot too. What a beautiful building it is. we stayed to the
Hotel till quarter past nine then started again on the cars.
when we were going to the Depot we were just in time to see
a steam boat pass. on the cars all night. slept very well,

considering the soft pillow we had to rest our heads on.
pleasant.

29th.   Saturday. this morning I woke & found myself far from
where I was when I went to sleep. got up, combed my hair,
had my toilet completed just sunrise, in Lena, [Galena, Il-
linois] arrived at Dunleave, went over to Dubuque (in boat)
just across the Mississippi[7] stayed in Dubuque to breakfast,
then took the cars to Manchester, they have a Picnic there,
about four miles from Uncles, arrived at Uncles at four
o'clock, we went to Mrs. Coffins to tea, came back & prepared things for breakfast.[8] . . . have seen today some
beautiful prairies & groves, some the largest hills I ever
saw, they are rock & very high, here I am about five hundred miles from home. Uncle has a great brick house and
everything for convenience, think I shall like to stay very
much. pleasant.

30.   Sunday. have my work done and sit down to write mother a
letter and write in my Diary. yesterday I chanced to meet
with a Mr. Eddy Esq. he has a farm about thirty miles west
of Uncles of four hundred and eighty acres, he asked my
permission to call, we are so often deceived by strange persons that 'tis well to beware who we choose for associates.
* * *

JULY. 1861.

Tues.   made cookies & pie, washed the windows & done rest of the
2nd.   work, this afternoon Uncle, Susa, Hattie Bailey & me went
to Manchester   Uncle bought me a pair of shoes, cost
$1.75   I got $.15 worth of paper and envelopes; this evening Mr. & Mrs. Smith came here, I am now in my room
writing in my diary.[9] * * *

Thurs.
4th.

this morning Uncle took Susa, Hattie & me to Delhi to a celebration.[10] . . . did not enjoy the fourth as I usually do because the people were all strangers however 'twas very pleasant. I would indeed love to see my friends at home but I will try to content myself to stay until December if providence permits me to live, and may I hope then to find my friends alive & well should I perchance go home.

Monday
8th.

* * * arose this morning just five, John, (Uncles hired man) was building fire when I went down stairs; done the washing this forenoon. this afternoon done the mopping in three rooms and pantry & hall, the house is all cleaned below and has five more up stairs, rain most all day quite hard. * * * this evening called on Mrs. Nellson & Mrs. Smith both families live in Uncle's old house, to night Hattie stays with Susan. Uncle said he would go home with me next fall if I would agree to come back with him   heigh ho would not that be a capital idea—I will lay my writing aside for to night and think about it.[11]

Wednesday
10th

done ironing. baked bread cake & pie * * * received a letter from Mother & Harriet. this evening answered it, Pa sent a few lines; was very glad indeed to hear from home and learn the good news that my family are all well.

Thursday
11th.

at Uncles. did not do much of anything to day only the housework. * * * Mr & Miss Parker came to hear John play on the Guitar, we all went in the Hall awhile, do not believe there is any *very great gentlemen* for beaux if [Truman] Parker is called one, but it is of little consequence to me for I would choose for my associates those who are more refined in their manners. how true the saying of Mr. Hathaway "one prefers the company of those whose thoughts and principles are like his own." I repeat the language of Mr. H—— and yet I know him not, only that he is well educated, and may I hope to know him some day as a friend.[12]

Saturday 13th.

Arose this morning half past five   get the morning work all done by eight. went to the garden to pick some currants to make jam. made six pounds, this afternoon finished my Saturday's work and tried to read some French in a grammar that I found up stairs   can not pronounce any of the words; Mr. Hathaway said he would learn me but I do not think he will ever come here, if he should he would never learn me much french I reckon for it seems to me I could not learn. I cried today the first time since I have been at Uncles, what for? because S—— was saucy, however she is a good girl, yet it seems a task to have the care of one old enough to use reason and will not, may I hope that in time Susa may govern her disposition and be an amiable young lady! * * *

Sunday 14th.

had broiled chicken for breakfast, went to meeting this forenoon, the text Hebrews xi, 6—. * * * it is two weeks last night since I came here, am in my room writing, yes, and am thinking, thinking of the past, of my friends at home, yes as the minister said today "The Mother prayed for her daughter who was far away among strangers in a land of temptation" how quick did those words remind me of being far away from my Mother & Father. . . . * * *

Thursday 18th.

'tis now 'tween four & five P.M. this forenoon done all my morning's work; scoured the kitchen floor; did not have much time to sew. I have just done my work for the afternoon till supper time. made bread & ironed four dresses & two aprons, am quite tired. I will lay aside my writing till evening & read in the magazine,—Petersons, 1857. read some good stories. after the supper work's done, called to Mrs. Nellsons, came back, read an article in the paper aloud to Uncle; he can hear real well today   (the piece was "no cross, no crown.") quite good, pleasant, very [13]

Tuesday 30th

* * * Today done the work as usual, called on Mrs. Smith a short time this evening. . . . how strange it is that ones

thoughts will be when they most try to not have them. I know
not why it is but every day in spite of myself my thoughts
are on one whom I have never met but once. perhaps 'tis
wrong yet in the conversation of H—— there was something
that was, or seemed, different from any one I ever conversed
with before and yet why, for I have heard others say even
more on that same subject and it had no effect on me whatever. my prayer is that if it be wrong for us to meet again
that we never may and that I may forget, adieu then for to
night, but a thought of home.

AUGUST 1861.

Monday
5th.

Susa helped me a considerable, commenced to wash 20
minutes of nine. had quite a large washing. did not get done
and ready to rest till after four. then lay down on the sofa;
should have gone entirely to sleep. Susa came and kissed
me & woke me up. after tea and the work done I commenced
reading a story in the Ledger (Maggie Burns) by Mrs. Southworth.[14] warm   Uncle writes a letter to Mother.

Friday
9th.

done the work today as usual. 'tis not pleasant for one
to feel sad, but alas, I do and know not why it is. * * *
yesterday commenced writing over my old diary; wrote
from March twenty ninth 1858 to April 22. today pleasant
but warm.

Wednesday,
14th.

done the work, made some cake. sewed the facing on lawn
dress. after tea was talking with Susan; she was angry and
did not talk very kindly, ah, the trials & troubles of this
world. cried. Oh how I thought I was not at home to hear a
mother's kind words, but as it were, am alone to bear all my
sorrows. but may I have the mercy of One who is ever watching our deeds and may my prayer be that I may ever do that
which is for the best * * *

Thursday
15;

this forenon done churning, mopped all the rooms (4) below stairs. * * * after tea Mrs. Craig and me went to visit the grave of her mother; she is planting some roots around her grave, it does not seem to me, that I will ever visit my mother's grave, may it be that she may live many years yet, yes, & live happy. much would I that my parents and brother & sisters would visit my burial place than I, theirs. pleasant today. * * *

Tuesday
20th,

done all the work today; the ironing, baking bread and cake &c. after tea called on Mrs Smith, Milton [Nelson] came in then. I philipened him. ha. ha. was glad for he philipened me yesterday.[15] today have not felt really well. ah, that I could be at home to night. may I hope to do that which is right in everything I do, and if providence permit may I be content to stay till December. this afternoon Uncle came in and gave me some of his medicine. O how kind he is, may I endeavor to make him happy while I stay. . . .

Fri.
23.

to day work about the house most all day. Milton went to Manchester. I sent a paper to Pa by him, he brought me a letter from Edna. this evening am writing an answer. pleasant. last night dreamed of sailing in a ship on Lake Michigan, out of sight of land, was away on the top, up by the flag.

Sat.
24.

* * * finished writing Edna a letter. good news to hear they are all well at home, ah. would that I might see them.

Dost thou think of me, sister,
Now I am far away—
Dost thou think of days past, sister,
Days when we were happy & gay

. . . .

Sunday
25.

. . . went out to listen to the preaching, they had too much Abolitionism that I came in the house. would not endure to listen to their blackguardism. am now in the ball room writing. Milton is here, too. * * * ah, ah. here comes Mrs. Craig, well I have got to go down and get supper for the minister and a gentleman that is going to stay here all night. it is now ten o'clock, am in my room writing. the gentleman that stays here to night has enlisted for the war. we had quite a conversation about that and some other things, his name is George Bowman. ha, ha, Milton, Mrs. Craig & me laughed about him, I said if he was not a married man I should be for setting my cap for him but I must say adieu for to night.

Tues.   done the work today, get breakfast for three of the threshers,
27.   dinner for 7 of them, eleven with ourselves, get tea for ten (with all of us) * * *

"Last night I dreamed my Mother
Was standing by my side,
And by me sat a stranger
(I was to be his bride.)
Then, too, I saw another,
He was listening I thought
But I saw no more of Mother
For she vanished from my sight."

* * *

SEPTEMBER 1861.

Thus.   done the work. finished Susa's dress, do not feel really well
5.   today; Uncle received a letter from Uncle Harvey, he wrote that one hundred soldiers leave Morenci, or did leave yesterday, no doubt there are many of them that are my acquaintances. rain quite hard this morning. * * *

Friday.   * * * commenced my dress today, alas, am thinking of
6.   home & friends would that I were with them but it can not

be now so will stay and be contented and then there has been so many of my associates gone to the war, gone, perhaps, to return no more. ah, they die for our country, die for what our forefathers died years and years ago. * * * this evening Milton here, him, Uncle and me had quite a chat on spiritualism. Hurrah for our union noble and brave, Brave soldiers are fighting our country to save.

Tues.
10.

* * * rain most all day. Ah, I'm sad today, why is it. ah, tis because my thoughts are wandering back to childhood,—to days when I had nothing to to [sic] make me unhappy. yes, then all was happiness. would that it were so now, but it cannot be, no, there are the cares, trials and sorrows to encounter with that a child has not, but enough of this, may my prayer be for a contented mind, content with such as the Lord see'est fit to give me. * * *

Thurs.
19.

* * * this evening Mrs. Smith, Emily, John, Henry and Milton Nelson here, they brought their violin. there was just enough of us to dance a quadrille. they have just gone home. I am here in the Hall writing, the rest are all a bed Ah, what a time for thoughts. 'tis raining real hard, Ah, that I were home, but may I pray for a contented mind. good night.

Mon.
23.

this morning arose (am almost ashamed of it) fifteen minutes of seven, cooked chicken and had breakfast at half past seven. Milton here at work today. * * *

Tues.
24.

done the usual work. ironed this forenoon. this afternoon Emily Nelson here, she helped me get tea, Henry, John & Milton working for Uncle today. this evening went to Mr. Alcocks to the party. only five ladies, first dance in I.O.A. they had a very good time though I should have enjoyed it had I been well, got home about two o'clock, even.

Mon.
30.

this forenoon done the washing. Mary [Evans] helped some about the work. * * * this evening had to laugh to see the fun with Mary & Jno. wonder if old maids always act *love sick*? ah, that to night I could see home friends. but home is far away, and I in the far west.

OCTOBER 1861.

Fri.
4.

done the work today, commenced Susan plaid dress. * * * this afternoon Milton caught me some squirrels   I dressed them & cooked them for supper, knit some on stocking * * *

Sat.
5.

done my Saturday's work. mopping, baking. Emily Nelson here to tea, am quite tired this evening, been on my feet most of the day. am now in the Hall writing. the Democrats hold Caucus in the bar room this evening. do not like it very well for they will get the floor so dirty. knit some &c, pleasant. * * *

Sun.
6.

got my mornings work done and ready to go to meeting. * * * this evening Milton here, he has just gone and I have come up stairs to write in my Diary   ah! may my prayer be that God's will be done in everything; that I may ever be true to my word in all that I say, and may I never hurt or mar the feelings of anyone. * * *

Tues.
8.

work all day. made bread, cakes & pies &c. today election. got dinner for nine men. this eve Mr. & Mrs. Smith here. we played cards. I never knew anything about it before, Susa at Mrs. Smiths in the afternoon, I was alone. enjoyed a good cry, was little homesick, pleasant,[16]

Sunday.
13.

ah, 'tis Sunday again, another week has passed away and I am far from home. Uncle has got so very deaf that one can

hardly make him hear a word. this morning finished my preserve, done my morning's work &c. am now in the Hall
writing in my Diary. yes, my thoughts are on home &
friends, ah, that I were there. * * * Uncle said James
Galispy was here this afternoon[17] Milton here a short time,
after evening meeting, pleasant. 'tis ten o'clock. I'm writing. wonder where I may be one year from now ah, I know
not, no.

Tues.
15.

* * * just got things ready for breakfast (tomorrow morning)
when Milton came in and told me he had enlisted to start
for war tomorrow, as tis the last night he stays here, thought
I would make a kind of party for him [The names of twelve
persons attending follow.] Emily & her mother feel very bad
indeed. I can see how my Mother and sister *felt* at my leaving home. Milton gave me a book "Oasis" for a philopena
present, Uncle came home about dark. pleasant,

Wed,
16.

after my morning work done went to Manchester to see the
Soldiers start, there were 94   Mrs's Nelson & Fisher &
Susan went, too. one lady fainted away because she heard
of the death of her daughter. others were crying, some for
brothers, some for husbands & some for sons, cousins &
friends. ah, indeed sad the parting farewell to those that are
dear. Milton bade us adieu, he gave me his Deguerotype,
and the last we saw of him he waved his hat to us. we got
home about two o'clock. I done sweeping up stairs, dressed
chickens &c. tis now nearly four, went over to Mrs. Nelsons
to get my bread. Emily baked it for me to go to Manchester.
* * * pleasant. ah, home, I think of thee today.[18]

Tuesday
22.

this forenoon done my usual work. this afternoon done ironing &c. . . . . have not been as angry since I have been here;
it was because this morning when my work was done was
going to sew some. my knitting and sewing was in the Parlor, could not get it for Susan had locked the door and car-

ried the key with her, I was quite angry, it seems I could not help it; have made up my mind to go home in five weeks. * * * Susan talked worse to me today than she ever has since I came here.

Sunday
27.

went to meeting this forenoon to listen to the preaching of Br. Bishop (Universalist)[19] * * * ah. what gives greater happiness to ones soul than to hear the true teachings of Christ. this evening Henry Nelson, Mr. & Mrs. Smith here. pleasant. Uncle not very well today.

Tues.
29.

this forenoon done my ironing. made some fruit cakes; Uncle churned for me. this afternoon cut & fitted my dress lining, just as tea was ready, I was looking for our folks to come & who should I see but Milton . . . he has come to visit his folks & friends before they go to St. Louis (which is next week). * * *

NOVEMBER 1861.

Friday.
1st.

this forenoon made some pies, the rest of the work & sewed some on my dress. Milton came about ten & stayed till after dinner. . . . this evening Milton came for me to go over there . . . before we went we came up stairs, I wrote a verse in his testament, we had a good visit, Milton came home with me and stayed till about ten, we had a real good talk, yes, he said things I never thought he would, ah, can it be the last time we meet, no, for tomorrow when he goes away, we meet again. * * *

Sat.
2.

it is now nearly nine. I have my work done and have come up stairs to write in my diary. Milton has just gone, he came to bid me another good bye. . . . Milton put a ring on my finger with a wish, he told me to keep it till he came from war. Uncle, Susan, Emily & me went to Manchester we went to the Depot, saw some soldiers start on the cars. Milton kissed and bade us adieu and we came away, we last saw him wave his handkerchief we waved ours to him. * * *

Mon.
4.

tis now 'tween two & three, I have my washing done, and have come up stairs to finish my beds so I sit down & write in my Diary. ah, why do I stay here when I can so well enjoy myself at home; is it that in the future I may be rewarded? * * *

Mon.
11.

done my washing (quite a large one) cleaned my buttry and done the rest of the work, am real tired, have just come up to make my beds, tis most five, my supper is commenced & I must go down & set the table. * * * O dear, my tooth aches.

Tues.
19.

got up this morning. O dear how it had been raining. my clothes were all down   had to rinse them over. and then I went in the pantry; the floor was all covered with milk,—a pan leaked, done the work as usual, sewed some & knit some   rain & blow all day. * * *

Fri.
22.

this morning Emily brought me a letter to read from Milton to his folks. they [the soldiers] start for St. Louis tomorrow so I cannot send my letter till I hear from him again. tis now nearly noon, I have mopped & done the rest of the work &c, dressed chickens for dinner. cold. snow all day.

Sat.
23.

done baking cake, bread, pies & cookies &c. this morning Jackson Sullivan came for me to go & set up with corpse (Mr. Johnson's girl.) sat up all night. cold   snow all day.

Sun.
24.

Jackson brought me home this morning. 9 o'clock. this noon, Mr. Sullivan came for me to make the shroud for them. I went this evening. Jackson brought me home again, cold. pleasant. sleepy.

Mon.
25.

got my morning's work done & washing all but rinsing my clothes. we went to the funeral. . . . I got dinner, we then went to Manchester. I sent a letter to Mother, received one from Edna Hattie & Mother. Pa sent his likeness in their letter taken with Carlo & how glad was I to get it, pleasant.
* * *

[A one-page essay called "Time" is included in this section of the diary, as is the following essay.]

Home.

Ah yes, a *father's* home. how little do we know how to prize that blessing, until we go from our home to some distant land. We have not then a father's kind advice, a brother or sister's love or a Mother's tender care. no! but we are alone in the wide, wide world, with none but strangers to cheer us in our lonely hours of sorrow and sadness. tis true we may have friends among strangers; but, ah, they are not parents, brothers nor sisters; in sickness they may watch over us kindly and affectionately; they may administer to their best ability, but there is not that love, that *pure love* of a *Mother.* no. no! but we can not always have a father's home; we must like they have homes of our own, for death comes sooner or later to every door, and the aged must die, and tis true the young may die, but when father and mother are gone, we are alone, yes, and forever,—not alone for friends but for that *care* & *love.* When are we more happy than when at home, in an winter's evening engaged in a pleasant chat around the fireside? never, no never. Ah, may we not look forward to the time, when death has taken us all to meet at last in Heaven, to part no more through an endless Eternity.

Emmie

Emmie to Edna.

Sat.
30.

done my work, mopping, baking &c. this evening a wagon load (18) of us went to Mr. Trumblees visiting.[20] they treated us on cake & pie, popcorn, walnuts & molasses candy. we enjoyed ourselves with plays &c. till near twelve, then came home, I went with Sammy Sullivan. * * *

DECEMBER 1861.

Tues.
3.

done my work & sewed some on my factory.[21] this afternoon went to Mrs. Smiths, a number of Ladies met to form a society; we named it "The Soldier's Relief Society." Mrs. H. Gardner chosen President   Mrs. Smith, Treasurer, *I*, Secretary, our next meeting, week from tomorrow, at Mrs. Gardners.[22] * * *

Wed.
4.

done the work as usual today. this evening Mr. Smith here; he brought me the list of signers that Mrs. Smith got today for Relief Society, $5.25. Uncle gave me twenty-five cents. * * *

Thurs.
5.

this morning arose at 15 minutes past five, made 5 mince pies, done part of my ironing & the rest of the work & got ready to go to Mr. Duttons, Uncle & Susan went, too. . . . they had some oysters and roast turkey & other refreshments & dined at three, this evening a whole wagon load came here visiting. [Names of guests follow.] we enjoyed the evening by playing, eating apples, &c. * * *

Wed.
11.

done lots of work this forenoon after dinner Uncle carried us to Mrs. Gardners to the Society, we had a real good time, we got home about 11 o'clock in the evening. received another letter from Milton, he is in St. Louis.

Sat.
21.

done my work &c. Rev. Mr. Bishop [the Universalist minister] here to tea & all night. this evening I read to him the second Epistle of John, he then sang & made a prayer, ah, how sweet would be the thought to be as good a Christian as Mr. Bishop is. am real tired to night.

Sunday 22.

this morning we all went to meeting   Br. Bishop preached * * * am now alone in my room, all are abed & sleeping, may I retire to night hoping to some day embrace Universalist Salvation, become a member of the Universalist Church & be a true Christian. good night.

Tuesday 24.

this forenoon made twelve mince pies, & done morning's work. this afternoon made 52 small tin cakes & one large cake. Esther Nelson here most all day. she helped me some. I gave her five cents. pleasant.

Wed. 25.

Christmas day. this forenoon made my beds, swept below stairs, mopped bar room, pantry & kitchen. cooked three chickens for dinner, this afternoon & evening we give a picnic for the benefit of the Soldiers Relief Society. * * * this afternoon we tied off three quilts, finished a number of pairs of shirts & drawers. about two they commenced coming, I helped to wait upon them till about eight o'clock in the evening then got dressed to join in the dance. . . . there were 75 different ones to eat supper. we took in about $17.00, very pleasant indeed.

Thursday. 26.

this morning after the party had broken up (about 5) and all had gone to their homes I went in the parlor thinking to lie down on the sopha & rest, but James Gilespy came in, commenced talking, so we sat and talked till nearly eight (may we never forget the conversation that passed between us, how much would I give to know if he really means all he said) then I went in the kitchen to get breakfast. O such looking rooms I never saw, nearly every dish in the house dirty, but I went to work, washed enough to eat on. James stayed to breakfast   Mrs. Nelson & Mrs. Smith came over

& washed up the dishes & I done the sweeping & picking up of the things   Mrs. Smith stayed & helped me till after dinner, then I went home with her & stayed till supper time, pleasant, but cold wind, retired early and slept like sixty.

JANUARY 1862.

Friday
3d.

done my usual work and baking &c, this evening Susan & me went to the dance. Susie with Ed Ayers. I went with James. We (James & me) came back about 11 o'clock. when we came in all was still. we sat down by the fire and enjoyed ourselves in conversation that we may never forget, no. never. ah, those words, "I love thee with all my heart, and ask yours in return" Oh, may it not be wrong that thy wish be granted and should our hearts be made one may we never prove false & untrue but ever live the life of happiness & love. —to day has been snowing all day & last night, too. James stayed all night, retired about two. my last prayer to night that the will of God be done & not mine, & that all may yet be well.

Wednesday
8.

this morning done my work   stewed some sauce. Mrs. Gardner and Mr. Gillespie here to dinner, the Society meet here today. I got tea for thirty-five different persons. they stayed till about nine o'clock in the evening   after they had all gone James stayed with me, ah. may we ever remember the vows we made. we conversed till about two. he, James stayed all night. pleasant. ah can it be possible that we so soon exchange hearts and hands   only been acquainted since Christmas but tis done and may it be the will of God if we change not our minds.

Friday
17.

done my work, ironing &c. finished Chimee [chemise], Mrs. Smith here most all the afternoon. this evening Mr. Nelson,

Wm. Trumblee, Edd Ayers & James were here. James stayed after the rest had all gone home   well, twas just as it always is when we get engaged talking; tis late before we are aware of it. pleasant. had to laugh though before Edd and William went home, Uncle says, "bed time, I guess." ha ha don't blame him for twas most eleven so they took the hint & started & off went Susa & Uncle to bed. I went too a little before one.—*great*

Saturday 18.

done my usual work. & made some pumpkin pies. this evening we all went to the Temperance lecture at the west schoolhouse given by Br. Bishop   snow some.

Wednesday 22.

done my usual work &c. cut and partly made me a night dress. Eliza here till afternoon, I mopped barroom & kitchen &c. this evening is the Lyceum. Uncle & Susan went   I lay down on the lounge (no one here but John) thinking to have a nice rest & sleep for I got up so early (before five) this morning. had but just got to sleeping nicely & who should come but James for me to go sleighriding. we went. got back about ten. pleasant.

Saturday 25th.

this forenoon done my work &c. got a large pan of material ready for some mince pies, done mopping in barroom, and kitchen. this afternoon James came for me to go sleighriding. we were gone two or three hours, came back, made pies & biscuit for supper. * * * Uncle says, "did Jim pop the question?" ha ha guess he'll find out.

FEBRUARY 1862.

Mon. 10.

didn't wash today because could not melt snow soon enough. made some cakes & pies. James stayed till after dinner. this evening there was a sleigh load of some others came &

danced till after twelve. O dear I had such a cold it seemed they never *would* go away. after they had all gone I lay down on the lounge to rest thinking to sleep there the rest of the night so as to be up early and who should wake me, James. I told him to go to bed but no he must stay and talk with me, so no more sleep till after he went home (about five). I slept nearly two hours. pleasant. may I not forget, no never.
* * *

Tues.
11.

got my work done &c, did not feel well enough to wash so Uncle got Mrs. Parker to. she came & washed & mopped. am just about sick with cold. * * *

Sun.
16.

this forenoon went to meeting. Br. Bishop preached from the text "of the sinning against the Holy Ghost." this evening went to hear Mr. Babcock preach   there were a number spoke on (the foreknowledge of God) such talking I never heard. I certainly believe it a sin to listen to such conversation. pleasant.

Wed.
19.

This forenoon Mrs. Nelson here visiting. she stayed till after dinner, Esther here too. Camps folks (7) and five travelers all here to dinner. 18 with ourselves.[23] * * * this evening we all went to our Lyceum, (snow some in eve.) James came home with me. we sat & talked awhile after the rest had all retired, ah, those questions "do you love me, Emmie, & will you be my bride?" and my answer, *yes*. O, my prayer, that we may ever prove as we now think each other to be, ah, true tis a life *journey* and may it be for the best, but, ah the trial to leave parents & friends, to live far away, but, I trust that all may yet be well.

Fri.
28.

done my work & sewed some, Susan went home with Esther to stay all night. John went to singing school, so Uncle & me were left here alone, not long tho for James came. we had quite a long talk, sent a letter to Mother.[24]

MARCH 1862

Thurs,
6.

have been sweeping the chamber rooms (6). am tired. this evening we went to Mr. Trumblees visiting. just as we were ready to start James came to go to the Lyceum, he went with Uncle & me. there were about 25 there, had a good visit. James came home with us. * * * James stay all night. we sat in the barroom & talked awhile after the rest were abed, ah, can it be, but if no preventing providence & James or me do not change our minds, that the first day of next March is to be my wedding day? Yes, James said to night he wished it to be then. my consent was given: O may it be right, my prayer is that the will of God be done, not mine for tis a great thought to think of leaving childhood's home to take a companion, yes indeed.

Tues.
11.

done my usual work. covered 4 dozen buttons for my dress. done baking and mopping. pleasant.

Fri.
14.

done my usual work. finished my dress. * * * To day heard the news of Milton Nelson's death. he died in the Hospital, at St. Louis with typhoid fever. the 18th. of February (last month) I composed some poetry on his death today. this was yesterday instead of today I heard of his death.[25]

Sun,
23.

* * * this forenoon went to meeting. . . . James came home with us, stayed to tea and in the evening (pretty late, too). Henry Nelson and Jackson Sullivan here in the evening. pleasant. James thought it best not to set any day in particular, for fear of some disappointment; well, I thought so all of the time. I will wait a year, if he proves true till then I hope I may place more confidence in him then than I now do, but enough of this. I will trust to God that whatever be my fate be His will. retire about two.—early isn't it?

Wed.
26.

done the work &c. this afternoon Mrs. Smith here visiting, got tea for eleven. this evening went to the Lyceum. read an essay on the negative of the question—Resolved that hatred is a greater passion than love.[26] * * *

Saturday 29.

done the usual work &c, after tea called on Mrs. Smith. pleasant. O dear, work, work all the time.

Sunday. 30.

* * * two men were buried today in sight of Uncles. they were drowned yesterday. they had started to go home and crossing the creek they fell in, and, being under the influence of liquor, died. thus ends the lives of two more victims of intemperance, leaving wives & children to mourn their loss. cold.

APRIL 1862.

Fri. 4.

went to Smiths this morning to bid them good bye, they are moving about 12 miles from here. am sorry. it will be so lonely when they are gone. done my usual work, baked 5 pies (mince) 4 cakes & biscuit   retire early; tired & sleepy. James called here but I did not see him to speak   Uncle came out in the kitchen & said, "You don't know who is here," laughed.

Sun. 6.

not very well. not any one here, snow all day: wrote part of a story (I am composing). the title Robert Burton & his Daughter, or "A Tale of Intemperance."

Mon. 7.

last night I dreamed a curious dream. that I was riding down hill with some others on a hand sled. I was riding alone. I rode on & on till I came over deep clear water, it was mostly covered with snow. I looked around and saw a large brick building. I went in there to stay all night for I was lost, its occupants were an elderly gentleman and lady, they were very kind, then there were two other ladies, I took them to be their daughters but I did *not* like *them*, for they asked too many questions as to who I was & how I came to be there &c. I was about to depart; the old gentleman urged me to stay, but, no, I turned to go and saw James there, *he* told me not to go. that they must now mind their business for he had come, then they were friends to me; done my washing this forenoon, this afternoon sewed some. * * *

Friday 11th.

this morning I am alone. I sit myself down in the kitchen and write in my Diary. tis my twenty-fourth birthday, tis a pleasant morning but look out and see the snow   Henry & his father were here a few minutes   I talk of going home in five or six weeks & think I shall if no preventing providence, Mr. Nelson says "he thinks I will not go   if I do I will come back soon for James will have something to say about it." his words are more true than he thinks for if we do not break those solemn vows we have made. but enough of this as Mother says, there is many a slip 'tween the cup & the lip, done my ironing this forenoon, this afternoon finished writing a letter to Edna,—four pages of foolscap full. this evening Wm. Trumblee here. we played a game of chess. thinking of home. ah, would that I were there.

Sat, 12.

tis now some past nine, I have my mornings work, sweeping & mopping done, have come up here (in the Hall) to write in my Diary. O dear how can I stay here any longer; Susan is so saucy. but may she, as she grows older, learn to use more judgment. * * * forty-one weeks to night since I first saw this house, ah. it seems a long time: am I now free as when I came here, ah, no, I have made vows which I dare not break, yet I have no desire to now. my prayer is still the same that the will of God be done. Should James see fit to recall that solemn promise my best wishes will ever be with him and may he ever prosper in his doing   what an idea. why do I still doubt his confidence. while a something seems to tell me tis right. not any one here this evening. retire early.

Tuesday. 15.	got breakfast for 9, dinner for 15. tea for five. O such a looking house I never saw. they all went home about 4 o'clock. I was glad enough, too for I did not sleep two hours last night. quite a thunder shower in the evening. retire early.
Wed. 16.	done my usual work today, mopping in barroom & kitchen. Esther Nelson here in afternoon & all night. I cut her a dress. pleasant to day. I finished Mother's letter, commenced it yesterday. ah, thinking of the past again. May I do not again the evil deeds which I know to be wrong. ah, may the will of God be done. not mine. . . .
Sun. 20.	have just got home from meeting, am writing in my Diary. ah, why am I sad. 'tis a beautiful day & kind friends my every want supply and still my heart has some longing desire. Yes, I know not what it is. Wm. Trumblee was here. I went to Smiths with him on horse back; the horse had never been rode by a lady before, he did not go very good, I walked back home horseless. pleasant.
Wed. 23.	do my ironing & mopping this forenoon. quite cold but pleasant, have been some homesick this three weeks and think that I will go home in June. * * *
Fri. 25.	this forenoon done the usual work, & mopped. * * * this evening called on Emily Nelson. * * * when coming home we saw in the west a prairie fire. it looked like a huge rock of fire most beautiful indeed.
Sun. 27.	* * * went to meeting but did not stay they preached Milton's funeral sermon. text the 9th chapter of Hebrews, 27 verse. James came to Uncles with me he gave me a gold ring. * * *

MAY 1862.

Thursday. 1st.	done the housework, broidered some &c. this afternoon went to Masonville with Uncle. got $.15 worth of pens; called on Mrs. Duttons. Mr. Dutton says if I will teach their school next summer I may make it my home there.[27] * * *
Mon. 5.	this forenoon done my washing &c. about twenty minutes of two thought I would lie down on the sofa and rest till two, but forgot myself and e'er the clock struck was in the land of dreams, when I woke twas past four. ah, me if I didn't have to hurry some, my dinner dishes & 12 pans to wash, beds to make & supper to get, & work to do up, but 'twas done by six. . . .
Fri. 9.	made some Rhubarb pies. ironed my light lawn & buff calico dresses, & three fine shirts. broidered some, & done rest of work. Uncle went to Manchester, brought me an apple and a lemon. this evening am writing in my Diary. * * * tis a pleasant May evening, yes. just 45 weeks ago to night we took the cars for the west; Susa has been gone since Wednesday. I am alone sitting on the floor by my trunk, all is still, save now and then, the mellow notes of the whippoorwill & the voices of the men below,

Ah, home, that I could see thee
Meet once more the warm embrace
Of those I loved so long. Aye, those
Who last gave the parting kiss.

Sun. 18.	got my morning's work done about nine. ready for meeting. * * * I came back, found Corrells & James here. James had exchanged my ring for another like it (only for my ring finger) well, he stayed to tea & till past the hour of midnight. heigh ho, if didn't laugh though when he came to go in the barroom for his cap it was not there. he found it though in

Uncle's hat: John had put it there to play a joke on him. real pleasant. only cold.

Sat.
24.

finished dress about one, then I made 5 pies (three rhubarb & two custard) one cake, a custard, & a pan of cookies * * * they hold grove meeting here this afternoon, pleasant. went to meeting this evening.

Sat.
31.

Uncle carried me to Delhi to be inspected . . . am to receive a certificate [to teach] by mail. we took dinner at the hotel. * * *

JUNE 1862

Sunday.
1st.

went to Mrs. Coffins this morning, stayed till meeting time. . . . James was here; he stayed till about eleven in the evening. Alas, that bitter must ever be with the sweet   James is sad today, he wept but told not why. today has been pleasant.

Tues.
3.

sewed on my dress (purple calico) most of the time, this afternoon Emily Nelson came. I cut her dress. tonight there is a family (8) of movers here all night & another gentleman, too, & Mary Williams too,—pleasant.

Wed.
4.

* * * now I am writing in my Diary. . . . but ah, this dreadful War. a Battle is being fought in Richmond. since Sunday morning thousands upon thousands of true hearted young men are being killed. what for? *O Slavery accursed wrong*: may peace soon be declared.—

Fri.
6.

got breakfast, done up the work. done churning & mopping, got dinner, am just going to do up the dishes. 'tis now after tea & am writing. my day's work is done and I am at liberty to think of the past, aye, of the present. another victory gained, Corinth taken & thousands of Rebel prisoners. . . . but I must put by my writing & go to the Concert. James came about eight, we went   it was a concert of *Bell Ringers*, beautiful indeed. after the concert, they danced. had quite a pleasant time. we came back about three, enjoyed the ride about as well as the music & dancing. very pleasant.

Sat. 7.

made cookies & pies & done rest of work. slept awhile this forenoon & afternoon, too. to night Br. Bishop, Mr. Brice & wife here. all have retired but—me—. 'tis past ten, am writing in my Diary & listening to some one *snoring*.

Sun. 15.

* * * tis now near evening, I am pondering on the past, thinking what may be my future lot, & writing in my Diary. cool but pleasant. this evening (after tea) called on Mrs. Nelson. Emily went with me to Corrells. they were strawberrying so we went out where they were. When I came home; found James here. we sat in the Parlor & talked &c. till near two, it most probably will be the last time this summer as I intend to commence teaching school next tuesday. * * *

Tues. 17.

Uncle brought me to Mr. Duttons. I commence school in Masonville this morning, had twenty scholars, work on sack.[28] at Mr. Duttons. my schoolhouse a new one situated on a large (high) prairie where we can see the [train] cars every day, not a tree to be seen only in the north east. pleasant.

Sat. 21.

tis now evening have just finished the first week of school— right glad I am, too. am at Mrs. Duttons. * * *

Thurs. 26.

received a letter from Mother & Father   work some on broidery, morning & evening   teach school, had 26 scholars. . . . this evening James called to see me. at Mrs. Duttons.

Fri.   taught school today &c. this evening Uncle came for me;
27.   here I am sitting by my trunk writing in my Diary. * * *

Sat.   done my washing this morning. about ten went to Mrs. Nel-
28.   sons. stayed till after five, then Emily & me went to Mrs.
            Coffins   I am now sitting on the steps at Uncles. Yes, am
            visiting here now, a year ago today I came here, ah little
            thought I then that I would be here now. but tis so. and how
            differently do I look forward for future providence than did
            I then. but God knows what is best for us, & it seems, to
            me, His will that I have so long deserted my father's home.
            but I trust in providence, faith whispers, I may at the end
            of my school,—once more meet them. work some on my
            sack. pleasant. * * *

Mon.   work some on broidery. this morning Uncle & Susan brought
30.   me to school. Mr. Dutton has come from Chicago, he
            brought me a hat $2.80, set of skelletons $1.00 & belt $.25
            = $4.05. have not paid him yet. am boarding at Mr. Mar-
            tins this week, pleasant.

JULY 1862.

Thurs.   in school today. real warm. * * * just heard the *glorious*
3.   *News* that the North had taken Richmond   Uncle came for
            me. . . . * * * a mistake, Richmond is not taken.

Fri.   today is the fourth of July, there is a celebration here (in the
4.   grove) today. this evening James & me went to Manchester
            to a dance. got home about daylight. warm & pleasant

Tues.   sent Henry's letter—am [boarding] at Mrs. Hiltons   had
8.   for breakfast, chicken half done potatoes, bread & butter

&c. well, I guess I can stand it a week. am here to night. like to stay very well, done some broider &c. took dinner at Mrs. Duttons.

Tues.
15,

in school, had to reprove one of the larger girls (Emma Bing) for being rather indifferent, that is not having good lessons & not seeming to try to do anything. was sorry to do it, but I *must* have some kind of *order*. 20 today. * * *

Sun.
27.

* * * this afternoon James came to see me. have not seen him in three weeks   he brought me to Masonville (to Mr. Martins) this evening. he thinks best that I do not go to Michigan in the fall, but stay here till another year, well, it will be full as well for our happiness that I stay. it seems but tis as the words of God & may it be His will, the first of October if no preventing providence may perchance find me in another home, ah, my dream of last June (1861). pleasant as can be. * * *

Wed
30.

could not eat any breakfast, was real sick, but sick or well will have to go to school, went to school & stayed till about half past ten, could stay no longer, was so sick, came to Mrs. Martins, took some pills &c. * * *

AUGUST 1862.

Tuesday
5.

in school today, am not very well. at Mr. Bings to night. am making pair of drawers for Mrs. Dutton, pleasant. carried Mother's letter to the postoffice

Wednesday
6.

taught school today, too, sewed some &c. called on Mrs. Rose & Mrs. Dutton after tea, this evening there is a lecture given at the lower schoolhouse to get volunteers to go to

War. O dear, 300,000 more men called for to be ready by the fifteenth of this month or they are going to draft. ah, horrible indeed to think that so many of our associates & friends must be slain on this dreaded battle field, but let us all do the best we can,—be content with such as is sent to us. Yes, *my* prayer is that the will of God be done, not mine   rain quite hard today & this morning   am at Mrs. Bings to night.

Friday
8.

in school all day, O dear am real glad that school is so near done. have 27 scholars today, Uncle came for me this evening. * * *

Sunday.
10.

I am sitting on the seat (where the preacher does) in the grove, writing in my Diary. * * * Gilbert came for me to ride with him, he goes to war next Thursday, ah, me this awful war. James came to see me, he stayed till after one in the evening. I teased him some to stay but how could I help it. —he has not been to see me in so long a time—all of two weeks. James says he will not go to the war unless he is obliged to. may I trust to providence to restore to me one friend but should he have to go may the will of God be done, and if it be right may he again return. at Uncles all night.

Wednesday
13.

* * * ah that I could go home—to fathers but I must wait with patience until school is done, only three weeks more. O.O. (I went to Mr. Duttons to dine, some of them said) James had enlisted, ah me what shall I do if brother & James too should go. I cried but may I place all confidence in God to bring them safe to me again. another great battle fought yesterday but not a victory on either side. O *awful war* if James should go, but I *can* not believe he will. I will try to do the best I can for I know he will sometimes think of the pleasant hours we have spent together and when he comes home, O happy will be the meeting to part no more till death * * *

Thursday 14.	another morning has dawned. not very pleasant for last night it rained most all the time, ah, my thoughts are sad and yet I know not really why. yes, tis of the fear that brother & James may be called to go to the battlefield but I must be aware that others, too, have parted with dear ones. and O may God give me strength to submit to His will; & be content with my lot, 'tis all I ask, Amen. * * *
Sunday. 17.	* * * about three o'clock James came with horses & carriage for me to go & take a ride. we went. through the grove & over on the prairie quite a long ride. * * * James brought me to Masonville to Mrs. Martins, he says he is not coming again in two weeks. but I almost believe he will. pleasant.
Monday. 18.	another Monday morning & ready to begin another week of school, tis pleasant. O.O. Mrs. Johnston brought me a letter from Henry; he is not going to war unless he is drafted. * * *
Friday 22.	am in school today. . . . tis now recess and I have a few minutes to spare, so I write in my Diary, ah, that some one would come that I would be,—O so glad to see. tis a pleasant day and Emmie has but eleven days more to be confined in this place. ah, happy thought,—yet may I hope that what I have taught the young idea here may prove useful to their minds. . . .
Sunday 24,	have written a letter to Edna am in my room alone [at Uncles], 'tis after four, they are having a meeting in the grove. I can hear them sing & preach, too, but I rather be alone to think. * * * James has not been here today, oh it seems a long time since I *saw him*. but I will wait till God sees fit to bring us together to part no more till death. . . . * * *

SEPTEMBER 1862.

Tuesday
2.

in school, 27 scholars. * * * O, me how many times does a teacher have to weep for the misconduct of some pupil. Yes, I cried to think that some larger scholars were saucy,—

Friday.
5.

today is the close of my school. this forenoon we had an examination of all our studies. * * * the scholars rehearsed their pieces, sang &c. and then remarks were made by several; thus closes my school—am glad it is done. stay at Mrs. Duttons to night, rain in night.[29]

Sunday
7.

pleasant all day. James was here all day, most & evening, too till eleven. can it be that next week Emmie is to be a bride? yes, yes, if James fulfills his promise—but may I trust that all will be well, that the will of God be done.

Tuesday
16.

sew on my dress &c. this morning Mr. Ayers paid me my school money. $30.00.

Wed.
17.

finished my net and dress & done other fussing—to day Uncle went to Delhi with James to get license—James came home with him, we sat & talked till past eleven   pleasant. sent $10.00 to pay for my dress &c.

Thursday
18.

James here all day. about half past twelve Molly & Alice came over. Uncle asked Mrs. Parker, Mrs. Aubry & John, Susa was here too. Uncle says, "You may stand up"—none but Susa knew anything about it, & in a few minutes we were pronounced husband & wife. What a pleasant day it has been, just sixty-four weeks ago today I started for Iowa with Uncle now there is to be on my mind new cares, yes, I am married now—and may it ever be my desire to make James a happy home. I hope we may both put our trust in God to lead us in the way we should go—stay at Uncles all night. commence Mrs. Correll's net.

Fri.
19.

at Uncles today, James went home this morning. * * * in the evening Henry Nelson came for me to go over to the old house to a dance. Uncle & Susa went, I came back about ten, the rest stayed till most morning.

Sunday
21.

James came to see me this morning. him & me went to meeting. * * * after tea we went to see James' Parents. . . . * * *

Tuesday
23.

settled up with Uncle. he gave me set of dishes $11.57. so we passed receipts & called it even, some rain. James came to see me awhile this evening, he thought my dishes real nice.

Saturday
27.

done up about twelve pounds of melon preserves. sewed some on Susa's dress &c. James came for me to go home with him. I went & stayed all night. we talk some of going to Michigan to spend the winter.

CHAPTER THREE

Emily Hawley,
Unmarried Woman

The journey west to Iowa was an allegory for the complex and sometimes contradictory drives that motivated Emily Hawley. At twenty-three, she desired to see more of the world than the rural township of her birth; yet she also longed for the comfort and security of her father's home. If going to work in Iowa represented an irreversible step into adulthood, living there with an elderly uncle and a cousin provided some of the protection of remaining a girl among family. She was neither the single woman emigrant—a statistical rarity indeed in 1861—nor the dutiful daughter who had followed her mother's advice and married a local boy at age twenty.[1]

Life in Iowa for Emily Hawley was, alas, really not that much different from what it had been in Michigan. The exciting frontier period had ended in this part of the state by 1850. If the hope of increasing her prospects for marriage was a reason for traveling to the Far West, it was unfounded, for in 1860 the male to female sex ratio for Iowa (1.14 : 1) was actually marginally poorer than in Michigan (1.15 : 1).[2] Emily's work at the inn simply repeated and enlarged the cycle of household chores she had performed at home, only now she served more people and was responsible for a much larger dwelling. She was still living in a rural setting on her uncle's property and was still dependent on pleasing the head of the household, who was now also her employer. In some ways, then, Emily Hawley's life situation deteriorated upon her arrival in Iowa, as reflected in the sad passages of her diary.

What had happened at home to motivate her to leave? At age twenty, when her diary opens, Emily Hawley has "a home at father's," where she is both an asset and a liability: she is a female worker contributing to the household and an unmarried eldest daughter. (Throughout the early diary home is called "father's"—she longs for her father's *home* and her mother's *love*, terminology demonstrating the gender division in her mind of property and sentiment. She also describes other families' homes via the male owners' names, again acknowledging men's property rights.)

Although Emily Hawley's description of her father's and brother's farm work and production is sketchy, one can judge from the size of the property—thirty acres—that this was a subsistence-level farm typical of the pre–Civil War Midwest where enough crops were raised to support the livestock but there were not enough for trade. On this type of farm, according to John Mack Faragher, historians and anthropologists have estimated that "women were more centrally involved in providing subsistence for the farm family than men." Given women's responsibility for the half-acre garden required to support a family, the poultry and egg production, and the processing of meat after slaughter, from one-third to one-half of all food produced on the farm resulted from the labor of Sarah Hawley and her daughters.[3]

Emily Hawley mentions few food-processing chores in her journal; to her fell several other women's household tasks that then "freed" her mother to work in the kitchen. She notes making soap, candles, and clothing for the family's use. Not only did she hand-sew garments and linens, she was responsible for producing woolen fabric from the farm sheep. To supply a family of four's annual need for homespun required two full weeks at the spinning wheel and loom—time mercifully abridged in an edited diary but nonetheless Emily's task (see entries starting September 21, 1860). One day's work at the wheel could produce two miles of yarn, which would make about three yards of woolen material. Home dyes such as Emily mentions making were quite rare by the 1860s, indicating perhaps a family pride in traditional ways or a lack of cash with which to purchase commercial colorings. Within the home, then, Emily Hawley was a contributing worker and literally the spinster who clothed her kin.[4]

But only a portion of her labor went toward the support of the family unit. The diary and her meticulous account books record a variety of services Emily Hawley performed for cash or goods in trade: teaching; sewing for hire; instructing women in crafts such as making hair flowers; housekeeping for invalids and new mothers; peddling books. With her earnings she purchased items for herself such as fabric, stationery, and books. She does not mention giving any of her earnings to family members, although she does note lending them cash. It is clear from Emily Hawley's accounts and comments in her diary that an income of her own was extremely important; she does not express misgivings or guilt about spending what she has earned.

The secondary scholarship on what was typical for a nineteenth-century unmarried daughter to do with her income is contradictory and unsatisfactorily documented. Historians disagree on whether girls employed at the Lowell Mill, for example, kept their wages or sent them home. (The realistic answer probably lies in the middle: some girls did, some did not, and some divided their earnings.) But there seems to be agreement, based on sparse autobiographies and letters, that in comparison to urban women workers, farmers' daughters had less or no discretionary income to spend; their labor went more often to their families. In agricultural settings, Thomas Dublin says, "women undoubtedly kept some of the income from the sale of products they had made, but the largest share probably went to the family as a whole and more particularly to the husband and father as household head." If this were generally so, Emily Hawley would be an atypically independent or ungrateful daughter.[5]

However, several factors should be considered in evaluating historians' differentiation between farm and factory girls. First, much of women's work on the farm was enacted, as shown above, in a cashless setting. A daughter's work would obviously benefit the family but also assist in her own upkeep. Likewise, the factory girl paid part of her earnings to a boardinghouse, her surrogate family support system, for her upkeep. Secondly, products produced by women on a farm relied on the entire unit—eggs require chickens kept in a henhouse and fed on grain raised by men. Thus giving a part of her egg money to the family would merely be a justifiable repayment of a woman's overhead. However, in Emily Hawley's case, she earned cash from selling her services instead of produce dependent on the farm unit. These services were often performed away from home, a distancing that would reinforce her sense of the separate nature of her work. By earning money even a mile away from home, Emily Hawley achieved that degree of economic independence sought by eastern girls through going to the mills. The retention of her income, then, seems more comparable to the findings about urban women workers who also sold their services—as hired servants, typewriters, and loom operators—and who kept their wages.

It is difficult to tell from Emily Hawley's diary whether questions of what was her money and what were her financial responsibilities to the family caused strife. Whether her "hiring out" was seen by her parents as an irresponsible desertion of the home where her labor was needed or as a respite when there was one less mouth to feed is unclear. We are privileged to hear only one side of the conversation. Thus we cannot tell whether Emily's sadness and tears about money were the result of the general Hawley poverty or of arguments about her role in the family's income. Disagreement about the cash value of women's work would be an ongoing motif in her life.

If Emily Hawley's unpaid household work was an asset and her independent income a family conundrum, her unmarried state at age twenty was a definite liability in her mother's opinion. The issue of marriageability again put Emily and her mother at odds and may have influenced her major life decision to leave home. Sarah Hawley pronounced Emily "not married yet," a twentieth-birthday comment that carried both criticism and expectation. The prospect of the eldest of the Hawley daughters not marrying first may have troubled the family, for even in the mid-nineteenth century over 70 percent of young women married in birth order.[6] Some people believed that if a younger daughter married first, suitors would suspect the elder daughter flawed. By the time of the Iowa decision, Emily's younger sister Edna was herself twenty and courting. There may have been mounting parental pressure for Emily to marry first.

But it is clear from the diary that the question of marriage for Emily Hawley was not *when* but *if*. For many women in the mid-nineteenth century, the marriage decision could be the most important of their lives. It can be argued that at this point in American history a number of social and economic factors combined to give the prospect of marriage unprecedented weight. In *The Bonds of Womanhood*, historian Nancy Cott describes the confluence of pressures: "The marriage choice determined women's life experience to a greater extent than it had earlier, when married women's household roles were less specialized, the conjugal relationship more dependent on wider kin connections, and the ideologies of individualism and romantic love less dominant. It is also more conclusive than in a later period when the incidence of divorce increased." As a result of such pressure, some Victorian women experienced what Cott calls "marriage trauma"—a sort of emotional paralysis in the face of an enormous decision requiring contradictory responses. "As long as the wife's legal subordination persisted, in combination with romantic love ideals that stressed personal attraction and emotional motivation for both partners, women faced an overwhelming irony: they were to choose their bondage."[7]

The combination of both romantic and rational decision making evidenced in Emily Hawley's diary is typical, according to a book-length study of courtship by Ellen K. Rothman. Relying on nineteenth-century women's and men's writings, Rothman discovered a heavy emphasis on three factors also found in the Hawley diary. Both women and men insisted on self-determination in the marriage choice, which Emily exercises in her rejection of suitors favored by her parents. Secondly, Rothman says, by the mid-nineteenth century romantic love was no longer considered frivolous; rather, it was considered a prerequisite for a happy marriage. Given Emily Hawley's list of sentimental reading and her comments about her lack of such feeling for her suitors, she too had expectations of romantic love. Thirdly, even betrothed women showed many misgivings about the prospect of marriage, describing themselves as "anxious," "mortified," and "fretful" in their diaries and letters. One sympathetic marriage manual writer explained a woman's fear this way: "Does she not submit, at least prospectively, to a long train of circumstances and consequences which, in her father's house, she would be able to escape?"[8] Emily Hawley's positive feelings about her father's house (despite the fact that it offered no escape from the "insult" her own uncle offered on July 10, 1859) gave her little incentive to risk marriage.

Emily Hawley's rational and critical skills in the courtship process are evident in the diary. The efficiency she shows in dispatching unqualified suitors may seem coldly unromantic to modern readers, but this opposite face of the Janus-like marriage decision was highly recommended in a variety of marriage manuals of the time. The characteristics of a good prospective husband, according to these advisors, were religious concurrence, excellent health, and good character (i.e., sobriety). By inverting Emily's criticisms of her suitors' faults into her approval of opposite characteristics, one can trace the logic of her quest for "the *right one*." She sought a man who did not drink, did not brag about his property, was not too old, and was not ignorant or unmannerly—a genteel, educated, modest, and sober man. Of the forty manuals (written mostly by men) studied by Michael Gordon, only one mentioned the desirability of romantic love. More representative was this statement: "True love is founded on esteem, and esteem is the result of intimate acquaintance and confidential intercourse."[9]

The opportunity for such confidential contact, as shown in this diary and in Rothman's study, was far more accessible to couples than the prescriptive literature of Victorian America indicates. Emily Hawley had much freedom for courtship both while living at her parents' home and when away working for others. These opportunities would increase both her sense of responsibility for self-regulation (her pride in being chaste is mentioned several times) and her sense of self-empowerment regarding the marriage decision. While historians like Cott have argued that factors controlling women's lives at this point in history made the responsibility to "choose their bondage" a cruel irony, at least the *perception* of choice such as that documented in Emily Hawley's diary gave her some sense of power, if only for once in her life.

Of course the process of such monumental life decision making is far more complex and interactive than our bipolar terms *romantic* and *rational* suggest. As Daniel Scott Smith noted when he reached the interpretative endpoint of demographic data in his study of parental power in courtship decisions, "The actual process of decision making and bargaining is forever lost to the historian of ordinary people. . . . the dead cannot be interviewed."[10] The closest we can come to such an interview with Emily Hawley is to analyze her diary. Besides her parents' opinions, her resistance, and her mixture of sentiments regarding herself and her suitors, there are other factors embedded within the diary that suggest deeper reasons she might leave home and eventually decide to marry.

An unalterable fact of Emily Hawley's life was that she was a female child in a family with a son. Given the modest size of the Hawley farm, it is clear that the property could not be divided among four children and remain economically viable. It would most likely go to the one child who could farm it—Henry Hawley. This section of the old Northwest Territory had gone through the stages of growth and stagnation previously enacted in the Northeast; out-migration was one alternative for adult children in such a situation. So despite her sentimental words about the pleasures of a "home at father's," Emily Hawley was probably aware that in a practical sense she could not live there forever. Spinsters were pitiable, as Mary Chesnut recorded in her own diary on February 25, 1865: "Girls who live on in their father's houses are slaves."[11]

Emily Hawley's social world outside her family was also changing. She records the marriages of close female friends and of former beaus. Several of her peers in her visiting network were already mothers, although comments in the diary do not seem envious of their lot. But the "school days" which Emily Hawley fondly remembered probably appeared more remote as one by one her friends established homes of their own.

Then there was the troubling rumor circulated about Emily Hawley which she heard from both her brother and her aunt (see entries of July 3 and July 8, 1860). Because Emily keeps the rumor a secret from her diary, it is impossible to measure its impact on her status in a small Michigan community. Was it omitted from her life record because it was immaterial or because it was painfully true to the mark? Nancy Cott observes, "Without some corollary information a present-day reader cannot tell what was left out of a diary, letter or memoir, and whether items were left out because they were unimportant or the very most important to the writer."[12]

The corollary information in Emily Hawley's case could be her coding of her menstrual cycle in the margins of her diary. Other nineteenth-century women used similar coding. Paul Rosenblatt detected it in three diaries: one woman marked her periods with "xx," similar to Hawley's mark; another used the code "# . . ."; a third wrote several times in "bad French" that she was not pregnant. Mabel Loomis Todd also coded her sexual activities in her diary using methodical detail, according to biographer Polly Longsworth.[13] While the marks in Emily Hawley's diary do not necessarily mean she was sexually active (they could simply be a young woman's method of predicting her next period), they served to assure her that she was not pregnant. The large gap in the marks, however (from April 1860, three months before "the rumor" reaches Emily, to six years later, when she is the mother of the number of children she desires), is puzzling if they were to serve merely as a record of her menstrual cycle.

One way to estimate the statistical probability that Emily Hawley was sexually active before marriage is by reconstructing levels of premarital intercourse through historical data about premature pregnancy rates in the nineteenth century. The rate of premature pregnancy at this period (1841 to 1880) was lower than at either the beginning or end of the nineteenth century. Still, one out of eight married women (12.6 percent) bore a child conceived before she was married. If this figure represents the portion of couples "caught" by premarital sex, an even greater number of women no doubt engaged in sexual intercourse before marriage, taking advantage of numerous contraceptive methods available in the mid-nineteenth century. As Carl Degler has noted, "In summation, before the Civil War all of the methods of birth control that would be known in the first half of the 20th century, with the single exception of the diaphragm, had been discussed, described, and advocated in books and pamphlets intended for lay readers and to which access was relatively easy." Contraception will be discussed in greater detail in Part II. [14]

By mid-1861, then, home was becoming less comfortable for Emily Hawley. Given her status within the family, her estrangement from her marrying cohort, and the unflattering rumor, there were negative incentives against staying in Michigan. But there would also be positive inducements to leave Home for the World, a conceptual dichotomy familiar to the Victorian mind. Although usually women left home under the care of their new husbands, sentimental literature often featured single women (orphaned or widowed) wandering the Wide World, encountering exciting opportunities and titillating perils.

Emily had already asked permission to go to New York City for art training (see entry of October 10, 1858), but this had met with disapproval. Perhaps if kin had invited her East instead of acquaintances, she would have received parental approval to go and would have made a life in the city. But both the Hawleys and the Bakers had lived in Michigan for two generations and there were few familial ties to the East. Thus Emily Hawley's destiny lay in the West. If one maps Emily Hawley's world as reported in her diary, for the first twenty-three years of her life she existed within a twenty-one-square-mile sphere. Clearly she aspired to broaden her vistas (and opportunities) by going east. That being impossible, she at least finally got to see Chicago between trains on her way to Iowa. Its wonders were not lost on her. The effect that the brief excursion (and her encounter with "Mr. Hathaway" mentioned September 13 and 20, 1861, in the diary) had on her suggests how open she was to ideas and worlds beyond hers.

Perhaps, then, at her Uncle Henry Baker's busy inn in Iowa she would find what Thomas Dublin says appealed to the Lowell Mill girls who left home: "Individual self-support enabled women to enjoy urban amenities not available in their rural communities, and gave them a measure of economic and social independence from their families."[15]

Once established at the Baker Inn, however, Emily Hawley found life little enlarged by the World. She was confined by her obligations as housekeeper and as caretaker for her uncle's daughter, held within a kinship system that was sustained by the labor of single women. Marilyn Ferris Motz found in her study of twelve motherless households in southern Michigan that, "none of the widowed fathers attempted to care for children without the assistance of female kin and none hired a housekeeper to care for the children."[16] Hawley's accounts show that she was saving little of her earnings from hard work at her uncle's, instead spending her wages on purchases in nearby Manchester. As her options narrowed, the advantages of "the political economy of marriage," Suzanne Lebsock's apt term, must have appeared more and more attractive.[17]

Teaching, idealized in Emily Hawley's Michigan diary when she could not get a position, was clearly a tedious option, judging from her Iowa diary record. Employment as a teacher, an experience typical of perhaps one-fifth of young women like Emily Hawley, often preceded marriage. (In her case, she was informally betrothed and teaching provided a rapid way to earn $30.00.) Given the lamentable comments about the stress of teaching in many women's writings, one wonders if this type of work did not provide the final bitter taste of the World that convinced them to choose marriage: poor facilities, a salary lower than a mill girl's, too many children to teach well, the indignity and vacillation of boarding around.[18]

During her first few months in Iowa, Emily Hawley often thought of another option—returning to her beloved childhood home. Content analysis of her diary for July 1861, one month after her arrival in Iowa, shows home, family, and the past mentioned eleven times, letters received mentioned eight times, letters written home eleven times. Of the six times she explicitly mentions her feelings during that month, five are negative—homesickness, doubts. Many of these sentiments are omitted from the edited diary because they are repetitive; but this same repetition shows her feelings were heartfelt.

In his study of grief in nineteenth-century diaries, Paul Rosenblatt found that separation from loved ones was second only to death in causing pain, especially to the person leaving. Grief was often stimulated by mail from or about the beloved. Much such correspondence was going on between Emily Hawley and her family, according to the diary and her uncle's observations. Women's diaries, especially those of overland emigrants, are filled with profound longings for home. Julie Roy Jeffrey also found separations from family often expressed in death imagery: "That women so often compared leave-taking to death was at once a realistic assessment that it was 'not at all probable that we ever will meet again on this side of the dark river,' as well as a symbolic recognition that the emotional void was like death itself."[19]

As Emily Hawley's plans to return to Michigan were postponed time and again, she must have realized that home as she remembered it was metaphorically dead. By July 1862, she mentions home only once and correspondence has dropped to half the level of the year before. One factor in women's fear of marriage, according to Ellen K. Rothman's study, was that for women it meant separation from home. In Emily Hawley's case, circumstances had already severed the home ties. She, too, was looking for a home of her own. If such a home at father's was irretrievable, then Emily Hawley would have to achieve it as over 90 percent of her peers did—through marriage.[20]

By the time Emily Hawley wrote to her parents about her decision to marry James Gillespie in Iowa, she was only a month away from her twenty-fourth birthday. While marrying at twenty-four was typical for women in the Northeast at this time, the average age of marriage on the frontier was closer to twenty. (Most marriage age statistics, however, are based on small samples.) In the middle of this range—neither in the East nor the West—was Emily Hawley. More importantly, by age twenty-four Emily had a less comfortable situation than she had had at age twenty when she ridiculed marriage.[21]

While working at her uncle's inn Emily Hawley met James Gillespie, a twenty-five-year-old man who lived nearby on his parents' prosperous farm. Information about James's other assets is difficult to infer from the diary, for Emily Hawley wrote remarkably little about his personality, conversation, or appearance. What romance there was to this courtship is also lost to us. Since Emily and James were not separated while they were lovers, no correspondence documents their affection. (Considering the vast quantity of materials saved by Emily Gillespie, including love letters from former suitors, it is unlikely that James' letters would be discarded.) While the romance between other nineteenth-century couples like Lester Frank Ward and his fiancée Elisabeth Carolyn Vought is immortalized in letters, no such record of Emily Hawley's and James Gillespie's feelings for each other remains.

In the diary where she freely recorded her opinions of other people, Emily Hawley was quite circumspect about James. There are no critical evaluations (and few positive ones) of James, in contrast to her assessments of previous suitors. In the nineteenth century, some women called their fiancés "my best friend" and "confidant," terms that show an emotional closeness that would prevent an objective critique of the beloved in the pages of a diary. Perhaps a new sense of the *couple's* privacy kept Emily Hawley mute about the details of their courting. In several past situations she withheld specifics of a tryst from the pages of her journal (see, for example, June 3, 1860). Thus phrases like "we had quite a long talk" may have coded for Emily scenes with James that she preferred to keep as private secrets, even from her own book. The implications of this decision are discussed in the concluding chapter on autobiographical theory.

Thus the historian is thrust back to corollary documents to confirm what one senses between the lines of the diary. Seventeen years after this courtship, Henry Baker wrote of Emily's days as his hired girl to her mother (his sister) in Michigan: "I might of kept Sister Emily but then there was a large family of us and all unmarried folks & I sometimes got disgusted with so much sparking."[22]

Very few nineteenth-century diarists wrote explicitly about sex. It was a subject considered deeply personal and may serve as a boundary marker for just how inviolate people considered their diaries to be. The exceptional diary of Lester Frank Ward, for example, was written in French—a barrier against most readers of his time, a translatable gift to ours. Although nineteenth-century women wrote about childbirth with the euphemism "being sick," historians have found little in their diaries about sexuality. In his study of fifty-six diaries, Paul Rosenblatt found that only Ward discussed his sex life. In his survey of 169 personal documents of the overland trail, John Mack Faragher concluded: "These historical sources allow not even a glimpse at sexuality; this was one of those human concerns too dangerous to commit to paper."[23] In sharp contrast, Elizabeth Hampsten criticizes Faragher's observations in her book *Read This Only to Yourself*: "I am astonished at this omission because sexuality is consistently present in the North Dakota–based writing I have seen."[24] Julie Jeffrey, also working from trail diaries and letters, found oblique references to women's physical longings, such as a wife writing that she wanted to hug her husband.[25]

The difference between these two observations can be somewhat mitigated. First, the interpretation of sexuality, especially if elliptical, is in the eye—and perhaps the gender—of the beholder. For example, within the context of the Hawley diary, the verb *talk*, when used for courtship (with women the verb is *visit*), probably carries far more weight than its denotation. However, in a rapid content analysis of such a diary, the phrase would receive a less loaded classification if the scholar were not reading between the lines for buried sexuality, sometimes interpreting the diary language as symbol, as Hampsten does. Secondly, the conditions on the trail, as Hampsten herself admits, might not be conducive to sexual encounters. Therefore the omissions of sex also found in overland trail studies by John Faragher and John Unruh might be documenting a particularly chaste experience in American history. Third, Hampsten's and Jeffrey's studies rely heavily on letters between women, and we know from studies such as Carroll Smith-Rosenberg's that this communication had much freedom and candor. A woman might feel her privacy more secure when she wrote to a dear friend "read this only to yourself" than when she committed words to a diary over whose eventual readership she would have no control.[26] (Emily Hawley, for example, mentions her sister Edna reading her diary.) Samuel Pepys's clever code for masking his sexual life in the seventeenth century had been cracked by 1813 and several abridged versions of the diary were available in the mid-nineteenth century, a reminder that no journal was inpenetrable to later readers.

The tension between what happened in Emily Hawley's life then and what she permits to "happen" within the pages of her journal is particularly evident, intriguing, and frustrating for the historian in this area of sexuality.

The gulf between what Emily Hawley did and what she wrote occurs throughout her diary, reflecting the tension within her life. This interaction occurs on at least three levels. First, there is Hawley's selective portrayal of her life—a self-edited version of it—that results in the diary. Secondly, there are conscious encounters of the individual and ideology, those rare moments when one realizes that a compromise is expected between character and conformity. Such is the case when Emily Hawley rebels against the norm of early marriage voiced by her mother: Emily suggests she will not marry, but succumbs four years later. A third, more subtle interaction of individuality and expectation occurs *within* Emily Hawley on a less conscious level. The internal ironies and contradictions between what she wishes, what life offers, and what she finally accomplishes and accepts can be excavated from her diary. Her book documents what all people experience but rarely record: the daily bargain that occurs and eventually accumulates in a satisfying or dissatisfying life. For a nineteenth-century woman, I would argue, the gap between desire and reality was particularly large.

One such desire in Emily Hawley's diary is her ongoing aspiration for those personal accomplishments that would thoroughly ground her in the middle class. Although she never mentions class (an unpopular concept in America), her list of middle-class goals recurs. She desires a better education, worthy gentleman companions, a home of her own (property), and freedom from care (a comfortable income).

The Hiram Hawley family fit C. Wright Mills's definition of "old middle class" by owning a farming enterprise of their own, however meager. At the beginning of the nineteenth century, according to Nancy Cott, as a middle-class daughter Emily Hawley would have stayed at home and spun. But by the mid-nineteenth century, with the rural economy increasingly reliant on cash, Emily was compelled to sell her services. She was typical of girls "whose families or priorities made factory work unlikely for them." She fit the pattern of woman's sporadic genteel employment—teaching interspersed with needlework. This type of irregular employment by women often does not apppear in labor statistics. For example, one source says only 10 percent of white women worked at this time. Emily Hawley's labor was hidden from the record books because she and other women were listed in the census as "at home" or "housekeeper." [27]

While Emily Hawley acted as a paid domestic helper in the homes of relatives, it is clear from several comments in her diary that she did not perceive herself as a mere "hired girl." This aversion to domestic work was echoed by one woman interviewed for a six hundred—woman survey conducted in the late nineteenth century: "The very thing you would do without a thought in your own home for your own family seems menial when it is demanded by a stranger." When Emily Hawley went to work at an inn, even though it was an uncle's, the perception by others that she was a hired girl must have bitterly clashed with her middle-class image of herself.[28]

Emily Hawley had wished to graduate from the new local academy in Michigan, another middle-class aspiration. Since the Oak Grove Academy was coeducational, she might have been exposed to a less gender-typed curriculum than was typical for all-female academies. The rationale for female education often focused on preparing young women for their future roles as wives and mothers. Emily Hawley never mentions such pragmatic and limited goals; rather, she desires simply to learn more and to graduate. Histories of nineteenth-century women have noted the correlation between education and feminism, arguing that the enlarged horizons and self-consciousness received through formal education may lead to political awareness. But the causality does not go only one way. Surely the self-selection of girls who attended such schools, either through wealth, precociousness, or supportive parents, predisposed them toward independent thinking. Something in Emily Hawley drove her to desire as much schooling as she could afford and to participate in local lyceums, another forum for adult education. Given her wish for more education and the lack of means to complete it, her frustration over her inability to achieve this ideal is understandable.

The diary also records the disparity between an individual's moral ideals and actual behavior. Such gaps between theories and reality make Emily Hawley seem all the more human and history a living, organic, negotiated entity. While the possibility of a gap between Emily Hawley's belief in chastity and her real-life interactions is merely suggestive, in two other areas the dissonance is decisive.

One such case is Emily Hawley's opinions and actions regarding the Civil War. If a historian only looked at the public record, Emily Hawley's role as secretary of the local Soldiers Relief Society in Iowa would indicate support for the war effort. Many such women's groups existed throughout the state, and Iowan Annie Turner Wittenmeyer became a national leader in the Sanitary Commission effort. If a daguerreotype had been taken at the Manchester railroad station on October 16, 1861, Emily would be in the crowd of well-wishers sending Milton Nelson and other infantry volunteers off to war. But Emily Hawley's comments about the war in her diary—her condemnation of John Brown and other abolitionists, her hope that her brother and fiancé do not volunteer—tell a different story. Her diary entry of June 4, 1862, shows her inner turmoil over the ideal and its cost: "but ah, this dreadful War. a Battle is being fought in Richmond. since Sunday morning thousands upon thousands of true hearted young men are being killed. what for? *O Slavery accursed wrong*: may peace soon be declared." Glenda Riley's study of Iowa women shows similar antiwar sentiments in the diaries of those who no doubt wore staunch faces and held dances to raise money for soldiers in the state that provided the most men, proportionate to its size, to the Union effort.[29]

The focal points in Emily Hawley's personal conflict over the Civil War were individuals. While she supported the cause for which the Union troops were fighting, she resisted the idea of individuals she loved—brother Henry, James—going to battle. Parents, siblings, lovers rarely happily give up their young men to war. When Emily Hawley found that individual soldiers, although unknown, could benefit from quilts and shirts in the field, she joined the effort for their relief. Personalization of the war caused Hawley much anxiety over the prospect of losing loved ones while at the same time compelled her to join the home front war effort to assist young men already on the battlefield.

Another case of ideals appearing in conflict is young Emily Hawley's support of women's rights and her increasing attraction to the traditional domestic sphere. While still living in Michigan she wrote a story called "Woman's Rights." Given its context in the family papers, it was probably written sometime between 1854 and when the diary begins in 1858. It is a short story of a wealthy young woman who independently drives her own carriage to an artist's home and proposes marriage to him, saying "she had no particular objection to sitting for another picture but as she was in pursuit of a husband if he would become hers it would obviate the necessity of having another picture, as the one already taken would be sufficient for both." The story goes on, "'R' after due consultation with his mother and obtaining her consent, informed Miss C he was much pleased with her proposal but as he was not infallible she must not expect with him to enjoy perfect happiness at all times." The heroine retains her own name in marriage and takes her new husband to her beautiful home, sharing her wealth with him.[30]

Her youthful story can be interpreted in several lights. It boldly deals with a woman's right to choose a marriage partner first, rather than only after a suitor approaches her. The ideal of a woman's right to choose her future is reflected in Emily Hawley's letter home announcing her real-life betrothal: "The whole responsibility rests on Emmie, for she has been influenced by no-one, but *herself*."[31] Such a right, implicit in the *Declaration of Principles* on woman's equality drafted at the Seneca Falls convention in 1848, later became one of the milder reforms proposed by the "free love" movement of the 1870s. Feminist Lucy Stone had kept her own name in her much-publicized marriage to Henry Blackwell in 1855. Thus the story plays with radical feminist ideals of the time.

But on another level, it is a wistful fantasy in which the heroine (Emily herself?) has material wealth but still seeks to complete her life in her beautiful home with a husband. While the word "love" never appears in the story, "happiness" and "happy" recur four times. The story, however feminist in ideals, still ends happily-ever-after-with-husband. In real life, Emily Hawley had resisted the idea of marriage until numerous pressures made James Gillespie a most attractive suitor.

A second essay, probably composed later, is called "Evenings at Home." It argues that "in our haste to be rich,—to find pleasure and amusement, we fail to discover the true riches" of home life. It encourages young people to stay under "*Home influence*" and to improve their evenings by reading. (However, in her diary, Emily mentions such home-based improvement very little and livelier entertainment quite frequently.) The essay again divides the home folk into gender roles—Mother is kind, Pa instructive.

On first reading, "Woman's Rights" and "Evenings at Home" seem to argue opposite sides of the sexual politics debate and represent the scope of Emily Hawley's ideas as an unmarried young woman. But while the first essay experiments with a reversal of traditional roles, it ultimately ends at home—the same idealized home of the second essay.

In real life, Emily Hawley also chose Home, an idea she loved, over the World, an idea that had proved disappointing in reality. The only way she could attain a home of her own, rather than a room as a dependent spinster in a relative's home, was through marriage. Yet the choice was not easy, for her awe and misgivings at this marriage choice are apparent in her diary. Marilyn Ferris Motz found similar themes in Michigan women's letters and diaries: the desire for more, the ultimate and late decision to marry rather than face "unloved solitude."[32] So with no dowry and no husband's home to go to, Emily Hawley planned to wed James Gillespie. It is ironic that Emily chose a man who did not have a home of his own. She wrote to her father, "I have always thought and said I would never be married to *any one* untill they first had a home but I may however."[33] Her decision attests to James's attractiveness and to the ever-present disparity between what the individual says and ultimately does.

Emily Hawley had wanted more education, art training in New York—and home. She had tried needlework, domestic work, and teaching. In the end, this ambitious young woman who desired to be more than a farmer's daughter chose to be a farmer's wife. Living in rural Iowa determined what men she would meet. Had she gone East, perhaps she would have chosen differently. A journalist observed in 1858, "The most intelligent and enterprising of the farmer's daughters become school-teachers, or tenders of shops, or factory girls. They contemn the calling of their father, and will nine times out of ten, marry a mechanic in preference to a farmer. They know that marrying a farmer is a serious business. They remember their worn-out mothers."[34] In her search for a home, Emily Hawley would also return to a farm.

PART TWO

"We Are a Happy Family Circle": Emily Gillespie, Wife and Mother

Overleaf: Henry, Sarah, James, and Emily Gillespie, February 14, 1873.

CHAPTER FOUR

"Seems Good to Know We Live at Home": 1862–1874

Emily Hawley and James Gillespie were married on September 18, 1862, but did not actually live together until the first of October. James and Emily spent their wedding night at Henry Baker's inn; the next morning, James returned to the family farm. The couple took no honeymoon trip, in keeping with their modest wedding. On the night of her marriage, Emily wrote home, "I wanted to be married in silk, & was real sorry, but I guess it makes no difference I shall live just as long. . . . I will send you a piece of my dress—it was only $5.30."[1]

The newlyweds' first "home" was in a wing of the house of Hiram and Lorinda Rawden Gillespie, James's parents. They lived on a two hundred–acre farm two miles southeast of the Baker Inn and two miles west of Manchester. Emily Gillespie's new family consisted of her elderly in-laws (Hiram was sixty-two and Lorinda fifty-eight), whom she called "Ma" and "Pa" in her diary. James (twenty-six) and Dennis (seventeen), their only surviving sons, lived at home. (Six of the ten Gillespie children had died of consumption, according to a family history.) Their two surviving daughters, Margaret (twenty-nine) and Mercelia (twenty-three), were married to Manchester merchants.[2]

The Gillespie family, of Scotch-Irish descent, had come to America before the Revolution. The Gillespies then followed the same pattern of westward migration as had Emily Hawley's ancestors, the Bakers and Garlicks. The Gillespies first settled in southern New York state in the eighteenth century, then moved to Jackson County in southern Michigan in the 1830s. They moved to Iowa in 1854, thirteen years after Henry Baker's arrival.

The changes in Emily Hawley's name, status, family, and home are reflected in her diary. It becomes a daily record of her husband's activities in addition to her own. In fact, when Emily is particularly inactive, James's accomplishments dominate the journal entries. During this decade, the diary contains a record of domestic tasks and farm production undertaken by the Gillespies. It also traces their work toward building a home of their own and forming a family circle.

OCTOBER 1862

Wednesday
1st.

rain. rain. * * * crochet on net. finished it. commenced Edna a letter. James came for me. I carried all my clothes. at Pa Gillespies to night.

Thursday
2.

quite pleasant. cut two shirts for James & partly made one. . . . like living here very much.

Friday.
3rd.

finished one shirt & commenced the other. helped Ma some about her work. received a letter from Henry & Edna. my folks feel quite bad about my staying in Iowa, but may I hope to meet them soon.—& they be resigned to my stay. James not very well today, he works in the sugar cane. he gave me $15.00 for oats that he sold.[3]

Tuesday.
14.

tis now evening. for the first time since I was married sadness is in my heart. but alas, for naught save my girlish actions. James says tis not very ladylike for a young lady.— but I know he meant not to hurt my feelings. O, may I try hereafter to give a reason for reproof & O, my prayer that I may never speak an unkind work to him that God has seen fit to give me. this forenoon I finished a pair of sheets. * * * am writing in my Diary, there are travelers (4) staying with Pa to night. * * *

Wednesday.
15.

done the ironing. made one sheet & helped considerable about the work, those travelers stay all day & night, & 4 more came. it is about all Ma & me can do to cook & wait on them. James taking care of taters.

Thursday
16.

Pa received $9.00 for the trouble of those travelers, this forenoon I put on comfortable and partly quilted it. this afternoon I went to Manchester with James. got some groceries &c $1.53. James plowing for wheat in forenoon. he says, "write in your Diary that roses are in bloom yet." . . .

Friday.
17.

finished my comfortable; made some ripe cucumber pickles &c. James plowing for wheat all day. tis now evening. James is real tired, how glad I will be when he does not have to work so, I done some. he does not work around the house.

Sunday.
19.

this morning James & me went to Manchester to get Mrs. Doolittle (James sister). I like her very well indeed. after tea Pa & Ma carried them home. tis evening now & I am up stairs writing. Ah, that I may ever be happy as now never doing evil or wrong. — [4]

Tuesday
28.

done part of the work &c. done the ironing this forenoon. Pa went to Manchester to get our stove. got it, the stove & furniture (boiler, heater, gridiron, 2 spider, kettle, & pot dipper, tea kettle, coffee boiler, skimmer, 3 drippans 2 tins) and freight altogether cost $18.55. * * *

Thursday
30.

finished Ma's apron. washed the windows & put up the curtains in the parlor, am nearly ready to keep house. today James made me a present of a nice cane-seat & back rocking chair, $4.50. he has been plowing for wheat is real tired, — just six weeks ago & all around was beauty   yes, it was my wedding day, —

Friday
31.

cleaned out our bedroom & the parlor, we are going to live in there. *tis quite* a nice room. finished one of James mittens. he is plowing. I went to the field where he was.

NOVEMBER 1862.

Monday.
3.

done my washing &c. knit some on James mitten. he has been husking corn all day. a family (7) stay here to night. cook their own victuals and make their beds. why am I sad;

Thursday
6

we moved to day in our part of the house, (parlor)   got tea for the first time this evening. * * *

Sunday
9.

my mornings work done. combed James & Denis' hair &c. this afternoon James & me went to visit our farm & see where we intend to build. ah, we are happy now & may it be the will of God that we may never cause each other pain

Saturday
15.

tis now about four o'clock, I have done my Saturday's work, baking & mopping &c. & am now writing in my Diary. James sharpen fence posts till this afternoon he has gone to get some furniture. Pa came back & told me James had run away—&c. he has gone to West Union to take a load of folks, he gets $5.00 so I had to take tea alone. O.O. what a lonely old bach *I* would make, but tis time to retire & so good night to all & a prayer for all to be well & that James may have good luck on his journey (26 miles)

Sunday
16.

breakfasted with Pa & Ma. James got back about three o'clock this afternoon wet & cold as he could be for it has rained most all day. this evening we sat by the stove (sparking, James said).

Monday
17.

got my washing done before eleven. James has gone to Manchester . . . he brought home our chairs (6) & table $8.00   this evening Emily, Orville & Esther Nelson & George Zerfass were here. ha. ha. a good visit. * * *

Thursday
27.

Thanksgiving today, snowy & cold. James is drawing wood. I done my usual work &c. made a small bouquet of hair flowers for Mrs. Dutton. James came home about three o'clock. what you think we had for dinner (a meat stew with dumplings)

DECEMBER. 1862.

Saturday
6.

done mopping, baking &c. & other work. James draw one load of wheat today $.71   this afternoon he stayed in the house with me;—the first afternoon we have spent since we were married, only Sundays. James got new ax, $1.25

Monday
29.

* * * Pa was here to dinner. Ma *gave James a deed of one half of her* (James Mother) farm the *east* half.—one hundred acers, today am alone this afternoon. wrote a good long letter to father & mother. will send it to PO. at first opportunity. Uncle made out James' Deed, James chops this forenoon.[5]

Wednesday
31.

done the usual work. knit some. James chopping, he cut his ankle quite bad—this evening we went to Mrs. Nelsons to a party. did not stay long for James ankle pained him so, Alas, the year is ended & I cried because James did not want to go to Nelsons, ah, may it never be again I done the ironing, too. ah, how foolish to cry, for James is too kind to have his feelings hurt by my silliness of crying.

JANUARY 1863

Thursday
1st.

ah, another year has passed away & with it what a change, done the usual work &c. James chopping, as pleasant as a March or April day.

Saturday,
3.

done my mopping, made pies & crullers, James chopping. guess James & me will never forget when we went to bed how I chased him in the Hall & he fastened me out of the room. O, how pleasant   seems like spring.

Sunday.   James at home all day. I was not hardly ambitious enough
18.   to eat, let alone working—but thank God that I have a kind husband, may I ever be as ready to assist him in days of trial as he is me.

FEBRUARY 1863

Saturday.   this forenoon did baking mopping & other work. * * * this
7.   afternoon we went to Manchester to get our miniature taken, we get them to send to father & mother, cost $1.00, and once [*sic*] for ourselves to keep $2.50. * * *

Sunday.   this morning we did not get up very early. my work done
8.   however & writing   this afternoon Jerome's [Doolittle] folks here. he starts for Ohio tomorrow, I sent James & my likeness by him to our folks, as he is going past there & will call & leave them. I wrote a letter to Harriet; wrote some to mother & father, too, in it.

Monday.   did my washing & other work. snow all the forenoon &
9.   windy rest of the day. * * * this evening Pa & James pass receipts, James is hereafter to pay Pa for all he has, Pa to pay James for all he does for him.—

Sunday.   my morning's work done; the day passed as all Sundays.
15.

MARCH 1863

Tuesday   this morning James went to the Grove, Susan went home;
10   did my usual work & washing. this afternoon I looked in my box [received from Michigan] & see what Mother has sent

me. O. O. real nice mess of things, my bed, some fruit, cheese & etc.

Saturday.
28.

did my morning's work & finished cleaning up. about ten A.M. Mrs. Smith, Mrs. Craig, & Mrs. Correll came to visit me.

APRIL 1863.

Tuesday.
7.

this forenoon did my ironing & other work. dressed my doll. this afternoon do churning. James drag for Pa all day.

Friday.
10.

ah. ah. today the last of my 24th year. but one year ago & I was wondering my destiny for now will there be as great a change in another year? Yes, methinks there will. James drag & sow wheat for Pa &c. pleasant.

Wednesday.
15.

did my morning's work, baked, & commenced sewing on sack (making it of my black lawn skirt) O.O. the fire got out in the field, Ma & me went with mop pails & water to help them put it out. * * * James plowed for our garden this morning.

Friday
17.

finish my sack, made some long sleeves for my wedding dress, & do usual work &c. * * *

Sunday.
19.

do my morning's work &c. after tea James & me went walking to our place. we gathered some flowers. the first this spring

MAY 1863.

Saturday.
2.

clean bedroom & bedstead & do my mopping in forenoon. work on flowers in afternoon. received letter & currant cuttings (18) from Edna & Harriet. James plow &c for Pa.

Wednesday. 13.	do my ironing, other work & made a little night dress. commenced broidering little shirt. James planting corn &c

| Tuesday. 26. | James carried me to Manchester this forenoon; bought me a dress $1.71; 1-1/2 yds. pink $.37 . . . 8 yds. diaper $2.00 . . . total $8.38. James paid to store, $.05. * * * |

JUNE 1863

| Saturday. 20. | do mopping & churning & other work. James hoe corn for Pa. Lyda Zerfass, Uncle & Susan here to tea, John [Schmidt] to breakfast, sold 12 lbs. butter, got 1 lb. saleratus [baking soda] $.10 & $1.10 worth of sugar about 8 lbs.[6] |

JULY 1863.

| Saturday. 4. | this morning James carried his folks to Manchester to the Celebration, came back & plowed corn till noon, after dinner he called on Mr. Alcock's folks, their little girl is dead. about five o'clock we went after our folks; stayed to Yeomans to tea, I worked some on tatting, did my usual work. James is not well. I fear something ails his heart, O, God my prayer that there may not be, will thou give him health & strength & prosperity as thou see'est the needs; may we be enabled to get us buildings on our own place that James may not worry so much, for, O. God, it seems I could part with all the world aside from him, may he have a contented mind. we enjoyed today better at home alone, than we would than we would [sic] at town among such a crowd of people. we had a good dinner with all the lemonade we could drink— |

| Saturday. 11. | do my mopping, baking &c; ah I am sad. O, why? 'tis this that James came home last evening late. I had been waiting |

for him a long time—& then he had been to supper, when he told me in the morning he would be home to tea, & I, foolish girl, did not eat any either. O, I know I did wrong & pray God it may never be again. O, Lord wilt thou & him forgive; for James is too kind to be spoken harshly to & God forbid that ever an unkind word or thought from me again. ah, I feel forgiven now; James plow corn for Pa. * * *

Sunday. 12.

Yeoman's came to Pas, they had him make out a note of $500.00 five hundred dollars to be paid to them at the end of a year & wanted James to sign said note; I did oppose it, it caused anger, yes, deep anger, to me; for it seemed wrong that James should get in debt so & for unknown cause, he did not do it however & pray God he may not but, ah, it seemed for awhile I could hardly live, grief was so heavy. I feel better now; tis evening & James has gone to Uncles.[7]

Sunday. 19.

am alone for James has gone to look for his ox. so I will write sister Hattie a letter. James came back about noon, then went to the funeral of Mr. Alcock's little boy, tis the third child of theirs that has died since two weeks today.

Saturday. 25.

do my mopping & usual house work, broider some. * * * Joseph Jones came for James to watch with corpse; he went & stayed all night. their little boy is dead, too—they are to be buried tomorrow.

Thursday. 30.

do my usual work. finish broidered white dress. James work in wheat for Pa in forenoon & part of afternoon. he is real miserable; took some pills on going to bed. Dennis did not come from work very early so Ma & Pa went after him, they were *very angry* indeed. Yes, it makes James about sick. they do act so. O how glad I will be when we go away from here. that we may be more alone then. I think James health will be better, too,—when his mind can be more at rest & quiet.

AUGUST 1863

Thursday.
6.

do my usual work, broider some. James went this morning after a coffin for Mr. Jones' little girl. it is the third one that died within two weeks. tis not noon yet, James has gone to the funeral. I am sad & have taken this book to pen down a few more words to add to the Diary of my life. why am I sad? 'tis that James is so miserable   I think he is better however & hope he may continue to be., for. O. Lord it seemest thou hast given him to me, my nearest, dearest friend on earth. Mother, father brother, & sisters are all near & dear but, ah, my companion,—tis him that is nearest of all. . . . James came home just as the cars went along. (3 o'clock)   he found me asleep, after tea we went to the field after some potatoes. he commences to sleep up stairs to night. perhaps it will be good to change sleeping rooms. * * *

Friday
7.

do my ironing, broider some & other work. * * * James seems some better today. ah, how kind he is, this morning about daylight he came down to see if I was lonesome sleeping alone. I *was* too, but I can deprive myself of any happiness for the sake of James health improving. * * *

Sunday.
9.

this morning James & me went to get some blackberries for tea. we took a sleep after we got back. James pretty well, only tired. did the churning this morning. * * * Pa tried to make James settle with him again, ah, me it makes James nearly sick.

Saturday,
15.

James real sick all day. could not eat hardly anything. O, my prayer that he may yet be *well* & spend many years of happiness, may it be the will of God. for *His* will be done, not mine. I made Reticule & do my usual work. tis now evening   James sitting in the big chair & I am writing. I ask what I should write for him today? he said, "You need not write anything at all."

Sunday.
16.

to day finds us at home as usual   I finish Mother & fathers letter; after my morning work done I went after a pail of potatoes alone James was not able to go with me, 'tis sad when he is sick. he is better today though so he sits up most the day. I read him the letter I wrote to my folks. I had said in it a few words about his being sick; the tears came trickling from his eyes & which made me feel real bad. I did when I was going after my potatoes: give vent to tears & grief & cry aloud, ah. what a relief are tears, to grief. tis near tea time, am writing & James is sitting on the porch.

Tuesday
18.

bake loaf of bread, & a few crackers   do my usual work; take care of James, he has a fever all day, does not sit up but very little, he went to the grove though this morning & got some catnip. Dennis took the horses & wagon & carried him. I have made up my mind tis a "nervous fever." O, that it is so, but I have all reason to believe it is there has not been the time since last winter but that his mind has been completely harrassed from him, as it were, by his folks, they have harped & bothered him ever since they gave him the Deed for his farm. they seem to think he ought to give it back or pay them something. but never mind now. if he gets well we will not stay here longer than his corn is taken care of. they did not act so, till about 6 months since that they thought perhaps James might not live long & they cannot bear the idea of his leaving an heir to his property, O. I hope he may live to enjoy the pleasure with his child, as he anticipates.

Thursday.
20.

do my work &c. sew on collar some of the time. James sits up about half the time today. . . . I wash him & make him some catnip tea, rub his stomach with liniment   he said he felt better. O. how good he is; he said he did not know but he was as ready to go now, as ever, if his time had come and if he found out he must die, he would settle up his business & die in peace with all. O, with what composure of mind he

talks, O, God I pray that when I die I may be all well prepared to go as James is. * * *

Friday.
21

'tis about eleven o'clock, my mornings work all done. I take
my pen as usual to write a few words in my Diary, ah, what
a change since one year ago, then I looked forward to naught
but a happy future when James & me would live together &
all would be well, & it has been the happiest of my past
days have been spent with him, that God gave me, my companion. but, ah, sickness now hangs over him. . . . this
morning James went to town with his father. Pa has come
back but he stayed down there, he is going to get something
more to take. O, that it may give him health again. James
came back about eleven, he bought a cat fish, some peck
apples, a paper of corn starch & a half pint of wine. . . . I
went to meet him for he came afoot lugging his box of things.
I carried for him. he stood the walk better than I thought he
would. I cooked some of his fish & starch for dinner   he
ate quite hearty for him. * * * James went for the cows to
night.—about tired him out.

Saturday.
22.

this forenoon I bake 1 loaf bread & crackers, churn, do my
mopping & ironing & other work. cut & nearly made a little
sack of my blue dress sleeve this afternoon & usual work.
James not quite as well today, he worried around too much
yesterday & got tired out. he feels better this evening, however. reader, do you not feel to sympathize with Emmie? ah,
too true.

SEPTEMBER 1863

Friday.
4.

ah, me, what have I to write for this day; was real sick all
night (last night), did not sleep a minute, nor neither did
James sleep but little, about daylight James sent for some

help to take care of me. Pa went, got Mrs. Lewis, Mrs. Coats, Mrs. Parliman, & Margaret, Ma *was* here. Mrs. Lewis was the Dr. (paid her $2.00) she is a real good woman   Baby was born about half past ten A.M. then could we thank God for our boy, & hope he might grow to be a man worthy of his name & the respect of his fellow beings; that he may be upright & truthful   O, that we may live to teach him in the "way he should go." about three o'clock I felt that all was well; was lying comfortably in bed; the boy beside me, the Ladies, all but Margaret went home. Mrs. Lewis kissed me, O. she seemed like one kind deliverer, & they were all kind. James felt real bad to see me sick, but he need not, it seems there can be none more kind & true than he. Uncle & Susan called to see me.[8]

Saturday. 5.	Mary Evans came to work for us, she will stay a week or two. Margaret washed me & combed my hair, I felt pretty well. she went home in forenoon. James took some wheat to town to sell he got $14.34 for 20 bushels . . . he came home happy enough thinking he was about (or quite) out of debt & got a boy.[9]
Sunday. 6.	this morning I washed & dressed my baby. & sat up some. James is rather tired being broken of his rest so much but it will not have to be long, I hope. Uncle, Susan & Jane Minkler came to see me.
Wednesday. 9.	sat up most of the time. knit some & finish Edna a letter. James threshing for Coffin, he felt quite well this morning, he slept with his boy last night, for the first time. this evening Ma talked worse to me than ever she did before. I did feel really grieved * * *
Thursday. 10.	rain this morning so James went to town; got breast pipe $.55 & paid for bitters. . . . this afternoon he got me some plums. am quite well, knit some.

Sunday.
13.

I commence to do my own work again tis some time past noon. James & baby are asleep & I am writing in this book. am real well I think. * * *

Tuesday.
15.

I made a plum pie. knit some, do my work, bake three loaves of bread, knit some &c. guess I will find that baby will take up all leisure moments, however good he may be. James cuts his hay, he gets real tired. now I must take our boy   he has slept a good while.

Friday.
18.

just one year ago today since we were married. ah, what changes happen in one short year, aye, a little boy now blesses our family, may we ever be true in *years* to come, as in the past, & train up our child to be kind. I do my usual work, James is working in his hay. * * *

Thursday.
24.

do my work, churn. James tends baby some. he finished his haying this forenoon. . . . O, dear, baby is crying, I have to hold him, he is not well.

Saturday.
26.

baby sleeps good share of the time today, he is better. I do my mopping—usual work, make two pies. James husking corn. ah, me, Mrs. Dutton came to make me a visit, how glad I was & what a good visit we had; she stayed till late in evening. * * *

OCTOBER 1863.

Sunday.
4.

do my usual Sunday's work. bake two loaves bread, James at home most of the time; he called at Mr. Jones. I cried, I was sorry but was tired & almost discouraged to think James wanted to put on his flannel shirt & I had not mended it for him.

Sunday.
25.

this morning I made cookies & pies & do other work. James go to Uncles, Ma came in & got Baby & carried him in the other room. I guess to let James' father see him, would I live in a house with a grandchild for eight weeks & not go in to see him? no, I think not! well, I commence writing & have to take up Baby & hold him, too.

Friday.
30.

do usual work. clean house some & other work. Ma gave me nearly two knots yarn to finish James' socks with. * * * James went to Mr. Jones to make a bargain with him for John Evans place. we are to have it for $30.00 to keep one year, commencing the 15 of November 1863.[10]

NOVEMBER 1863.

Monday.
9.

do my washing & other work   mop, too. * * * I received a letter from Henry stating that Fred Sims & Lida Crampton were married, & Nelly Baldwin to Sarah Sims, & Julia Gardner to a Mr. Fisk. that's the way the world goes. If I were to go home it would not seem like the same place, or rather like the same people. James plow (on Evans) about 1/4 day. Mother & Hattie wrote me a few lines, too. how glad to hear from my childhoods home & friends.

Monday,
16.

do my washing. pack up most all our things for James to carry away. Mrs. Coats called on me. this evening will be the last I suppose that we stay in *Pa's* house. right glad I am, too. we have go all away except the bed, one table, stove & things to get breakfast, do ironing in evening.

Tuesday.
17.

this forenoon I clean bedroom then room we lived in & got the remainder of our furniture ready to move. * * * we took dinner with Ma & Dennis, got to our place (Evans) about one o'clock. then James drew 100 bushels of corn (ears) down here, & I did the mopping in two square rooms, & bedroom, got tea. we sleep on the floor tonight. are real tired. * * *

Wednesday.
18.

do work as usual, regulate some of the things. . . . * * * Baby is real good. we shall like our place very well, I think.

DECEMBER. 1863.

Friday.
4.

tis nearly tea time. James is husking corn. while I have done my regular routine of work & writing in my Diary, am holding baby. James says we will name him Henry La Fayette Gillespie for Uncle & brother Henry & James' brother Fayette. he is not much help to me in writing, but may he grow to be a kind man and worthy the name which his father gave him.[11] * * *

Sunday.
13.

wipe off the floor &c. rather cold & snowy. today finds James, Baby & me at home enjoying ourselves & happy in each others' company. ah, my prayer that it may ever be so, may no discord ever enter our family circle & may the will of God be done.

Friday.
25.

ash, with a fond recollection do we look back to two years ago when first we met & now a precious boy is numbered in our family. We went to Jeromes with Pa & Ma to eat roast turkey. this evening Orville & Esther Nelson here. James got me a spool of thread & set of knitting needles $.15, Jeromes gave baby a rattle box $.25

Thursday.
31.

today the last of the old year, & O, what a stormy day it is. I can scarcely do my work—James out all day, helping Pa fix a place for his cattle, ah, with what fear did I look with an anxious eye to hear his footstep; at last he was welcomed to come in. we knew then he was safe—Good bye, old year.

JANUARY 1864.

Sunday.
10.

real pleasant. we were at home all day. do our usual routine of work. Henry is getting so he laughs real hearty.

Tuesday.
12.

do my usual work &c. James went to Uncles. . . . in the evening he went after pail of water; did not come back till he had been to town. I felt real cross about it. O may it be the last time an unkind thought or word ever passes my lips to one so true. I did feel real sorry. I made baby a shirt, fixed over his dress & partly made him a cloak. * * *

FEBRUARY 1864

Monday.
8.

do my washing & other work. commence me a sack of my raglain—James work for Uncle. the hogs were trying to eat the calf; they ate off its tail, it got out of their way, however, by going on the top of a straw pile. I took it in my arms & brought it in the house.

Sunday.
21.

we were at home enjoying life finely.

Monday.
29.

do my washing & make James a necktie of my silk waist for his 28th. birthday present. * * *

MARCH 1864.

Friday.
11.

do mopping & other work. O, dear me! I have just got little Henry to sleep. I pinched his little forefinger in the table leaf. real bad. * * * I pray God it may get well & not pain him any more. O so much rather it had have been my own. James worked (he said) for James Gillespie.

Thursday.
17.

make one of Henry's shirts. commence the other (had to be up with him considerable last night). in the evening I put some sweet oil on his nose & he rubbed it off in his eyes. Oh, he cried. * * *

Saturday.
19.

do usual work. patch James' coat. . . . this evening Dennis came to bring me a letter from Edna. she sent me her likeness. she's changed to look older since I last saw her, but is that same Edna. O. how it calls my mind to thoughts of time spent in the family circle at home. I did cry about it *not* for sorrow—for what.—

APRIL 1864.

Friday.
1st.

knit some & other usual work. James sowed three acres of wheat, & drag it in partly   quite pleasant. I did "fool" him to get the bucket out of the well,—it wasn't in.

Monday.
11.

today am 26 years old. do my washing. patch some. tend baby. James sowed & dragged in some wheat. this morning it commenced to rain. & rained till nearly two. * * *

Sunday.
17.

today is rainy. we are at home all day. O how warm is our love. may it ever be so? just as it is now. even warmer.

MAY 1864.

Sunday.
1st

I was at home all day. James went to town.

Friday. 13.	do usual work. *James* went to town & got my box of things that Mother sent me,—some apples (9); some dried apples & peaches, & cherries; my hair flowers. * * * Mother sent Henry a new dress.
Tuesday. 17.	do usual work & finish baby's dress. bake bread. * * * I asked James to get me a few sticks of wood to bake by. he said, "write it in your Diary," for tis the first time, he is not very well. his heart troubles him. too bad. churned.
Wednesday, 25.	sew some &c. James carried me over to Smiths & then he drew logs to mill came for me & stay to tea; had a good visit

JUNE 1864.

Sunday. 5.	we were at home all day. Dennis brought a letter from Harriet. she said Edna had married a grasswidower with a boy 9 years old. I've nothing to say, only am sorry & hope it will be for the best. they were married the 7th April
Thurs. 9	churn etc. work on flowers, too. James plow corn. *Henry has the first tooth* just cut through.

JULY 1864.

Monday. 4.	wash etc. I cut my new dress. James draw stone.—after dinner baby & I went with him to where he is going to dig the [new house] cellar.
Friday. 22.	mop & churn, cut rags &c. James work for Mr. Coats. there is another call for 500,000 more of our men to go in the

battle field to be slaughtered. O, dear, may it be the will of God that James may not go. I milk the cows this evening.

Saturday,
30.

mop all the rooms, (4) do what ironing I had to do, etc. knit some. this afternoon I went to Mrs. Nelsons visiting, draw Henry in his cart. * * * had a good visit. shower of rain.

Sunday.
31.

Esther Nelson here to dinner. Henry just begin to try to go (walk) alone, today for the first. O. I *will* be glad when he can walk without his being led. * * *

AUGUST. 1864.

Tuesday.
2.

braid some &c. run the first curd for a cheese, James went to Mrs. Nelsons—she lets me have rennet & take her [cheese] hoop. this forenoon Ma came here a little while. * * *

Wednesday.
3.

knit some & run up another curd & put my *first* cheese in the press   rainy. James binds & set up wheat. I braid some.

Sunday.
14.

James was real sick all last night, he is not well today: him, Henry & me all have the summer complaint. * * *

SEPTEMBER 1864.

Sunday.
4.

we are having a nice shower of rain. James went to town & got Jerome to come & help him stake for the cellar. Henry is one year old today, he can walk all round, & this morning he went up stairs, (steps) alone. I took hold of the bottom of his dress however for fear he might fall. he has 4 teeth & is just tall enough to stand under the table leaf & that's all. he fell down, bumped his forehead on the floor & cried about

it,—is now on the floor trying to get me to play with
him. . . . * * *

Saturday.
17.

do my mopping. bake bread, cookies, pies & crackers. knit
some, & iron. James & Dennis finish topping out their hay
stacks in the forenoon, & in the afternoon they went to the
grove to drill, or elect officers for a company,—to practice
so as to be ready when called on to kill their fellow men to
the best advantage. James does not want to go at all. but
those who resist have to pay $100 & be imprisoned for 20
days. O this awful war! when will we witness the end? * * *

Sunday.
18.

James killed the old rooster this morning. I cooked it for
dinner,—we had *quite a good dinner* to celebrate our wedding day. ah, we know not what the third year of our lives
may bring forth.

Monday.
26.

do my washing, & knit some, bake bread & 2 pies. Mrs.
Evans was here. James commence to cut the buckwheat
then at nine o'clock he went to the grove to train. they were
there most all day,—got up or organized a club to raise
money to hire substitutes,—they raised $850.00 James
paid $25.00 it is to be divided equally among those drafted
in the club.[12]

OCTOBER 1864.

Sunday.
2.

James went to . . . Manchester to get some of the window
frames,—got them. I went with him. Ma & me went to see
the new house, & cellar—the sills are all on, tis 20 feet by
31 feet. * * *

Wednesday,
5

James went to town this morning,—got some more lumber
&c. got a list of the names of the drafted men of this town.
O, how glad I am that James is not one to go. I feel to thank

God—that my prayer is answered. am sorry for those that do have to go. may God be with them in a safe return to their homes. I knit & do other work, as usual. * * *

Wednesday, I knit (commence) on the second pair of stockings & do etc.
12.   James shingling the roof. I & Henry went to see him awhile in afternoon.

NOVEMBER. 1864.

Sunday.   my morning's work done; am writing here. James & Henry
6.   are down to Pas. it commences to rain. I'm afraid I will have the ague. James got some meal to Pas & we had some pudding. — Yes, I did have the ague. . . .

Wednesday. run 2 dozen candles—make a fur for Henry to wear around
9.   his neck—James finish lathing forenoon. snow & rain & freeze all day.

Sunday.   I rather break the Sabbath by working; bake bread, biscuit,
13.   crackers & pie. James does his chores. * * *

Wednesday. James went to town this morning, came back & said we
16.   would move this afternoon so I got dinner, packed up the things &c. Dennis help us move so we take tea in our new house this evening. I clean some &c. Pa called.

Thursday.   clean house & put up some things. James husk corn for
17.   Dennis. our house is not plastered yet, nor the kitchen finished off—bake.

Saturday.   mop, wash windows & nearly get settled again; seems good
19.   to know we live at *home.* * * *

DECEMBER, 1864

Saturday.
10.

mop. get mince ready for pies &c. James husk corn. more pleasant,—have not been very well for three or four weeks.

Sunday.
25.

this morning Dennis came to invite us to take Christmas dinner at their house—we went,—had a good visit, Mr. Yeomans were there, too. ah me, they tell us another draft is to take place by next April unless 300,000 more men volunteer ere then.

Saturday.
31.

mop, bake jelly cake, some tarts & crackers—James chop for Mr. Coffin; he bought an (red) cow & calf of him & is to pay $25.00   he brought her home tonight. Mrs. Smith here visiting, Mr. S—— came to tea, they stay awhile in evening—yes, another year is ended—may we ask ourselves—what have we done?

JANUARY 1865

Tuesday.
10.

do my wash.—finish shirt—my cow has a calf this morning. James chop wood & kill the calf.

Sunday.
15.

we are at home. Eliza Camp called. O. I do wish I were well & did not feel so fretful about everything.

Monday.
23.

wash & make a needle cushion on the bottom of the sugar bowl that was grandmother's. James . . . carried calf skin to town,—got for it $.65

FEBRUARY. 1865.

Friday.
24.

Mr. Lillibridge came along, I went home with him. James came to tea. Mrs's Smith, Craig, Correll came; were all

there, too, & Mrs. Brooks, Henry one of the *best* boys to go
visiting.

MARCH 1865

Tuesday.
14.

commence Henry dress that Uncle gave him, bake pie &
cake. Brother Henry came to see us; was real glad, too—he
is a great big boy. Mother sent me some yarn.

Saturday,
25.

cannot do any work at all hardly. Henry is real sick. James
at home a part of the time. . . . * * * James went to town;
got some expectorant, $1.00 & some soothing syrup $.35.
Brother talks of going home, he thinks he can do better
there—would like to have him stay, but may we trust to
meet again.

Monday.
27.

wash, knit some. Brother started for home this morning. . . .
I sent Mother cloth for a paramentta dress & sent Edna my
glass sauce dish. was sorry & cried to see him leave us. but
we will trust to meet again * * * I do my churning 6 lbs.[13]

APRIL 1865

Monday.
3.

wash, sew on hat &c. James churn (12 lb. 2 oz). * * * Good
news—Richmond is taken by the North but it seems cruel
that the city is to all burn up.

Saturday.
15.

make a shirt for Henry & a pair of shoes—James plow door-
yard & garden; Miss Mitchel & a lady called. we hear that
President Lincoln is *shot dead* yesterday by one John Wilkes
Booth.

Thursday.
27.

finish flannel skirt, cut out 4 shirts for James—commence
one, & cut 4 sheets & 4 pillow biers. James work in garden
& set out some trees.

MAY 1865

Sunday.
21.

James is gone—to his fathers,—Henry is asleep & O how glad I am to hear the news that soldiers are returning to their homes. war is nearly or quite closed. the Confederate President was captured the   of this month.

Monday.
29.

wash. commence me a new dress. James work on road. carpenter here, build privy. . . . little Henry is asleep,—poor little boy, he fell down cellar—O, I hope it did not injure him. O. my prayer that with the help of God that I may be or do by my children as a mother should.

JUNE 1865.

Monday.
12.

James churn 7 lbs. 7 oz. butter, he did most of the washing. I do what I can. * * *

Tuesday.
20.

nearly make my 2nd. chemise. * * * Paulina Stephens [hired girl] commence work here, today. she wash & bake &c. I sew on shirt, James hoe corn, John Evans help him. James bought of him two soldier's blankets, an overcoat & roundabout. . . . Ma called in evening.

JULY 1865

Sunday.
2.

I am all alone. * * * O dear a me. I will be so glad if I ever am well. my prayer that I may be patient with such as God sees fit to place before me & for me to endure—& O if it be my time to die may God watch over & guide my little boy in a way that he may bear an honorable name through life, & at last accept him at His right hand in Heaven; & may my James be reconciled that I go.—may he ever prosper through life & finally when we shall all be called to that final resting place,—may we meet to never part again. Amen. Uncle & Susan here awhile.

Friday.
7.

ah. ah. can it be possible that we have a little daughter born this morning—that weighs 5 lbs. 7 oz—her twin brother did not live to even breathe—I do not know but it was right—however we would have done the best we could had he have lived—may our little girl be in the world as virtuous & pure as has been our prayer for little Henry—Mrs. Lewis here all day.—Ma here in forenoon   pay Mrs. Lewis $3.00. Paulina Stephens here to wash.—pay her $.50   James sent by Pa to get 1/2 pint of camphor.

Sunday.
9.

sit up some. go in kitchen to eat supper—James gets it. * * *

Sunday
16.

James, Henry, baby & me at home alone all day. I got dinner. Mrs. Stephens borrow 8 lb. 10 oz. flour,—tis *borrow,—borrow,—borrow* all the time.

Monday.
17

commence baby a pink dress. James hoe corn.

Saturday.
22.

I do my own work today   finish baby's dress. * * * Stephens brought flour home—borrowed wash board, wagon & the flatirons, bring irons back before they use them, because I told them I would get some of my own before *I* would borrow so much.

Monday.
31.

do my work best I can. am not very well. Paulina do our washing & ironing.—James work for Uncle in hay.

AUGUST 1865.

Tuesday.
1st.

knit some,—pack down about 100 weight of butter. Jas. help Uncle in hay.

Thursday. 17.	do my work as usual, put the 4th cheese in the hoop. (make one every other day) this afternoon I went to Mas. James came to tea. . . . * * *
Tuesday. 22.	do up my gooseberries—(3 lbs. of them). James went to town, carried one firkin of butter (103 lbs.) got $21.63 for it. . . .[14]

SEPTEMBER—1865.

Monday. 18.	do my washing,—make cake & pie James dig potatoes in forenoon, went to town in afternoon. . . . Uncle here to tea: (our 3rd. wedding day)
Thursday. 21.	threshers here 1/2 day, 3 to breakfast, 6 to dinner; had 52 bushels of wheat. . . . Susan [Stephens] work for us all day, paid her $.40.
Wednesday. 27.	do my work best I can, Henry is not well, his teeth do plague him. Sarah can sit alone on one's lap; can laugh & crow. churn 2 lbs. butter. James go to town in forenoon, get 3 yds. calico $1.05 paid. rain. * * *

OCTOBER—1865.

Wednesday. 4.	bake bread. knit some etc little Henry went away down in the field to follow James to Pa's—I had to go after him. I was too sponky & scolded him too severely. I *know* I did I was in such a hurry about my work, but may I be forgiven, I pray, O God, & may I never get angry again with my dear little boy. * * *
Friday. 20.	knit some & do what I can—James . . . went to town in afternoon brought home a window & our new bedsteads

(2) $12.00, they are real nice. borrowed 14 lbs. 12 oz. flour of Pa.—took up a mare that is turned out to die

NOVEMBER 1865

Wednesday.
15.

cut out pair of slippers for James & pair of shoes for Henry. knit some, bake bread, pies and cookies. Dennis help James husk corn.

Wednesday.
22.

bake bread; broider on slippers & knit some—James . . . bought pair of pants $8.00; 2 balls candlewick. $.30; & 2 apples $.10. sent Henry & Edna each a letter. James' Father sold out for $5590.00

Monday.
27.

do my washing. James plowing.

DECEMBER—1865.

Monday.
25.

Christmas. wash, mop whole house, make cake. Mr. & Mrs. Thomas, Mr. & Mrs. Bacon, here to dinner. Mr. & Mrs. Hull, & Mr. & Mrs. Bly here. * * *

Tuesday.
26.

Uncle & Susan here to tea, Pa here. James get old Gray shod. . . . I sew on my dress & commence to make a fur (of cat skin) for James to wear around his neck.

JANUARY 1866

Monday,
1st.

New Years. we went to town & took oyster supper at Yeoman's. Pa's & Doolittle's folks there.

Thursday.
4.

patch pants all day. peddler came, sold him 12 lbs. paper rags $.30 & bought quart basin & 6 tart tins $.45. * * *

Wednesday. 24.	James carry grist to mill, I go with him to Smiths, stay all day. Mrs. Craig there, James to tea.

FEBRUARY 1866

Sunday. 4.	we stay at home & try to keep warm.
Sunday. 25.	we are at home, & may we not safely say all is well? yes, we are a happy family circle; little Henry just learning to talk, & baby (Sarah) just begins to be cunning—James is so kind, O may I thank God for giving me such a kind husband & may I try to return his kindness.—
Monday. 26.	wash, knit &c. James went to town. Pa was here, he gave James $70.00 for our cows; he let me have $50.00 of it; he paid some store debts &c. * * *
Tuesday. 27.	pack up things, bake cake & bread, mop &c. get ready to go to Michigan. James help me all day.[15]
Wednesday. 28.	* * * James is getting up the team to carry us to the cars. O may we trust in God that we meet again. we started from Manchester 1/2 past ten $10.50 to Chicago. . . .

MARCH—1866

Thursday. 1st.	got home to Fathers about sundown, we were really glad to meet once more indeed. we rode on cars all night, paid $1.50 for sleeping car—James is 30 years old today.
Friday. 2.	little Henry is real sick so I do not enjoy myself much. send James a letter. yes, & wish I could see him. Mrs. Brower here.

Saturday.
3.

Henry is better,—am so glad, too. Mr. Brower came, O. how glad I will be when little Henry is well, home is home, yes with our own family circle.

Sunday.
11.

rainy all day. Brother went for Dr Chappell, he came & left little Henry some medicine,—ask me no pay at all, Tis better to have friends away from home, than enemies. Henry real sick.

Wednesday.
14.

Henry's fever has abated; it has run 12 days. we think he had mumps, too, Dr. Chappell pronounced it lung fever & worm fever together with cold—received letter from James, he is well. his folks live with him in our house, O. I wish I could see him, & my prayer to God that be it His will we may all meet again & be happy in future as in the past.

Sunday.
18.

I am at Fathers, Sarah well & playful, little Henry considerable better so he runs around some. Oh that I knew what James was doing & how enjoying himself. * * *

Thursday.
22.

knit &c. Henry gets better, O. I am so thankful. received a letter from James, he thinks of joining the Army in Mexico. O. I hope & pray he may not go—may God be with us & guide us in the way we should go—then all is well—

Thursday,
29.

sew some, Edna came home & her husband. I like him very well. O. what a fuss Edna did make,—yes, we are all at home once more & tis as [brother] Henry says, "we may never all meet again," if James were only here then the family circle would be together,—That it were.

APRIL 1866

Wednesday.
11.

28 years old today. Mrs. Brower . . . & a peddlar at Fathers. traded some hair for a comb & handkerchief & had a real time. * * *

Tuesday. 24.	write & send James a letter. . . . send some potato eyes to James, & a letter to Uncle Henry sew on little Henry's pants, pleasant.

JUNE 1866

Saturday. 2.	knit &c. go to Morenci with Henry this afternoon. borrow $.50 of him (brother). . . . Saw lots of people that I used to be acquainted with, O how people & everything do change; some for better & some for worse.
Thursday. 14.	finish Henry's drawers. Sarah just begins to walk. Brother received letter from James. James wrote me a few lines & sent me 50 cents,—I paid it, to Brother,—all I owed him.

JULY 1866.

Wednesday. 4.	pick strawberries &c. last mess for tea. Brother & Hattie go to Morenci to party. I wanted to go real bad, cry about it after they were gone. * * * . . . this perhaps is the last time that I spend the 4th at Fathers, but my prayer that we meet in a better home than this when we die. little Henry can talk quite plain, Sarah can walk & climb up alone any place where she chances to be, & says, "away."
Tuesday. 24.	work on Mother's flowers &c. * * * Mrs. Hall made me a present of 19 knots of yarn worth $1.50 & a can of cherries worth $.50—quite a present, pleasant Mother gave me about 6 run of doubled & twisted—worth $4.50,—a nicer present still, & I hope I may sometime do as well by them
Wednesday. 25.	Uncle Horace Garlick & Lucy Ann Sims & Aunt Mary Osborn, too—I wrote letter to James & one to Edna. Lucy Ann has been crazy,—is better now but acts real strange. Uncle Horace has had a shock of numbpalsy

Sunday.
29.

pleasant. this morning. Harriet sick yet. none of us are very well, summer complaint. * * * this, perhaps, may be the last Sabbath evening that I stay at my Father's house, for many years, if ever. Mother is preparing some squirrel broth for Harriet. the rest have all retired for rest. I am writing in my Diary thinking, & pray, if it be God's will, we may go home soon to meet him who is most dear *to us* on earth. * * * may we all be well & all ready to go & visit sister Edna next Thursday; then on Tuesday start for home, & be it God's will we go safe on our journey. Amen.

Tuesday.
31.

finish Henry's apron. sew on Sarah's dress. . . . Hattie go away to school this morning. we kiss good bye, perhaps for the last time. ah, what relief to shed a farewell tear, when parting with a dear sister. . . . Father & Mother dread the idea of our going away; but seems 'tis right that it must be.

AUGUST 1866

Thursday.
2.

Brother brought us to Hudson   Father goes with me to Quincy [Michigan], to make Edna a visit. Mother feels real bad indeed to see us go away, yes, it does seem hard to part with our parents but it must be. we arrive at Ednas at tea time, we were glad to find them well situated & well—* * *

Sunday.
5.

am at Ednas. tis the last Sabbath undoubtedly I ever spend with her. yet I hope to visit her again sometime. but much more will we be glad to get home to see James, & be again alone our little family, pleasant. we went to the barn to crack hazel nuts. Wallace [one of Edna's sons] kill some squirrels. ah, one can but think how bad Mother did feel when we came away from there—she said, "O. dear Emily, how can I part with my baby?"

Tuesday.
7.

rain most all day. Father goes away from Ednas just at noon. I shake hands & bid him good-bye, O. dear me, am afraid

I will never see him again but hope we may meet in Heaven if not on Earth, Why do I weep to part with Father more than with the rest of my friends, ah, I know. *He* is always so kind. * * * we start for home, pay $5.65 at Quincy, then by Omnibus ticket $.50 to Wellstreet Depot; arrive in Chicago at 12 o'clock (night).

Thursday. 9.	* * * we arrive in Manchester at noon—find James & Pa waiting for us. we get home all right only pretty tired,—glad to get home,—got supper—about all
Friday. 10.	wash. mop floors all over, bake bread & pies,—am awful tired Pa here awhile.
[Thursday] 16.	my box of things, had to pay $2.20. I send a letter to Father, things came all right.

SEPTEMBER 1866.

Tuesday. 4.	bake cake & bread; make 4 lbs. plum butter. sew rags &c. 3 threshers here to breakfast, 4 to dinner & 8 to supper, rain last night so they could not thresh till afternoon, little Henry 3 years old today. 145 bushels oats.

OCTOBER 1866

Thursday. 4.	make wall basket &c. sew rags. James draw wood . . . 1/2 day. O. Dear. how awful; he brought his team home,—has had them in the fire, almost burned one of them, Kitty, almost to death. he was unloading wood; they started & ran the wagon into a rut or ditch & stopped themselves in a bed of hot embers which had been thrown from the lime kiln; burned Nelly's feet very bad & Kitty's left leg & shoulder & neck & side of face & ears & mouth. *awfully*. James go to town get sweet oil & salts. $1.10

Saturday.
6.

iron etc. knit some. Dennis dig potatoes for us, James take care of horses, most all day, then dig potatoes; about all the neighbors call to see our team, Kitty some better, James put on them—potatoes, starch & sweet oil mixed together. . . .

Tuesday.
23.

make Sarah an apron, & patch shirts, knit some, &c. James get onions (1 barrel); potatoes (15 bushels) & carrots & beets & pumpkins in cellar, real cold, almost snow. * * * we receive a letter from Harriet *O. what awful news.* Lucy Ann Sims has killed herself & her four children—little children—ages—, Lucy Ann   years; Horace , Ella , the baby   months. O, dear, how bad Robert will feel to lose his little family, all, and in such a dreadful way by having their throats cut from ear to ear[16]

NOVEMBER 1866

Sunday.
18.!!!

mop, bake bread & pies. Dennis here to tea. we are at home. Kitty no better.[17]

Tuesday.
20.

knit, churn 6-1/2 lbs . . . . *Kitty died* this morning & my pig died last night. . . .

Tuesday.
27.

knit. churn 6-3/4 lbs. James plow garden. Pa here to dinner, James give him his note of $109.50 at ten percent payable in two years from date; they have now settled up & Pa has James' notes for all he owes him. . . . * * *

Thursday.
29.

today is Thanksgiving. we kill old rooster & have a good supper. I knit &c, James help Thomas husk corn with team. snow.

DECEMBER 1866.

Monday.
10.

do not wash,—so cold, & James not well. Dennis help thresh buckwheat, 1/2 day. we send $.25 by him for pills.

Sunday.
23.

we go to Uncles. have a good visit, Susan got us a good dinner. her beau, Hersey, is paying attention to her.[18]

Tuesday.
25.

we go to Mr. Bly's to spend Christmas. Mr. & Mrs. Hull there, roast chicken etc. for dinner, pleasant.

JANUARY 1867

Tuesday.
1st.

we go to Uncles to attend New Years, Coffins, Chapmans, Van Alstynes, Smiths, & several others there. a *tip-top* good dinner. we are all well except bad colds,—general complaint. * * *

Wednesday.
16.

tis now evening; the children are asleep & I am alone. James has gone to the Turkey. have churned 1-3/4 lbs. knit some & made 3 pies.[19]

FEBRUARY 1867.

Saturday.
2.

fair & clear. Paulina mop, iron, & wash dishes for me. I fix her cloak for her in exchange. a peddler here. I sell him 17 lbs. paper rags, & buy 2 spools thread, paper of needles & thimble $.40. . . . * * *

MARCH 1867

Thursday.
14.

we go visiting at Orville & Nathan Nelsons—most excellent sleighing   cold as fury.

Saturday. receive a letter from Edna   she had a pair of twins, only
30.   one of them lived. James drew some lumber home from
           town. mop, bake pies & knit &c.

APRIL 1867.

Saturday. knit, sew &c. * * * Old Nelly lose her colt. might as well
13.   have lost $30.00. rain

Sunday.   Old spot has a calf today. Thomas offered James $5.00 for
14.   it. rainy. loan Thomas a barrel. commence weaning Sarah.

Sunday   rain. James go to see Pa; he is failing all the time.
21.

Wednesday. cut & sew on Henry's pants, plant 24 hills potatoes & 50
24.   hills of cabbage   sell a pint of milk to Juliette Stephens.
           she paid me $.25. * * *

MAY 1867.

Wednesday. we went to town to see Pa. I bought Sarah a hat $2.10;
1st.   myself ribbon, buttons & flower $2.00. & pay $.65 for
           slates & books for children, & me a lead pencil. * * *
           James go & stay with his Father to night,—he is very low.
           send a letter to Mother.

Thursday. trim hats, sew on my dress &c. James came home this morn-
2.   ing, his Father died at 7 o'clock.

Friday.   finish my dress. we attend the funeral; the children all feel
3.   very bad at the loss of their parent friend. am sorry for them.
           we last saw the last remains about 3 o'clock. * * *

Saturday.   Bake for Mr. Webber enough to come to $1.00. churn
4.   4-3/4 lbs. James build fence around *grave* in forenoon &
             go to town in afternoon   Ma gave him $.25 silver piece that
             was Pa's. am sorry for him for he mourns the loss of his
             Father very much.

Sunday.   we stay at home all day. I write the following poetry on the
12.   death of James' Father:

             It has pleased God to call thee home,
             To that home which thou off hast told us
             Was waiting for us all to come;
             That blessed home, the home of Jesus.

             [Seven stanzas follow.]

JUNE 1867

Sunday.   after dinner we go to Uncles stay to tea. we met Hersey &
16.   Susan going to our house. O, dear, what will Uncle say or
             do when he knows the sad news which Susan told me,—bad
             indeed.

JULY 1867.

Tuesday,   we all go to menagerie at Manchester   saw many things.
9.   cost us $1.45. * * *

                          cheese
             milk warm, put in rennet enough to bring to a curd, then
             whey off till dry by cutting up or breaking & stirring the
             curd occasionally, then salt & put in press for a couple of
             hours; turn & put in press 3 or 4 hours, turn again & leave
             in press till time to put in another cheese (say about 24 hrs

in press in all); then take out & grease in hot melted butter with red pepper in. change cloths every time the cheese is turned so as to have a dry one. keep in an airy place & turn & grease every day till cured.

[Recipes follow for sweet pickles, fruitcake, silver cake, sponge cake, and catsup. There is also a note to "sow onion seed in *last qr.* of new moon."]

AUGUST 1867

Saturday 10.

do not work very hard today only to cook for 6 harvesters . . . 5 to dinner, 6 to tea. * * *

Tuesday. 13.

do usual work. Uncle call & give us a piece of pig. * * * in the evening Susan & Hersey came here. James went & got Prof. Russell to come & marry them, they were married about 11 o'clock in the evening. Mr. Russell went back home & we partook of some cake & pie which I prepared in the afternoon for the occasion. they stay the remainder of the night.

Thursday. 15.

* * * sew. churn, the people of Manchester & round about have a chicken hunt & go to Uncles to get dinner. I count   wagons, busses, & carriages all full. it seems too bad I cannot join in some of the meetings & festivals & be one among many as I was wont to do—but those days have passed away.—James is harvesting for Hersey & did not feel as if he could lose the time to attend picnics— [20]

SEPTEMBER 1867.

Tuesday. 17.

make a nice wedding [anniversary] cake for tomorrow; make 1 gallon of pickle peaches   do up a tureen of peach preserve. James go to town. . . .

OCTOBER 1867.

Tuesday.
1st.

some movers camp in dooryard last night; buy oats &
hay $ they let us have a Shepard puppy   pay them $.40
in money for it. was offered $3.50 before they were out of
sight. O. dear me we have another loss. *Fly died this morning.* James do chores, go to town, I knit & do usual work.

Wednesday.
16.

. . . we go to town & get our molasses 30 gallons—cost
$9.00 for making $2.50 for a barrel to put it in, $3.00 for
drawing it to mill & allow James $4.00 for his work to sell
the whole it would bring $27.00   then for my work I would
get (pay for making molasses) $10.00 for my work viz. for
planting, weeding & stripping 3 days work. * * *

Sunday.
27.

Ma came here & stay all day, the first visit she ever made
us; she gave a new dress to Sarah & a flannel sheet to
James. we carry her home. . . .

Wednesday.
30.

James gives me $6.00. we go to town trade $21.93: got me
2 dresses, calico for aprons, Henry clothes & children shoes
& 47 yds. of factory. . . . * * *

NOVEMBER 1867.

Friday.
8.

sew, knit. James top turnips. . . . Thomas & Hersey here
this evening—Susan has a baby girl.

DECEMBER 1867.

Sunday.
8.

. . . after tea we ride up to Uncles, call on Dutch John
[Schmidt], he treated us to grape wine. very pleasant all
day.[21]

Tuesday.
10.

took pills last night, was rather cross last evening. James wanted me to read to him, did not,—did not feel like reading—I might have said so & then saved all disagreeable feelings, will make amends. O. I do pray that God may help me to ever be more pleasant in our little family & never again refuse to read when James asks me so kindly—or tell him a reason why. today make Henry a waist. James finish husking corn. . . .

JANUARY 1868.

Thursday.
2.

made my new bonnet,—cost in all $2.85 besides the outside & velvet & some other little trimmings that cost (or would have cost) about $.50 then I could afford to sell it for $4.50 or $5.00 & make $1.70 for my day's work.

Monday.
6.

sew &c. James quite sick all day. cold, real cold—tis now evening, the children asleep & I have just laid aside my knitting to retire, too. James seems to be considerable easier than he did last night. I think he has symptoms of inflation on the bowels, have kept hot cloths wet with vinegar across him all day. O my prayer is that he may get well, for, O. Lord, what could I do were he to die.' . . . O. wilt Thou spare him to me awhile longer for I feel I have no other friend on Earth; this we ask for Christ's sake for thine is the crown & the glory forever & ever. Amen. Ah me all seems bad when dear ones are sick. James groans so mournfully,—and without the wind howls its most dismal sound, but we hope & trust we may say all will yet be well.

Tuesday.
7.

sew. knit &c. etc. James better, Sarah is quite sick however with *bad* cold. Susan here visiting. Hersey call & stay to tea. Susan tells me of New Years supper at Mr. S——, a 'company were invited & among them was a certain lady, Mrs. B—— (grasswidow), there seemed to be quite an object for her to get a beau therefore Mr. B—— [Uncle Henry Baker?] was invited to come & join in the tete-a-tete among friends & strangers, of course he attended & it being leap year, Mrs. B—— having considerable confidence & a little fast, on the long-looked-for occasion politely invited Mr. B—— to partake of the turkey with her. —was almost overwhelmed with joy when they sat there talking & devouring the dainties which were prepared for them & she thought without fail she had caught the old bird at last. but, Oh the downcast eyes & when she invited him to accompany her home to listen to the enchanting sound that she might play to him on her Piano, & he willfully declined we imagine she went home thinking why is it so? & shall I try again'— continued next week.

Thursday. 9.	bake, sew. Sarah's cold pretty bad James do chores &c. go to town & get a paper—just get the first Manchester Delaware County Union, costs $2.00 per year. [22]
Monday. 13.	do large washing, sew & knit some James go to town & saw wood for Jerome (rather hard work for money to buy papers) James sell 6 chickens for $1.00.

MARCH 1868

Sunday. 1st.	we went to Margaret Doolittles. James' mother & Dennis were there, too, Margaret invited all of the family to dinner to celebrate James' birthday. Ma gave him cloth for a pair of pants, Mercelia sent lining for them (a nice birthday present)
Friday. 13.	finish my apron. [A small drawing of an apron is on the page.] Mrs. Smith call. James do chores & saw wood. Old Spot cow has *twin calves*, both steers. an omen of our having

better luck. O. that it may be true, may we have good health
& be thankful to Him who bestows all blessings.

Monday.
16.

Hail big as walnuts & rain, do not wash because James is
so lame he cannot bring water. sew some & knit, help James
shell corn.

MAY 1868

Friday.
1st.

we finish setting out strawberry vines this morning. Henry
Stimson here to rent some corn ground, James is to let him
have 5 acres at $3.00 per acre in exchange for breaking 5
acres of land at $3.00 per acre. * * * *turkey commence to
set on 15 eggs*

Tuesday,
5.

mop. finish Sarah's dress, dress Henry's doll. work some in
garden. rain, James plow 1/2 day.

Wednesday.
13.

churn 6 lbs. 7 oz., James finish plowing in forenoon, we go
to town in afternoon, take 22-3/4 lbs. of butter; get for it
$5.55. . . . I get Henrys, Sarah's & my pictures taken 8 of
each (24) $3.00 . . . lent James $5.00. * * *

Thursday.
14.

commence James' pants; he got them cut & a coat & trimmings yesterday   let the tailor have 3 bushels of potatoes
$1.20 & now owes him $. * * *

JUNE 1868.

Saturday.
20.

mop, iron &c. pick over berries, have picked about 24
qts.—James plow corn.

Tuesday.
30.

make pants for Henry, churn, send $.10 for braid. James
plow corn. * * * there has been since first of March 344
mover wagons.

JULY 1868.

Saturday.
4.

some movers here last night, pay us $1.90. we attend Cele-
bration in Manchester & stay to dance in evening,—spend
$.35 for lemons & cookies.

Sunday.
19.

* * * Jas. go to town get mail—go to see how his folks have
settled up their estate, they charge us in addition to James'
note of $350.00 for every thing that his Father gave to
him. . . . O may we pay them their demands, with a willing
heart, though it seems like *giving* away what we have
worked hard for. . . . though we have been sorely wronged
may it be a lesson to us never to walk in the steps of our
enemies, that our children may arise & call us blessed.

Jimmy McBride & Sarah Bacon here to tea. rather think
Sarah will be e'er long Mrs. McB—that is the way the world
goes— [23]

AUGUST 1868.

Tuesday.
4.

James carry us to Uncles to chicken picnic in morning, my
cake said to be the nicest there. * * *

Tuesday,
11.!!!

do up melon preserves—6 lbs.—James plow in forenoon
. . . in afternoon, we go to town in evening, sell 25-1/2 lbs.
butter for $6.38, send for Detroit Free Press $1.00. . . .

Friday.
21.

James plow &c. I bake bread & pie, Oh! Oh!! Oh!!! what
awful news again   Uncle got hurt in the reaper—we went
to see him, he is in dreadful pain, the Doctors there, they
think his hand will have to be amputated; he fell off ahead
of the sickle while mowing & got his right arm almost cut
off between the elbow & hand all but a part of one bone;
had to be taken out of his arm, about 3 inches flesh, bones,

arteries, cords & all. Ah, dear a me, it seems too bad but we may be thankful tis no worse, & hope he may get well.

Sunday.
23.

we go to see Uncle, Oh, I am afraid we are to lose our best friend that we have near us—Jimmy came & got his threshing machine.

Sunday.
30.

we go to see Uncle; his *hand is all mortified.* rainy most all day.

SEPTEMBER 1868.

Tuesday.
1st.

we go to see Uncle this morning,—he had his hand amputated yesterday with great excitement about its having to be done, he had thought they were saving it, & the thought that it must come off almost, almost killed him. * * *

Sunday.
6.

we take a ride over the prairie   we hear that Uncle is better, quite cold

Wednesday.
16.

churn. I drive the horses & go to Uncles in the afternoon.—Uncle gives us a piece of fresh pig. * * *

Friday.
18.

the 6th. anniversary of our wedding day has arrived & finds us all well & may we be thankful to God for all blessings bestowed upon us, for the happiness we have enjoyed & pray that in future all may be well.—James help Sellens thresh[24]

Tuesday.
29.

churn. knit &c. James work on road for Thomas, Uncle Ben & Aunt Mary Osborn come here from Michigan (Morenci)—Mother sent me some yarn—we were real disappointed that Mother did not come, too.

Wednesday,   rain very hard last night. & this forenoon. we carry Uncle
30.   Ben & Aunt Mary to Uncle Henrys & stay to tea,—leave
              them there * * *

NOVEMBER 1868.

Saturday.   mop &c. knit, James build railroad crossing,—he sells
14.   Dave for $145.00   I felt real bad about it, think it is too
              cheap for he is a nice colt. * * *

Wednesday,   finish mittens for Sarah, James husk corn in forenoon. we
25.   go to Mr. Thomas' to get our turkeys—they all (29) went up
              there.

DECEMBER 1868.

Tuesday.   knit. patch, iron. James help Mr. Thomas husk corn in fore-
1st.   noon, he went to town in afternoon, buy crackers, cheese,
              & oysters $2.50. Mr. Thomas buy the same, we all go up to
              Uncles in evening. carry oysters & have a dance—I receive
              letters from Harriet & Aunt Mary—they are all quite well.
              * * *

Friday,   Christmas, very pleasant. I make the children night dresses.
25.   James saw & draw wood.

JANUARY 1869.

Friday.   fry cakes, bake pies & bread. James fix the old sleigh & we
8.   go on a sleighride. snow.

Thursday. 14.	knit &c. Augustine bring me some slices of smoked meat & get some turnips. tis lonesome. *James* stays away [at Turkey River] to night, too.
Wednesday. 20.	bake pies, bread, cookies & fry cakes. this evening there were 24 here on a surprise. we have a good supper & dance. James do chores &c.

MARCH 1869

Saturday. 6.!!!	sew a little, the children both sick. Sarah a little better but Henry real sick. O. we do hope & pray they may not be sick long; that if it be the will of God that they may both be well. . . . * * *
Sunday. 7.	finds us a grunting set—Sarah is considerable better—Henry seems not to have quite as much fever—but is real sick, O how thankful we will be when they are well—we are alone all day.
Monday. 15.	the children better so they sit up & eat a little today—I do a two-week's washing, James draw wood.

APRIL 1869

Sunday. 11.	is my 31st. birthday—we go to visit at Yeomans, Ma gave me a real nice calico dress—'tis the 48th. anniversary of James' father's & mother's wedding day.—a sprinkle of rain. we now have 4 cows. Spot has a calf today.
Wednesday. 14.	sew, churn. James go to town get me a letter from Harriet & she has given up coming out here this spring because Mother is sick—Julia Blanchard is dead. * * *

| Monday. 26.!!! | wash & churn, rain most all day—James plow in afternoon. we have found 96 eggs that 6 turkeys have laid. |

MAY 1869.

| Wednesday. 5. | churn etc. * * * James went to town, get plow sharpened $.50 . . . paid *uselessly* for ale $.10,—& get trusted $1.87 for 6 more tin pans. |

| Thursday. 13. | bake. clean house &c. James plow. I sell hay, milk, & eggs to emigrants $1.20 |

| Wednesday 26.!!! | —rain last night—so I have to bring in some of little turkeys   they almost die. James build fence & go to town; get me wine $1.00, some fish $.10. * * * |

JULY 1869

| Saturday. 17. | make cheese—James chop wood. Mr. Ikener here to dinner, we go to town, take 26 lbs. butter, get $4.65 for it; pay up store debt at Thorpes. . . . |

| Thursday. 22. | do usual work, James haying. I go up to Mr. Thomas'. they sent for me. Nell has a nice baby girl 5 lbs. 5 oz. |

AUGUST 1869.

| Sunday. 1st. | real pleasant & all good natured. except the old hog wants to get the milk away from the turkeys. |

| Saturday. 7. | churn. mop &c, James harvesting   Ikener has worked for him 2 days. . . . 7 harvest boarders to dinner. almost total |

eclipse on sun, commence 10 minutes past 4 & end 5 minutes past six,—beautiful indeed.

SEPTEMBER 1869.

Tuesday.
7.

sew some. stay at Mr. Thomas' most all day, their Baby is *sick.* * * *

Wednesday.
8.

bake, get dinner for 4 men, sew & knit some. about one o'clock go up to Mr. Thomas'—they bury Nell's baby there in the dooryard,—it died about 3 in morning. churn. * * *

Saturday.
18.

bake some, clean house in general. receive a letter from Hattie,—she starts to see us next Monday evening. O.O.O. can it be! how glad I am. James went to town . . . bring his mother home with him.

Sunday.
19.

Ma goes with us to Uncles—Albert & Susan are to start for Kansas tomorrow. shower of rain—* * *

Tuesday.
21.

make me a skirt, clean up in general.—James help Scanlon thresh—in the evening we go to the Depot for Harriet, she arrives at 11 o'clock, how glad I was to see her & to hear direct from home.

Tuesday,
28.

finish threshing, 128 bu. wheat & 180 of oats. I bake every thing, have 3 men to breakfast, 14 to dinner & 13 to supper & Mrs. Snell, she stays all night. Henry is better. I am about tired out.

OCTOBER 1869.

Wednesday.
13.

Today pleasant, Hattie & I quilt a coverlid & Hattie irons. James bet with Hattie that if she was at home one year from today that he would get her a new dress and if she was not she is to get him a new pair of pants.

Sunday,
31.

cook turkey. Hattie here. James go to see his mother, she is sick.

NOVEMBER 1869.

Friday.
5.!!!

Dennis come & tell us Ma is worse, we go & stay most all day, come home & do chores, then go back. I stay all night, James went home.

Saturday.
6.

Ma *died* just 23 minutes of 2 o'clock this morning.—died without a struggle. James came for me about 10 o'clock, I then sewed rest of time. Hattie does all my work.—how good she is.

Monday.
15.

we wash &c. I sew. Hattie commence attending the Teacher's Institute at Manchester. * * *

Saturday.
20.

clean up &c. James kill beef. . . . I sell my turkeys— 86—for $73.95—Hattie came back, has a certificate & a school engaged—received a letter from Mother. * * *

DECEMBER 1869.

Thursday.
2.

—sew &c. James go to town & get his things that were his mothers,—he has a very nice bureau—3 quilts—4 dresses—& quite a good many things.—sold 48 lbs. paper rags, bought chopping knife & a lantern $1.35.

Saturday.
25.

Christmas. bake chicken, pie—fruit cake & have a good dinner in general. * * * James work on sleigh. Hattie finish James' socks & I finish her cloak—pleasant.

Thursday.
30.

we go to town, I buy toys & candies for children $.20 &
$.15; New Years presents. toy for Hattie $.30; match box
for James $.40. . . . we visit Hattie's school this after-
noon—they have New Years tree,—a nice time in general.
(Hattie gave me a toy   real nice. $.75 cost—& James a
china mug cost $.75 & the children each a present $.25
apiece)

JANUARY 1870.

Sunday.
2.

we are at home. Mr. & Mrs. Collar call to warm. Jimmy
McBride here with his wife to stay all night, they were married the 26th. of December—a week ago today. do not think
he has as good a wife as he is a man.

FEBRUARY 1870.

Saturday.
12.

we are at home. sew &c. cold as fury!—Henry receive his
first letter from Grandma.

[The entries skip to March 8. Two pages of the journal are
left blank, perhaps indicating that Sarah Huftalen thought
she might locate the missing sheets during her transcription
project and left space for them.]

MARCH 1870.

Friday.
18.

make overskirt for Hattie—she goes with John McGee to a
surprise at Uncles. James go to Turkey & back.[25]

Thursday.
24.

sew. James chop wood. in afternoon we go to Masonville,—
stay to Billy Williams to tea,—roads very bad—start to go
through some water, ice break under horses & let Sam horse
clear in out of sight & Jane colt all in except her head—&

us in wagon half covered with water—feet wet—James'
boot full of water

APRIL 1870

Monday
11.

32 birthday [This line is framed by a hand on each side
pointing toward it.] Hattie does work for me, I build hens
nests. James *commence plowing.*

MAY 1870

Wednesday,
11.

churn, &c. James mark corn ground. Jimmy Proven brings
a span of colts here for James to keep—to work one &
Jimmy is to pay for pasturing the other, *too bad,*—Jimmy's
wife has left him & going to Scotland. * * *

Tuesday.
17.

churn, bake &c. James make fence. Jimmy Proven come
here with his little boy thinking he is going to keep him but
finally makes up his mind to let his wife take him to Scotland with her, O. dear tis a sad affair for a husband & wife
to part—I do not have very good luck with my chickens,
only 14 hatch out of 54 eggs.

JUNE 1870.

Sunday.
5.

all at home, no one come, all is right, 'till midnight, then
company come too late to be entertained. rain.

JULY 1870

Wednesday
20.

—wash etc. Henry quite sick. James work for Scanlons.
Mr. Bronson bring sewing machine here for me to try.[26]

Friday.   sew on Harriet's nightdress—we have an awful time of
22.   it—needle cuts cloth etc. James harvest for Scanlons.

AUGUST 1870.

Saturday.   frost a cake, &c. James carry Harriet, the children & me
6.   up to Uncles to a picnic   I thought James was going with
               us till we were all ready—when to our sorry surprise he said
               he was going to help Scanlons thresh & so he did & I did
               not enjoy the Picnic at all.

Sunday.   we & all of Uncles folks go about 10 miles to see a very high
21.   ledge of Rocks   ft. high, take our dinners & dine some   ft.
               up in air

               Where pines & cedars grow—
               & far, far down,—down below
               On either side is the gentle flow
               Of the river Maquoketa.

Saturday.   do little of everything. James cut corn   we all go plum-
27.   ming—get nearly 2 bushels.

SEPTEMBER 1870.

Thursday.   making sauce & drying plums & patching. churn. James
1st.   cut corn.

Thursday,   we attend the fair pay $1.00 for a family ticket, a right to
29.   attend the fair 3 days & enter any article for premium. we
               take some flowers. . . . Harriet go with John[27]

OCTOBER 1870.

Saturday.
1st.

we are at fair all day. I get premium on my flowers: (Diploma). Harriet go home with Uncle.

Wednesday.
26.

help James get oats up stairs, sew, James husk corn in afternoon. Clark & Webber came & got my turkeys (78) paid $89.75 for them. they weighed 718 lbs. at 12-1/2 per lb.

NOVEMBER 1870

Friday.
4.

sew. churn &c. James work on stable. Messrs Hull & Lowe bring a Howe sewing machine here. I buy it of them for $67.00.

Tuesday.
15.

make coat for Henry. * * * ground white with snow this morning. buy 2 turkeys yesterday of Jimmy Proven, am to do $3.00 sewing for them.

Friday.
25.

Harriet go with me to town, I take two jars of butter, sell for $17.37 (69-1/2 lbs) . . . pay for James' coat &c $7.00 buy 6 yds. cloth for overhauls. . . .

DECEMBER 1870.

Sunday.
11.

sell hay to mover $.20. *real snow storm.* we go to Uncles but James did not want to.

Saturday
24.!!!

we all go to Mr. Chapmans to Christmas dinner. James go to town, get pair skates for Henry $1.50, get wagon mended. . . .

JANUARY 1871

Sunday.
1st.

make chicken pie, bake spare rib &c. Uncle & Aunt, Frank & Viola & John & Lilly here to New Years dinner, emigrants here, paid us in 1 year past $21.50. there has been since year ago today, 1553 emigrant teams been past going west & 171 going east. James draw rock.

MARCH 1871

Tuesday.
14.

sew &c. rain, James sell my heifer. I felt real bad about it.

Tuesday.
21.

finish night dress & chemise. Harriet . . . paid me the $4.50 that she owed me. & she lets James have $20.00. that makes $100.00 he owes her. * * *

MAY 1871.

Monday.
8.

* * * Alfred Brower here to dinner, he starts to night for Pocahontas County to live, Francis Conley here to tea, he is to go to Nebraska to find a home in the wilds of the West.[28]

Sunday.
21.

Uncle came & Harriet & I go to hear the Dedication of the Universalist church at Manchester. Mr. Anson of Chicago preached the sermon. . . . (they took a subscription to clear the house from debt & raised it all, the Amount of $2600.00)   the house cost over $8000.00. * * *[29]

Wednesday.
24.

bake. make fine shirt for James & Harriet make a coarse one. I gave her $.15 for it. James clean dooryard & pick up

in general. Uncle call. John here all night. * * * Yeoman
here to dinner,—he let James have $30.00 to pay his ex-
penses to Kansas City. James is to drive Yeoman's team with
carriage (Yeoman goes by rail)—John McGee with James.

Thursday. 25.	we are alone today. James & John start this morning on their journey—some rainy. Henry Stimson is to do the chores & plow the corn—Uncle call.
Friday. 26.	sew some, churn &c. 'tis evening. all in dreamland but me—seems lonely indeed when James is not here—I do hope he is well

JUNE 1871

Sunday. 4.	am here alone. I have 236 chickens & 84 turkeys.
Wednesday, 7.	sew some &c. James come home last night on the 10 o'clock passenger train. I was in bed,—he came to my bedroom door—rapped & called for oats & permission to sleep on porch etc. asked if there were any men folks around. * * * he so changed his voice that I did not know him, was *glad* indeed that he came cost him there & back $36.00.
Monday. 12.	wash, etc. James plow corn—the children go to school to- day for the first time
Sunday. 18.	we are at home. little Henry was real saucy & struck me,—I had to punish him quite severely before he would be a good boy. indeed I was real sorry & do hope with the help of God I may never have occasion to so punish him again—may I know the right way to do & bring up my children as is good in the sight of the Lord.

Monday. 19.	"all is well," this morning—James at work plowing corn, the children gone to school & Harriet, & I must away to my washing

JULY 1871

Wednesday. 12.	finish me a silk waist & over skirt—of the silk,—I bought of Julia Blanchard (poor girl—she is now dead). * * *
Sunday. 23.	we are alone today all day. happy lonesome. Harriet churn.

AUGUST 1871

Thursday. 3.	quilt a quilt.—Susan start back to Kansas. I go with them to town, Uncle goes as far as Dubuque. . . . * * *
Sunday. 13. !!!	make chicken pie,—man to dinner,—he has been past here to & fro several times; he said he called to visit us,—after dinner he started and said the "good bye, James, take care of yourself." & James says, "You are not going without paying for your dinner, are you?" "Why, I'll willingly pay—but thought I was visiting." by the way that is the way he & family get their living most of the time—he paid (rather reluctantly) however $.20
Friday 25.	bake, make pickles, rain. James get out stone, help to take down partitions—door & window—butry to have shelves on one side & one end,—closet to have 5 shelves. . . . [Calculations of the cost of the construction and a diagram of the house and its new addition follow.]

August 1871.

25. Friday bake, make pickles, rain. James git out stone, help to take down partitions — door & window — butry to have shelves on one side & one end, — closet to have 5 shelves — move door & window and git ready for plaster $2.00, move siding, make butry 1 window & 1 door & shelves 2.00, move partition, make cellar way & closet 2.00, move cellar way & make floor in place. 2.00 Butry 5 hrs. window & door 3 hrs; move cellar way & closet 2 hours — move partition, make cellar way & closet 10 hrs. 10 + 5 + 3 + 2 = 20

26. Saturday. sew & bake. James help Webber thresh Harriet mop & go to town.
27. Sunday. after tea Harriet & John go over to Brooks, Uncle & Mrs. Bevins call — and Jennie Stinson & Mr C— . movers here. too. pay $.30 for hay.
28. Monday. wash — bake, Sarah stay at home — not well. James help Walker thresh half a

A page from Emily Gillespie's 1871 diary with her diagram of the new house.

SEPTEMBER 1871

Saturday.
2.

bake bre ., cake & pies—emigrants (Mr. Everets) 4 of them here to stay over Sunday. * * *

Monday.
4.

movers go,—pay me $4.00 in the house, and pay James $1.80 out doors.

Monday.
18.

bake 3 cakes, cookies, & bread—today is our 9th. Anniversary. Mr. & Mrs. Sellens & Uncle here to tea. *pleasant.*

Friday.
29.

James clean wheat in forenoon—we attend school picnic in our schoolhouse in afternoon—school is done for this term. I gave Henry & Sarah each a toy (dog & horse) for they reading their readers twice through   Henry step on nail.

OCTOBER 1871.

Saturday.
14.

Mrs. Houghton & I sat up all last night with old Mrs. Stephens, 74 yrs, she died 10 minutes past 9 this morning. we lay her out in black dress—I came home this afternoon, rain, rain all day. * * *

Sunday,
29.

* * * we attend meeting, Prof. Wood (Universalist) gave lecture on "The Lessons of the Burning of Chicago, a Loss of About $2,000,000.00."[30]

Monday.
30.

James plow. Harriet wash & clean house, I bake   tarts, 40 cookies, 7 + 2 pies, 2 cakes, 2 jelly cakes. Movers feed 30 head of cattle in corn stalks last night $1.50. I send $.50 for 2 lbs. raisins.

Tuesday.
31.

cook Bride's cake & 75 cookies, bread &c. snow all day. James go to Delhi with John after License.

NOVEMBER. 1871.

Wednesday.
1st.
!!!

Harriet & John are married today at half past three   By James Stephens, preacher. [Names of the eighteen people in attendance are listed.] a nice day.

Tuesday.
14.

iron, sew &c. James plow. this evening Harriet & John came after her things; they live with his folks.

Thursday.
16.

sew, churn etc. James plow. snow. Harriet came after pig.— *not get it.* no give.

DECEMBER 1871.

Wednesday.
20.

—we go to town; . . . buy at Congers two set Candall's Building Blocks for the children's Christmas presents $4.90.[31]

Monday.
25.

wash etc. James try tallow 70 lbs. it is worth $7.00. children get their presents this morning—they are *very* well pleased—play with them all day.

Thursday.
28.

sew, mop. children at home. cold   James kill 5 cats & go & get grist. I receive a letter from Henry—he says Dr. Sweeney, Alonzo Downer died, Old Mrs. Converse is dead, too. Aunt Mary talks go getting a divorce after being married over fifty years, how strange, it is too bad.

JANUARY 1872.

Monday.
1st.

wash etc. James go to town with Uncle. gets treated to oyster supper. * * *

Thursday.
4.

Children at school. I go to the mill with James, he took 14 bu. of corn—we stay to dinner at Dan Ryan's. Mary buys a sewing machine like mine—I am to have an embroiderer for influencing her to buy *it* in preference to a Singer—[32]

Wednesday.
10.

cut cloak & dress for Sarah, James help Estey kill hogs— Trumblee here begging for poor family—give butter & meal.

Monday.
22.

wash. bake etc. James take steers to town. . . . this evening read a story "Finoola" treats upon free-love—* * *

FEBRUARY 1872.

Wednesday.
14.

James help me wind over & prepare rags for carpet, *cold.*

Tuesday.
20.

* * * I clean up in general. James go over to Bly's to grind axes &c.—Bly is to take the job of building James' barn. James is to help. $27.00 for the job,—not *board.*

MARCH 1872.

Wednesday.
6.

mop, get tea for a visiting party: [Names of fourteen men and women follow.] good time in general. Mr. & Mrs. Chapman stay in the evening. I loan them 20 of my Woman Suffrage papers with a hope they may see rightly & understandingly. children at school.

Thursday.
21.

I & the children go & make harriet a visit,—last sleighride I guess for this winter. Harriet Encienta since Christmas. James & Bly frame.[33]

Friday.   patch. James go to town, *stormy*. get me a letter from Edna
22.   & the rest of the mail, our best paper is Woodhull & Claflin
                Weekly (may right prevail; may women vote & help to make
                the laws which govern them)[34]

APRIL 1872.

Thursday.   *birthday—34—windy*. mop. James drag. we go up to
11.   grove & get shrubbery,—get 1 doz. currant bushes of John
                Schmidt. he treated us to wine.

Saturday.   do usual work. finish vests &c. James sow wheat. Henry
13.   drag for the first time about an hour, *did well*. * * *

Thursday.   pick up rags. *Henry churn* for me for the first time, did well.
25.

MAY 1872.

Monday.   children commence to go to school. Miss Pope, teacher, to
6.   teach 5 months for $80; I wash &c. James plant potatoes &
X[35]   corn.

JUNE 1872.

Tuesday.   clean house &c. have fed salted meal to my turkeys acci-
18.   dentally,—killed 18. James make bedsteads in forenoon,
                plow corn 1/2 day.

JULY 1872.

Wednesday.   pick currants in forenoon at John's [Schmidt], get 10 qts. in
3.   afternoon visit Harriet, have a splendid visit; they are doing

well. live in stable; will soon have a house,—all framed
now.

SEPTEMBER 1872.

Saturday.
14.

James help McGee thresh, I drive the new horse & the children & I go over to visit Harriet.

Sunday.
22.

we are at home, last night McMillen came for me to go &
stay with Mrs. McMillen,—they have another boy.

Tuesday.
24.

clean up house &c. James help Uncle thresh   'tis the first
day of the fair, I would like to go very much indeed.

But when a man *wont*
A woman can not—
We must try to not despair
Our little children yet need care,
May God be with us every day,
To guide us safely through
And help us to endure
The trifles which crowd their way—
Then let us truly, safely live & tell
That all is well,—all is well.

Wednesday.
25.

we go to the fair but too late to enter my things, costs $.75.
* * *

OCTOBER 1872.

Tuesday.
1st.

John came for me last night   Harriet sick, her little girl
died about 2 o'clock this afternoon, Lilly [McGee] bake my
bread & get dinner for James, he plowed

Saturday. 12.	bake pies etc James dig potatoes, the children & I help him in afternoon.

| Wednesday. 16. | do usual work, knit . . . visit school, 'tis the last day of the term. the children just finished reading through their third readers the *second* time. the teacher gave them each a card, I gave them each $.50 for being good & to Henry $.55 for leaving off at the head 55 times; & to Sarah $.25 for 25 times. James do chores in forenoon . . . . * * * |

NOVEMBER 1872

Tuesday. 5.	Election,—candidates are Grant, Republican & Greely, viz. Liberal Democrat.—we go to Masonville, at Billy Williams to dinner. James vote for Greeley.[36]

| Friday. 29. | I sew. Sherwin came after some turkeys; sell him 41, they weigh 352 lbs. at x/7, $24.64, he paid James $1.00 for taking them down. * * * |

| Saturday. 30. | bake. finish Henry's coat. Mrs. Langford & !!! Harriet here, James do chores & go to town, get ax helve. |

DECEMBER 1872.

Wednesday. 25.	Christmas. Make me an apron, a skirt for Sarah &c. James do chores.—children get magazines & papers in their stockings. cold & snow.

| Friday. 27. | do usual work. James do chores. we go to town. . . . We subscribe at PO for papers viz. Peterson's Magazine $1.50, The Western Rural $1.75 & Inter Ocean $1.25.[37] . . . |

Monday.
30.

visit at Dan Ryans while James attend Covey's Auction.
* * * Mary is Encienta again. am sorry for her. *snow. snow*

JANUARY 1873.

Wednesday.
1st.

wash &c. we go up to Uncles. Harriet & John were there.
Harriet cooked a real nice turkey *good dinner indeed.* apples & wine. Harriet Encienta, too. I lent John $12.00

Tuesday.
7.

sew on my cloak, afternoon we go sleighriding, call at Mr.
Smiths. exchange gobblers, get a splendid black one. . . .
snow badly drifted & commence to *blow, blow snow.*

Friday.
10.

sew. bake etc. James shovel snow to get horses and cattle
out of shed. I went out with the children & rode down the
snow bank on hand sleigh; it pleased them very much to see
Ma dump off in the snow.

Friday.
31.

sew &c. James saw wood. pleasant   Mrs. McMillen here
visiting, she came on foot   brought one baby 4 months old
& led one 18 months old.

FEBRUARY 1873

Friday.
14.
xx

we went to town today. get our pictures taken (4 of James, 4
of Henry & Sarah together, 4 James & mine together, 4
mine alone.) $3.00. * * *

Sunday.
16.

we are at home; were going to meeting but found the time
too slow.

MARCH 1873.

Saturday.
1st.

* * * mop &c. we go to town, get letter from Mother. I buy
yeast of Toogood $.25; James pay Mosier all due $2.25.

those Irish Behans had to treat him to beer; he drank too much, great beginning in over 38 years. the children & I go to Mrs. Brooks, stay to tea, turkeys begin to lay.[38] * * *

Friday.
21.

Mr. Estey came after me last evening to set up with Mr. Stephens; he has been sick all winter, he died this morning half past three;—died in a sound sleep; passed into Eternity without a struggle. I finish fine shirt for James today.[39] * * *

Monday.
31.

wash, bake etc. James help Estey thresh—rain in night.

Musings of Midnight[40]

1. Thou didst tell me that thou loved me
   Many years ago
   Although I loved you in return, I dared
   Not tell you so.
2. 'Twas just fifteen years ago this eve
   I first did pen
   An answer to the wish you craved
   I loved you then.
3. Methought you wert jesting when you said
   "I love but you;"
   Thou art so often with me in my dreams
   I think 'twas true.
4. Ah well do I remember now. Alas!
   The words you said;
   "Our hearts may ever be united," as then
   When we are dead.
5. Down in the deep recesses of my heart
   A secret lies.
   Many is the time I have sought to tell you
   These binding ties.
6. Should you know the author of these lines
   Keep in your heart
   The secret which has ne'er been told before
   In silence wrote.

   7. I know your heart has e'er been mine
             In secret bound
      My heart shall e'er & e'er be thine
             The thoughts resound.
   8. When thou art called by Him who reigns on high
             My words of love
      May comfort thee in the last; thy dying hour
             We'll meet above.
   9. Could I know thy love was still unchanged
             Thy heart still mine,
      Just the same as fifteen years ago:
             The thought's devine!
  10.

APRIL 1873.

Tuesday. 1st.	sew &c. James go up to Uncles & get some buttermilk,—he fooled us in morning,—wild geese, snow all day.
Thursday. 10.	color rags—James commence to scrape cellar to barn. * * * Icicles this morning hung from the eaves of the house three feet long & large, like winter.
Sunday. 20.	we are at home. real cold.—did have 3 little turkeys but the hen killed two. today I would like to see Father & Mother

Aye ones mind oft wanders back
   To years in childhood spent.
Where sorrow, joy, love & pleasure
   All in so short a time were blent.

MAY 1873

Wednesday. 14.	sew on sunbonnet—bake. * * * Old Dolly (horse) lose her colt last night—I was indeed real sorry because it was ei-

ther killed by plowing with her last Tuesday week, or because she was out in cold rain last night. It would not have been if James had done as I told him, too, not work her & keep her in shed every night. children at home. rain.

JUNE 1873

Friday.
6.

do usual work; have from 23 to 25 pans of milk to skim & wash every day besides take care of poultry etc. * * *

Tuesday.
17.

finish Sarah's dress & drawers. churn bake. James plow corn. while sitting here on the porch I see a procession of carriages & a hearse pass by. Alas,—it is to convey the last remains of Mrs. Snell to its final resting place. Consumption has felled another in our midst, one that was ever ready to lend a helping hand in time of need & although the tongue of slander has been playing its part for the last year she will hear it no more now that she has gone they can only think, (it may have been untrue) & at last, like her, will be judged by Him. how glad I am I never said one Evil word about her. & hope I may ever say good if any thing about every one.

JULY 1873.

Monday.
7.

wash. bake 4 bread, 18 cookies, 4 pies, fruit cake etc. James finish plowing corn & get ready to raise.

Tuesday.
8.

bake jelly cake. mop &c. we raise (partly) our barn, Mr. Chapman, Mr. Bly, Mr. McMillen, Sellens, Smith, George Brook help James, they raise it with pulleys & long ropes with the team. Mrs. Smith & Mrs. Bly came, too. Jay & Harry Smith came to supper. the first (South bent) they raised, they pulled clear over, no one hurt, however, though it fell 24 feet.

Monday.
14.

cook &c—Mr. Bly & Peirs help Jas. enclose barn. children go to school. *very warm.* they need not go again when it is so warm; *'tis too* far   *1-1/2 miles.*

Sunday.
20.

do not feel very well. get real mad at James because he never seems to want me to go anywhere or to say anything at all about things (which he calls *his* affairs). It makes it very disagreeable, but I trust in God it may be better sometime.

AUGUST 1873

Sunday.
3.

in afternoon we go & make Harriet a visit—was *real glad* to see her, she has a letter from Mother saying Henry was married to Agnes Smith, the 2nd. of July. we called at Uncles awhile.[41]

Tuesday.
12.

we go to the circus,—cost for tickets (4) $1.50, I bought 3 packages of candy for the children,—they contained 2 rings & 1 pair of sleeve buttons. (it was money foolishly spent).

Sunday.
24.

I get home this morning about ten o'clock. * * * I stayed with Harriet in the Evening Mrs. Cook came, later Dr. Lanning, therefore about one o'clock this morning Harriet has a little girl; she is quite well & so is baby—it is not near as pretty as was the other though it looks well. * * *

SEPTEMBER 1873

Thursday.
11.

* * * cut my gingham dress—children real good to help me do the chores—O dear, what a world this is;—little Henry left the butry door open & my clean dishes, milk & all got covered with flies,—so I have to take them all out again. I am sorry I reprimanded him at all for he did not intend to

do it, he says, "Ma, I did not mean to, I'm awful sorry—I'll try & never do it again." Yes, indeed now that I am calm & can think how glad I am that my little children are once more in the land of dreams—. . . Oh, God with thy help I pray I may ever keep my reason; that through all the trials of life Thou wilt direct me as Thou desirest I should do. . . .
* * *

Sunday.
14.!!!

we go to tent (Advent) camp meeting today, Hastings of Boston, Mass. preach. (subject "What is Truth?") he is quite an able speaker—I will note one illustration: he said (in reference to husbands being obeyed by their wives)—it was more in the ruler than in the ruled whether they were submissive— . . .

[The following one-month segment of Emily Gillespie's diary is the midpoint of the document. It is transcribed here in full to illustrate the tone of her prose, the proportion of each day's entry given to various events and family members, and her accounting of her daily work.]

Monday.
15.

wash. twist rags & stocking yarn. James plow. Chapman here last evening—pay him $9.80 for threshing

Tuesday.
16.

sew some; twist a little yarn. James plow 1/2 day. Jack frost visit us last night. children at home; cut my dress (gingham)   James cut sorghum in forenoon.

Wednesday.
17.

do usual work. children read & play. James plow. lend, or rather pay Willie Grey $6.00 for John McGee.[42]

Thursday.
18.

sew on my dress. James cut corn. kill a chicken. we have been married eleven years today, all's well. John call. Henry went for the mail yesterday, got me a letter from Mother.

Friday.   sew some. James cut corn.
19.

Saturday.   bake 3 bread, 5 pies, cookies & fry cakes. James dig pota-
20.   toes, the children help us.—blessed little ones, we go to
               town in evening, buy pair of shoes for Sarah $1.75; a box of
               matches of Thorp & Co (not pay) & baloona [bologna] of
               Glisendorf $.25[43]

Sunday.   we go away below Delhi,—to Camp Meeting—& to look for
21.   Dolly [their horse, lost for several weeks].—some one stole
               all our cookies & friedcakes & baloona & drank all our tea.
               We only heard Berry sing a song; they are Methodists, in-
               deed. McMillen said John & Harriet came here, I am real
               sorry because Harriet has not been here in so long—but I
               told John we were going away—& that they must come next
               Sunday, if they do not I'll be afraid Harriet did not like it
               that we were gone. the children are in dreamland,—they
               are tired.

Monday,   wash,—James plow.—I churn. circus performer to dinner
22.   & peck of oats $.25.

Tuesday.   do usual work. James husk some corn. sell 1 lb. butter for
23.   apples $.20 & buy more for $.25.

Wednesday.   rainy. we go to town, sell 46-1/2 lbs. butter to Davis for
24. $9.30. buy me a pair of shoes $2.50 & 1 pair of gaiters
               $1.75; 2 bu. of onions $1.50.—6 yds. cloth $2.40: 8 yds.
               muslin $1.00 at Thorps (except gaiters at Browns & do not
               pay for).—broom of Davis $.35. churn.[44]

Saturday.   mop. can 12 qts. grapes make 2 qts. jelly &c. go to town on
27.   foot,—first time I have walked so far in 12 years. I asked a
               man if I might ride, he was very ungentlemanly—refused,—
               when he had two horses & double carriage with no load

except one little boy & himself. I was *real* tired, Mr. Scanlon was so kind as to wait while I did some shopping to let me ride home with him. bought 6 cans of Terrill $1.25 & a wrench $.10; buy at Thorps 6 bottles $.60;—1/2 lb. tea $.70; 8-3/4 lbs. sugar $1.00—James plow. children at home all right.

Sunday.
28.

this morning I bake biscuit, 3 pies—1 cake & 8 tarts, John & Harriet here this afternoon; their little girl is 5 weeks old—rainy all day. there comes Chapman,—he has gone & I am glad of it, he wants our team to work on machine, he *shall not* have it—I think I have a better right to use it than he has—what does he do that he should have the preference. here we have more than we can do to get ready for winter & I told him the other day that when James could spare the team I wanted it myself & then he comes & asks for it. I think it is a real imposition & if he comes again, I'll tell him so. If James had kept his horses at home when I wanted him to they would not have died as they did.

Monday.
29.

wash. churn etc. James plow.

Tuesday.
30.

commence pants for Henry. James plow.

OCTOBER 1873.

Wednesday.
1st.

patch &c. afternoon we go to mill 6 bushels wheat. I buy at Thorps 5 spools thread $.35; James pay on acc't. to Thorps $5.00; pay all due for lumber, $6.75, buy butter tub $.75. pay amount due to Freelove $1.00.[45]

Thursday.
2.

we go to Masonville; James make returns on road supervisorship.—then he went South of there to an auction; the children & I stay at Billy Williams to dinner, Lizzie has two boys (twins) 5 mos. old. O dear, I think she has her hands full & heart, too. five children (one little boy died a year ago)—all so young—why, the oldest is only seven years old the 10th. of last month, how thankful I am that I am not in such circumstances   it seems I could not endure so much trouble, Aye, the old saying is but too true,—"those capable of enduring most have most to bear." after we came home the children went with James for the grist. I churn twice.

Friday.
3.

bake bread & fry cakes, finish pants   James plow, children read, play &c. some rainy. sister Edna is today 33 yrs. old.

Ah, fleet is time, & life though dear
Soon goes to meet by-gone friends—leaveth here,
Then let us make *this* life our aim
A better home in Heaven to gain.

Saturday.
4.

call on Mrs. Sellens, ride to town with Bly—get mail & baloona, mop etc. James plow. misty.

Sunday.
5.

cold. at home, chicken dinner.

Monday.
6.

wash etc. James plow. children help

Tuesday.
7.

churn, twist yarn, Jas. plow. Henry twist some yarn, Sarah mop off the floor—they did *pretty* well.

Wednesday.
8.

do usual work. Jas. plow.

Thursday.
9.

twist some yarn. Jas. plow.

Friday.   patch, etc. James plow all day.
10.

Saturday.   go with Harriet to see Isabelle, she is sick, her baby 1 week
11.!!!   old. James plow 3/4 day—Margaret & Laura Doolittle here
               to Tea. James go to town in evening, buy boots, $5.50, pay
               $5.00 on them, children go home with Harriet, after dinner
               to stay all night.[46]

Sunday.   childen came back this morning   we go to Uncles awhile.
12.

Monday.   twist yarn. James fix place for horses & poultry. I help, the
13.   children help, too.

Tuesday.   finish twisting yarn yesterday. Michael come & get wheel
14.   head, I wash, bake, etc. James fix shed, go to Election &
               churn.

               [This ends the transcription of an entire month of the diary.]

NOVEMBER 1873.

Sunday.   at home. very pleasant, attend lecture on "Spirit Rappings"
9.   by Elder Russel   flat, flat, indeed. * * *

Sunday.   we attend a Phrenology lecture given by Miss May Chapman
16.!!!   last evening   *very* good indeed, put $.10 in contribution
               box for her.[47]

Friday.   finish Sarah's flannel, knit &c. Jas. draw manure, Harriet
21.   here visiting. . . . I am going to make her baby a cloak &
               she is to knit for me, John came to tea.

DECEMBER 1873

Saturday.
20.

we go to town, buy 2 books for the children, $1.50, 1 blank book for my diary $1.00. . . .

Wednesday.
24.

misty. James take children to school, go & clean wheat (10 bushels). I rinse clothes, make apron for Sarah, undershirt & cotton flannel socks for James etc. generally. children take their Geographies to school. this evening finds us all well & enjoying the annual time for putting presents in each others stockings which are hanging on nails—well filled & ready for tomorrows inspection, the children & James are in dreamland & I am just ready to retire, 'tis into the wee small hours at night,

Dec. 25.
1873.
Thursday

we arise quite early   the children are very much delighted with their books & mugs which they find in their stockings. & James makes a parade over his new match box, that Sarah bought for him, & I am well pleased with the two yards of calico that Henry bought for me—we go to Uncles. . . .
* * *

Wednesday.
31.

sew on coat, make pies &c. children go to school. this evening Jas. put some apples in the children's stockings & he put something in mine, he said I could not see it till morning. he took the Deed of his farm to town yesterday & I surmise he has given me a portion of it, yet I do not know, for he has never mentioned any such thing. * * *

CHAPTER FIVE

Emily Gillespie,
Wife and Mother

Emily Hawley Gillespie's diary of 1869 is noticeably different in style, content, and tone from that begun by young Emily Hawley a decade before. Her husband is a prominent figure and her children are becoming daily "actors" in her journal. The diary reflects the adult roles and contexts of Emily Gillespie's life—the cyclical routine of farm chores and housework, the network of Iowa kin and community, the labor and rewards of attaining a home and a family circle. It records Gillespie's ongoing struggle to live up to her expectations as wife and mother and those cherished moments when she basks in the joys promised by the ideology of True Womanhood. Also emerging is the portrait of an individual who questions some societal norms.

In four areas—the language of self-perception, work, finances, and emotion—the diary records Emily Gillespie's changed circumstances. The aggregate language Gillespie increasingly uses—"*we* are at home"; "*our* little girl"—signals her changed perception of herself. Now she is part of a group, a family. In addition to her record of her own work, she faithfully records her husband's activities and, upon occasion, his words (October 16, 1862, and May 17, 1864). Emily Gillespie's diary, then, has become the account of a family, especially as the maturing children earn increasing attention in the entries. She is now keeping the diary of four people.

Nineteenth-century women's use of the pronoun *we* in preference to *I* has been noted in other studies such as Robert Fothergill's. Fothergill interpreted the emergence of the *I* in twentieth-century women artists' journals as a symptom of healthy egoism, but in the nineteenth century the perception of oneself thoroughly embedded within the family was the ideal and is echoed in women's language choices. My survey of Iowa farm diaries also showed women using *we* and men using *I* even when it was clear from the context of men's diaries that their wives shared in the activity. John Faragher, on the other hand, found that women on the overland trail most often used *I* and interpreted this as a sign of their sense of isolation during the journey, which disrupted normal kin and sex role networks. Thus language can give us insight into a woman's emotional state. While Emily Gillespie still occasionally employs the singular pronoun to describe her individual work and opinions (especially when they differ from James's), her collective language is that of a woman who perceives herself as part of a circle. Hers is no longer the diary of a woman alone in the Far West without a home.[1]

The repetitive cycle of work that Emily Gillespie performed dominates her diary as the social interactions so predominant a decade earlier recede. Because this study's primary focus is on ideology, many of her descriptions of work in the diary have been foreshortened. Gillespie herself often accounts for the major portion of her day with "sew, churn &c.," emphasizing instead unusual events of interest. The one-month transcription of the diary (September 15 to October 15, 1873) is intended to show how work dominates the foundation of her life. Gillespie rarely omits even a short notation of her work and every day it precedes other items in the entry.

James and Emily Gillespie followed most of the traditional sex role divisions of labor on their farm. James was responsible for the crops and livestock, Emily for the family garden and poultry. In the area of butter, however, they cooperated, he milking, she churning. Each marriage partner was also responsible for unpaid work that supported the farm and home. The 1870 Agricultural Census records show that James produced one hundred bushels of corn, forty-five bushels of oats, and eight tons of hay, most of which would be consumed by his livestock. For her part, Emily produced linens and clothing for the family, cooked the meals, and maintained the house. The diary records the interrelated nature of men's and women's separate work on the farm that was no longer evident in urban families, where the man's workplace was isolated from the home. Including her own and James's activities in the same paragraph of her book, Emily Gillespie showed her sense of mutuality in the family's enterprises.[2]

My calculations from Emily Gillespie's financial records for 1870 show the following cash income earned:

Emily's labor (poultry, eggs, sewing)	$110.13
James's labor (wheat, hay, hogs)	42.95
Mutual (butter, boarding travelers)	76.21

If her accounts are accurate, her work provided 48 percent of the income, James's accounted for 19 percent, and together they earned 33 percent. While many goods produced by each spouse were used for trade and are therefore "hidden" income, these accounts show what a large portion of the family cash earnings Emily Gillespie provided. Agricultural historians have recognized that such "butter and egg" money earned by farm women was crucial to family income.[3]

During these middle years, Emily Gillespie made extensive financial notations in her diary which have been edited here in the interest of brevity. This careful record, however, shows that she was the accountant for the family and that she understood the economics of the farm very well. Unlike the widow in Ruth Suckow's *Country People* who had no idea of her husband's finances or how to write a check, Emily Gillespie seemed to relish money matters, keeping an account ledger in addition to her narrative of each transaction.[4]

Her accounting interest served Emily well, for the Gillespie farm was increasingly connected to the cash economy of Manchester, unlike the subsistence economy farm she grew up on in Michigan. She was able to ship her poultry to eastern markets, earning cash that she then spent on items she had once made as a young woman such as soap, candles, and fabric. If Emily Gillespie had not kept track of her earnings (she identifies income from poultry as hers), her diary would fit into the mold of other women's diaries Mary Ryan studied that "plot the subsequent eclipse of home production by a profusion of such shopping expeditions." In such a cash economy where woman's home subsistence labor takes second place to purchasing items with her husband's money, her work loses status. As Faragher argues in his study of midwestern farms during this period of transition, "To be sure, farm women's ills were exacerbated by the growth of the market, for under commercial pressures gender divisions were widened, men's economic activity was further divorced from the household, and family economic unity shattered; for farm women there was, in consequence, a further devaluation of their already questionable status."[5]

Emily Gillespie, however, resisted this devaluation with several strategies: (1) She produced goods that were marketable rather than merely subsistence. When egg prices were low, for example, she began to raise poultry instead. (2) She then confirmed possession of her own earnings by purchasing items she desired. For example, on October 26, 1870, she earned

$89.75 for selling seventy-eight turkeys. Nine days later she purchased a sewing machine for $67.00. (While it can be argued that a sewing machine would benefit the entire family by rendering Emily's clothes production easier, the purchase of this labor-saving device so soon after she had cash in hand indicates it was hers.) (3) She perceived her unpaid labor as worth money, as her calculations of her "salary" for her part in molasses production (October 16, 1867) show. This practice would reinforce the value of her work to herself and to the farm enterprise.

Thus Emily Gillespie's financial accounting becomes in a larger sense an accounting for the expenditure of her time. While the repetitive cycle of "usual work" might seem trivial, Gillespie's cumulative record of what her churning, rag saving, and egg tending amounted to affirmed the value of her labor in economic terms her society understood—cash. Because she documented her work and its subsequent profits, Emily Gillespie could indeed account for her time. She was far different from Amanda Snow, an Iowa farm wife who upon learning of her cancer at a clinic told her husband, "If there is something wrong with me, we may as well go back home, for I am of no account."[6]

Emily Gillespie's diary in these middle years seems less emotionally rich to the reader because the entries are often terse, short, and undescriptive. Content analysis shows they are indeed less emotive. Each July portion of the diary was classified, sentence by sentence, under topics growing out of the entries—visiting, sewing, weather, etc. One such topic was "sentiments," the overt expression of emotion. During Emily Hawley's early years (1858 to 1862) there were an average of 3.6 expressions of feeling in July; during the middle years of marriage and young motherhood (1863 to 1873) there was only 1 sentiment on the average, and it often concerned James rather than coming from Emily's own experience. While no such rudimentary method can trace correlations between emotion and other events in Gillespie's life, it does confirm what the reader senses—that the diary is constricting.

There are several explanations, not mutually exclusive, for this change. First, Emily Gillespie's social sphere contracted upon marriage, as content analysis again shows. As an unmarried woman in Michigan and Iowa, she visited 9.2 times during the average July and received 13 visitors; as a married woman, she visited only 3.2 times and received 6.3 visitors per

July. Part of the diminishment in Gillespie's diary, then, could simply be the result of her altered life pattern. Her interaction was constrained by a variety of factors—living in the home of her parents-in-law under some stress, then confinement during two pregnancies, then responsibility for two small children. During this same inactive period of Samuella Hart Curd's life, according to editor/scholar Susan Arpad, the diarist complained about her immobility compared to her husband's—then attempted to erase the entries after his untimely death.[7]

It is also clear from certain diary entries that the Gillespies sometimes *preferred* to be alone in the dyad that characterizes the early years of marriage. A close emotional bond with one's spouse was considered desirable by the mid-nineteenth century. Emily Gillespie's term for James—her "best friend"—is echoed in other women's diaries and correspondence. In 1848, Mary Butterfield wrote of this bond to her fiancé with an intensity we may find incongruous with our image of staid Victorians: "I can love you better from the fact that to no one have I made myself known as to you, to no one have I given such confidences."[8]

If Emily Gillespie formed such a tight bond with her husband, the lack of sentiment in her diary may be due to a shift of her reliance onto James as her confidant. If all her emotions were spent upon her husband, little would be left unresolved to write down in the diary where she once confided her innermost feelings. In fact, most of the emotional passages in the book during this period refer to sentiments she probably tried to mask from her husband—dislike of his parents, worries that he might die, fears before childbirth. Again, no correspondence remains in the family papers to confirm whether this bond between Emily and James existed, even though according to the diary they exchanged letters when Emily made her Michigan visit.

The sparse prose that characterizes Emily Gillespie's diary can also be interpreted through twentieth-century linguistic theory. During these years her style matches what sociolinguist Basil Bernstein calls a "restricted code." This code has unelaborate prose (few modifiers), concrete language, an emphasis on how instead of why, implicit rather than explicit emotion. The contrasting code Bernstein terms "elaborated." It is extended, emotional, explicit. He found the restricted code used when people assumed a commonality, while the elaborated code was used where social connections were weak and language was used to attempt to bridge the gap while still differentiating the speaker.[9] Marilyn Ferris Motz also found restrictive language in nineteenth-century Michigan men's and women's diaries: "There was little need to differentiate the self or to make explicit values which were generally accepted by the community."[10] In Gillespie's case, then, her restricted language may reflect a period in her life when she truly felt in harmony with others, when she felt little need to explain herself in her diary.

There are a variety of reasons why this irrepressible diarist continued the account of her life in such an abbreviated form. The contradictions and tensions between them are intriguing. Was she simply an exhausted mother whose narrow world of work was too boring to record elaborately? Were her emotions spent during talks with her husband/confidant, leaving the diary as a repository for financial accounts and minimal affect? Was Gillespie so at peace with her life of home and husband that a few plain words in her diary sufficed? Or did she repress most of her negative emotions even in her diary (which may not have been a private book) as she strived to be a good-natured wife and a patient mother? In some of the longer diary passages during these years she records the failure of her efforts to check her anger and her subsequent guilt. In these cases the diary acts as a confessional where Gillespie recounts her faults, then asks forgiveness and forbearance in her efforts to be a good wife and mother.

Who defined what a good wife and mother was? Writers of prescriptive literature on True Womanhood in the nineteenth century included male professionals—doctors and ministers—and female advisors who sometimes used demure pseudonyms like "Genevieve" when instructing the readers of women's magazines: "A good wife, a true woman is a real heroine and an accomplished actress. She puts her own grievances out of sight to drive away with pleasant smiles the clouds that gather around her husband's gloomy brow."[11] Other prolific domesticians were Catharine Beecher (who was not herself a wife and mother) and her sister Harriet Beecher Stowe (who took long rest cures away from her family).

Women's diaries bear witness to the struggles and rewards that trying to achieve True Womanhood entailed. It was not easy to be benign yet influential, patient yet purposeful. The good-natured wife and mother portrayed in domestic advice literature sometimes gave way in real life to other emotions, despite repression. Emily Gillespie's self-recriminations over her "foolish crying," her prayer that "God forbid ever an unkind word or thought from me again," are echoed endlessly by her peers, each privately writing of her failures in her journal. "Often wish myself a smarter body, & able to be a first rate mother, wife, mistress, & every thing—sometimes am quite discouraged on this matter," wrote Mehitable Dawes in 1831 in Massachusetts. Samuella Curd put it this way in her 1861 diary: "Oh! that I might become more reconciled to my *fate*. I feel as if I never could, I know it is wrong, I have so many blessings such as a good home, kind husband . . . & the best of friends." Agnes Stewart wrote in her diary from a covered wagon going west in 1853, "Sometimes I govern myself, but not always, but I hold in pretty well considering all things."[12]

On the other hand, women's diaries also record the rewards of domesticity: their deep joy in the pleasures of *Home* they often achieved, just as the domestic advisors had promised. Emily Gillespie: "Today finds James, Baby & me at home enjoying ourselves & happy in each others' company" (December 13, 1863). Another Iowa diarist, Elisabeth Koren: "We were alone—alone in our first home! Now for the first time I begin to understand rightly what 'home' means, our home, which becomes dearer to me day by day." Echoing the language of Gillespie's sentiments were those of Eunice Wait Cobb: "Yes the happiness which we enjoy in our little family may well be termed *uninterrupted* happiness. All is *harmony, peace*, and *contentment*."[13]

This domestic harmony, requiring effort and repression while offering sentimental rewards, was ideally suited to appeal to the nineteenth-century woman. It gave her responsibility for a small sphere which offset her isolation, the awesome task of creating a world in which she could be empowered amidst her confinement. As *Ladies Magazine* put it, "To render *home* happy, is woman's peculiar province; home is *her* world."[14] Thus Emily Gillespie could be both active and influential, as she had yearned to be in her early years, and safe in a home of her own.

The even tone of Emily Gillespie's diary during these years, then, is probably a reflection of her commitment to being pleasant-natured, even if it sometimes required acting. The tremendous effort of achieving the domestic ideal within the real world, however, is hinted at by her recurring prayers that the little world she has created continue. Her entry about the

joys of home, cited in part above, continues: "Ah, my prayer that it may
ever be so, may no discord ever enter our family circle & may the will of
God be done." This combination of responsibility for the home and pas-
sivity before the uncontrollable factors Emily Gillespie witnessed around
her—disease, dangerous farm machinery, fire—must have led to a great
sense of fragility lurking outside—and a hint of the delicate balance required inside—the cherished family circle.

The separate spheres of women and men prescribed by domestic ideology
and the changing economy meant that Emily Gillespie spent much of her
time in a homosocial world. Her experience is typical of that found in many
histories of nineteenth-century women: she visited with women, gave and
received birth aid, corresponded regularly with her mother and sisters.
Affection for other women in Gillespie's letters or diaries never reached
the intensity found by Carroll Smith-Rosenberg in her study of the female
world of love and ritual; this disparity is discussed in Part III. It is clear
from her diary, however, that she enjoyed visiting within a female circle.
When her younger sister Harriet Hawley moved to Iowa in 1869, Gillespie
achieved the happiest situation, according to Nancy Cott's study of women's
networks: she had both her husband, James, and a close-by sisterly
relationship.[15]

While in many ways Emily Gillespie appears typical (wife, mother, sister, community member), there are elements in her diary that hint at her
atypical individualism and ideas. The three children (one twin stillborn)
she bore were significantly below the average rate of 5.21 for a native-born
middle-class woman of the 1860s.[16] Her comments upon the stillbirth of
Sarah's twin on July 7, 1865, indicate that Gillespie thought raising two
children would suffice. The pity she records for her female friends with
large families is echoed by Samuella Curd in her diary: "Mary Dowden had
a boy last night, her next youngest only *13 months* old, she is to be pitied."[17] There is strong demographic evidence that Gillespie, while atypical
in her success in limiting her fertility, was not unusual in her desire for
fewer children. The U.S. birthrate fell from 7.04 in 1800 to 3.56 in 1900,
a dramatic decrease of 50 percent.[18]

Daniel Scott Smith has attributed this striking decline, despite little in-
novation in methods of birth control, to what he terms "domestic feminism," the increasing power of women over their fertility. Other women's

historians, including Gerda Lerner and Suzanne Lebsock, have suggested that smaller family size was also economically advantageous to men in industrializing America and may not be a symbol of women's growing power within the home.[19] In the Gillespies' case, family limitation served both partners' interests. A small family would conserve the hard-won wealth of James's farm and also meet Emily's concerns as a progressive woman.

On the other hand, several other factors would predict more children for James and Emily Gillespie. Rural well-off families were usually larger than average, and James came from a family of ten children. Counterbalancing this was Emily's parents' family, which was smaller than the average of 6.5 children for its era. Perhaps, then, Emily had inherited values and methods for limiting her childbearing from her mother. That women did indeed talk about and pass on such information in their letters has been documented by Elizabeth Hampsten. This openness about contraception, compared to women's reticence in writing about sexuality even in their diaries, shows the Victorian differentiation between reproduction and sex.[20] Given Emily Gillespie's proven fertility in bearing three children in close proximity, juxtaposed with her desire to carefully raise noble children and her quest for economic security, her atypically small family was probably carefully planned.

If and how the Gillespies agreed to limit their family size are only hinted at in this portion of the diary. If Emily's marginal code (!!!) indeed indicates her method of determining pregnancy, the reappearance of the marks after the birth of Sarah would indicate that she and James had resumed their sexual relations and that she wished to avoid future childbearing. However, so many theories on women's fertile periods abounded during the nineteenth century that her concept of the rhythm method would probably be inaccurate. Most available methods of contraception such as abstinence and withdrawal involved the cooperation of the male. Ellen K. Rothman found in her study of courtship correspondence that several couples mutually agreed to remain childless, relying on contraception and abortion.[21]

The Gillespies owned an 1863 edition of Dr. Edward B. Foote's popular book, *Medical Common Sense.* Foote offered for sale his "womb veil," considered by historians to be the first true vaginal diaphragm. Foote's description of the device is radical in its implications: "This prevention possesses the following qualities: Conception cannot possibly take place when it is used. The full enjoyment of the conjugal embrace can be indulged in during coition. The husband would hardly be likely to know that it was being used, unless told by the wife. . . . It places conception entirely under the control of the wife, to whom it naturally belongs, for it is for her to say at what time and under what circumstances she will become the mother, and the moral, religious, and physical instructress of offspring." Full sexual enjoyment without procreation. Use possible without the husband's knowledge. Woman's right to choose the timing of her motherhood. Foote also sold the "Apex Envelope," a rubber condom.[22]

Foote argued more conventionally in *Medical Common Sense* for the electromagnetic theory of intercourse, which promoted sexual moderation in order for each partner to "recharge." But Foote even recommended that "ladies should be allowed to 'pop the question,'" an unconventional opinion that would have met with Emily Gillespie's approval. While possession of Foote's book does not mean the Gillespies followed his contraceptive ideas or purchased his devices, it does indicate their exposure to information a decade before it was made illegal by the Comstock Law of 1873.

Emily Gillespie's adherence to Universalist beliefs is another marker of her individualistic viewpoint. Universalism's emphasis on man's responsibility as a rational moral agent, universal salvation, and deism contrasted sharply with other Christian beliefs of the time. The expansive nature of Universalist theology was radical, according to church historian Ernest Cassara: "The Deists put aside the Scripture with scorn and replaced it with what they considered god-given Reason which allowed them to read God's revelation writ large in the universe around them. There they thought they could see a God who was much too grand to treat man as the erring child the Calvinists and other Christians insisted he was."[23] No wonder "Universalists were viewed with suspicion and hate by their fellow Christians, who considered them immoral and subversive." Although there were over 800,000 believers in the United States by mid-century and an established congregation in Manchester, Universalists were considered extremists in Iowa, according to church historian Oval Quist. She notes a passage in Herbert Quick's *The Hawkeye* that says it was "a thing of shame not unmixed with danger to associate with Universalists."[24]

The Universalist philosophy, with its emphasis on open education for all and human potential, was conducive to women's rights. The correlation between strong-minded women of national fame and Universalist/Unitarians is striking. Judith Sargent Murray and Clara Barton were Universalists; Susan B. Anthony, Elizabeth Blackwell, and Lucy Stone, among others, affiliated with Unitarians after they left—or were asked to leave—more restrictive religions. One of the first woman ministers ordained in the United States was Universalist Olympia Brown in 1863. She argued extensively for women's rights, sometimes attacking the most cherished images of Victorian womanhood: "But, says some objector, women will no longer be angels when brought in contact with the rude world. Alas! the United States of America in 1874 is not a favorable place for angels, nor are the men of the nineteenth century suitable companions for them. . . . Since they are surrounded by fallible, suffering mortals, let [women] give themselves to the work of the world." [25]

Emily Gillespie's exposure to Universalist thinking connected her to such eighteenth-century proponents of women's rights as Judith Sargent Murray, who decried female dependency: "I would give my daughters every accomplishment which I thought proper, and, to crown all, I would early accustom them to habits of industry and order. They should be taught with precision the art economical; they should be enabled to procure for themselves the necessaries of life; independence should be placed within their grasp." Emily Gillespie, then, had made a good match between her religious convictions, her own youthful ambitions as a woman, and her motherly aspirations for her daughter. [26]

But Gillespie's interest in feminism went even further, as her subscription to *Woodhull and Claflin's Weekly* shows. The magazine's founders, Victoria Woodhull and Tennessee Claflin, sounded the call for "a new social order, a grand family in which every person in the world will be a member," which concurred with Universalist thought. On sexual matters, the *Weekly* advocated "a new sexual system, in which mutual consent, entirely free from money or any inducement other than love, shall be the governing law, individuals being left to make their own regulations." [27]

The magazine also contained articles on the activities and petitions of the National Woman Suffrage Association, Susan B. Anthony's and Elizabeth Cady Stanton's organization. The NWSA's call for reform in women's rights was more far-reaching than that of the rival American Woman Suffrage Association. Victoria Woodhull's support of the NWSA in the pages of her magazine and on the lecture circuit was a mixed blessing. She declared her right to vote before a congressional committee, became embroiled in the Beecher-Tilton scandal, and declared herself a candidate in 1872 for the U.S. presidency. Perhaps her most controversial opinion was her support of free love. In the *Weekly* she printed in full a lecture on the subject. It termed marriage an "impossible restriction" and criticized the double standard in which "man is already a free lover in the lowest sense, while woman is a slave to those laws, customs and superstitions which, with total ignorance of her true nature, force her to love and bear children, under barbarous restrictions."[28]

How much of this thinking Emily Gillespie agreed with is unclear. In her diary Gillespie notes distributing her "Woman Suffrage" papers to visitors. If this was her description for the *Weekly*, she perhaps overlooked the articles proposing free love and spiritualism in her hunger for national news of the suffrage movement. But other readers of Emily Gillespie's papers must have been shocked at the publication's extreme views. This would be another sign to them that Emily Gillespie was indeed living on the edge of the community in a metaphorical sense. Victoria Woodhull's ideas were sometimes so radical that they embarrassed even Stanton and Anthony. But at its peak, *Woodhull and Claflin's Weekly* claimed 40,000 subscribers. Iowan Emily Gillespie was not alone in her reading.

Iowa was in some ways amenable to women's rights. In 1854 women's rights lecturer Frances Dana Gage declared Iowa "the most moral and progressive, as well as the best-improved State, of its age, in all our country." The State University in Iowa City had allowed (while not at first encouraging) female students to enroll when it opened in 1856. After the eclipse of woman suffrage efforts during and immediately following the Civil War, Iowa legislators again debated the issue, and news about suffrage was in the local papers. In Dubuque, forty-five miles east of Manchester, the Northern Iowa Suffrage Association was formed in 1869 as a result of lecture tours to the state by Elizabeth Cady Stanton and Susan B. Anthony. More feminist speakers returned to the state in the 1870s, when it seemed possible that a suffrage amendment would be approved in the legislature. Then the internal conflict among national suffrage organizations and propaganda linking the movement to free love (such as that found in the *Weekly*) alienated lawmakers and meant that the vote for women would not be enacted in Gillespie's lifetime.[29]

While Emily Gillespie was exposed to feminist ideals and radical thinking through her religious beliefs and some of her reading, she was also a subscriber to *Peterson's Magazine*, a standard lady's publication promoting domesticity. These artifacts of Gillespie's ideological framework excavated from her diary may seem inconsistent, but they merely symbolize the complex and continuing mixture of desires young Emily Hawley wrote of in her stories: one about a woman who "pops the question" and another about pleasant evenings at home. In these years of early marriage and motherhood, Emily Gillespie maintained a balance between the selflessness expected of a wife and mother and her growing interest in wider opportunities for women.

PART THREE

"Woman Is Always Lovely—Until Her Strength & Beauty Fail": Emily Hawley Gillespie, Woman

CHAPTER SIX

"Tis the Saddest . . . Merely to Be Always at Home": 1874–1883

If James Gillespie gave the deed of his property to Emily Gillespie, as she suspected he might on the eve of 1874, he was publicly acknowledging his wife's true partnership in their farm enterprise. By 1874, the Gillespie farm was indeed prosperous. Physical testaments to its success were a new home, completed in 1872, and the large barn raised with the help of neighbors in 1873. According to the 1870 Agricultural Census, the James Gillespie farm was valued at $5,000, a high valuation for a one hundred–acre property. (For example, Henry Baker's farm, six times as large, was valued at $20,000.) The crop land produced wheat, Indian corn, oats, and hay. The Gillespies also listed 370 pounds of butter, 75 pounds of cheese, and $100 worth of home manufacture in the census.[1]

By 1880, census figures show that the cash value of the Gillespie farm production had doubled, from $551 in 1870 to $1,141. The number of cattle, horses, sheep, swine, and chickens also had more than doubled. The Gillespies reported selling 448 gallons of milk, which parallels the diary account of the decision to no longer produce butter, a cooperative venture in which James milked and Emily churned. The diary also records the growth of Emily Gillespie's poultry production in this decade, profitable through the sale of eggs and birds.[2]

What is notable about the Gillespies' success is that it occurred despite the agricultural recession that accompanied the national economic panic of 1873. While the cash value of their property declined to $4,000 in 1880, reflecting the drop in farmland prices during this decade, its productivity grew. Given the 71 percent decrease in wholesale farm product prices between 1870 and 1880, the actual value of the Gillespie farm production was three times that of 1870. The size of their farm and livestock herds was typical for Delaware County in 1880, but their productivity per acre was high, $40.00, compared to the average of $35.19.[3]

The fact that James Gillespie had no mortgage to pay, having received his land free and clear from his parents in 1863, surely accounts for some of this prosperity during the recession. But the personal initiative that led to the farm's success is recorded in Emily Gillespie's diary. Its narrative of long work days, a cherished savings account, and astute awareness of the cash economy provides a daily record of the process by which the Gillespies flourished in comparison to some of their neighbors and kin.

Emily Gillespie's diary tells two stories of this decade. One is of her efforts to contribute to the family farm enterprise, of her desire for and joy in the domestic fruits of her labor—a nice home, fine furnishings, attractive clothes, educated children. The other story is of indebted farmers, foreclosures, and economic malaise that affected many of her peers. Emily and James Gillespie lived in both the relatively prosperous world of their farm and in the uneasy world surrounding them. They found it impossible to free themselves of financial worries, even as their personal status and home surroundings improved.

Note: Volume 6 of the manuscript diary is the first book in Emily Gillespie's handwriting. (The first five volumes are holograph transcriptions done in the 1940s and 1950s by her daughter.) Sideways in the margin of the January 1, 1874, entry is written a dedication to Sarah L. Gillespie, dated 1887. However, the even penmanship of the entries suggests that Emily Gillespie's transcription did not occur in 1887, when her handwriting had deteriorated, but dates from an earlier period in her life.

> Another book is added to my journal of life,
> May it not be filled with sorrow and strife.
> Let pure & undefiled Virtue, its pages unfold
> May our hearts be as pure & bright as fine Gold.
>
> E.E.G.

JANUARY 1874.

Sunday
4.

Rather snowy & blow this morning. 'tis very pleasant this afternoon, however. we are at home all day & quite content to sit by the fire. this evening after the Children have gone to sleep—I look for the first time at my *New Years Present.* it proved to be just what I surmised it was—a Deed—yes, James gave me a Deed of his farm. indeed I can hardly express my feelings of gratitude for his placing so very much confidence in me as to entrust to my honor the keeping of his hard earned property. By the help of Him, who doeth all things well, it is my *earnest* prayer that I may never do aught to destroy that confidence, nor never again say one word to mar his happiness through life. that he may never regret his first New Years gift to his wife, if she did shed many tears in consequence. may they be tears of repentance & lead us to the more trust & love eachother [*sic*] & our little children.
* * *

Monday
5!!!

We arise quite early. James carry the children to school on the hand-sleigh, get water for me to wash &c. * * * my mind is more happy than it was last night because Jas. said he gave me the farm in a good motive, that in case he should die first, there would be no trouble about it being divided. and also desired me to keep it free from incumbrance, Which I *will* endeavor *to do.* warm[4]

Sunday
11.

We are at home. I intrude on the sabbath by baking bread. The children write in their journals &c. they improve well in their writing. Pleasant.

Wednesday.
28.

Knit! finish Henry mittens & commence pair for Sarah, this afternoon we all go & make Harriet a visit, how glad I was to go—yes indeed! I rather visit her than any one else this side of the Mississippi, but it sometimes seems almost im-

possible to get there. Harriet let me have 'My Old Clarks
Grammar'—(which Mother sent in her box of things,—)
that I used to study fifteen years ago—

ODE

Ah dear old grammar! all my own!!
Thy time-worn paged and torn leaves—mildewed—
All marked by idle fingers of loved classmates:—
Each tells a story of some dear one.
Thy covers, severed by times rusty mould,
Alas! but tell me I too am growing old . . .

FEBRUARY 1874

Friday
6

Finish my alapacca dress. James take the children to
school, salt meat &c. There is to be a Masquerade at the
New Hall this evening. Oh, how I would like to go; but alas!
I fear my days of pleasure are all in the past, yet I can not
complain, for when I look around me, and behold so many
who have far less privileges than I, I can but say—all is
well. and our children. it is pure happiness to see them
happy and growing up to man & woman-hood virtuous and
pure knowing no hatred—may they ever be as innocent and
loveing as now—snow

Monday
23

I only do what I am obliged to do about house work. James
done his chores this morning, much as ever though, I gave
him catnip tea, onion syrup and he went to bed. I put
around him cloths, wet with vinegar warm, with hot flatt-
irons & plates untill he sweat, his fever still continues, he
is real sick Henry went to McMillens to get him to come and
do the chores & go to town after some medicine. . . .

Wednesday.
25!!!

Just the same as yesterday. do all I can & take care of
James. this morning he seemed to think that perhaps he

might not get well, that he was glad every thing was settled up. that after I was done with the property he would like it to be dived [*sic*] equal between the children. Oh I can not write all he said—he was oh so calm he said I must not cry. that it was all right to talk about such things, but Oh no no I could not, it seems, give him up. Oh I pray, if it be God's will, that he may live to enjoy his hard earned little home. . . .

MARCH 1874.

Monday
2

It is 2 o'clock. I slept two hours & a half. Sammy [Doolittle] gave James his tea—untill one. his pain in side still bothers him & nerves are weak. Ah me I blotted my journal. all is wrapt in the stillness of night and I quite keenly feel the effects of the sleepless nights, hard work, days—and the great anxiety of mind. * * *

Sunday
8

Tis a lonely day, though all is pleasant—James is gaining quite fast. we all read &c. have fried chicken for tea & nice biscuit—have looked in vain for Harriet all day. the papers are literally filled with the "temperance movement of the ladies from all parts of the states—they go about from one saloon to another with suplications of prayer and singing of hymns"—they have my prayer too in behalf of their *good* work—may its effect, be of use in rendering peace and happiness to the now many degraded firesides; may it be *lasting*. More pleasant

Saturday
21

Mop—knit &c—bake a cake composed of milk, meal, ashes, sulphur, alum, pepper & salt; for our *poultry*, some *disease* is *killing* them *very fast*—their *combs* & *gills* turn *black* & they die with their crops full of feed. think it is *cholera*. am afraid we will lose them all, but *hope not* indeed. * * *

Sunday
29

We go to Presbyterian meeting . . . very good. * * * after supper—we attend a temperance—mass-meeting—it was indeed *quite* interesting. it is the first time we were in the new City Hall—it will be a beautiful room when completed.[5] . . .

APRIL 1874

Thursday
2

Bake pies—finish my dress. John McGee help James draw stone. now they are even again as regards wood & work etc—*except* the $100.00 note. *Chilly* wind

Saturday
11

I am thirty-six years old to day; the children wish they might make me a present. I kindly thank them—bless their little hearts. * * * I sew, mop etc:—

This life is but a pleasant dream,   Chilly wind
Things are not *always* what they seem.

Thursday
23

Finish Henry pants, they set sleek as a ribbon, he is proud of them   James sow oats plow little in garden   Children go to school. Pleasant

Wednesday
29

Sew some, go to town with Uncle—call on Mrs. [Emma] Brook stay to dinner. buy some cod-fish & sugar. hear lots of news about Temperance-crusade. 43 ladies were visiting the saloons this morning. * * *

MAY 1874

Monday
4

Wash, churn etc. James set out some trees & clean around shrubbery in forenoon. * * * 'tis so clear this evening we can hear the band music from town. Pleasant.

JUNE 1874.

Tuesday
2

James help me clean house all day. we slept in the barn last night for the first time, like it very well. think we will sleep there some time. * * *

Tuesday
23

* * * Though sad to day in secret thought.
        Time shall never tell
    The sad sad story of my heart.

Tis now afternoon   I am writing again in my journal. what a happy resort. James is at work & soon our dear little children will come from school almost roasted. how I wish mother and Father would come & see us. *Warm*

JULY 1874

Thursday
2

Do usual work &c. trim 5 hats. travelers pay us fifteen cents for grass. James plow corn. children go to school. I have now trimmed 144 hats & bonnets. Amounts to $36.00. Thorp [dry goods] sent for them this evening. Very warm

Sunday
5

We stay at home all day & *try* to keep cool. we went to Camp-meeting last evening. they are haveing a general time. . . . one man had *the Power* & several women acted rather powerful. I can not see where there is any religion in such actions   Dry & warm[6]

Tuesday
14

Do usual work. Mc[Millen] help James draw hay all day. Last evening the Comet [first noted by Emily Gillespie on July 12] looked very beautiful   its tail loomed up high above the horizon reaching nearly to the north-star. it is situated in the northwest, traveling southward   it is called Coggias' Comet & according to Prof Parkhurst, the tail is already 3,000,000 miles long. I remember seeing a very brilliant Comet in the year 1858. . . . Mother was afraid it was going to hit the earth and destroy it. how strange it is that many people are so ignorant about the works of Nature. Here comes little Henry. he has been mowing away hay. he must not do it, his face is all spotted with heat. Very warm

AUGUST 1874

Sunday
2

James is asleep, the children out around-about, & I am writing here. & now am just going to read the Beecher & Tillton scandal. after dinner we take a ride through the grove and back by way of Harriets & stayed there to tea. Pleasant[7]

Thursday
20

Bake 4 loaves bread, 2 pies & a cake, besides get dinner for threshers   yes they were here to breakfast too, three of them & 4 to dinner & (six to tea.) I'll set it down after supper. 'tis now three o'clock & here I am writing once more in my journal, the only confidant I ever had, & *thou* dear journal dost not know *every* secret. nay! nay!! now I will write to Mother & Father. Very Warm

Friday
21

Harriet here most all day, *was glad* she came for I had the blues. I sew some &c. * * *

SEPTEMBER 1874.

Wednesday
16

Sew some on Sarah a dress. the children have gone to school. Jas work on wood house   went to Town   got me three new dresses, the first I have traded on my hat money. * * *

OCT. 1874.

Thursday
1

The children & I go to the fair all day, 'Twas very good indeed, the children enjoyed the swing very much   Sarah got the second premium on her [quilt] blocks * * * I found red tags tied on my fruit cake, Peppers, Strawberries, Plumb butter, Wild Grape-Jelly, Tame Grapes, Strawberry-wine, meaning the First Premium: and blue cards, or second premium on Wild Grapes, Crabapples & Tomatto preserve. Well, well quite fortunate. Windy

Sunday
4

> We are at home.
> Will some one come,
> To while the hours away
> We have agreed
> That we will read
> And make merry the day. . . .

Friday
23

Do usual work finish pair stockings &c. Children read get their lessons play. James help Chapman thresh. we hear some very sad news—James Vanalstine hanged himself yesterday. no reason is yet known. only that he told his wife he was too much trouble to her & began to cry, he then went out of doors. Alas! to be brought in a corpse. . . .

> Ah frail indeed is the thread of life:
> His spirit hath flown to him who gave.
> He left his little children and wife,
> Alas! he must fill a murderers grave.

There James has come   the children are asleep & I must retire. Beautiful[8]

NOVEMBER 1874

Saturday
7

Knit, patch &c—James lay stone wall   he has rented that part of our farm above the railroad to George Brook. George to furnish seed, do all the work and deliver to us 1/3 of the wheat in half bushel at the machine and to plow land again next fall.[9] * * *

Sunday
22

We are at home. read &c. I write off some of my old Diary, ah! different now, then it was 16 years ago—is it better? or worse I can only ponder an answer: twas well then, tis all right now—then I was happy at Fathers enjoying youth— now we are older & happy with our own little family   Rain

Saturday
28

Tis evening all have retired, I am writing. we have been to Manchester to day. Buy a new eight-day clock, it has round face, square picture of Grapes & cherries, walnut frame, with columns on either side. Guilted, it costs eleven and one half dollars   how its ticking reminds me of my child- hoods home, of my school days. flurry of snow

DECEMBER 1874

Thursday
3

* * * it is now fifteen minutes of eleven   all are asleep, save me. I am telling you, my dear old and tried friend, my journal. you are my only confident. am telling you that I have been *very* unhappy this evening—because them Doolittles almost make me insane   only for the help of God I surely would despair, they keep wanting a horse pastured, some corn or hay or something else the whole time, & James can never refuse them, he rather let them have it, it seems sometimes, than his own family, yet I may & *hope* I do judge nothing wrong, yes I hope I may know & see aright, that I may have a contented mind, that I may do nor say naught to mar the happiness of any one, at least of James and Henry and Sarah. . . .

Friday
25

The children were awake early & wished us Merry Christ- mas   they were very well pleased with the various things I put in their stockings. i.e. candy, apple, Gingersnaps, Al- manacs and new No 7 Writing Books   Henry gave me a spool of Black silk. Sarah gave me calico for an apron. indeed I was pleased with their gifts because they so much enjoy the pleasure of bestowing them. well we have all spent a happy day. James chop wood. Henry helped him. Sarah helped me sweep   I commence me another hat. Beautiful

Saturday
26

* * * James has been getting wood &c—I have been sewing on my hat, taking care of milk & butter & bake. James came in this evening & said he had business to town and thought he would go. I do not know but I was too hasty in my reply, when he asked if I had any objections. he asked in such a manner that I said 'if your *business* is *urgent*, why it is nothing to me.' he did not like it and so did not go & said considerable more than was necessary. and I told him there was no use of angry words, that 'turn about was but fair play'—O my dear journal if it were not for my little children, sometimes I would hardly know what to do. it seems the more I do to make home pleasant the more unpleasant it is. yet with the help of God I will try to do right always, the great difficulty seems to be he does not want me to go any where at all.

Tis hard to live a hermits life.
Ah my little ones I live for thee.
Bright prospects before thee rise.
May I live to help thee gain the prize.
                        Warm

Sunday
27

We are at home. read & do usual chores. James and the children have retired. I write to day with a lighter heart. All is well. Pleasant

JANUARY 1875

Friday
1!!!

Sew on my cape &c. cook our oysters & biscuit. James go & invite Uncle to dine with us. flurry of snow. We recieved

a *letter* from *Mother* this week. she sent her *picture*. I think
she looks about the same as She did ten years ago. * * *

Sunday
17

We are at home. * * * we all read our papers. Uncle gave
us a piece of meat. a stormy day indeed

Sweet, oh sweet are the joys of home,
When all in love are united;
May never a sorrow to us come,
May our fondest hopes ne'er be blighted.

Snow

Monday
25

* * * tis now twenty minutes past eleven. Mr & Mrs Morse
& 2 Children have been here this evening, they have just
gone, the children have a great time, though I would rather
they might always with Society more gentle & refined, May
the Lord guide, and be with us evermore, Amen   Pleas

FEBRUARY 1875

Saturday
20

We do usual work, the children get lessons. we go to town
after mail. * * * while waiting for Jas, Mr Quackinbush and
me have *quite a conversation* on the *Woman Suffrage question*, both are in favor of *the* cause. Pleasant

MARCH 1875

Friday
12

Mop, iron, etc. * * * N.B. I let James have 8.00 for twenty
bushels of corn. *thats hat money.* * * *

Tuesday
23!!!

Do what I can, not very much though because I had a severe
head ache untill near two, it feels bad yet. I hope I can hear
the childrens lessons tomorrow, they pity me, & help all
they can to do the work. * * *

APRIL 1875

Sunday   John & Harriet here all day   visit and read. Bake bread &
4   cake. Pleasant

Thursday   Have just been reading a query in the Inter Ocean. some
8   one asks 'the religious views of Darwin, on the origin of
              Man.'—and here is the answer—
                  In 1871 Mr. Darwin published the "Descent of Man and
              Selection in Relation to Sex." in which the Author infers
              that "man is descended from a hairy quadruped, furnished
              with a tail and pointed ears, probably arborial in its habits."

              Then, O. man! why boast of an immortal soul
                  Art thou better than thy horse,
              Better than thy dog? stop and pause awhile
                  It may be, they have souls like us. * * *

Sunday   Well, Journal I am permitted once more to record another
11   birth-day   am thirty seven. Ah how little do we know what
              a year may bring forth, and just now Mr Sellens has called
              to James to come up there soon as he can, I think perhaps
              his father is dying—. * * *

Tuesday   Do usual work. we go to town get us a new stove, it & fur-
20   niture costs us fifty dollars. * * *

Wednesday   My work done for the morning. * * * a gentleman call &
21   tell me we have friends at the Delaware house, to drive
              down for them. we can *not* untill noon, I almost think it is
              Father & Mother yet think they would ride up with some one
              if it was. O I wish I knew. Tis now three o'clock. our friends
              were Susan Hersey [Henry Baker's daughter] & her four
              little children. they rode up home to Uncles. . . . * * *

Saturday   We do usual work, visit at Uncles this afternoon. Susan has
[24]   lost her teeth, indeed she looks like a wreck. Warm

MAY 1875

Thursday
6

Sew. knit &c—James is dragging, Henry & Sarah are gone to school. tis real *cold*   I just read in the Bazar of the 'Pallace House' in Sanfrancisco Cal. it has 755 rooms, with a Bay window at each outside room which is 348, and 377 Bath rooms; 2000 easy chairs, 600 rocking chairs & 350 Sofas. I would be glad & think we were aristocricy if we had *one* Sofa even with *half a doz easy chairs. Contentment*—* * *

Sunday
9

Dear Dear! what a long day. no papers to read. Henry went to get the mail but was too early. I bake a cake & pies. Shower of rain

Sunday
16

To day Father is 68 years old   Ah me! his allotted span of life is nearly finished. how I wish it were so we could live near together. * * *

Thursday
20

Well I have house about cleaned   looks pretty well, if 'twould only *stay* clean. But *no.* house-work is one monotonous round. * * *

JUNE 1875

Wednesday
9

John McGee came along last evening & I went home with him have had a *good* visit with Harriet all day James & children came for me this evening. they have been to school. Jas said he got lonesome, knit, &c. ah yes 'tis sad to be alone, lonely: Rain

JULY 1875

Sunday
11

We have *raspberry short cake* for tea. We read &c. as usual. * * * Father sent us some papers. Beecher Jury

disagree *nine* for *Beecher* to *three* for *Tilton*. Rumor says
they are to carry up the suit & have *change of Venue*. Ah
bribery—money wasted. * * *

AUGUST 1875

Saturday
21

Ah me, we arose this morning to find that some one (there
were barefooted tracks of two). had been in our house last
night while we were asleep. . . . came in the room where
we all slept, took James' pants from foot of bed & left them,
with our umbrella in front yard. . . . thanks to kind providence they only looked at our pictures, toys etc, & left them
unharmed. think we will fasten the doors however, after this
for awhile at least. Susan was here visiting [before departing
for a return trip to Kansas with her husband, Albert, and
her children], Uncle & Albert to tea   she wants to stay with
her father, indeed she reaps the reward of her deeds, we all
work &c as usual, Jack frost   Pleasant

Sunday
22

After dinner we drive over to see Harriet & John. she is
encienta again. since fourth of July, am sorry for her,
pleasant

Wednesday
25

Joyful *day*. Mother has at last come to visit us. Aunt Mary
[Osborn] came too. . . . John & Harriet were here to dinner
too. . . . they are real tired and retire early, we all do usual
work.

How dear to our hearts are those we love;
    Though care-worn & old in years
Tis sweet to hear their voices, once again
    And talk of by-gone days.
                                    Pleasant

Thursday
26

Bake cake & pies, James work in garden. children are very
much pleased to see Grand-Ma, as we all are, & to see Aunt
too. we are haveing a splended visit, we walked over on the

big hill where they could view the prairies, they looked till
their eyes ached. John came after them this evening. * * *

SEPTEMBER 1875

Saturday   Do usual work. James draw manure. children help do
4   chores &c. Mother came back this forenoon, she is tired out
                & glad to 'get to Emily's again' she says. . . .

Sunday   John & Harriet & Aunt Mary came here. well, well. They
19   said we had forgotten when our anniversary was! sure
                enough it *was* thirteen years yesterday since we were mar-
                ried; I cook chickens   Bake cake etc, we have some nice
                mellons too, Pleasant

OCTOBER 1875

Wednesday   * * * Uncle and Aunt came to tea, we all went with Mother
13   & Aunt to the Depot, they start for home on this evenings
                train, at half past six, tis just seven weeks to day since they
                came. Mother felt real bad to leave us, & I equally as sorry
                that she should go. * * *

                [Volume 6 ends with forty-seven pages of account records,
                from December 1873 to May 1876.]

Thur   We begin, this Journal, another book added to our Diary, to
28   day. have a plenty of work to do, am glad to have a cheerful
                mind to do it. * * *

NOVEMBER 1875

Sunday
7

'Tis a beautiful day. we are at home. James says he wishes we had a carriage   I do too but rather have a new house. we all read &c. Pleasant.

Thur
25

Patch, sew & knit. children read and play. James still persists in working for Sellens, we think tis a lonely thanksgiving. makes all *sad* to have Pa *working* for other folks, when tis so very unnecessary. there is plenty to do at home. * * *

Sun
28

Have been reading the Life of Cleopatra . . . have almost come to the conclusion that the indolent enjoy life best. yet, we can not too highly prize an accomplished well educated mind. and we are thankful indeed for the knowledge we possess, and would that we might gain more. Pleasant—

DECEMBER 1875

Tues
7

Sew etc. Henry is going to bring in wood—& Sarah wash the dinner dishes this week, for each 10 cents. Jas chop wood. Henry help him. Misty & snow

Wednesday
15

Sew &c. children at school   We go to town, sell some butter, we made just 28 lbs of butter from 482 lbs of milk (of 5 cows) in 7 days—we pay some little debts. ho [*sic*] nice it is to think we owe (as the saying is) no man a shilling. Real Pleasant

Saturday
25

Christmas—children find each, a pencil. Sarah string of Beads & Henry pair Tweezers, in their stockings. Jas wished us all Merry Christmas. we wished him the same * * * I sew &c   Jas do chores & Sarah chrochet on a mitten. indeed Christmas has passed pleasantly away. Colder Tis evening. I am sitting here alone. James & children are in the land of dreams. yes I my thoughts are of the past, just fourteen years ago this night was the first time Jas came to visit with me. ah it does not seem one half as long ago. nay we have never regretted the termination of that visit. may we ever live as happily in the future as has been the past, & too we are thankful that our dear little ones are as bright stars shining in our little home. All is well. Pleasant

JANUARY 1876

Saturday
1

Tis the beginning of the Centenial-year. being just one hundred years since Independence was declared to the United States. . . . in Philadelphia has been arranged a place for a Centenial-celebration, to be in session from now untill January 1877 in which all nations are to be represented and participate in the Great-fair-of-the-World. would that we might join with them, but we only can with our best wishes for success. * * *

Saturday
8!!!

After breakfast & the chores done we all went to make Harriet a visit, we stayed to dinner. they are usually well. three o'clock we went to Uncles, were coming home, after tea, but the Grangers (a kind of society) were to meet there in the evening to have an oyster supper, so we stayed to visit with them. twas 10 min past 12 o'clock when we got home. do not think I would be a Granger   can not see any real benefit to be reallized from *any* of these secret or other societies.[10]
* * *

Fri
28

Finish James *coat*, took me *forty eight* hours. used 9 spools silk and 2 spools black & one of basting thread (12) * * *

Sun
30

We read in our new papers, we have seven, Phrenological journal; Live stock journal; Western Rural; Harpers Weekly; Youths Companion; Champion: (sent by unknown). and the Manchester press. am writing as usual in my journal, nearly ten

'Yes journal, I love thee, and who shall dare
To chide me, for loveing a friend so fair.'[11] . . .

FEBRUARY 1876

Thur
3

Patch, all day. James do chores & chop. * * * James says I may write in my Diary, to have warmer feet when I come to bed. *Coldest* day this winter, *Cold*

Sun
6

do usual work, bake bread, have been reading. Father sent us papers too—we are well supplied with reading, James has piles tis too bad. * * * tis so warm to day we scarcely need any fire, yes and too there are two Notices in the [Manchester] Press, that leave a bad impression on every one who reads them   one is—Mrs Quakinbush sues for divorce, the other—Mr Barnard says My Wife has left my bed & board &c—the former were leading members in the Methodist Church, the latter deacon in Presbyterian, let me ask, are they fit for an example & guide in society? no—no. Warm & Pleasant

Wed
9

Bake pies & cake, cut & Baste self wrapper (striped Gingham). Nelly Tyler and Harriet here all afternoon. James went to town with John, one Barber treated John to Liquor—tis really too bad, for Harriet feels so *very bad* about it. seems to me a person that induces one to get drunk, is a *most direful enemy*. Manchester to day is infested with saloons of the lowest degradation. you will see the business men of the City—those who ought to be a guide in society, comeing out of those dens, red faced and staggering on the sidewalks, tottering home to abuse and disgrace their wives and families. Ah tis worse, far worse than death. with Gods help we pray our boy may never enter such a loathesome place, no never. Warm. Misty

Thurs 24

tis just 9 P.M. ironed &c—, finish Jas socks. I will have 8 new gowns when I get them all finished and Sarah 6. Jas chop &c. * * *

Sat 26

Do usual work. we all go to town. Deposit, for the first time, money in the Bank. (James drove hogs to town yesterday.) * * *

APRIL 1876

Sunday 2

We are at home all day, I bake bread. read some in Book of Mormonism, By Ann Eliza Young, his nineteenth wife. think it is not a book that will give much refinement of thought to any one who reads it.[12] * * *

Tuesday 18

We do usual work. * * * John has come for me to go & stay with Harriet to night. Pleasant

Wed 19

Came home this evening, 3 more hens & Bronze turkey dead, others sick. James & Children have kept house, Harriet has a Boy baby, born five minutes of 12 last evening, looks very well, think he weighs near ten lbs. Dr Reynolds was in attendance. Rain

Frid 28

Finish sunbonnet. help James work in yard. he is makeing flower beds for me in door yard. *looks real nice.* * * *

MAY 1876

Fri
12

Do usual work, sew &c. James do chores, resting to day, he is some better. children go to school. I have been to town, got a piece of Card Board 22 × 28—am going to draw a picture on it. got too some new Geographys for the children. * * *

Friday
26

Iron, cook & clean generally. James finish hog-yard. children at school. I spend (2 hours) on my picture: James says tis more beautiful than the original, children say tis very nice. Henry said "I would give five dollars ma, if I could draw as nice a one" Sarah says tis not like *the* picture but nicer. Very warm

JUNE 1876

Sun
4

Am at home. make out Bill of Lumber etc for [building] our house. children busy gathering flowers and read. Jas do the chores & sleep. * * *

Wed
7

Iron, help weed onions, sew. * * * have been to town with Mrs Thatcher. got the Frame for my Picture. Bought of Mr Eldridge, nails, Door and window trimmings. they cost twenty one dollars. *rather* James would get such things but he says I must, if I build a house, do it my self. Rain

Thur
8

Finish my Picture (The Rendezvous.) *I* think it is *very* nice indeed. the drawing is 20 × 22. frame, 26 × 32 outside. there is 4 verses of poetry (12 lines each) written on the bottom margin. It has taken about 40 hours. * * *

[After June 9 entry is an account of lumber costs for the new house.]

Sat
24

No! tis Friday evening, and I thought I would write a line more in my journal. James rather seems to think we must wait till another year ere we can put up our new house. because we have not just at present got the money ready at hand. to me however, it seems as though we can get it enclosed at least. because, if no preventing providence, we will get fifty dollars in money (now due). besides the seed oats, 277 bushels. . . . They are due when threshed; Yet, if we can not, without getting encumbered, I think we better wait, though great would be the disappointment. *Warm.*

Sat
24

* * * I have done usual work & been to town. paid some on bill of lumber. we have paid for Material to build with *two hundred & eighteen dollars* & there is yet some more to get   Warm

Mon
26

Wash, can 2 qts Strawberries, and do usual work. Children go to school. James plow corn. there were three men here to see about getting the job of putting up our new house. James has concluded to get it enclosed, ready to lath. I am glad, for it seems that now is a good time   We can but think "Fortune favors the Brave." * * *

JULY 1876

Tues
4

John, Harriet, Babies, Henry Sarah James & I were at Uncles to dinner. roast turkey and other good things. Lemon-ade—tis our *Centennial* Celebration. looks like rain. Pleasant

Tues
11

* * * I do usual work, pick berries. a ~~Jipsy~~ Gypsy Girl here this morning—says I am to recieve a letter from a distant relation & am to recieve a large property, and she she will tell me who from and when if I will pay her 3.00   think I'll wait. Warm

The 1876 house.

Wed 19	Still tearing down house, move beds in barn last night. sleep aloft. work on Rug—James went to town. Children help to do every thing. we move stove out in shanty, are really camping out. we all like it quite well. Pleasant
Thur 20	Work on Rug do usual work, pull onions (all of us). James took down last of old house. Adieu old house, thy Walls will shelter us no more. no more pleasant hours beneath thy roof, yet we part with thee in fond hopes of a new one in thy place. . . . and wilt thou keep all past sorrows, and leave on memories page, the joys of bygone days. * * *

AUGUST 1876

Wed 9	Do usual work. James tend Mr Andrews (Mason) he is building our chimney, indeed—we have a fire place 2 feet clear in front & 8 inches deep. Children study & help all they can Henry hurt his back, he has gone to see Charley Noyes. Sarah is laying brick. there was a *gentleman* here to day to see about the product of our cows for 1875. he intends to start a Creamery in Lynn County. Shower
Sat 12	Do usual work. * * * Mrs Brook here visiting this afternoon. she brings me *quite a compliment* from Mr Houston (the gentleman that was here last Wednesday) he said I gave him the best account of dairying, the most accurate, general information of any one he had seen and that he had been investigating for four days, though I must not let it excite my vanity. * * *

SEPTEMBER 1876

Tues 5	*Rain* last night, makes unpleasant camping. we lath (children & me all day) Jas go to town all day Rain

Sun
17

Am up stairs writing in my journal. we have got all our things in the house, all topsy turvey. * * * James has fire kindled to get dinner   children cracking hazelnuts. * * *

Tues
19

Do usual work, Jas make Mortar. he gets the blues every time he is tired & bad weather. children at school. Pleasant

OCTOBER 1876

Sun
1

We, all, visit at Harriets   there to dinner. her & John are quite discouraged. well they may be, they owe debts to the amount of *twenty-six hundred dollars*. (2,600.00)   Wheat a failure they sowed 55 acres & only had 64 bushels, & that *poor*. I am sorry for them, & yet they were advised to do different. * * *

Wed
25

Commence to clean chamber. * * * children at school. Mrs McBrides little boy used profane language, so she sent word to the teacher, by *the* boys sister, to whip him within an inch of his life. Oh! what a *Mother* she must be, it seems some people think more of their dumb animals than of their children. the way our school is taught by the present teacher, is a mere state prison, the pupils move, act, speak etc, at the thump of the bell. how sad to think that in this age of civilization, our little innocent children must be treated as convicts. pleasant but cold.

Thur
26

* * * James is husking corn, children gone to school, & I am talking, to you, my old & tried friend, my journal. bread mixed dishes to wash & house to clean. * * *

Fri
27

James has been husking corn, children been to school, I just finished cleaning the chambers at five o'clock, looks real nice & closet clean too. * * * we intend to have a dancing party next friday evening if all is well and pleasant   Nice day

NOVEMBER 1876

Wed
1

Bake ninety cookies (motto candied)   James go to Johns after pigs. . . . Then he took some butter to town & engaged music for *the* party. 'twill cost five dollars. * * *

Sat
4

Tis about noon, house swept and mornings work done. we had our party last night. . . . There were twenty-three numbers besides several others. fifty-four all told to supper including ourselves & children. Rain

Thur
9

Do usual work. * * * Children bring their readers home. I think that they better read at home & not at school, because Miss Gill interrupts them so much they can not understand what they read, and it induces them to repeat while reading—which to my taste spoils ones reading entirely. . . .

DECEMBER 1876

Sun
24

We are at home, read & talk. James & children have retired, their [stockings] are hung beside the chimney awaiting for their Christmas-presents, ah how innocent, how confidential, and I must not disappoint their trust. though I could buy nothing new. I give to Henry my 'old History'—and to Sarah my 'old English Reader'. and each some nice yarn for mittens. pleasant

Sun
31

The clock just chimes ten. Ah! this memmoriable Centennial year has but two more short hours, and its life has ended. methinks perhaps a hundred years hence may not

win a greater name than thee who art about to leave us forever to join thy sisters and wait for all to come. [Two stanzas
of poetry follow.]

JANUARY 1877

Mon
1!!!

Wellcome new year, we are all at home. James chopping
wood. I wash etc as usual, help the Children do examples
in arithmatic. . . . *they commence to keep a journal.* Clear
& cold[13]

Wed
10

Do usual work, finish Sarahs dress & commence pants for
Henry. they go to school. James take pig to Mr Clark. We
were all reading a piece of poetry this evening—James
did not like it because I laughed, though I meant no
harm   Cold.

FEBRUARY 1877.

Sat!!!
3

Have a lame neck. we all do not seem to feel first rate to
day. * * * Sarah help me quilt on my diamond-quilt that I
pieced eighteen or twenty years agone. * * *

Wed
14

A Valentines day. have made pies, broidered some. * * * I
am writing, and meditating on the past   Ah how many
changes have been wrought since *I* was a school-girl, enjoying all the pleasures of school-life, and of Society. aye well
do we remember our last term of school, it closed with a
grand exhibition, almost a theater. it was seventeen years
ago last fall. the winter following every one seemed to
have,—well a *panic* for writing valentines. I wrote one, and
for the fear of the Reciever finding out who the author was,
did not send it. therefore afer [*sic*] a time I wrote another,

and kept *it* too. and now will copy it here, except change
the date to the present time. No! I'll write it just as it was.
it was first written in February 1858.

[The poem that follows is a longer version of "Musings of
Midnight," which Gillespie wrote in her diary on March 31,
1873. In "Musings" Gillespie says that she loved the person
in the poem fifteen years ago, which would also date it at
1858. The 1877 version of her Valentine poem ends:]

How I would to see, and speak with thee once more
Once more behold thy face as in those days of yore.
Methinks it can not be, that years have past and gone
Since first we met, and loved,—and I— /
thou are still alone.

Valentina.

Yes *he* is yet alone, and undoubtedly will ever be, he is
now an old man, near sixty—. I am quite content with my
own dear family, a *very* kind husband, and our two children,
inteligent, perfect in form. . . .

MARCH 1877

Fri
2

Finish my Sopha cushion Cover   tis indeed beautiful, there
are 96256 stitches on it. could broider at the rate of 100
stitches per seven minutes, which would take   days, providing it was all plain. it is worth at least 15 or 20 dollars to make it. the cost of material was one & one half
dollars. * * *

Wed
7

Well—as I expected, this morning we must have our happiness marred again on acct of Doolittle wanting us to help
him. . . . if James could only see that one can not do his or
her own family justice, and at the same time try to care &
do for other folks, even if they are brothers and sisters; most

truly I can leave *my* parents, brothers and sisters for him, and him alone. Oh! if he could only do the same for me and our little ones, we might never see a sorrowful hour. * * * we have two new milch cows this evening. Cold Snow.

Sat
10

Have been in Manchester all day, attending the *'Teachers Examination.'* they do far different here than they used to in Michigan or Ohio. . . . I answered correctly 38 questions in 43, which is .928 percent—90 pr. cnt. being required for a first class certificate. . . .

Tues
13

* * * saw the article I wrote for the paper in the press to day, tis the following—

A DEFENSE.

We the undersigned, write in behalf of our teacher, our Children and ourselves. . . . We as Citizens believe in a free government. therefore do not desire to send our Children to teachers who have such arbitrary rules as to injure their pupils both physically & mentally. . . .[14]

APRIL 1877

Thur
5

do usual work. Quilt. help Children cipher. they are just through cube root. Sarah *cried* because Henry done 4 or 5 examples ahead of her, before she came in from play. am sorry she does as she does sometimes, yet think it was because of her excitement through hard playing. they are both such *good* children, I hope I may ever govern my own thoughts so as never to speak too harshly. James draw manure. Cloudy

Wed
11

Tis my 39 birth day, it seems but yesterday, as it were, that I was only 19. how fleeting is time. when mother was 40, she thought she was old. *old.* though our hair is silvered and furrows begin to trace our once smooth face, our thoughts are yet as young as twenty years ago. only that some experience has perhaps taught us, that all this worlds doing is not quite a dream, but a calm reality. . . . * * *

MAY 1877

Sat
5

Children & I go fishing we catch 28 small fish. James plow this forenoon . . . he has the piles real bad. oh, if he would only get over them. * * *

Tues
8

Tis a beautiful morning. half past five, how sweet the children sleep. James is milking. I must get breakfast while my three Gobblers, noble fellows, are strutting hugely. * * *

Thur
10

Do usual work, make garden &c. I put up a sign board "Seedcorn for sale". have sold thirteen bushels now, & had we five times as much we could sell it all. Mr Esteys folks have lost their place by mortgage. *tis too bad.* however, if people give mortgages they must know payday will surely come. * * *

Fri
18

Work in flower yard all day   am *very* tired indeed. and oh so thirsty—yet I can not drink even one swallow of cold water, without it making me sick. Children at school, James plow & do chores, I hope he will be better natured, over 'the blues' tomorrow   Very Warm

Sat
26

Do usual work, children & me help plow garden. * * * two gentlemen called to dinner, Messrs Baskerville, one of them just from Manchester England, last Monday arrived in N.Y. I felt quite highly flattered indeed, *the* one said "he had visited Art galleries in London, Paris, Liverpool and in Manchester, and never saw *any thing* in *hair work*, nor in *drawing with pencil*, as *nice* as *mine*, that they out [*sic*] to be on exhibition in a museum or some other public place of art." am thankful for the high praise of a D.D. of Manchester England. Warm

Sun
27

We read & while the time pleasantly away. when I see Henry & Sarah strolling over the fields together in search of flowers, it reminds me of the time when sisters & brother and I done the same. where are *we* all *now*, since twenty years agone. and *they*. Ah where may they be twenty years hence. time can only tell. yet we hope & trust they may be as virtuous as now, guiding stars, as it were, in society, financially comfortable. may no deep sorrow ever bedim their brow. Amen. Warm

JUNE 1877

Sat
2

We all go to town, pay Mr Buckley *all* we owe him—we do not owe any thing now on our house, total cost to now is *$552.87—if no mistake*. Sarah & Henry think themselves quite independent, they have their own money to trade with   Warm.

JULY 1877

Wed
4

We all went to Manchester to the Celebration. twas *very* good   'twas called A Reform Club Celebration   the drunkards of all the states are forming reform clubs (Red Ribbon) to refrain from all intoxicating drinks. glorious resolve! may they *never* get drunk again. *68 deg in cellar*   Very Warm

Thur
5

* * * I am working   just finished canning (30th can) strawberries for this year. have picked from our bed . . . good *six bushels*. O dear! tis extremely warm. picked one qt more, so there was 190-1/2 qts. *Warm*   warm

Sun 15	. . . had a good visit with Harriet. O dear! am sorry she is so changed—she is quite discouraged. (*There now.* I too am in trouble, wind has just blown a plate of drying raspberries off on the ground, & wasted every one of them.) However their crops look well at present, but they can not begin to meet one tenth part of their obligations. too bad, *too* bad, yet they are young enough to begin again. if they do *I hope* they will do different than they have in the past. *especially* Harriet. she works beyond all reason: surely ones intellect must be injured, to rise before four in the morning & then, from that time till nine even'g, to so over tax their physical strength. . . . * * *
Fri 20	Do usual work. * * * There are beggers stop almost every day wanting us to give them a bit of something to eat. would that all might have good homes, and were competent to take care of themselves. * * *
Sat 28	We all do usual work. * * * we all go to Uncles stay to tea. Mrs Smith call here this evening. she said they had taken *Mrs Brook* to the *Insane Asylum* last tuesday. Shower
Sun 29	We are at home as usual. am sorry for Mrs Brook I only wonder that more women than do do not have to be taken to the Assylum. especially farmers wives, no society, except hired men to eat their meals. hard work from the beginning to the end of the year, their only happiness lies in their children. with fond hopes that *they* may rise higher. that *they* perhaps may be an ornament to society—in fact be all that is chaste & pure. Warm

SEPTEMBER 1877

Tues 18	Work as usual, make cake &c. Went to Uncles & get some butter. Mrs Preston told me there were several of the neigh-

bors comeing to surprise us this evening—complimentary
to our 15th Anniversary * * *

Wed
19

Well *they* came, Mr Chapmans (6), Mr Morses (5), Mr Sellens (4) Mr Smiths (3) & the teacher, yes & Harriets (4),
they presented us with a very pretty set of glass,—Sugar
bowl, spooner, creamer & butter tureen, Henry gave me a
bottle of Perfumery & Sarah gave me 6 salt cups—for their
share. nice presents indeed. I commence to draw a picture
to day (Vanity). James dig potatoes &c, Children go to
school   Pleas.

Thur
27

Children go with us to the fair to day, I help arrange the
things, I have first premium awarded to me on my rug; my
hair-work, my hair-wreath, & also on collection of hair flowers; the first on my Landscape; Animal; printing & on the
collection of drawings. . . .

OCTOBER 1877

Sat
6

Cut dress &c. * * * we all go to Johns this afternoon, get
wheat. Harriet says she has had the blues for *two months.*
there was a hard frost last night the first to *kill* every thing
that was bright & green only yesterday, *now* how seared.
Pleasant

Sun
14

* * * James said we would go to meeting so we started, but
came back because we heard there was none. James is cross
about riding in a wagon wouldnt even speak while we were
gone. I think it will not be a very pleasant remembrance for
the children to think of, but we can only *hope* it may *not
ever* be so. for *my* part I like to make home pleasant. most
surely there is nothing to be unsocial & unpleasant for, tis
only one of his moods, Shower

Mon
15

Do large washing. James help me all day. he feels better natured to day, do not blame him if he does get
cross—* * *

Mon
29

Sarah is driving team for James to husk corn. Henry is digging the potatoes. . . . I am doing up work. wash etc. ten
oclock. I & Henry too, help husk, in afternoon. Pleasant

DECEMBER 1877

Sunday
16

John & Harriet here all day. Her & the children intend to
start for Michigan Tuesday, to visit our folks. how I too
would like to go, but can not. We are all at home read &
visit, tis a beautiful day, doors open. Warm

Tues
25

Christmas. Children up early   after breakfast they distrib-
ute our presents, James get a Book—'The Royal Path of
Life'. I get slippers, and shell Basket Sarah made me, and
a Cross Henry made, & Motto "The Lord will provide."
Henry gets Purse, Slippers and a Motto "No Cross No
Crown", Sarah gets Slippers and Motto with Chromo "What
is Home without a Mother"   we all get apples. Would that
all might get as much   Clowdy

JANUARY 1878

Wed
16

Finish James' pants, do usual work, Children have gone to
School, James has gone to town. I, I'm sad—do not know
but tis foolish, but the tears will sometimes start, perhaps
tis 'the Blues,' I *did* so want to go and hear Miss Susan B.
Anthony lecture last monday evening, and *might* have
gone, only that it seems to be so much trouble to take me
any where, that I am, seems to me, almost a hermit, tis the
saddest of all things to give up, as it were, the Idea of ever

being any higher in society than merely to be always at home, except sometimes to go where necessity compels us to, but I must *not* give up *no, no,* my children are too noble. I must use every effort to help them to be, what I might have been, tis my only pleasure to see them happy   yes and James too is ever as kind as one can be, ever ready to do any thing to promote others happiness though it make himself miserable, therefore knowing as I do, I never let him know, how great my desire is to go more in public. no blame to him, he may some time see differently. I hope, still hope on as ever for a contented mind, that we may all gain wisdom, all do right.

Harriet came back to day, said our folks were all well, she is tired. the air full of frost   Foggy[15]

FEBRUARY 1878

Sun
3

John and Harriet here visiting. Tis evening and all is still   James and children retired for the night. I do indeed feel sorry for Harriet, Alas! she is like so many, many others who has married a *very kind* and *pleasant* man, when every thing is just to *his* liking   I some times think, woman is but a mere tool. Warm like spring

Fri
8

Do usual work, get 4 more comfortables ready to tie. * * * O dear a me. we must have trouble yet, about his [James's] relatives. *why can he not let them alone.* Sarah went to school. Henry felt real grieved that I felt so bad. 'Oh Ma do not cry any more' he said and so pathetic too, how reasonable how just & true he is. Aye I must live for my children, and forbear with all sorrow, though great it may be. * * *

Sun
17

We start to go to meeting, Henry felt really grieved, on account of having to sit behind on a low seat. indeed, I do not blame him, he is too noble minded to be put off with any thing not as good as others, *I did not* want it so, but we must often submit to things which are most unpleasant. James was so offended that he drove around back home, so we did *not* attend church. Henry will never forget no never, but there will ever be written, one sad word, on his memory, *misused*. May he forgive however, and we will trust to kind Providence that all may be well at last, Chilly

Fri
22

Henry & I finish a seat to put in carriage, James take it & waggon to town to get ironed & mended. * * * I forgot to say that we all done usual work yesterday, & that it was a *rainy* day. We all go to Mr Morses this evening. I tied a quilt too. Pleasant

Tues
26

I visit at Mrs McBrides. * * * John came for James to sign a note with him, he *did* of 100. dollars   I hope it may be all right, yet it seems to me if ones own name is worthless they better not ask others to be their security. *I* would not sign with *any* one   they might go to jail first, still I *am sorry* that John & Harriet must lose their place, yet I can not help it, A beautiful day

APRIL 1878

Thur
11

Go to town get me cloth for new gown & some pearl trimmings for Sarahs & my dresses. Children stay at home. * * * Dreamed, last night, of conversing with Queen Victoria   Am 40 to day, seem but twenty in mind though my hair is near half gray.

MAY 1878

Mond
6

Tis afternoon, Children have gone with James to fix fence. they got their lessons well. I must now wash, bake etc. I do wish I may not be so nervous, the children are so good, how thankful I am they bear with me patiently, and are so kind to help me, when I have so much to do. I too well know my mind sometimes fails in strength to what it used to do. My hope & prayer, that I may never lose my reason as many have done at my age of life. * * *

Fri
10

We all do our regular routine of work & Study. This afternoon we with the rest of the neighbors in district meet at the school house to consider the wellfare of our school & to talk over the trouble now existing. . . . Mr Evart the Superintendent . . . brought Authors to try to sustain his argument, as regards the present system of teaching viz signals, then too about pupils obeying the teacher etc. I too believe in promptness, and dicipline, but not by arbitration, & I claim not *one Author can be produced who advocates* that *children shall obey through fear.* . . .

Thur
16

* * * Harriet has another Boy it was born to day tween four & five o'clock. I have been there all day, rode home with Dr Sherman. Ah what suffering one can endure. James & Children at home. Rain   O yes tis Fathers birth day *he* is seventy-two. Cold.

Fri
31

Have done usual work, so cold & Rainy that I have lost some of my little turkeys. Set 208 eggs, hatched 168 chicks and now have 117 & 7 ducks. it lightens & thunders now, tis *quite* discouraging to lose so many little turks. * * *

JULY 1878

Mon
1

Wash, use wringer for the first time, one here on trial, like it very well. James hoe in garden, Children get their lessons. we put up or rather hang our door screens, they are wood frames with wire canvas, they *are nice* to keep out flies & musquitoes. Warm

Mon
8

Wash, go with James to Wool-Mills—he drove through the creek—Fox laid down in the water. I thought I would get out, when Betsy jumped & threw me out over the wheel, hurt my ankle so I could not step on it. broke the harness some. we took forty five lbs wool to market (off of four sheep) * * *

AUGUST 1878

Sun
4

O dear. believe I am quite discouraged. ever at home   can not go any where even to meeting. hope on Emily, however. never give up. Children too, you may some time have a chance to do. it seems little enterprise, to alway live one continual round of hard work, be it in ever so nice & good a place. we like change   then we can the better & more appreciate our home, Warm * * *

SEPTEMBER 1878

Wed
18

Our Anniversary, 16 years ago to day—O how changed since then. John Harriet & children here, we cook a duck. do not like it. * * *

Mon
23

James & I go to town this morning. I got some frames & other things, take my broidery to Mrs Houghton to work, first time ever got any work done away from home * * *

OCTOBER 1878

Sun
20

We attended meeting to day, both morning & evening   Rev E. R. Wood preached his farewell sermon this evening . . . "Lessons of Lots Wife." His prayer was so fervent, indeed many shed tears. thus our meetings close for a time at least, it really seems too bad, that the congregation—members of this Church are so few, as not to be able to support a Pastor, one who teaches such good morals. . . .

NOVEMBER 1878

Sun
24

We go to meeting to day, to the Presbyterian Church. Russell preach a sermon from 2nd Soloman about 'Little foxes spoil the vine'   does not sound much like the sermons we have heard by Mr Wood, giving to us such pleasant thoughts—good morals, and pure advice, while Russell lays forth all the evils & ways of sin imparting to one impure thoughts toward downward degredation instead of Progressive hope and dare-to-do-right ways to gain a happy life, and be, as it were, light not darkness, or day instead of night. For me I like pure Universalist reason logical and truth. Pleasant

DECEMBER 1878

Sat
7

We attend the funeral of Mr & Mrs Tirrils little girl, sad indeed. now both & all their children have died within one short week. . . . Aye we are thankful that our children are yet spared to us. this evening we hear the Lecture again on temperance   o I can not find words to express the curse that whiskey causes. Pretty cold

Tues
10

We go to town take more turkeys, have now sold 102 for $61.16—put $50.00 in Congars Bank, we pay up all debts only 5.05 [16] * * *

Tues
24

Sew & do other usual work. James bank some around house. Uncle invite us to come there tomorrow, Susan came back last Saturday with her four children, they bring all the things they have   she says she will never go back to Kansas. Alas I pity Uncle. an old man with all them on his hands. Children at home, we put Christmas Presents in one anothers stockings   *Cold*

FEBRUARY 1879

Fri
28

Children at school   James & I attend the Dairy Association. tis very good. I go to Mrs Houghtons to dine; Bake & sew. Snow

MARCH 1879

Thur
6

Make Broidered Chimese for self, James do usual work, Children at school, Henry has gone to a Phrenological Lecture at Manchester this evening, tis the *first* time he has ever been alone, any place in the evening, I hope harm may not befall him. one can not always expect to have their children near, tis well for them to go, especially to good places. James went & came home with Henry, Pleasant

APRIL 1879

Tues.
1

Usual work, sew & knit. * * * Foxy *very* lame yet, they put rowel in her shoulder. Henry cried about it   him & Sarah both are very tender hearted, indeed I hope they may never be cruel to any thing as are some *men*, I think if horses were treated kindly & rightly worked they would never be lame. Children cipher and help me, I bind quilts & knit, Cold

Wed
9

Make sun bonnet for Sarah, she help. * * * John & Harriet move to town to day. they rent a house for   per month, it does seem too bad to lose every thing they had, may they prosper better in the future.

Fri
11

My birth day, 41. Sarah gave me a shawl pin, she is indeed an affectionate little girl. Henry wanted to make ma a present, but he had to keep his just-enough money to buy a swarm of bees. all right Henry. *James* go with *John* to finish moving * * *

Tues
29

Go to town, stay to Harriets to dinner, she has boarders. frost Pleasant

MAY 1879

Wed
28!!!

More pleasant, to day, rained last night too. every thing begins to look nice. Children go to school James help me, about an hour fix turkey pens, (he *does not like* to do *any* thing with the poultry, but *never refuses all* the *money* they bring!) and sprout the potatoes, Warm * * *

JULY 1879

Sat
12

James help mop in morning Henry paint porch roof. Sarah help on her gown in afternoon, I sew, on & finish it, tis a *beautiful white gown* trimmed with [eighteen yards] broidery & tinted pearl buttons, sewed on it from one P.M. till half past eleven in evening. * * *

SEPTEMBER 1879

Tues
23

I went to town with James he took quarter of hog to Doolittles Ill be so glad when we don't have to be giving

them so much. I think charity begins at home first, most
surely *we need all* we can get & more too. * * *

OCTOBER 1879

Sun
5

Children and I go to the Creek after dinner and stay till
night. Catch few fish, get few grapes   look about for pretty
stones etc. James stayed at the house, Warm

Wed
8

Harriet & her two boys here all day. She is quite discouraged, & no wonder. John leaves her to chop all her wood,
& bring watter to wash with etc near a half mile. she said
he even wanted her to clean the hog-pen. *tis too bad*. methinks he would be surprised to find his washing undone, &
nothing cooked to eat when he came home, if he had to
depend upon me to do it under *such* circumstances. I *am*
indeed sorry for Harriet, she is too good to have married
such a man. but Alas! all must bear their own burden of
trouble. James help *Willie* husk corn all day, & do usual
chores. Children go to school. I have got perfectly sick of
tea, & drink Coffee instead, have drank tea since I was
seventeen years old, think I feel just as well without it,
though I think, by quitting its use sudden, it causes me to
perspire when asleep of night, and in fact nearly all the time
seems as though i were sweating. . . . I took Harriet home,
baked, & done ever-so-much work. * * *

NOVEMBER 1879

Mon
10

Wash. sew on shirt for H. James do chores &c, take Children to & from school. They Commence, to day, to attend
an Academy, tis new to them. there is 68 students, mostly
young Ladies & gentlemen. They are to attend the last half
of this term, their studies are Arithmetic; Grammar, reading

& spelling. . . . Henry & Sarah were much pleased & had good lessons to day. Rain [17]

DECEMBER 1879

Thur
4

Well I walked, to Harriets, yesterday. last night she went with Sarah, Henry and me to the Lyceum. Sarah read *a very good* Essay on "Cities & Towns." Mr. Kirsell paid me quite a compliment. he said—*'Henry & Sarah are splended readers* they are far *far* advanced in their studies, & more. they are most worthy noble Children.' . . .

Thur
25

Christmas—Henry start to go to Harriets about 10 AM, Sarah & I start about 11 A.M. we all walk. James stay at home, because he did not want to go. Harriet had a *very good dinner*. she was quite disappointed because Uncle and James were not there. . . .

JANUARY 1880.

Thur
1

Leap Year. * * * Henry & Sarah came to Uncles this morning. Griffins family (8 of them) and Bailies (8) came about noon. Uncle felt real disappointed because James did not come, and the reason,—because he did not want to. we had a general good time; set table for twenty seven. * * *

Thus
22!!!

* * * Children study. Henry is very much pleased with Bookkeeping, & wishes already that he could go to work with it as a profession. Sarah has not received hers yet, and is impatient. I well remember, my Air-Castles, of what I could have done, had my parents have seen a way to have sent me to College, yet it may perhaps be as well as it is. however, I often wish I might have graduated, as I might have done in the terms of only one more year. I only wish

that Henry & Sarah may attain an education such as I had
not the privilege of doing, because 'money I had none', &
all is well. * * *

FEBRUARY 1880

Wed
11

Finish shirt for Henry & commence overhauls. * * * I almost have the blues, wish I might ever be content, though
how can one when their wants are so many, and ne'er a
penny. yet we may well be thankful for what we do have and
trust to Providence that we may have all that is right & just.
we should have, health the best of all. All is well   rain rain
all day I wish I knew how all my folks are to night. my best
wishes with them

Sun
29

End of Winter. We are all at home. Sarah not very well,
(Menses first). Snow.

MARCH 1880

Tues
23

James go to Mill, Sarah & I go with him & stay in Town. he
gave me *forty dollars* that Uncle paid him for hay. I put
twenty of it in Bank to send Children to school. * * *

APRIL 1880

Fri
2

I went to town with James. we called at Mr Walt. Butters,
to see about sending Henry & Sarah to the Academy next
term. paid him their full tuition for twelve weeks, to commence next Monday. I called at Mrs Bailies too, and saw
Mrs Hulda Lewis. she thinks of leaving him, bad—bad—
they can not agree, her first husband was Mr Dr Morse. he
died. After his death she recieved a pention of nearly

300.00 a year, which she could not get after a second Marriage. she—alas! like many others sold herself, at too great a price.[18] * * *

Wed
7!!!

James go to Mill. I go with him to town. * * * call at Harriets a few minutes; they have got to move again. O dear. I do not know but she may have to go to the poor house, if John goes west. tis too bad, for she is a good girl & works hard. I stayed at the Soldier Reunion of the "12th Iowa Co F." Twas very good indeed, recalled reminicences of the soldiers that went to fight in that awful war of 1861 to 1865. . . . * * *

Sun
11

Real pleasant. * * * The *wolves* have caught two of my geese so we lost them & all their eggs. * * *
42 years old to day. All is well.

Mon
19

Wash, bake & usual routine. Children go to school. Sarah is not going to study *Book-keeping* any more this term. she get too tired. * * * *Birdie* [canary] commence to make a nest again. hope she will raise some birds next time. freezing cold

Wed
21

Children gone to school, James gone to town. * * * I am as usual doing work. intended to have gone to visit Mrs Glover to day but am disapointed about it as I most always am about going away from the monotonous round of kitchen work. ah me!

Hush my soul, thy sad repining
    Never, Oh never despair Emmie
Better times by & by are coming
    Wait and watch for them patiently.

[Two more stanzas follow.]

Tis two oclock. am alone. James said I could go to town now, though Ill wait till after supper. feel better than I did this morning. I often wish I might never be sad. but Ill read my poetry and can see myself getting happy again. Went to the Lyceum this evening *very good indeed.* * * *

Sun
25

* * * John is going off tomorrow to work on the *railroad.* Harriet & Children have moved, over on north part of town, they & Emma Brook & her children live in same house. George [Brook] is going with John.[19] * * *

MAY 1880

Sun
9

Children & I go to the woods. I am sorry to say—I got mad to day—yes *mad*—Warm   tis annoying to ever be found fault with because—work not hard enough, *forgive & forget.* Henry has asthma tis too bad. O if him & Sarah only can be able & competent to go through this life better, if may be, then I have done, it will be happiness to me. . . . * * *

JUNE 1880

Wed
16

Go berrying. do usual work. paint flowers on window-screens * * * *At last!* Well—Susan and her children have had to go back to Kansas. . . . she 'was never going back to Kansas again' but was going to stay here & take care of her property, till Uncle could not take care of it—then 'Albert was comeing too.' *Thanks to Providence. Uncle can attend to his own business yet & I hope* he can 'yet forty or fifty years hence'. . . . Tis far better for every one to get homes of their own. . . . * * *

Mon
21

Sew on my Gown in forenoon. James take me to town. I go with the Children to Coles' Circus in the afternoon. the Sea-Elephant is indeed a curious animal, as is also the Sea Lion. A Mr & Mrs Bates *the Giants*, were on exhibition too. . . .

they are each 7 ft 11-1/2 inches in height & weigh respectively 478 & 413. . . . . the rest of the show, to me was worthless   Awful warm * * *

JULY 1880

Fri.
23

Bake, sew & do usual work. Sarah help me. * * * Henry go peddling, he sold goods to the amt of 1.11 which cost .61; he is at home again to night, all is well. . . . Dreamed I put on beautiful black gown last night. Omen of the death of a friend.

Thur
29

* * * Sarah & Henry and I go fishing, get near 2 dozen, we take our lunch & get as tired as can be. Musquitoes thick as bees. Warm

AUGUST 1880

Mon
2!!!

James & I go to town, get Sarah cloth for 2 gowns & an apron; Suit for Henry, and material for myself 3 gowns. * * *

Mon
9

Do general *work*. work has no end. Sarah is making over a gown. she does it *quite* well. Henry commenced a window screen for me. he will be a scientific carpenter or cabinetmaker, if he chooses as a profession, either. James draw manure, wish he might do something, not such disagreeable hard kind of work. Sultry

Sun
29

At Harriets all day. George Dodge came for me to go. *Rain*

Mon
30

James came for me this morning, & brought home their [McGees'] children. *five* of *them* stayed at our house yesterday & night. Sarah says they need never leave so many for her to take care of again. 'twas mean. I went this morning to get hired girl for Harriet, & to pay some debts for her etc. She has another 9 lb Boy, born last evening at seven P.M. I just think it too bad. it seems to me as if John left his family to the mercy of the people. I do lots of work after I get home. Rain

SEPTEMBER 1880

Wed
1

Tis near the wee hours. James & Sarah have retired. O that I knew where Henry is, hope he has a good place to stay all night, that he has good success selling his things, that he is well & all right. tis lonely indeed when him or Sarah are away, especially at night. we all miss thee Henry, our good night kiss. . . . * * *

Sat
4

Henry is seventeen years old to day. James & I go to Town. Henry & Sarah at home. they felt *very* much disappointed this morning because James said he could not pay their tuition (16.00) to go to school. they feel all right this evening however—as he changed his mind & paid 12.00. Henry pays 4.00 (1/2) for himself. we call to see Harriet   they all think her boy looks like me. I bake, can peaches &c. * * *

OCTOBER 1880

Sun
10

All at home. yes our little family are together, I often wonder and think, how long may it be our happy lot to thus be—Henry & Sarah are, as it were, Children still, yet they are larger than I am, and are styled as young-folks, Pleasant

Thur
21

* * * I went to town sold the feathers that Mother sent to me. bought a *couch* for 9.00; bed-stead 3.75; curtain &

picture knobs; and get 3.00 to buy me a ring. I got for 45-
3/8 lbs 20.40. * * * I sold a bird to J. A. Brown. I keep a
singer, give one to Sarah, & keep Birdie—she raised 10.00
worth of birds for me this season. Cold

NOVEMBER 1880

Wed
3

Bake bread & pies &c. * * * we went to the Lyceum, it was
post-poned untill next wednesday evening, on account of
every body was so very jubilant over *the victory* of getting a
majority of *573* to have the *County-seat removed* from Delhi
to Manchester. the whole *City* was *illuminated, speeches*
made. *Torch Light procession* etc. they burned (in Effigy) the
old Court house. . . . Pleasant [20]

Sun
14

Have the Blues—well—try to work them away by baking
Bread, cookies & pies. Children read. * * *

Mon
15

Henry & Sarah have gone to school. James plaster in the
cellar-windows. I knit, wash & do all sorts of work. sometimes I almost despair. No! No!! I must *never* give up. what
would my children do. Snow

Sat
27

Children at home * * * James & I go to Town. call at Harriets. John got home Thursday. Pleasant

DECEMBER 1880

Thur
9

Children at school. Jas do chores   I sew. Mr Mead send for
rest of my poultry. . . . they alltogether come to 105.75—I
keep 29 turkeys & 50 hens & chickens. the old Gobler
weighed only 19-1/4 lbs. *his spurs an inch* long & his *Bristle
over 7 inches long.* am really thankful for my good luck in

raising so fine a lot. [Calculations of poultry-raising costs and profits for 1880–81 follow, plus a margin note: "Ship poultry to Boston."] Leaves 142.78 profit.

Sat
11

Cook, knit etc. * * * James go to town for load of brick. I went too. paid the taxes 25.15   paid childrens tuition for this term 16.00. got them each a pocket-Book. let Sarah have 1.50 & Henry 3.00 * * *

Thur
16

tis morning. James doing chores. Children not up yet. I have breakfast about ready. hash, potatoe, bread & Butter & Mince pie, 7 o'clock. Tis evening. I have been to Town. bought 22-3/4 yds of Brussels Carpet 22.75 for my Parlor & oilcloth carpeting for bedrooms, & Ingrain for stair-steps. all cost 50.40   bought myself, James & Sarah each a Porte-monnaie [money-carrier], & Collar-button for Henry (our Christmas), & skates for Sarah. *Colder*

JANUARY 1881

Mon
3

* * * Tis getting late—just one o'clock.
Have only done—half my days work;
Children soon come—tired & hungry,
James doing chores—all in a hurry.
Wonder if there will be—all the year through
Just as much work—every day to do?
Work on and wait ever
Despair not no never.
Always look on the side that is brighter
Pleasant.

Tues
18

Sew on my gown. do work. James do chores & chop. Children gone to school. Im going to the Theater to night. they play Merchant of Venice. is Shakspiere. now I wonder if I

spelled S——— right. no! its *Shakespeare*. Very Pleasant and
warmer & Excellent sleighing.

MARCH 1881

Wed
16

I have mornings work most done   James took the Children
to school. when he came home he said Henrys example is
right—At the close of last term, Mr Butter gave an example
in Algebra to be solved. the first one that got it right was to
have this term's tuition free. well I done it, but twas not for
me to do, & I was very glad that Henry got it right too   Prf
Butter said he had given it to a great many—& not one had
ever got it before. good for Henry. here is the example. [Half
a page of algebra equations follows.] . . .

Sun
20

Five o'clock. Bake. snow drifts are bad as they have been
at any time, almost impossible to get through them. in front
of the house, sleighs go almost as high as the fence. there
are three Engines—now—trying to get through the snow-
banks—might as well say snow mountains—they have been
at work—in sight—all the after-noon—they get stuck every
few rods & the Engine is almost burried in the snow, & is
just being pulled out by another Engine so as to get another
start. . . . there looks to be as many as 75 or 100 men all
shoveling out the snow. . . .

Thur
24

Do usual work, bake. * * * Harriet has been, some-where
visiting, west, has just gone past. think she might have
called, if no more. she feels offended because I have not
been there in some time, Ill try to go some day next week.
* * *

Tues
29

Do usual work and paint. Children go to school. James do
chores & go after them. *John & Harriet* have rented Mrs

Carpenters place & moved there to day, about 80 rods east of our house. * * *

APRIL 1881

Sat
9

Children go to school; James do chores & clean barn-yard. I paint, have the Parlor & Bedroom white, Henry's, Sarah's & north Bedroom Cream collor, & the Hall Grained in imitation of rose-wood with center pannels of door Light-oak. looks *nice*. I cook & iron too. Thaw. Pleasant

Sun
10

* * * To day ends my 42nd year.
　　　For something, unknown, I have all day
　　　　The children say—Been sad.
　　May to-morrow dawn, on my birth day
　　　To make us all—more Glad.
　　　　　　More happy.

Mon
11

Half past ten. mornings work done, a goose set, and work enough for *one to do*. Children gone to school. James doing chores. I am warming my feet & writing in my Journal. just 26 years ago to day, I was inspected, at Medina Lenawee, Mich—the first time. received a certificate to teach school for a term of two years. that was in 1855—then we lived at the old Mill—where are we all now. . . . [Three stanzas of poetry follow.]

I washed, cooked, cleaned generally　James do chores & go after Children. when they came home they must give me a whipping. well we did have quite a time. 22 years ago *the time* was with Mother—now with Henry & Sarah. . . .

Sun
24

We are all at home. * * *

Harriet has company. they either go some-where every sunday, or some one or more comes there. *I* do not like sunday company. *Warm*

MAY 1881

Wed
4

I go to town, ride with Uncle. at Mrs Houghtons to dinner she is going to California. wish I could go with her. * * *

Thur
5

Go to town. Paint Hall-floor &c. * * * I received a *letter* from *Edna* yesterday   she is very much offended because Father & Mother sold their farm, says they have trouble, *trouble* all the time. *I* am sorry, & do wish they might spend the last of their lives in happiness. if [brother] Henry has all they have for taking care of them he ought to make them comfortable, & do all he can to promote their well-fare, long as they live. yet I fear for them—& hope for the best. Warm

Mon
9

Chore & work all day   go to Harriets after fork—*ours.* * * * I wanted to dig some roots in the garden this after-noon. our potatoe-fork was down to Harriets. I *was* provoked that I had to go after it—when I was so tired. I would not stay because I wanted to use it before it rained, well it *did* rain before I got done. tis *raining* now. James has gone after the children. Harriet just came & brought home our crow-bar   she was real wet, would not come in, said she would not trouble us any more about borrowing—I am sorry she feels so, but I can not help it—when I work & get things to use I do not like to have them gone when I want them. . . . I hope though it may be sorrow to her & me too, it may learn them a lesson that they can not always expect some one of their relatives to help them. they must work to a better ad-vantage for them-selves. . . . I can & do remember them in my prayers, but can not work for them. tis more than I can do to keep my work half done a great deal of the time with-out even thinking about keeping things on hand for others. I will say once more Im sorry indeed to offend Harriet for she is a good girl. . . . I surely will go to see her as often as I can. she said she would never come in my house again unless I sent for her. . . . Tis evening, just nine o'clock.

James & the children have retired to sleep & Im ready to go
too, hoping tomorrow will be not as sad as to day, I go to
bed. . . .

Fri
29

Same old story. *Work.* hoe in garden, tend Birds & Turkeys.
Children at school. James churn, chop & chore. * * * Harriet here for pie-plant. Im sorry she has to work so hard
(chop, carry water etc)

JUNE 1881

Fri
3

Make coops. take care of turkeys & hoe in *my garden.* Sarah help me. her & I both—the worse we feel—the harder
we work. Henry hoe his garden & work on gate. James plow
corn. * * * Tis happiness to retire to rest feeling that we
are enimie to none—friends to all. . . .

Sun
5

* * * I got up this morning just 7, got breakfast ready, then
watched a turkey, to find her nest till after nine, before I
ate. *tis* a real tiresome task to raise turkeys & birds—
yet—had I not so much else to do I would like it, in the
morning it seems, almost as if one was in the woods—they
so merrily sing together. . . . * * *

Wed
22

Sarah & I put our Brussels carpet down, to make, this morning before breakfast. James says tis too nice to corespond
with the other things. Henry says it is *real nice* & we must
make the other things corespond with *it.* *I* think so too. I
never saw any thing *too* nice for *me* yet. Sarah looks at it,
makes it match etc, says she feels like a king on such a
pretty carpet & wont it be nice to all clean & dress up sundays & sit on it. in fact it seems at home, to have nice
things. oh that all could have just as good. * * *

JULY 1881

Sat
2

Sew on Sarahs gown. she is not well, helps me what she can
* * * we hear by telegraph that Garfield was shot, seriously,
at 9 o'clock this morning. Assassinnated. Warm[21]

Sat
9

Twilight. I am sitting on the east porch, writing, and occa-
tionally drops of rain *blot* my book. it *lightens & thunders*—Ah me, if I would give up to my feelings, I should
almost despair of raising any poultry this year. I have but
few left, perhaps a hundred out of 265. wolves, minks etc.
I can only say tis too bad, & trust to have better success
another time. would that I knew how mother & Father are
getting along. * * *

AUGUST 1881

Tues
16

Do general work, indeed I can not do work as easily as I
could twenty years ago. it seems sometimes as though I
would have to give up were it not that Henry & Sarah help
me. . . . John has threshers here to day. James & Henry
help. tis as ever, not much Happiness for me, when James
has any extra work to do. I sometimes think of words which
different women have told me in my girl-hood—that—
"woman is always lovely—untill her strength & beauty
fails, then—she is—only in the way"—it seems almost invariably true, yet we will try to say & think—all is well.
Henry helped hang barn-door too. if James could only appreciate what he does for him, he would do many many more
chores for him. but it seems as if all men can only find fault
with what *is* done & are mad if every thing is not done.
Warm

Sun
21

Henry, Sarah & I go fishing. we call at Harriets & stay to
dinner, then they all go too. John waded through the creek

& carried us all over. he said I was light as a feather. * * * well we had a general good time, tired & a good apetite for supper. . . . We hear Garfield is worse, he will be apt to die. . . .

Sun
28

Tis 10 o'clock, evening. am up alone—writing. Henry, Sarah & I went to the 'Devils Back-Bone' were gone twelve hours. well I can not say it was a gala day—it was not: Henry did not want, very much, to go at all. he said so much & in such a way that I cried about it. *it* made him feel bad too, and Sarah. . . . Oh if I could but controll my mind to be more steady, it would be such a blessing. tis my prayer that I may never get so nervous again.[22] . . . * * *

Wed
31

Bake, mop & do usual work. Sarah went to town this morning & got Mrs. Butter. she stayed all day, then I carried her home. * * * James went out in the field to work just when Mrs Butter came, & stayed untill she went home. I like to see people that are respectable, treated with respect at least.[23] * * *

SEPTEMBER 1881

Thur
8

We went to the fair this morning, I took my 4 cakes & 2 pies, making in all 26 Entries. . . . The committee wanted to open all the cans of fruit to *test its quality*, they said, *I* objected. then there was a few roiled tempers & some spicy words said. . . . Tis not so pleasant, sometimes, to *make* people *do right.* though when obliged to, and succeed *tis glorious.* Children went to school in forenoon & to the fair in afternoon. not many went to day. * * *

Tues
20

Bake, etc. James draw manure, Children went to school this morning—no school to day. President Garfield died last night ten. 15 o'clock. the City, the whole country in fact are draped in mourning. Tis indeed a sad affair—yet I can not feel that he is more human than millions of others who have died, and been consigned to their last resting place, quietly, with but a few to mourn their loss—forgotten, as it were, ere a year had passed oer their graves. Alas! what a polittical state this Country is in—tis almost monarchial, there are many who would like to govern the people & make law just as old tyranical Kings and Lords of olden time. sorry it is so. this sad event may be a lesson that will give thoughts to purer & higher motives among leading men. * * *

Thur
29

Do usual work, knit—* * * James asleep. Children up stairs. I am writing. There is an offer, for a *prize-story*, in the *Companion*. I have a mind to try for it. all is well. Rain Think Ill have for my Subject "The Declamation Contest" or Reminicinces of boarding school.

OCTOBER 1881

Mon
3

Wash, bake & iron, Children go to school. James draw lumber we are to have a kitchen built south side of house. Pleasant

Wed
5

First frost last night. cold all day. Trenchard [carpenter] & his three men here, they have got the frame of kitchen up. tis 16 × 20. James help them all day. * * *

Sat
8

* * * we retire to sleep, our hearts filled with sorrow, yet with a prayer and trust that all will end well. James has one of his fits of—well I do hardly know what—whenever he has to pay out any money for any thing he seems to think, I ought to get every thing for myself & the Children without calling on him for it. Henry & Sarah went out & got him to come in, they were afraid he would hang himself—well he *did*—as he has done many times before—get a rope &

threaten. Alas! the trial to get along with such a disposition. we can only know & trust that God will help us to brave it through. he does not want the Children to go to school. thinks there is no need of it—but wants them to stay at home & work—tis well for all to work—yet it seems to me we are placed here on this earth, for something higher than merely to use our hands, toil and toil—merely to eat, and die in debt to our brains—to hoard up money—he does not like me to raise turkeys because I use the money they bring to send the Children to school. I *do pray* that I may *know* and *do right*. they love to go to school—with Gods help I will try to educate them that they may through life have the advantage of a good education, with their noble hearts, their virtue and industrious habits. . . . James told me to pay Mr Trenchard. I could not make the right change with his money therefore, I took the money that I got for one of my birds & a turkey (2.50) to pay them. I told him how I done—he flew in a minute—said now I was planning to get all of his money again—that I grabbed every cent he got. most truly I never spent one cent of his—except to buy something necessary to wear or to eat. I never get any clothing for my self only when I am obliged to—and then the money comes from my poultry—never give up—but strive for the right shall be my aim—commending ourselves to God I retire once more. Warm

Sun
9

Thank God we are all spared another day. Sarah & I drove up to Uncles a little while   Henry did not go. he said he would stay at home with James * * *

DECEMBER 1881

Mon
5

Henry went to [blotted]   their *sixth* term at the Academy commences to day. Sarah coughed so she could not go. her & I put down the parlor-carpet. it looks real nice. we filled our Bead hanging basket with flowers. *it* is beautiful. we put

up our lace curtains, too. James do usual work chore &c.
Pleasant

Thur
15

Do usual work. Children go to school. James chop & Chore.
Henry bought himself a pair of skates last evening. they cost
him 3.00. James said 'may be *you* can afford it, but *I* cant.
I always had to work and never spent money for such *trash*'.
I am real glad he has got them. we need be thankful for him
& Sarah being so pure and steady. they never yet strayed
one step from virtue   I feel they are noble and pure. may
they ever be so. saloons and bad places of resort has never
been any charm for them. all children and every one ought
to have some thing for diversion, not ever the monotonous
routine of all *work*. I can not be thankful enough for their
good name and so worthily bestowed. *I* will as ever do all *I*
can to help them. Cold.

Thurs
22

Do usual work. finish writing another story. "Sunshine after
Shadow or How we spent Vacation," of 3825 words. It takes
at the rate of ten minutes to copp [*sic*] 125 words, & about
the same to compose . . . 31.25 evenings at 2 hours each
evening. Well I will know whether they are worthy their
acceptance for publication or not, after awhile. the offer is
$1000.00 for the *two best stories* one for boys & the other
for girls. * * *

Sun
25

Christmas. We have no presents to day. tis too bad, but may
be we can another time. it does seem lonely indeed, to go
no where and no one come here. we can only hope it will
not always be. Children and I will try another year if all is
well to make a party. Tis a beautiful day.

JANUARY 1882

Thur
12

Sew & do usual work. * * * Henry brought the stories that
I sent to Boston to me. they returned them, with a letter,

saying they had re'cd near 3000 manuscripts. Stories for the prize. there will be many disappointed. Cold.

Fri
13

James & I go to town   pay debts etc. I have my Bird-money (40.00) in the bank. only have *7.00* left of turkey-money to get clothes for myself. * * *

Sun
29

All at home: traveler call to dinner. well we hear Guiteau [Garfield's assassin] is found guilty in the first degree. woe to him. it seems to me very wrong to hang. 'tis murder in first degree too. Pleasant

FEBRUARY 1882

Wed
1

Tis a nice day. * * * I—well I have so much to do, do not know what to do first. Sarah has gone to a concert at City Hall, with Frank Mead   tis her first time to go any place with a young man. I hope she may never go with worse. he came for her with Covered Carriage. Very Pleasant.

Fri
3

* * * I do usual work. Children & I go to the Lyceum this evening. . . . James stayed around town & waited for us. *he might go* to the Lyceums as well as not if he *would. School & Lyceums* nor *meetings* has no charms for *him.* * * *

MARCH 1882

Thur
16

* * * I went to Harriets twice. baked for her. there was not a mouth full cooked & nothing to cook until John got some flour. all hungry. *Harriet sick   abortion.* Dr Sherman her physician. tis a shame   Mud[24]

Sun
19

Sarah breaking out with measles. she feels real bad, too bad. Henry went out of doors, the first for 11 days. looks puny enough. James chore &c. I went to see Harriet, she looks very bad indeed. I am really sorry for her. *Ah* me! such is the life of most women. Pleasant

Mon
27

I went to Town with James   we carried the Queen Sewing-machine back to Mr Bronson. I bought The Domestic of Mr Cross. paid him 32.00 of my Bird money, owe him 3.00—. * * * Paulina Stephens is going to work for us awhile. * * *

APRIL 1882

Tues
11

My birth day. 44. no one has thought of it however. clean onions, sew, *work*. James & I went to Town this afternoon. . . . took my old Sewing machine to the Pawn-shop to sell. * * * Adieu years forty-three. [Three lines of verse follow.] I would like to know how Father & Mother are to night. with best wishes for all I retire. * * *

Tues
25

Sew & work * * * I took Paulina home, she is going to Wisconsin. now I will have to do my work alone again. have patience. keep up good courage Emmie! Sprinkle

MAY 1882

Sun
21

James has another freak of being *ugly* to his horses. *'tis too mean* to tell. I—well I did get very angry at him—am sorry tis so, yet I can not endure the seeing of kind animals abused. Sarah & I went with him to take Uncles plow home. Henry stayed & watched the bread to bake.

Minnie was mine, a colt. But a horse now, mine no more. * * *

JUNE 1882.

Sun
4

At home all day. after tea Sarah & I call at Harriets. I received a letter from Elisha Hawley wants me to go with him
to Mich—how *much* I would like to go. it makes me have
the *Blues* to think I can not go. Fear not but trust in providence to go some other time. What cant be cured must be
endured. Warm [25]

Fri
9

Tis evening, almost twelve oclock. all are asleep beside me.
I sit on the floor in front of Sarahs bed writing. how sweet
she sleeps & Henry does too may their dreams be happy
dreams ever, & James' too. may the Lords blessing rest
upon all. we have worked on dress, taken care of turkeys,
hoed in our garden. * * *

Sun
18

We are at home all day. Sarah & I go over in the field to get
our first mess of strawberries. Frank Mead here to tea. Sarah
does not fancy him very much, says 'he has too red a face
and blotches on it.' it *does* look bad. he seems however to
be a very kind hearted boy. think he eats too much butter,
at least Henry *says* he does. Warm

Sat
24

We read the 'Prize Story' (The little Keeper), in the Companion. *I have read many better stories*, it seems simple,
and quite improbbable. * * *

JULY 1882

Thur
13

* * * Harriet came in crying. she had a letter from brother
saying mother has a stroke of paralysys or palsy of the right
side—she can not talk and does not seem to realize any
thing. O dear: I wish I could have visited her and Father
once more, but alas—such is life—yet I know tis best perhaps to be content and reconciled with every thing. I could

Phrenological study of Henry Gillespie.

do her no good—yet I would like to be with her. my presence perhaps might comfort her in her last moments   may
it be Gods will that she survive this. if it is not, we trust that
all is right   it is well.

In sadness we retire to night, hoping the morrow may
bring good news of Mother

Tues
18

Harriet came this morning & brought a Telegram that—
Mother died this morning and is to be burried tomorrow. It
seems as though we can not give her up, yet we know tis
right. . . . He spared her to us to a good old age. 66 years
5 months and 11 days old. she prayed as all mothers
pray—'that she might live to see her children all settled in
life'. that prayer was answered. Harriet is the youngest—
she is 37—Tis the first time death came into our little
family circle, and this to take our dear Mother. we can say,
All is well. . . .

* * * Henry finishing inside of house. I got for him, yesterday, his Phrenological Chart or a discription of Character. Tis indeed a model Chart, gives him the highest rec-
ommendation as to the different scientific works which he
might do—or adopt as a business—to succeed in life. Mechanic. Piano-Forte Cabinet. Doctor. merchant. Photogra-
pher. in fact every thing scientific—even down to a dentist.
and said his hope was like the head-light to a Locomotive.
All of it *was good*. . . .

Wed
19

Tis four P.M. Alas, our Mother is dead and gone. Ere this
they have laid her away in the silent tomb. Mother fare you
well—you can be with us no more. it seems I can almost
hear the last sound of earth as tis thrown upon your coffin.
adieu adieu: until we meet above. I can think of no more
fitting words than those I composed two years ago when Mrs
Tyler died.

To my own dear Mother.

Adieu our dear Mother, forever adieu

Until death shall claim us as his own,
May we at last be prepared to meet you,
In heaven above where no sorrow is known.

Oh the thoughts of thy gentle voice Mother
We will cherish the more, now thou are gone,
To never forget thee, will 'eer be our prayer
That our lives be as pure & unblemished as thine.

Mother—how I wish I might have seen thee
Once more, ere thou went to thy long home.
Aye in that home I know thou will welcome me
Mother, when it please God to bid me come.

Though far away, I grieve for thee Mother
It seemed almost 'twould break my heart,
Yet I would not wish thee back Mother
Soon we will all meet to never part.
                    Cool & Pleasant.

* * * I do usual work, though I scarce can think what to do.

Sun 23   Tis a beautiful day, a cool breeze is gently blowing. I commenced to keep a journal in March 1858 just before I was
twenty (was 20 in April 1858), twenty-four years ago. Ah
me how every thing has changed since then. but the saddest
of all things which I have written in my journals was that
Mother died last tuesday. I bid my old journal rest with the
past, & welcome this new one. may its pages be filled with
all that is good and true. * * *

Sun 30   * * * Tis afternoon. Henry brought me a letter from brother,
he speaks about Mothers sickness and death. . . . he
speaks of dividing her things   it is sad indeed, yet tis
right. Henry seems to think that most of her things ought to
be given to Harriet, for he thinks she needs them. It may be
she needs them—yet—I think what belongs rightfully to
[me?] should not be given to some one else, except by the

owner of such things. I am sometimes sorry for Harriet, tis true she works hard & gets little recompense, & why. I can only say that two strong healthy persons without brains or good use of what they do with their hands can never prosper, it makes no difference how much may be given to them by their relatives—tis only bestowed to be used up through extravagance—and they only look for more when tis all gone. pity their ignorance. Raining

AUG 1882

Wed
2

* * * our new kitchen is very nice—but we do not need so much house room. I rather have the money to send Henry & Sarah to school, perhaps we can send them to school too—yet I can not see just how. . . . * * *

Sat
5

* * * we are all tired. Im sorry I get so nervous when I am warm cooking over the hot stove, it seems just as if I burned up twenty years of my life by the heat off the stove. but for all I must try to always be pleasant. tis so much better for the Children and me too. May thy will O Lord be done in all things. . . .

Mon
7!!!

I answered Ednas letter last night, after all the rest of us were in bed. * * * Henry & Sarah have gone to the Normal. it commences to day. costs each 1.00 to begin with. tis a preparatory school or review of studies of three weeks prior to examination of teachers for Certificates, they walk. . . . * * *

SEPTEMBER 1882.

Wed
6

James help Wm Scanlan thresh. Henry chore &c. Sarah & I go to Manchester get Henry some things to peddle, 10.66 worth & let him have 2.00 in cash. get *Sarahs pic-*

tures for a *chart*. we called at Harriets, hear her usual scolding. Warm

Mon 11

* * *Henry has gone—he started just twenty minutes past eight to go to Mahaska Co. west of south of here about *120* miles. Cousin Elisha Hawley lives there, at Rose Hill. Henry took his satchel (weighs 24-3/4 lbs) and started across the field south   I watched him to the railroad—took him just 20 minutes to get there. indeed I feel grieved to see him go and though I can not help but cry at parting with him, I feel tis all right—but it does seem pretty hard for him to start out in life so young. . . . Henry cried too as did Sarah & me at parting—Oh how thankful I am that they both are so noble & kind   I feel my prayers have not been in vain that all I have done is appreciated by them & now if I can help them to graduate in College—their education will be praise worthy & repay me for all my efforts. . . . James seemed sorry that Henry went, too. he said he felt sorry too, but that he was big enough & could take care of himself
     * * * now I must get my things ready to go the *the Fair*

Mon 18

This our *twentieth Anniversary. Uncle* was here to supper. I asked Harriets—they did not come. we had 3 kinds of premium-cake, pie & Turkey. * * * we got a card from Henry he is at Traer [a town halfway between Manchester and Rose Hill] & is well. . . . * * * In thought to day, I feel as young as I did twenty years ago, though care & hard work has told upon my then youthful looks. then my hands were like a lilly—now they are like a faded rose. yet tis all right. I have now a son & daughter just as fair as I was then. . . .

OCTOBER 1882

Wed 11

Sarah help do the work   I canned my grapes have twenty-five cans. 100 lbs would can about 33-1/3 qts. 3 lbs to the can, at 5-1/2 cents per lb a can is worth 35 cents counting

& can too, besides three or four hard days work—tis cheaper to buy sauce of all kinds already canned. costs .50 per can to put up peaches, can buy them for 30. * * *

Fri
13

Sarah & I went to town twice. I received a box of some of Mothers things. . . . I will keep those little relics that Mother kept, in remembrance of her I love. she is gone. I can see her here no more. It seems too bad that she worked & worked so many years and the things she intended for us (her girls) are to be kept by Agnes & Henry, let them go. tis all we can do. I am sure they will not enjoy them.
* * *

Saturday
14

* * * Sarah & I go to Harriets. she got 14 dresses, 3 bonnets, a close [*sic*] basket full of white clothes, 4 prs of shoes, rubbers, 1 Broche, shawl and quite a number of other things (about five times as much as I did). Harriet came & saw what I got, Sarah & I went to town, sent pair drawers & socks to Henry. * * *

NOVEMBER 1882

Wed
1

Tis 20 minutes past nine   Sarah started at 5 minutes past nine to go canvasing for her Album. . . . though I grieve that she has gone, I feel tis all right. she wants to do what she can to make money so as to get ready to try to go to College. . . .

Yes they are both gone. . . . O but I miss their society so much, though if I know they are doing well, I feel better about it. now I must go to work. . . .

Wed
8

James help Sarah & I put down sitting-room-carpet. *hard work*. I went to town with James this afternoon. we bought a new stove. 'tis a Coal Stove   name of it is The West-Point

Base Burner. it is real nice, though too high a price for such a stove. $44.00 . . . . * * *

Mon
27

Nearly Finish Sarahs Cloak. she done small washing &c. James draw manure & chores. Pleasant   Henry came home just as we had sat down to eat our supper, he said "how do you do?"—we were all glad to see him. he is well.

Thur
30

Thanksgiving. James going to Harriets, Sarah Henry & I going to mr Cunninghams. Cold.

DECEMBER 1882

Sun
3

* * * Henry Sarah & I went to Anamosa last Friday to visit the *State Penitentiary*, there are 203 prisoners there all at work. . . . Tis indeed sad to see men & boys—that look as though they ought to be bright stars in society—shut up—yes every night must be locked in a dismal prison cell—away—as it were—from the world. I often wonder why, can not all *do right*. no I do not wonder that either. I more wonder why there is not *more there in that dark place*, when I think how many parents drive their noble sons and daughters away from their homes   send them into the world alone, long before they can live unaided by the protection of parents. . . .[26]

Thur
21

* * * Tis now half-past-eight P.M. Henry & Sarah have gone to Mr Smiths to a party. Harry Bird came, with Mules & Cutter, after Sarah.—Henry said he 'didnt bother to take the girls—cost too much.' I only wonder if he will always think so. *Snow*, & tis *raining*

Fri
22

finish Henrys pants, commence vest, make 4 pies. * * * Children got home last night 2 A.M. too late by two hours.

they think such parties are about as I used to think of them. too much bussing. Colder

Sun
31

Well, I have ended the year in *work*. made bread, pies & cake, dressed a turkey etc. * * * May every year prove a blessing to all, especially Henry & Sarah. . . .

JANUARY 1883

Sat
20

Rip up the delaine dress that was Mothers. (the one I gave her sixteen years ago)   I bought it when I lived at Uncles 22 years ago. am going to make it over and trim it with black. * * *

FEBRUARY 1883.

Tues
6

* * * Sarah received her Phrenological Chart last evening she is highly pleased with it. I *am* so *glad* she has got it, it is a splendid examination. the principle things they told her to do as a profession is to study *Medicine* first, *Teaching* second, *Short-hand* & reporting third, for professions. only think of it both my Children *Doctors*—well I am proud of it & will help them all I can. . . . If Mother had have lived until to day she would have been sixty-seven years old.

MARCH 1883

Sat
10

Finish my third bird-cage. they are real nice (made of wire & tin). Cost just $.65 each, the hooks and springs $.40   tis worth $2.35 each to make them. * * *

Sun
11

All at home . . . . Last Thursday—I sold 21 lbs of dried apples that Mother sent to me, for $2.10. I want to get some memento with it that I can keep—tis the last Mother ever done for me, to dry those apples. * * *

Sun
25

We are all at home to day. The time as usual spent in reading and work. * * * James is at the barn, he went without his supper because of a very unpleasant time we had—tis too bad—but I can not always endure everything   he would turn us all out of doors if he could. (when a man lays his hands hold of his wife & Children I think tis time something was done.) especially Henry—& for nothing—only that he wants him to do kinds of work that he can not. we must not despair. I hope and trust all will be well at last. they want to go to College—and I will help them, all I can, to go. . . .

Tues
27

I finish my night-gown &c. go to Town with James. he feels better natured—I am thankful he does. I *sometimes think* tis *a real disease that some people have to have a time every so often.* they seem to get so full of some undefinable thing they *must explode.* * * *

Thur
29

Beautiful morning. my head aches. I will try to be happy. * * * Jas doing chores, will try to believe tis natural for him to fret & find fault. . . . Henry got his paper, (*The Fayette Union*) last evening, in it is *his Article* on *"Temperance Reform."* he is proud of it, yet says not a word. it is indeed nice that Mr Butter published it. we *are* proud of it, espicially Sarah & I. there comes the *sweet. all* is *not* bitter. * * *

APRIL 1883

Wed
11

Am forty five to day. tis past nine. All have gone to bed only me I am writing. * * *
    I am as old now as Mother was when I came away from

home. how changed since then. our family circle was then broken. and now Mother is gone, gone forever.

MAY 1883

Thur
3

We all work. James chop wood & chore. Henry help me clean & fix an old Bee-hive. * * * Sarah received a Certificate to teach school. I *am* glad, average 85%

Sun
6

James churn & go to Uncles to get team. Henry, Sarah & me go to Meeting, drive Mr. Hynes' team. an alarm of fire was given during services. about 3/4 of the Congregation were not long in getting out of doors, at indignance of the preacher. he said they lacked faith & that he sometimes thought Satan had something to do with such things. * * *

Mon
7

Sarah wash & do work in house, Henry help me plant my garden seeds. *James plow.* I am going to sleep up stairs to night, hope I will sleep better. * * *

Fri
11

Sarah and I paint porch. James plow in forenoon. Henry plow in afternoon (finish above the railroad.) *tis his first trial at plowing*   took him from one to seven. James is sick with piles. * * * Henry says "he rather tramp or work for a dollar a day at carpenters trade than plow." Pleasant

Tues
15

Sarah wash, Henry help me set out raspberry bushes. . . . Henry has felt grieved all day. James must misuse him or some one else, about every week. he told Henry he was here living on him—and he must leave etc. it is the first time I ever saw Henry mad, and I do not blame him—he told James he would not go until he got ready. nor shall he. . . .

Wed
23

* * *

Sarah & I call at Harriets. she got a letter from *Brother Henry*   he says he starts for Tennessee: thence to Arkan-

sas, then to the Indian Territory, in about ten days in pursuit
of a home. he wrote *'they had sold their place* and it gave
him *a chance to look* for a home.' More likely it gives him a
chance to spend the rest of *What Father & Mother worked*
for, I feel as if tis the last of their earthly possessions, gone,
gone—. . . .

Thur   * * * Sarah and I went to Mrs James Smiths visiting this
24   afternoon. Mrs S—— really has the *blues.* Im sorry for
                her. another victim to the sorrowful fate of man. being all
                I—while family may work, & work,—and yet have no
                credit. * * *

Thur   Half past two. I went, this morning to take Henry and his
31   tools to Mr Lawrences'. *Henry* is going to work for *Mr
                Parkhurst* at the Carpenters trade. he is to have 26.00 per
                month (26 days) and expences paid besides. he said 'good-
                bye Ma. Ill come home when I get hungry,' & laughed. I am
                glad for his sake he has a chance to earn something for
                himself, that he can feel he can use as he chooses. he would
                gladly work at home, could he do it to any advantage. but
                he might stay here & work early & late the year round and
                James would think him paid if he had enough to eat and
                common clothes. . . .

almost seven. supper ready. James has one of his crazy
spells again. he has got the idea into his head that he wants
a deed of the place. I think I had not best to give it to him,
but Ill try to do right about it, I want it so we will all have a
home while together. then if Henry & Sarah both outlive
James & me it shall belong to them equal. . . .

James also has another idea that he will come to want or
be turned out of doors—. no one will ever turn him out of
doors—as long as he lives. he knows he will have a home
here and none but himself ever thought otherwise. I do hope
and pray, if it be Gods will, I may do right,—and that I may
always keep my right mind. . . .

CHAPTER SEVEN

"No Home Here": 1883–1888

The final section of Emily Gillespie's diary records the growing tension between her aspirations and values and those of her husband, James. James Gillespie announced in 1883 that he wanted back the "deed of the place" that he had signed over to his wife in 1874. Emily Gillespie, on the other hand, wanted to retain the deed "so that we will all have a home while together." The complex reasons behind this tension over the deed unfold in the last part of the diary, as do the differing perceptions the Gillespies held of their property—a place versus a home.

Home in 1883 was a fine large house, the Gillespies' third, built in 1876. When all its additions were completed, the two-story structure contained two thousand square feet and was decorated with spacious covered porches. Emily Gillespie took pride in furnishing the house. She wrote in her diary on June 22, 1881, "in fact it seems at home, to have nice things." She continued, "I never saw any thing *too* nice for *me* yet," in response to James's criticism of a new carpet she and Sarah were installing. (The "Brussels carpet for my parlor" was purchased with $22.75 of Emily Gillespie's poultry profits after she had paid $25.55 for taxes, according to her account book.) Their home was becoming the stage upon which the Gillespies argued their differing aspirations. While they had successfully weathered the economic crisis of the 1870s and were in prosperous midlife, they had increasingly divergent views of what they had been laboring for.[1]

While James Gillespie's opinions can only be inferred from his critical comments as recorded in Emily Gillespie's diary, her desires were clearly articulated and enacted. For her children, she wanted the highest degree of education possible and was willing to help them financially. Although the Gillespies were country people, Emily Gillespie enrolled her children in the private Manchester Academy and encouraged their participation in activities such as the Lyceum, something she had enjoyed as a young woman in Michigan. Her child-rearing philosophy of nurturance and rational discipline was continued in her support of Henry and Sarah as adolescents.

For herself, Emily Gillespie took pride in her domestic and farm production accomplishments and renewed her interest in drawing. While she seemed unable to totally indulge in her artistic endeavors (she recorded the hours spent on a drawing and counted words as potential prize profits in her fictional attempts for *Youths Companion*), Emily Gillespie pursued her interests despite her perception of living a "hermits life." Ironically, as her physical home became more comfortable, Gillespie found it increasingly confining compared to the cultural offerings of Manchester. Although the Gillespie farm was less than two miles from town, the effort needed to get horses and wagon, energy and escort often overcame Emily Gillespie's desire to "go more in public." There was also a social gulf between city folk and country people that probably frustrated Emily Gillespie's aspiration "of being any higher in society than merely to be always at home."[2]

A similar gulf was growing on the family level between Emily Gillespie and her kin. She criticized her sister Harriet McGee's husband, who had lost his property and now rented a nearby farm, and she was upset when James helped his sister Margaret Doolittle's family. After Emily's mother's death in 1882, a rift opened with brother Henry Hawley over his management of the Michigan homestead.[3]

Closer to home, Emily Gillespie's growing sense of separation from James enters the journal in subtle shifts of language that reveal her changing perception. For example, her Christmas Day entry of 1875 codifies the gulf between Emily and the children on one side, James alone: "Jas wished us all Merry Christmas. we wished him the same." It is impossible to know from the early diary how long this tension existed in the household, although Emily Gillespie's allusions to sadness and the blues may have been her elliptical attempt to remember hurts without disloyally detailing them. But at last the quarrel—perhaps the secret to be buried—pours out into the life record. The growing length and vehemency of the daily entries indicate both the rising level of hostility between the Gillespies and the emotional relief Emily Gillespie found in her diary as her "only confident."

JUNE 1883.

Frid
1

Friday. Half past seven. well I begin this June morning in sadness. James did not come in to supper last night nor to his breakfast this morning. he will not answer when spoken to. he has done his chores and gone with the team up west, but I do not know where. It is indeed trying to my nerves to live as I have had to for years. I am sorry it is so but I think something will have to be done. I do hope & pray it may be for the best. I think he has gone to Uncles. I dare not give him a deed of the farm, but want to do right. I did not sleep but a little while last night. laid awake till after two—and then woke at every sound. yes I have not dared to go to sleep many a night, and it wears me out—I feel tis not right to live so. . . .

Mon
4

We are all up early this morning. Sarah and I do the work, James churn. we went with him to town   bought a pair of long-wristed-kid-gloves for Sarah cost 1.25—and a pair just like them (only a little soiled), and a pair of 2-buttoned-kids for myself, cost 1.25. we stopped and fished awhile   James did not wait for us, caught 9 fish & walked home. * * *

Thur
7

* * * Sarah & I called at Harriets. not much pleasure in going to see her. she is a perfect slave to work, feeds hogs & calves, *milks eight cows night and morning.* poor foolish girl. I too once was no wiser. James chop wood at the door. *would that every thing might be as pleasant as to day.* we are all at home to sleep to night. Pleasant

JULY 1883

Wed
11

* * * Sarah is asleep. I do hope she will enjoy going to the Normal & that she will get a certificate, because she would be disappointed if not. I would so like for her to stay at home

with me, yet if she wants to teach, I am willing & wish her the best success. no no I would not keep my children at home away from doing what is right & best for them to do, though I am so lonely without them. yes I will help them all I can.

How well do I remember, dark days of youth
I could get nothing to do—almost despaired.
And well do I remember too, the happy truth
That most my life is happiness treasured.

Sat
21

* * * I got a letter from Edna, she says: her boys are like men, that they work like nailers. that she supposes Sarah helps me lots & that Henry is big enough to carry on the farm. carrying on the farm is about as high a position as Edna can think of. it is all right, those that like it. for me I like some other occupation better and so do Henry & Sarah too. . . .

Tues
27

I took Sarah to school this morning. * * * I had so much to do this morning I got real nervous, let the tea-kettle of boiling water fall on the floor, burned the mutton too. Henry says "Ma Im sorry to see you feel so" Sarah says "Im sorry commenced to go to the Normal there is so much to do." . . . I must try to never get nervous, it makes every thing seem bad. I will try to ever be pleasant & make it bright as I can for Henry & Sarah. . . .

Tues
31

Away goes July. tis a nice day. Sarah walked to Normal James raking hay. I am writing in the midst of work on all sides. my chicken (old hen) is boiling. * * *

AUGUST 1883.

Fri
10

Half past eight. I am *real grieved. I started to take the girls* [Sarah and Miss Gibbons of the Normal] *to school. we had*

gone about half a mile, they said they rather go on foot than
ride. James jerks and hits Beauty with the pitch-fork and
hollows at her so much that she is almost uncontrollable. she
jumps & scringes at every noise & every move as if afraid she
was going to be kicked or pounded. I may talk & reason—tis
of no avail—and my tears for the team seems all in vain. I
can only hope & trust it may be better sometimes, though I
fear that cruel spiteful disposition of James' will never allow
him to have a nice team.

    * * * Beauty got so she went all right before I got home,
but tis too hard work for me to have to break her over every
time I drive her, I can not when James uses her. * * *

Wed
15

Well I am about as tired as I can be, pull onions etc. * * *
I called at Harriets a few minutes when I was looking for my
turkeys. O dear! she does seem to have fallen from all the
refinement she ever had. . . . she was driving an old horse
(round & round she followed it) to churn. she looks more
like a beggar than any thing else. a perfect Slave to mans
will & hard-work. indeed I am sorry. I do think woman
ought to retain enough of their pride to keep themselves in
a shape proper to their sex. no woman need to get so low as
to do such filthy work, I should despair if my children, when
I am gone, should remember me less than nobody in society—I would be as high in looks, in acts, and thoughts, as
nature will allow. . . . * * *

SEPTEMBER 1883

Mon
3

* * * *Henry has made up his mind to attend the College at*
Adrian Mich. if he goes I do hope he will have good success.
him & I went to town. he bought a *trunk* 7.00 & a *pr shoes*
3.50. I got cloth for him a suit of clothes. Warm[4]

Sun 9	Have cooked all day, tis now 15 minutes past five. I got as good a dinner as I could, Sarah helped me. Henry went to meeting . . . his trunk & Valise are packed—all ready to start James is after the horses now to take Henry to the cars. . . .
Mon 10	Just six A.M. James doing chores. Sarah not up. I am writing, tis a beautiful morning. Henry is not here. . . . he is just about entering the great city of Chicago, but 17 years since I was there. * * *
Thur *13*	Sarah & I go to the fair James churn & take butter to market. we rode home with him. he did not like it because we walked this morning. do not think he cares so very much about the *jant* [jaunt] as the thought of the people seeing us. *I* think it *much harder* work, to work in garden & *other* work I do, than to walk to town, *that*, however, is quite unnoticeable. tis not as public. *Well*, we had a good time, saw & visited as usual at fairs. * * *
Sun 16	Sarah went to meeting, heard a *mulatto* preach. she brought to me a card & letter from Henry. he wants his tools & says he got there & settled in his room all right. he has a job of repairing the College doors & windows, etc. his studies are Rhetoric, Trigonometry, Latin and German. * * *

OCTOBER 1883.

Thur 4	Work. finish writing an article on "Womans Sphere", 26 pages. Sarah fixing over her bunting dress. James chore & chop wood. he is tired & has one of his bad spells again. I am sorry and hope he will feel better in the morning. it makes my blood run cold & I shake like a leaf as did Sarah,

too. * * * James said—'Give me what you have of mine & you may have the rest'. I said, 'I do not consider I have any thing of yours'—'dont eh, then you & I are done forever on earth'. I sometimes hardly know what to do.

Sat
13

Tis evening. I feel better to night. I was real sick yesterday. I have had a real nervous-chill every day for over a week. was afraid I would have a fever. my head feels bad yet. the top seems pressed as if my brain was swolen & I think it does. * * *

Sat
20

Sarah do most of housework. James churn & go to Town. I cut rags. *takes 10 days to cut 40 pounds*, & 'tis *disagreeable nasty hard* work. Cold and Pleasant.

NOVEMBER 1883.

Sat
17!!!

Sarah and I do the work. I sew on Henrys coat 1 hour. patch James' coat & pants. * * * we attended the funeral of *Dr Reynolds*. . . . The church was crowded full, almost every woman and nearly all the girls too cried. in my opinion the Dr was to them a physician as was H. W. Beecher a minister. it indeed looked ridiculous. I could see nothing sublime about it. * * *

Sun
25

* * * The first thing Sarah and I done *yesterday* was to go to Mr. Porters to let him know she will teach. she is to have $130.00 for teaching 4 months (80 days) to commence monday morning, the 26th of this month. We then went to see if she could board at Uncles, he said she might & that he would not charge her much. we came home. I finished Henrys clothes. . . . took me just 49 hours to make coat, pants and vest. I hope Henry will like them. I do hope Sarah will have good success in her first school. . . . Sarah get a letter from Edna too. Edna asked Sarah if my hair is gray and if I wear glasses. she wears glasses, is gray & smokes. I hope my eyes may keep as good as they are. yes my hair is *gray*. Hail.

Mon 26

* * * Tis eight o'clock P.M. Dear-a-me Sarah is gone to night. the evening seems so long. I went to Harriets after supper a couple of hours. * * * How much more a teacher can get now than when I first commenced to teach   I commenced Monday, May 7th 1855. I received $6.00 per month (22 days). Sarah gets, now for a month (20 days) $32.50 5.4166 + times as much. * * *

DECEMBER 1883.

Sun 2

Sarah has a great time arranging her program etc for teaching. I am so glad & thankful she had such good success last week, the first two or three weeks always seems to be the worst   she says she hardly knows how to get them to come in promptly at bell call, and wants to change some in their seats. I told her of several ways I thought would be good, and that she must act on her own judgment. * * *

Wed 12!!!

. . . *my head is dizzy. feels bad.* * * * May the Lord be with and guide us all, especially Henry & Sarah that they are gone. . . . the house seems so big. nine tenths of it is used only for storage, as it were. we only occupy two rooms to sleep in—the kitchen serves for all else. south wind. now I must write to Henry. a good-night to him & Sarah. though I can not hear them answer, I think they remember me too and often wish to see Ma. Pleasant.

Wed 19

Mr Evans came for my turkeys, let him take 59 goblers and 50 hens. they weighed 1099 lbs. am to get for them $109.90. . . . It costs about $25.00 to raise 150 turkeys & 75 chickens. [Emily Gillespie's calculations follow.] Think it pays to raise poultry. it requires *care* for about five months. * * *

**Fri
21**

Do the work as usual, mop. I see after I pay for feed, and for several things bought, send some to Henry & pay for Sarahs things that I will have about twenty dollars left for myself. here is to days settle-up etc.

To James for feed	21.00
Cash to Henry	50.00
" " Sarah	2.00
For Sarahs Books	3.85
" " Journal	2.50
" " Shoes	2.00
" " Velvet	2.00
" " Christmas Toys	1.50
For Bazar	3.20
Myself a Journal	1.50
	89.55
109.90 − 89.55 =	20.35

It seems good to make ends meet at the end of each year. Tis better to have 20. ahead than to be out 20 dollars. * * *

**Sat
22**

Harriet called, this morning when we were eating breakfast. she was going to Town, so were Sarah & I too. James took us all, *real cold.* * * * offered James 21.00 for feed he furnished for turkeys, he said he would not accept it, so I will get him some clothes. * * *

**Sun
23**

Evening. Sarah has gone to stay with Harriets children until John comes from Manchester   he took *Harriet* to the *Depot*   she starts to night to go to Fathers. I wish her & them a *good visit.* Oh, how I *would like* to go too, but I can not now. it is to me a greater pleasure to help Henry & Sarah to go through College. . . . * * *

Sun
30

James, Sarah & I at home. * * * I went to see how John & the Children get along. cooked Chicken & got dinner for them. I could not leave Henry & Sarah like that. * * *

Mon
31

Goodbye old year. it is the last time we can write December 1883. We are thank [*sic*] for all the blessings bestowed upon us, and if may be we hope to make the New Year better. may no future year ever be worse than has been this old one. Sarah is teaching. Henry in College, and James has plenty to do, and I too. my health seems good only a *dizzy feeling in my head.* . . . * * *

JANUARY. 1884.

Thur
3

* * * Harriet came home. I went up to hear the news. she said Henry [Gillespie] was at Fathers & looking *real well.* . . . But of Father—by what Harriet says—he can not enjoy life very much. Henrys [Hawley] boys call him *bad* names. it is too bad, & brother—he is a drunkard. dear, dear, why will he so throw himself away to vice, when he knows the folly and the dreadful consequences. Im sorry, indeed I am, but what more can I do. * * *

Fri
4

Wash, fry cakes, mop etc. James do chores. it is 20 below zero, has been that all day. 3 P.M. James just gone after Sarah. he said if he "freezes take care of yourself the best you can. next time may be you will get some one that will suit you better." I never said I wasnt suited, & I do not like to hear him talk so. . . .

Thur
17

Do the work, sew. James do chores chop & help me clean out the hen-house and make hens-nests. *I am tired* * * *
    I was speaking . . . to James this evening—when he said

in one of his tones, which means he does not like to hear a word said, "It seems to me your voice has a peculiar *whang* to night." I asked him why? he did not reply. Dear old journal, none but you greets me a welcome, when Henry & Sarah are gone. it is not very pleasant, to always keep still & only listen.

Wed
23

* * * *Received a letter* from [Henry], and sent one to him, & also sent some pieces on "Woman Suffrage" and my article on same subject, he is to debate on the question, "That if the Negro votes, why not woman?" * * * *Sent $1.00* to *M. A. Dauphin, New-Orleans Louisiana* for a ticket-drawing of February. Should I be *so* fortunate as to *draw* a prize, I shall try to take care of Father the rest of his life, & hope for wisdom to do what is right.

Mon
28

Sew & work. James chore & take Sarah to school. dear! I almost wish sometimes she did not have to go. it is so lonesome when she is gone, & Henry away too. . . . James & I went to Town. he is better to me this winter—than he has been before since—well I can say—since we were married, I *am thankful.* pleasant

FEBRUARY 1884

Fri
8

have been cleaning up my birds & cages. I feel sad to day,—last evening James was making calculations to build a hog pen and shed, as to the cost &c. I said "Henry may be home time [*sic*] to build it?" his reply was—"There's no use your talking about Henry working for me. *him* & I cant work together," and several other things he said—but no matter. I did not say another word—but O! it seems too bad. . . . he does not like either of their ways of work—

they are too fine, too high—for him to comprehend. . . .
* * *

Thur
14

Valentines day, James asked me what he should give me for
a valentine, said a kiss was good as anything & gave it me.
* * * I had thought I would go to Mich about this time, but
think I will not go as long as Sarah feels discouraged about
her school. James has gone after her. The Director had
been, or rather was there to see her, said Cooks, McGees &
Trips wanted the school closed so as to save the money for
next term. I am glad Sarah would not do it. . . . * * *

Mon
18

Evening. have been gone all day James take Sarah to
school. I went too . . . then go to Mrs McGees. * * *
McGees acted guilty enough. Harriet told James the reason
they wanted to close the school, Irvin told them yesterday,
"was to *Spite Sarahs mother*, they would let her know she
was no smarter than anyone else. they liked Sarah though
& could not find one word of fault." I can only say to them,
they will spite themselves the worst. I never laid a hairs
breadth in their way, & I feel far above them. they will get
their reward.[5] * * *

MARCH 1884.

Wed
5

James has gone to take Sarah to school. I intend to start for
Mich this evening. . . . May Sarah & James get along all
right & I hope to find Henry well & doing well. . . .

To day is April 21. I will copy my visit to Michigan.

Thur
6

Left Manchester 7.20 P.M. last evening. . . . Arrived at
Fathers about five o'clock A.M. walked on track half a

mile. . . . Father did not know me at first, but is real glad
to see me. Aggie [Agnes Hawley, brother Henry's wife]
looks real bad. she seems glad too. *I* am glad to see them
all and expect a real good visit. . . .

Fri
7

Had a good rest last night and Agnes feels better. she has
to be up too much nights for health. Henry (brother) is gone
off on an excurtion   was sorry not to have seen him. * * *
Father is stronger and looks better than I expected to find
him. he walks with two canes, can get in wood &c. he is
just the same as ever to talk on subjects of Religion, Politics, Temperance and Woman-Suffrage, he still thinks it is
not quite in place for a lady to vote, yet he said if ever he
had an opportunity he would vote for me to be President for
he thought I would make a good one. Aggie believes about
as I do, she has her heart and hands full to live. . . .

Sun
9

* * * Agnes said they did not look for me at all. I asked
her why. she said because Harriet had written—'that I
had given up comeing'. Agnes let me read Harriets letter.
It was written the 23 of February—& such a horrid letter
as it was to write. it is full of slander about Henry, Sarah
and me. I will not write such talk in my Journal. I have
often thought she was trying to make disturbance between
[brother] Henry, Edna,—well in fact, all of my folks & me,
there is nor truth in one word she has written. she can re-
pent at leisure, I shall never forget. * * *

Sat
15

* * * When we came to Morenci, yesterday, we stopped at
the Cemetery, to see where Mother is burried. . . . Mother
has nothing to mark her grave only three oak trees standing
on the lot, it seems sad indeed, that she worked so hard all
her life, and then to be so unappreciated, as to be burried
all alone, no tomb to even tell her name. if ever I can I will
get her one. * * *

Tues
18

It is evening, am at Cousin Elizabeth Hendersons. . . .
Henry [Gillespie] met me at the Depot. I was glad indeed to
see him, he looks as if he had been studying too hard,
though quite well, he has gone back to the College. . . . I
was happy to meet Sylvenus [Hamlin] at Lucys last evening,
though his hair & beard are silvered—he looks the same
pleasant look as he did twenty-seven years ago. he said
"Emmie—you like myself are older and hair white—I *am
glad to see you.*" we both visited all the evening, and stayed
with Lucy all night. . . . It seems almost that it has been
but a few days since we met, and the saddest for us to part
of any one I have seen. he bade me good-bye several times
just as he did the evening I went with him to a party in
Canandaigua, 19 years old I was then & he 24. I can but
say Au-re-voir. * * *

Fri
21

Am ready to go to bed. Elizabeth is tired & has plenty of
callers. we went to . . . the Lyceum at the College. . . .
Henry was assigned a declamation for the next meeting, I
am sorry he can not be with them, for he seems to be a
general favorite with all. it may be for the best. . . . Elizabeth is a *genuine Universalist.* . . .

APRIL 1884

Sat
5

Just up—Father is out trying to see to the chores. poor
old man—how lame he is. he lies on the lounge a great
share of his time. Aggie and I sat up and talked 'til most
twelve last night. they are much discouraged about Henry
[Hawley]. I fear he is drinking and spending all the little
they have left. *what will they do.* Aggie says she has not
more than $40.00 and Father has only $5.00. . . . Evening
again. Henry [Gillespie] & me went to Morenci this fore-

noon, got some corn, oatmeal and rice for Father & Aggie. after dinner Sarah Baldwin & me went to Robert Sims'   he has his 3rd wife. * * *6

Tues
8

Am at Agnes'   Father helped Henry put the hoops on our box of things. I have my little [spinning] wheel. it was Great Grand-Mother Garlicks then Grand-Mother Bakers; then Mothers; and she gave it to me. * * * this afternoon we drove around where we lived when I was at home. I thought I would stop & see the old house once more. no one was at home. it did indeed seem sad that not one of us remained to welcome me there. when I came away in 1866, Mother stood in the door. she said "good-bye Emily" through her tears. and now she is not here. no, no, she closed the door to never open it again for me. . . . We stopped in Canandaigua to see Dr Chappell   he was standing in the door when we drove up to his office, he knew me in an instant. he talked of old times, of the days when he came to see me. he said "he was sorry to see me look so bad and if I was careful may be I would be healthier after awhile," that he wished we might have a longer visit—at last when we came away he said good bye and asked if he might kiss me. I too was sorry for him. he is just recovering from a stroke of paralysis. he cried and said "Emily this may be the last time we meet on earth." we are at Agnes' to night—Father & all are well. I think they will soon be obliged to break up their home entirely, & what will they do—no place to go—and nothing to live on. . . .

Wed
9

Evening [at Quincy, Michigan]. it is 18 years since I saw Edna. she scarcely knew me, nor I her. she looks as if she had seen *trouble*, it causes a sigh perhaps when we see that we are growing old—not in mind, may be—but nearer so much nearer our time to leave this world. Ednas boys are nice looking & work on the farm. they do not seem to care or respect any thing she says. she is a type of a slave to work & mans will. my head aches   Edna is making maple syrup. Snow & Cold

Thur
10

* * * we visit, but there seems to be something back some-where, as if some unpleasant feelings existed. I try to make all agreeable but Edna acts as if she had had orders what to do and say, and too she has lost all her pride in keeping her things tidy and clean. fate, fate; * * *

Mon
14

* * * Good bye to Michigan again. we start for home at eleven, hope to get there all right and to find James and Sarah well. it is warm and pleasant as summer. dear me the fumes of tobacco in a depot are enough to suffocate a per-son. Warm.

Wed
16

At home. we were glad to get here. . . . Harriet came down a few minutes this morning. I could hardly feel glad to see her after knowing she has written such untruths about Chil-dren & me. I am sorry she is so envious, yet I will try to treat her well & wish her no harm, and hope she may some-time see that I have never done aught to injure her, *for I never have*. Sarah has kept every thing all right. * * *

Sat
19

I went with James last evening to Mr Richmonds to settle calf-keeping account. . . . we were coming home through a brushy dismal place and talking about the calves &c. all as I thought was good nature & all right. when to my very un-pleasant surprise he said '*Emily* I believe you mean to kill me sometime, I want you to tell me if you do. I want to meet my God prepared'—I was perfectly terror struck, & though I did not really fear him, I was afraid he might attempt something wrong. I only said 'you have no reason for such unjust talk,' 'I *have* many reasons' he said. I asked him 'what are they', but he would not say. I *was very thankful* when we arrived *safe* home. it seemed like riding with a maniac in a *dark dark* night alone. and yet *not* alone for I feel protected by him who doeth all things well & guards us if we but ask Him. . . .

Tues
29

We were up early so that Henry could go away. they are to build a house for Mr Belcher about eight miles south of town. Henry said "I wish I did not have to go off to work." I wish he *could* stay at home, but it seems we can not always be together. if they go to College they will have to earn the money to pay their expenses. * * *

~~MARCH.~~ 1884. *MISTAKE* IT IS MAY.

Sat
3

* * * Sarah & I planted our melon seeds by *lantern light*. dear how tired we are, but it seems nice that we are all at home. Henry came, he has done well this week. we finished our garden about 10 this evening. tired, tired; tired; Warm.

Thursday
15

Half past 4 P.M. James is planting potatoes, Henry and Sarah are finishing fence, I am writing in my journal, old & true friend. I can scarcely believe that Father would have come here, but he *did* come last night about eleven o'clock. he said "he came to stay awhile until he hears what brother will do, that he has a box of clothes and my beauro come-ing." I believe thay have sent him here & that he intends to stay as long as he lives   I think a great deal of him and respect him though I feel it an imposition upon us all (after Henry [Hawley] has squandered all he had, then leave him, poor old man, in the streets.) we will trust that it will be all right. I will do the best I can and see what we can do about it, most surely I do not feel able to take care of him. my health is too poor and I can not concienciously keep Sarah at home to do the work. she wants to teach and earn something for herself, & it would cost more than we could earn to hire help. * * *

Tuesday 20

Sarah & I clean up, make up a bed in the sewing room for Father. it is nice   he feels very much provoked at Harriet, he says she tries her best to set him up against me but that she could not, he said one time when they were at home & Edna, Henry & Harriet were talking the worst they could about me, he told them all they had against me was that I knew more than all of them put together & if I did have a deed of the place I knew enough to keep it. * * *

Tuesday 27

* * * Sarah do most of housework. her and I clean up my beauro. father brought it to me it was mothers that she bought with money she got from her mother. When I was washing the last drawer (the same small one that I kept my trinkets in when I lived at home) I beheld on the underside of it where Mother had written on two diferent times that she wanted me to have her beauro when she was dead & gone   it seems to me as from the dead. One time was when she was fifty-seven years old, and the other she was sixty-one. Alas! it is sad that dear ones must die, but happiness to know we will meet again. I always felt that Mother loved me above all others, but could not know it until to day. it seemed almost when I read her gift to me that she came to tell me, that I might have proof that it *is* surely mine and *not* Harriets as she claims it to be. *it is well.* how glad father was too   he got to talking about everything, said he wanted to pay his way, that he wanted to stay here this summer and all he had I might have.
* * *

[The entries that follow, until the beginning of volume 10, January 1, 1885, are in a different hand. The handwriting appears to be Sarah's.]

JUNE 1884

Mon.
16.

James churn & chore. I went to town with him when we came home he commenced "What about Sarah" he said. . . . O dear, there is no use to worry, it is the same old story—want to divide up, is bossed, & everything else, anything to vent his feelings, I have felt for a number of days that he would say something, for he must have a time about so often. . . . He said, "when Henry is at home, he sits around & reads, or tinkers a little & Sarah *works* & tante fair.". . .

Tues.
17.

raspberries ripe, work in garden &c. Sarah work. * * * Sarah rode up to Sellens with Mr. Seger; it was nothing wrong, but it gives a chance for talk. am sorry the people are so fond of evil thoughts, one can hardly dare to speak to any gentleman even to be civil, especially in presence of the third person, how much better would be society if all could be free & innocent to speak & be sociable. a good night to Henry, Rain.[7]

JULY 1884

Tues.
1st.

there was a beautiful cloud encircled the eastern sky last night. * * * Henry came home abut 10 o'clock,—he is well but looks as if he works hard; he went to town this afternoon he commences working on the M.E. [Methodist] Church, will come home nights. *warm*

Mon.
7.

Sarah's birthday anniversary—19 yrs—it does not seem possible . . . I bought a toothbrush for her present, am glad I could get it & would like to have given her something better, how thankful I am she is so pure, so noble of purpose. * * * . . . I must retire, 10 P.M.—arose at 4 A.M. *18 hours work*—a long day. I dreamed I saw Mother last night,—she laid some silver dollars on the table to take off her bonnet, it seems she looked as natural as life & had been traveling. I took the pieces of money & took care of them, and to night while looking over some papers I found that *Ma* [Lorinda Gillespie, James's mother] had not given her right-of-dower for "right-of-way" to Railroad, it still must be good for her heirs of which there are 4—that must be the omen of my dream. I will see about it. all is well. light shower. I have concluded that the right of the railroad passing through our place belongs to me now for it [the deed to the farm property] belongs to me & I will see about it.[8]

Sat. | finish cutting Father's coat & vest, & Henry's coat, vest
12. | & pants. Sarah hang out clothes & do up the work. we
commenced to pick raspberries at 11:A.M. & quit at 7:P.M. sold . . . 30 qts. total worth $2.40 for 14 hrs. work . . . per hour . . . would be .438 while a man would want & get $2.00 for same time, *Equality.* * * *

Tues | Sarah & I pick berries, I canned 16 qts. this evening. * * *
15. | Father saw wood. I read in his paper (The Morenci Observer) that *Dr. Chappell is married* to Lovina Rorick & gone to live on his farm in Alegan Co. Mich. Alas! poor old man; his life is short at best & I fear will not be happy, for it seems to me no refined lady would have married him; he has palsy, is old, & large from excess in drinking beer; yet I think of him as physician my best friend & the news gives a feeling of sadness, I hope his wife will be kind to him,—though I believe she married him for his property; knowing that his days are few. * * *

Thurs. | * * * we were talking this morning on various things. I said
31. | I thought if I were able to fix it as I would like to I thought could raise 500 turkeys as easy as 100 now. Father said, "Why don't you fix it then? You've had the money." I said I had to use the money for things to wear & to eat but he still

persisted in a different answer. I *said* because of surrounding circumstances; then James had a chance to say that was the reason he was not rich &c. considerable was said until I told Father I had trouble enough to get along with my own family without anyone else helping. he said he was sorry & did not mean to make any trouble, I cried about it & Sarah did, too. . . .

AUGUST 1884

Sun
3.

9:00 P.M. am sitting on the floor at the end of Sarah's chest; she sits on it. we are writing in our journals, Henry & Father are in bed. Sarah & I tramped in the woods in search of blackberries,—found 3 mandrakes. well,—I cannot say I am quite happy—for James caught me alone & as usual commenced about the property   he said, "I am not going to do another year as I have this." I made no reply. "If you are going to give me any of this property back I *want* it." I said, "when you let me have the deed of it, I agreed to keep it, & have done all, & more than I was able to to help. I have done as I agreed & we have a good home; this dividing up has ruined many a family & I can't do it, but will settle, now, James how much money do you think you ought to have & let it all go?" "just say how much & we will have it righted," but he would not say because Sarah came in just as he had last spoken & he stepped in the barn, he *looked daggers*   O what a terrible look, he would take hold of me if he dared. . . . I dare not give him a deed for I know he would turn us all out of doors soon as he got it, such threats are dangerous weapons. I think I will see Mr. Bronson & get his advice, hoping for the best I retire to rest. sprinkle. cold.[9]

Fri,
8.

* * * I was alone all day; horses got in garden. Sarah came back to help get them out. am tired of so much work. I

sometimes wonder what *was* designed for woman to do, seems as if there is no end. * * *

SEPTEMBER 1884.

Sat.
6.

can tomatoes & make sweet pickles. * * * Father went up to Harriets; he is cross every time he goes there, James cut corn. Mr. Seger here to supper. Father said he thought if he was an Insurance Agent he better tend to his business & be gone not be visiting with women, I said if it was with *men* a half day it would be all right, & women liked to visit as well as men. * * *

Thurs.
18.

Our 23rd. anniversary. James churn, he took a fat cow to Mr. Work. Sarah & I went to the fair. Henry work on church; we saw him up on the spire, putting the vane on top; it looks dangerous but we hope no harm may befall him, that they may raise & finish it all right. we walk home & am tired. * * *

Sat.
27.

Sarah & I do the work. Father help James hoe corn, he has been very cross to me all day; will not answer anything only in an insulting way, as he does every time he goes to Harriets. I told him I was sorry but had stood it long as I could to be bothered by her & would try to do all I could to make it pleasant for him, but if he lived with me I thought it would be best for him to stay away from there. . . . I do hope Father may feel contented & enjoy himself. I do not mean to do wrong. may God's will be done & all for the best. I will tell Father in the morning I am sorry if I said anything to hurt his feelings,—if we get a carriage we will try to take him round about sometimes for he is an old man without a home. I could not see him suffer. . . . * * *

OCTOBER 1884.

[There are no entries from October 2 to October 6.]

Mon.
6.
1884.
Oct.

O dear I can hardly write in my Journal, last Friday noon Mr. Morse came for me to go to Manchester that Henry was hurt. O.O. he had fallen from the church spire—I could not be thankful enough that he was not killed. . . . The first place he hit anything was 9 ft. then 20 ft. to the roof & from there it was 45 ft. *Oh, terrible.* I have been with him all the time. The first thing he said was when I asked him how he felt, "Oh, I guess nothing seriously" & in a minute he said, "Ma, I do not think it was any of my fault." . . . it is too bad, terrible to think of,—to fall 74 feet, not a bone broken. . . . he is seriously hurt it seems as if he is bruised in every place, O. how thankful I am that he was not killed & now if it be God's will may he get well all right & rational. I am thankful, too, for the kindness manifested by friends, hundreds have called to see him. words cannot express my thoughts. *Thy* will not mine be done & all is well. he is at Nelly Smiths. it is now about 20 minutes past 9, it is indeed the hardest time in my life. I could not cry, until this morning I cried myself to sleep, & it was relief to my overstrained brain. . . .[10]

Sat.
11.

we are at home, James got the omnibus to bring Henry in. Dr. Sherman came with us, O dear I never felt so bad about having to do anything as I did to bring him home before he could sit up, yet if he gets well I will feel so glad. He is very tired & is in more pain; it seemed as if the jar hurt his hip. cloudy. pleasant

Fri.
17.

James plow, Father saw wood. Sarah do the work, I help all I can. Henry can come in the kitchen on his crutches, is better. O, how glad I am. my hands are almost useless as to feeling. I do hope if it be right they may again be well as ever, that I can do my work. * * *

Wed.
22.

James plow. I help work. Henry gaining slowly. Father sarcastic & cross, thinks the weather cold. James looks at me with such a stare sometimes it almost makes me feel a fearful dread to see him. why, O, why is it & what can he be thinking of.

NOVEMBER, 1884

Sat,
1st.

10:00 A.M. Sarah knitting, Henry at barn. James plowing, & Father gone to Harriets, he is very mad. I told him some truth; he does not like to hear it but he must not come into my home to make trouble for I have enough to bear without it. . . . It is sometimes as much as I can endure such a care or continually being obliged to be on my guard to be able to be calm at all times—two such men to deal with. he commenced before Mr. Seger to tell his belief that if a woman voted she must bear the responsibility of supporting the family, etc. Mr. Seger came to our protection "that it was not a woman's duty to support the family as he termed it she more than half supported them in her care of the children etc, that the most of the responsibility was on her." no more to say. pleasant.

Tues.
18.

I do most of work. James husk corn, Henry pretty well, I am glad he is getting well. Father came here. he said he came to have a settlement. I told him if he wanted his things, they were ready any time, he said he wanted me to pack up the bureau & all his things that he had made arrangements to stay with Harriet this winter, that he had a good backer & had good counsel. I said the bureau was mine & I should keep it; he left right off & was very angry.

I told him Mother bought the bureau with money from her mother & it was never his; he said he would acknowledge that, he did not dispute it but "when she died it belongs to him." after he went away, I told James of it, one thing & another was said & finally . . . he commenced about being a waiter &c., that I had it all in my hands, meant to keep it along & then turn him off.[11] . . .

Wed.
19.

* * * Henry & I went to town, 'tis the first time he has been any place since he came home, he is real tired to night, O how thankful I am that he can get around again & hope he may never have another such a bad accident. I saw Mr. Carr [lawyer] & asked him about my bureau; he said not let them have it, but if I had possession of it to keep it. It seems as if they were possessed of an evil spirit. * * * there was a Barbecue, a cow roasted whole in Manchester today in honor of Cleveland being President.

Sat.
22.

* * * I put straw over grapevines, 'tis now evening   Jas. & Henry in bed. Sarah warming her feet, I writing. I felt so discouraged that I cried today two or three times,—there is relief in tears. I always try to be cheerful but it seems as if I have had almost more than I could endure this fall. Harriet & Father & the rest of my folks do so wrong; James talk as he does sometimes   Sarah soon to go away to teach; Henry's accident & he talks of going to work soon, too & I will be so lonely; & my hands & feet feel so bad, yet I think they are a little better. I hope & trust they will get well, & all will be well at last. I can say, *Thy* will be done & now to sleep. Rain all day.

Sun.
31.

11:30, o'clock. James has gone to take Sarah to Mr. Alcorns, she is to commence school tomorrow. . . . Henry is in bed, he has a cold; he carried out a part of drink to the turkeys & got sore, it was too bad, I am afraid it made him more lame. * * *

DECEMBER. 1884.

Wed.
3.

sew on my drawers & work, my hands feel real bad & in fact I have a singular feeling all over; when I rub my flesh it gives a peculiar sensation—a shudder—almost hurts. my nerves must be in a bad condition. I hope I may be better sometime,—am near sick today. work & I disagree. warm.

Sat.
13.

Benj. Smith came here. Father is about to sue me for his things, my bureau, too. I will have to let it go. . . . James & Mr. Smith went to see Father,—he is so mad they can do nothing with him; then James went alone, but just the same, now he has gone again this evening. I hope he will be more reasonable & that we can get along with him without serious trouble. James says Harriet is perfectly wild about it, & declares he shall not bring his things there.—I think she will get enough of her folly.[12] . . .

Wed.
17.

* * * James commenced his talk the first thing, said there was one thing troubled him a great deal, that he wanted to divide up & have what belonged to him. I told him, very well, I had stood this fuss every time we were alone long enough & I would divide up with him & give him a divorce if he wanted it. he said he did & that I would regret that I was like Father etc. . . . I said I would see when I went to town, I knew what was right but I would see [lawyer] Bronson. . . . * * *

Fri.
19.

sew on coat. * * * I *am* nervous today, I hardly can tell what course to pursue. I do not want to see a lawyer & make known the reason why I keep the deed of our place, nor can I endure much longer to be tormented about it. . . . O if I were only strong. Henry & Sarah dare not leave me alone with him. I asked him Wednesday his reason for doing as he does, & what I had done that was wrong. he only said, disinterested in his business & unfaithfulness to him. I

asked him how. he only said,—in a *good many ways*. well,
what is one? I asked. why by asking me to do things that is
not my business to do. tell me what things, I said. one is
filling the [stove] reservoir & keeping fire & you don't have
any thought about the calves or anything. "Well," I said
"there is no use—you have told me time & again you
wanted me to mind my own affairs . . . do you want me to
feed the calves, pigs & take care of the horses?" Ah, me,
there is no reason in him. I will try awhile longer & if he
still persists I will do the best I can. Cold.[13]

Sat.
27.

* * * when Henry & I went to town yesterday we got some
Christmas presents from Harry [Jeffers]. Sarah's was Byron's
poems, *very nice*—with a letter asking her to remember
him, it was fine language & of more than friendship in the
words. we all joined together & send him a year's subscription to the Phrenological Journal. * * *

COMMENCING JANUARY 1, 1885.

In the past year trials and sorrows has been ours to bear,
yet there were many pleasures intermingled, to day is clear
with sunshine and our surroundings bid fair for a bright and
happy New Year. Henry's was indeed a very sad accident,
his falling 74 feet from the Church Spire, on which he was
at work, the 3rd of October. . . . Sarah is away from home
this winter teaching near Edgewood, 14 miles. she enjoys
her school of 27 scholars and can come home Sundays,
though it is lonesome without her. . . . May we leave all our
sorrows and troubles with the Old Year and strive for right
and happiness in the new. * * *

Thursday
8

James do chores and go with Mr Bailey to his farm, he is
trying to sell Beauty. she is the nicest traveling horse we
ever owned. I *shall* feel *sorry* to see her go. * * * Mr Bailey

thinks Beauty too fast—am glad of it—but he wants Minnie—her I have thought so much of—she is mine by
right—but alas it is the same as it was with my beauro.
Father took it just because he could. . . .

Monday
12

James and I attend the funeral of Henry Fox. Rev Brindel
preach from 1st Kings—"a Woman was asked if it was
well that her husband should die, and she answered *it is
well"* * * *

Wednesday
21.

Do the usual work, sew on Sarahs dress. I *did* get real tired
& felt, well not really discouraged, but nervous—have always been *very sensitive* inconveniently so *many* times, at
any disagreeable oder, so much so that I have vomited time
& again from the effect offensive smell & Kerosine is one
thing & every time the lantern is lighted it *is disagreeable*
to me, & *too* I think it unhealthy & bad for ones eyes, therefore I always have used candles, though they cost about five
times as much. we mentioned about kerosine this evening,
James seems to think I imagine every such thing. . . . I felt
grieved about it & in spite of a great effort, I had to cry. . . .
I could not help it, it seemed as if my heart & head must
burst—O there *is* relief in tears. * * * Alas my new Journal
begins with sadness. May it end in happiness?

Friday
23

Henry went after Sarah this morning almost half past eight.
Harry [Jeffers] was going too. * * * I have cleaned up *all*
the rooms, made the (4) beds, washed, made pies etc.
James help me & done chores. O! if he could always be as
pleasant as to day how nice it would be. how thankful I am
that all is well to night. it reminds me of how Mother
watched my comeing home when I was gone, just as anxious
as do I for Henry & Sarah. they come. . . .

FEBRUARY 1885

**Wednesday
11**

Do usual work, sew, large ironing & keep up fires. James chore &c. bring an black sheep & twin lambs in the house had to sew bandage around her, she is bursted, it is not very nice to do such things, but it is too bad to let them suffer. * * *

**Thursday
12**

Near eleven P.M. I dreamed of seeing Edna last night. . . . *Now the omen.* I visited Emma Brook this afternoon—she told me that Harriet had received a letter from some relatives saying that *brother Henry had been* at *home for more than two months.* for all I have sometimes imagined he was there, I am astonished, that he can be what he is, and I do think it strange that *Agnes does not answer my letter.* it must be Henry will not let her tell where he is. Miserable, can only express my feelings to his apparent designs. I will call him Henry H. after this to not get him mixed with Henrys name. * * *

**Friday
13**

* * * I have just got my work done up—Birds & all asleep, the clock ticks as it has done for years, it is my only company *many times.* I wish Sarah could be home to night. . . . Harriet came out when Henry was passing there—asked him if we knew Henry H. is at home & that she is having a terrible time with Grand Pa. I *am* sorry—for all they have done & said I *do* wish them well & happy with all my heart. *Snows*

MARCH 1885

**Thursday
12.**

Sew & work all day. Sarah sleek up her things and help me. James churn, chore and go to Town. he said he saw Lawyer Sumner again & that the only way for me to avoid the supporting of Father is to deed the property back to him and

that I could do it as soon as I pleased. . . . it *is sad*. Henry
went to the barn—he cried about it, when he came in he
looked out of the window crying. he said he thought as soon
as Pa had a deed he would disinherit him, for he had threatened to lots of times, that he thought him & me could hope
for no home here. I think the only way is to give a deed so
that he can not sell nor encumber, but can have the use of
as long as he lives & then it shall be Henrys & Sarahs. . . .
The Children go to bed to night feeling the worst I ever saw
them, the saddest and most discouraged. my prayer is that
it may not be as bad as it seems. Gods will be done.[14] . . .

**Friday
13**

* * * Children have just come in from doing the chores, it
is their first experience trying to milk. the funny part was
they did not know which nor how many cows to milk, they
milked one however. Warm. * * *

**Sunday
15**

It is two P.M. can it be that this is the last sabbath day that
I have a home that I feel no one could turn me out into the
streets. alas! *it is a sad sad thought*. . . . When Harriet was
here Wednesday . . . again she said "I dont blame James at
all. he has always been a perfect slave to the children and
you." what has he done that he had not ought to? I asked.
"he has done everything." well, what? "he has done *all the
running* there was to be done." *what* running? what is it?
"he is a perfect slave. worse than the niggers in the south."
who told you this & how do you know? "you ought to help
him milk—every body knows it" well how do they know it?
then James said "they dont *have* to be told—they can see it
for themselves." ah me such talk about a wife & mother,
right in her own home, by a sister & he who *ought* to be a
protector. *it* looks dark, but with Gods help I feel I am to
come through all right. Snow

**Friday
27**

* * * I saw Uncle & Susan coming—so thought I would go
out to the road and see them. heard her say "there Emily

Gillespie is comeing out to waylay us." I went however and
and tried to show respect by asking after her & families
health, to come down &c. she answered, but not *one* word
of *enquiry* of how I done. he asked me to come up, and I
intend to. can not say that it very much hurts my feelings,
for I too well know the cause, and purchance, some time all
will know the truth. then I feel I shall have many many
friends, friends that will be sorry they were ever anything
else. * * *

Monday   Am tired to night I walked to Town this morning, to see
30   Messrs Bronson & Car, in regard to arrangeing our property.
              they advised me to give James a deed of *all*, if not I will be
              obliged to support father. *May it end well?* * * *

APRIL 1885

Thursday   * * * *I gave James a deed of the farm. indeed I felt as*
2   *though it was signing myself out of a home.* I said to Mr
              Bronson "it seemed pretty bad to be *compelled* to do such a
              thing as this, that I should *never* had done it had I not have
              been *obliged* to." he said a deed was good for nothing if one
              was compelled to give it.[15] . . .

Thursday   * * * Henry went to see Mr Segar. Mr Segar told him he
9   would let him have the job of [building] house & barn for
              $2500.00—I am glad he has got it. . . . James seems to be
              very kind & obliging all at once, like a june frost, since
              twenty years—but never mind tis too late. so much sorrow
              can hardly be turned to joy by some [unreadable, blotted].
              forgive. but forget *never.* my head feels bad it sounds so like
              the swashing of water. Chilly, sprinkle.

Saturday   It is my birth day anniversary. Sarah made me a present of
11   a white glass cross candlestick this morning before break-

fast. it is real nice. Sarah is so thoughtful. . . . James says he thinks it is time I done something that I could not be sitting around here all summer. I said 'to just let me alone is all I want.' & it seems so. * * *

Monday
13

James churn chore & go to town. I went too, & get tired. * * * Mr Segar came across the street & was talking with James about his house. James said—"I know Henry could not run a mess of work hands. a lot of men wont be bossed by a boy." "no!", says Mr Segar "thats so." then he told me that Trenchard said Henry could not set a window frame to save his life—and other things just as bad, so much said, that Mr Segar seems to be afraid Henry can not build it. . . . if people ever want their children to rise & prosper in their undertakings *most surely* they must not go about telling they can do nothing. but that is & always has been James' trait to think none only himself knew how to do any thing. he must quit talking such a lingo of perfect wrong. . . .

Sunday
19

Sarah went to meeting, Henry did not. I think he stayed at home because he does not like to have me stay alone. first him & then Sarah stay. Noble son and daughter. James do his chores. Frank Mead here to dinner he will take Sarah to her school. he is a good young man, temperate and industrious, but—who he may get for a wife can expect to leave all society, all that gives happiness to a woman's life, and take *hard work & solitude. Mud*[16]

Wednesday
22

* * * Henry went with Mr Segar this morning, to have a carriage ride. it is the first time he ever went with any one for diversion. O how often, how *many* times I have wished they & I too might go more in society. Still we enjoy visiting together, perhaps better than with others—it is a bright & happy thought. . . . * * *

MAY 1885.

Monday
4

I done all I could this forenoon. O dear how tired I do get. my heart beats so fast every little thing I do, and my head, it is bad or at least feels bad. *Miss Ada Hoskins* came here, at noon to day to work. she is to have $1.50 per week, is not very strong, but think she will do very well. she done up the work &c. James chore &c. we went to town. I went up to the P.O. could hardly get back to where the team was. had to rest two or three times because I felt so faint. * * *

Friday
15

Father came here one year ago last night. Ah me. I have been obliged to deed away my home on his & James account. but never mind—there is always some place for all. I can truly say that father, James & Harriet have nearly crushed my heart. but with Gods help I hope to outlive all the trouble they have caused. * * *

Thursday
21

Girl iron &c. James chore & fit cornground, Henry work as usual. I help a little, can feed the turkeys by lying down on the ground to rest. my heart beats fast. my feet swell & I *am* weak. Warm

Saturday
23

How good it seems for us all to be at home. I went with James after Sarah yesterday. . . . *dear* I was so glad to see Sarah & if we both cried, it seemed as if it the more expressed our joy. James got a covered Carriage to go in. * * * Mr Segar call. I think he is quite upset in his affection for Sarah. I am sorry for we like him as a neighbor, but married men ought to give all their *love* to their wives. I will have to talk with him about it. *Warm*

Sunday
24

* * * Cora Brook call. she walked to church (2-1/2) through the dust with a 40 dollar silk. *Vanity*. it is not Sarah. Ada thinks no corset, with short hair parted on one side looks "awful funny & boyish." *her* corset is so tight she breathes like a lizard.[17] * * *

**Monday
25**

Ada do nice washing &c. Hulda Lewis came here & stayed all day. * * * it seems James has been complaining to Hulda about me working him to death. she is so plain hearted, she spares no words. she said to him "got *five* cows to milk, put in five acres of corn, is that *all* you do?" yes he said & had to hire the corn mostly put in. "G—— G—— I cant see for H—— S—— what you complain of Emmie (me) working you to death." harsh talk, but it cuts him close to the truth—so much so that he will not reply. I was afraid they would get into a dispute. am thankful I am clear of such wrong doing. * * *

**Sunday
31**

James do chores &c. he does not like to have any one say any thing to me about dropsy or being sick. it is his way to let one sicken & die. tell them "nothing ails them, they look smart etc—as he says by me that I do not have dropsy any more than tobys tail." and in a few days things are forgotten as though they had never been. Charley Thorpe was here after seed corn—he said his Mother died with dropsy just as I have it. Harry came home with Henry from meeting, he says he knows a man in east where he lived that *cures dropsy*. he will write to him for me. it seems as if it is my only hope. if it should cure me I would know it was sent me by God through hearing my prayers to live as long as I may be needed here. . . . O dear, it is very unpleasant to be obliged to keep a hired girl. it is tell, tell, tell, what to do all the time, until one is tired out.[18] * * *

JUNE 1885.

**Monday
1**

James plow &c. * * * I take care of my poultry—have over a hundred real nice little turks. it is so hard for me to walk, though I do not see that I get any worse. am very weak, my eyes too see [*sic*] to be weak. tire easy. my ankles I can scarcely dent them they are so hard, & if I do the indenture stays for hours—as if made in warm wax.

If I should not get well, and am to leave this world it is my earnest desire that Henry have the west half—and that Sarah have the east half of this property (this that I deeded to James the 2nd day of April 1885.) . . . May this be right & done   I can not say it is sad to leave James for it has so long been his wish I should. I wish him no harm & hope he may have all he needs long as he lives. . . .

Saturday
6

* * * Father applied to this county for help, Johns folks agree to be [*sic*] to all his expenses & take care of him for one dollar ($1.) per week. *disgraceful affair*. I feel that he has caused me too much trouble to make right. I *can* forgive, but can *not* forget a willful injury. * * *

Monday
8

Girl wash &c. James churn & go to town. . . . I went to Manchester too—done some trading. Mr Morris is in town giving Phrenological Lectures. I went to his room. he examined my head & I got a Chart. he told me about the same as others have. Said *it was the most remarkable head he ever examined. that it was almost impossible for a person to reach as high a position as I was capable of doing & also desirous to do. Why it beats all—you scarcely live in this world, but from your high knowledge & great desire for right you live, as it were, heavenly, and and [sic] when in the other world you can only find ideas of the beautiful fulfilled. (& much more he said) That I could be one of the finest poets, one of the best authors, & in the finest arts I could have reached the very highest.*

Ah Me. I must say with the poet.
"The saddest words from tongue or pen,
Are these—it might have been"

All is well. My Children amply repay me for all I have been obliged to—well—give up.[19] * * *

Saturday
20

Dear a me. I almost get discouraged   Girl is so slow, here she has been seven weeks getting the house *partly* cleaned

& a few quilts (6) washed, besides what little cooking &c there is to do for three of us & herself. she was not very good natured to day because I had her wash or rinse over some of the dishes, when she poured hot water on them they made a perfect suds from the soap that adhered to them. . . . I think it my right to have what I eat clean & *will* as far as possible. * * *

Friday
26

* * * James churned & we went to town in afternoon. he spoke of getting a mower. it is all right he should if he needs & wants it, though I did not say any thing about it until he said he could get it if Henry & me calculated to get our buggy. I replied . . . I thought if I had good luck with my berrys I thought I would have enough to pay for it. he then said, here we owe 8 or 10 dollars now, who do you expect to pay that? I dont see how I can pay so much, and who do you calculate will pay the hired girl. I told him *him*. then he commenced the same old story that I didnt help him, worked against him etc. I was disgusted. . . .

JULY 1885

Thursday
2

Have had company to day. Emma Brook & May (Brook) Douglas. had a good visit, was real nervous though—had to do so much to help do the work & get dinner. Henry work as usual, Sarah gone. Jas plow corn & chore. I am sorry my love or friendship for him is broken. I try to overlook his deceit—but can I? when any one is here he is O how nice—but when alone will scarcely answer or speak. . . .

Monday
13

This is a *sad* day for me. one flock of 80 of my turkeys are all dying from feeding them meal that James had mixed salt in. *this is the third* time he has done the very same thing, said it was an *accident,* & that they were his as much as mine. I can see no excuse for it whatever   I think if *I* should do such a thing I could not help but think of it. 30 little chickens died out of a flock of 38. . . . * * *

Wednesday
22

Adays father came for her to go home this morning just as we were done breakfast. . . . I paid her alltogether $16.00 . . . it was the understanding, that she must pay for articles she carelesly broke or injured, when she first came here, I retained 1.00. . . . it may be all right that she went sudden, gave her no chance to pilfer anything. I caught her ransacking my boxes & drawers more than once. * * *

Monday
27

Sarah wash, mop & do up the work before eleven A.M. O so much nicer than it has been done for three months, but it makes *me feel bad* that she has to do the work when she has been gone so long & can only stay a short time. . . . Henry too works as usual, he gets along real well but it seems as if he has not the force or strength to endure when he could before he was hurt. his hip near the spine is yet lame. . . . I see no change in his disposition except that he may be more irritable or not have quite as much patience, like one perhaps who has been sick & not fully recovered. . . .

AUGUST 1885.

Saturday
8

Do all the work I can, take care of turkeys. my head is not quite as bad as it was. *I believe it to be congestion* of or on the *brain*, and but for cold water it seems it would burst. . . . perhaps a few seconds it *did* seem as if my head was being crushed through the entire portion of the brain in the vicinity of the Whole top of my head above the ear   I had to hold it with both hands with all my might to even have the least impression toward keeping it together. with a great effort I called Sarah & she came to my assistance or it might be I should have died of it. * * * My head feels literally to have been smashed to pieces, it hurt so badly that it affects my eyes so as to make an appearance of stars among waves, so I can hardly write, and when the worst makes me dizzy too.

Monday
10

* * * 8 A.M. It is a beautiful morning. . . . *In fact I am happy* for I feel I have ever tried to do right, am willing the world know all. Monday 10 afternoon continued. I have just ate a piece. James came home he put up the hay, then ate a piece of bread & things for dinner, he began to wash the dishes—he also began his lingo again, said he should charge Henry & Sarah for their board after this fall and then he could hire a girl. I did get out of patience & told him some *facts* about the threats he has made. . . . ugh. yes. was all he would say, & twited me of getting good meals of victuals when Insurance agents or a young man came from town etc. . . .

I have never seen a happy day since less than two weeks after we were married. he told me how he had been tempted to kill himself as far as to get a rope & go to the barn to hang, he has threatened it many time since. O what an anxious heartbreaking sorrow to me it has been and for it I have spent many sleepless nights. I thank the Lord that he has given me wisdom to find out his iniquity & it affects me no more. I feel that I have done my duty & still will try to do. . . . Sarah get Vira Philips to come & do the work while she goes to the Normal. Vira is a good girl to work—but was so unfortunate as to be obliged to be married. her baby is 9 months old, its father will not support them: promises in vice are only to be broken at the ruin of its victims. Alas! sad fate.

Monday
17

* * * Segar called . . . he said James told him that the Deed I gave him of the farm is not good for anything that it will have to be made over. it may be that is the cause of his being so unpleasant for so long. What can I think? . . . I will try, as I have done, to keep our little family together just as long as possible. yet—sometimes—yes often, I think it is dangerous to be with him alone. O if he could only be & do all right. Mr Segar told me never to give another deed, & for Sarah & Henry & I to live together. I told him how we were so near being separated, how very disagreeable & unpleasant it was for us. he said he was perfectly astonished and if I did not say it, he would not believe it, that every one thought Mr Gillespie to be one of the best men to his family that ever lived & that I had kept our trouble to myself & kept the children from ever saying a word & we always seemed so happy & pleasant, that it would be apt to throw the blame upon me. *I fear not, for I am right.* at least I *feel* that I am. I only regret that I did not go away and leave him when I first knew and found out what a terrible despondent disposition he had. then I was well. I could have taken my children & taken care of them, yet I have ever prayed for wisdom & to do right. . . . Ill keep up my courage yet.

Wednesday
26

Bedtime. we are all at home again. have worked all day. Henry has been settling up all round   he made $61, building Sanrings [? unclear] house. he felt quite cheerful, until this evening Sarah & I went out of doors—Henrys hip pained him—he was heating his feet—James commenced as soon as we were out, called him lazy—told him he could not stay here unless he paid for his board and other insulting things. Sarah came in soon as we heard them. James went out without saying another word,—he was *awful mad*—Henry was grieved & mad too. . . . he said *"Ma I have no place to go"*—O I can *never* forget how *bad* he felt & how *sad* sounded those words. I told him as long as I lived and had a home he was welcome him & Sarah too & that they should have a home too, to not worry. . . . Vira said "she was actually afraid of Mr Gillespie—he walked around so, and talked & looked so—she was afraid he would pitch right on to Henry, that it seemed any man that had a heart in them could not use a child so mean." . . .

Thursday
27

I went to town with Uncle, bought cloth for Sarah a dress, green flannel with silk velvet for trimming, 1.00 a yard. . . . Henry feels better this even'g we all do. none of us slept much last night. we all work. I put a chair at the head of the stairs every night & have done for a long time, so that if anyone should come up they would hit it & wake me up. * * *

SEPTEMBER 1885.

Friday
11

Do all I can. my hands & feet feel bad yet, as if the cutus [cutis?] or skin was *real thin.* * * * Henry . . . said "Ma come take a walk with me, you need exercise." and accordingly put his arm around me and took hold of my hand—we walked out on the porch, around the house and in at the back door. it *pleased* him and I think it *did* do me good. at least it cheered dull feelings. we are all at home to night & all is well. Rain

Sunday
13

James, Sarah and I go to Uncles. . . . I can not talk with him, he is so deaf and my voice is weak, and then he seems to rather talk with James since he told him his pitiful story of the Children and myself. he *was* before that my very dear friend. let it pass. * * *

Tuesday
15

* * * I could not find three of my teaspoons this morning at half past eight, so after I had *looked considerable,* I asked Vira if she had not laid them some place where I did not happen to see them? she flew mad in an instant, she was just ready to commence washing. "Ill *go home.* Ill pick out my things, Ill not stay where Im twitted of stealing." I told her "very well if you wish to, but you are mistaken and you will be sorry, for I merely *asked if you knew.*" I did not ask her to stay though I know she *was* sorry before she got ready to go. she was *cross every time* she washed or if I asked her to do anything, especially this morning because I asked

her to get up, then it was nearly six o'clock. I paid her and asked her to come & see us, no reply—she stopped at Harriets an hour-and-a-half—she called her in and then went to get Emma Brook to help her digest the news. . . .

Friday
18

Our 22 Aniversary, been married 23 years to day. Mr Parkhurst came for me to visit at Mrs Beals, had a good visit and enjoyable ride. when he brought me home he came by Quaker Mill, all round about 12 miles. he is quite proud of his horse and carriage. Mr Segar here to dinner   Sarah & I seem to have friends among the other sex—more friendly than we like, or rather more than most *they says* would approve. I often wonder why Etiquette so restrains us from that freedom of familiarity to express our thoughts with decorum without some green eye to whisper it too loud. James cut corn & chore. I embroider & visit. * * * Mr Segar told Sarah if she would let him pay her schooling to graduate in Medicine, she could commence now. he is very kind but I think Sarah done right to refuse & try to work & earn enough for herself to go & then she is free. yet it does seem to almost tempt one, when so much needed. it *might* be right, it *might* be *wrong*. keep safe.

Wednesday
23

* * * Sarah takes care of me with *fan* and *camphor* several times a day. I hope I may fully appreciate *her* sympathy & *Henrys* too. James cut corn. he gets real tired. I am sorry he is not stronger. I feel better this evening & all is well. Pleasant.

Saturday
26

I went to town with James. * * * . . . brought home *my Carriage*. I am intending to buy it of Mrs Tipple, will cost $65.00 it is realy worth nearer $150.00 a *Phaeton*. . . . The cover & cushion is new & cost $65.00 alone, they have had no use for it, it has been in the barn for over 4 years & therefore sell it cheap. . . . I have wished for this or some other carriage for years which I might have had. [A drawing of a phaeton is in the left margin.]

Sunday
27

* * * James, Sarah & me went up through the Grove to try my Carriage. *it is splendid,* but James is *too harsh* for anything *so fine.* . . . Henry & Sarah think it just as nice as I do. Henry says it ought only to be used with fine clothes & for nice, Sarah says it *shall* too. if I only could have had it for their enjoyment when they went to school, but it is well to get it even at this late day. Father & Johns folks were at Uncles, father will not speak to us nor answer when spoken *to.* it is unpleasant, but let him go. I feel he has finished up my ruin as regards having to give up the deed to my home. * * *

OCTOBER 1885

Monday.
5

Sarah went to Town, she paid Mrs Tipple for my Carriage $65.00—I give my note to Sarah for the amount due January 1, 1886 at 10 per cent. I help do the work. * * *

Tuesday
6

We all work all day. Henry & I ride to Town in *my new Carriage.* . . . I am thankful for it, and when I pay Sarah it will be mine. I have raised turkeys to get it & if nothing happens to them I shall have more than enough. *counted 143 the other day. trust for success.* * * *

Tuesday
13

Better of cold, sew on Sarahs dress and help work. * * * A man shot a *black-bird. I cooked & ate it, it was good.* saved its head & wings and tail to put on a hat. We have fall weather again, the summer has gone, a long winter is before us, eight long months before we have warm sunshiny days. * * *

Friday
16

Mend three cupboard doors where mice had spoiled them. it was a hard job for me to do. *am too tired to write,* and feel discouraged—it seems as if I had worked & calculated so as to help to get us a home . . . and now I have not one cent to say *is my own.* . . . I said this evening I would be glad when the shed was done so there could a place be fixed for my carriage. "you better take it to bed with yeh"—James replied. . . . O such cutting words—in perfect ridicule. . . .

NOVEMBER 1885.

Sunday
1

* * * Uncle brought a fresh ham. I fried a piece for dinner. James was much pleased when he came in—said "beats all my wife knows whats good to eat on a cold day"—but changed his tune when he saw such a big piece; asked "how much did you get?" there is 10 or 12 lbs.—"what you get so much as that for?" so to have enough to last awhile; "did you pay for it?" *no I had no money*? "well I dont want you to be runnin me in debt unless I know whats for." he does not even dream I have to work & help to pay his debts when he borrows money. . . .

Harry [Jeffers] here to day. he came with horse & Carriage to take Sarah riding, and, as I conjectured he would—he asked her to become his wife. she told him she had not thought of ever getting married that she intended to teach & go to College, to study and practice medicine. Harry cried, indeed I am sorry for him—it is his first love, & may be a real disappointment. I hope he may meet & love another & all be well with him.

Sunday
8

It is almost eight o'clock. James in bed   he does not look very well. I wish we might ever lived happily together, and we have when compared with many that I know. we have not had many words in dispute. *I am glad* that I have almost always kept still when he had his bad spells. I said the most & so did he too the day that Vira came here to work that we ever did. let it pass. may I forgive as I wish to be forgiven. I pray for Wisdom. Segar—last night—took advantage of Sarah standing near him when he started—and kissed her. he must never do it again, for Sarah is pure & inocent. . . . * * *

Wednesday 11

I fininsh painting Carriage almost, get out of paint   Sarah & I made a cover for it. When James went in the barn he said *he saw a ghost*. it looks nice. we cut rags too, we *are* tired to night—but it makes me rested to know *all is well*. * * * Oh how grand it would be if one could live two hundred years, live to see the wonders wrought, to see the progress in art & science. *not* live for mere life alone. it almost enraptures us in reverie of thought to even have an idea of such a life. *There is one invention which I do believe can be made to be a perfect success*, & that is *perpetual-motion as I dreamed it about 15 or 18 years* ago. it must be done by weight and pressure by springs on an inclined plane, similar to a machine used by putting a horse into a sort of treadmill—

The frame was silver and sparkling stones,
The horse was gold-tied with a golden chain,
Beneath his feet was an inclined plane
. . . .
Within this golden horses feet, cut in notched form
Were diamonds, to fit & drive the bars of gold
On which were notched plates of dazling brightness.
Standing near this wonder of art and skill
Was the inventor: his raiment—gold and silver thread . . .

If I only had money to make a model & get a patent, just as I dreamed, three diferent times. I should surely try. Oh! my dream was rich in gold & silver   The man said so plain "*It is perpetual motion*"

Sunday 15

Sarah went to meeting. . . . Sarah said Mr Joseph Hutchenson caught up and walked with her through town. I *do realy believe* he is seeking to gain Sarahs favor and will eventually offer his hand & heart to her wishing her to be his wife. it will be far diferent than Harry's proposal, for she seems to take a diferent view of Him than any one she has seen. . . . his father is supposed to be worth several hundred thousand dollars. Joseph is his Secretary. financial riches. is he as rich in goodness, is he worthy of Sarah. his appearance is gentlemanly. Sarah is much like myself when I was her age. it seemed as if young boys, young and old men, bachelors and married men admired, though I can not tell why unless that it was that I made it my aim to use correct language, never to jest and always treat every one who was respectable with propper decorum. Henry was much pleased when I gently told him about Sarahs lovers. . . .

**Tuesday
17**

It is ten o'clock. we did not eat breakfast *very early*. I finished at nine, *late*. it takes me a long time to do up my work. am resting now—*think I am fully determined to buy a lot in Manchester, can build a small house on it—then we might rent this. it would be such a help, to Henry and Sarah when they are at work in town they could board at home & not cost them so much. I could keep a girl for her board to do my work & I could do what I was able to, & James might get plenty to do. capital idea. it is not new for I thought of it strongly so much, that I would liked to have done it & would have if I could have paid for it 15 years ago* when I was well and could have worked at Millenary work & done well. perhaps I might do it now. . . . I will speak to Henry and Sarah about it, and after I buy it then I will mention it to James. . . . [Half a page of house plan drawings follows.]

Friday
20

James washed . . . it rather pleases me to see him wash dishes &c. because he has always intimated that I have done nothing. now let him do *that nothing* (of a thousand chores or more everyday) and see how he likes it. We went after Sarah. . . .

Sunday
29

Five Minutes past one. I can hardly write. the tears blind my eyes. James said "he was going to sell one of the horses, that he meant to try and pay the taxes this year, but if he couldnt the turkey money would have to go to pay it." I only said (I was going to pay Sarah what I borrowed of her to get my buggy, that I needed clothes, and she had worked & wanted to get her some things, and I wanted a little of my own so if I wanted any little thing I would not have to beg for it & then not get it) he did not reply & went up in the field. O there is no use to think how I feel. . . .

[The following month is the last of three fully transcribed in this edition. The length of the entries demonstrates Emily Gillespie's growing reliance on her diary as her confidant.]

DECEMBER 1885.

Tuesday
1

James is loosing his love for housework. he cleaned up barn or stable &c. churned too. I sew some and do what work I can. Henry and Sarah are gone. I am in thought with them each day and night. My last thought before I sleep is ever with them with my best wishes. Now I must try to get something for supper: pleasant.

Wednesday
2

Henry came home last night. pleaster too damp to finish. he is not very sociable, is lost in study what is best to do. I hope he will not get discouraged: he balanced up his books this forenoon. we went to Mill & Town this afternoon. we were talking of his falling from the spire. he too blames Harry just the same as I always have, from the very first—that he did not fasten the chain as it ought have been was why the hook turned—Oh it is too terrible to think of. It may be considered an accident, yet I think it was carlessness by Harry tyeing the rope, that fastened the chain, on the wrong side. if it was so—he will sometime allude to it in a way that we may know. Henry helps me do all the work & takes care of my turkeys. he feels better to night. Chilly James proposed to me—that I sell my turkeys, for Henry and me to go to Kansas City, rent a couple of small rooms and go to work. that the turkey money would last till Baileys note was due and when that was gone of it—we could not do enough to make a living. said he wanted us to make up our minds—when he came in—well have you made up your minds? I told him I meant to make my little money count more instead of use it up that way, that he could go best—perhaps he could work for Gill Yeomans. [In margin:] might as well turn us out of doors one way, as well as another.

Thursday
3

Henry write a piece, *Experience*, for the paper—it is real good. he helped do the chores in the house & out of doors, too. he seems to feel more encouraged to day, though he would not stay at home at all if it was not for me, he said so, and that he wanted to save all he could to go to school, poor boy I pity him—for there is seldom a day but James hints that he wont do any thing. he does however and I tell him to never mind, providence will make all right at last. he will see a way to do and get as much as he is able to do, that he has done well, *better* than any sensible person thought he ever could. we must fear not but trust in the Lord to save and protect us. all is well, with good wishes that Sarah too be well & happy and getting along all right—I must go to bed. Henry says I must sleep and rest all I can, James do chores clean up stable. Cold.

Friday
4

I baked pies and tried to get the work all done up nice for Sarah will not have so much to do. James gone after her & to Mill. I went out to cover up some plants &c. with straw. Henry helped me, he did not want me to but I thought I could, I worked too long at and got so tired and nervous that I know I was clear discouraged—Henry said he felt real sorry, he got the big chair for me to sit in, and rubbed my head, how dear he is. I *will* try to never get so nervous again, I only could find relief in tears.

Well it is now bed time. Sarah & James have come. Henry feels better, I do too, O how thankful I am. all at home. all is well. there is a very hard blow and snow storm all the afternoon. Cold. [In margin:] Sarah is getting along all right. how glad I am, may she continue as well through her school.

Saturday 5

Sarah clean up & wash, James is in a perfect stew & works to try & get a falls work done in one day   he said he thought Henry might have framed a post or sill such a pleasant day, I told him Henry could not do a half dozen things at once. he had been at work all the forenoon, he churned after dinner & went skating. Sarah & I went after him. Cold. [In margin:] Henry was real mad at Pa, but he feels better to night. he held the robe around me all the way home & Sarah drove.

Sunday 6

It is seven oclock, *cold* and dark. I am all alone. James has gone to take Sarah to her boarding place. they started so late, fifteen minutes past five, it takes about four hours. Henry went to meeting this forenoon, he has not come home yet. I must not worry, for he may have gone home with Mr. Segar to dinner and stay to evening meeting, though I would hardly think he would because it is so very cold   60 right here only six feet from the stove. I think he will be all right—except that he might have started to come across the ice alone and fallen into an airhole. Oh! Lord I hope not. Oh, if it should be it would be almost unbearable, fear not but trust in Providence for his safe return & may James be all right too. *Cold* & hard wind. Good night and best wishes to all.

Monday 7.

Henry came home at half past seven last night. James came a few minutes later. he drove *12 miles in two hours* Henry went to Mrs Bates' to dinner. his hip some lame. I do hope it may get well, though I fear it may trouble him all his life.

he helped me do the work, bring in wood, keep fires & take care of my turkeys besides he helped James make sheep shed. he is figuring on the cost of building Mrs. Bates' a new house. a good night & best wishes for Sarah too I go to bed. snow

Tuesday
8

James has gone to bed. he acts as if he could not bear to see Henry rest or study one minute. it makes Henry feel unwelcome and as if every mouthfull he ate was begrudged. Sarah is just the same, it is just the same with me I might work until I died & then he would think & say I done nothing—it would be impossible to do enough to suit him, I do all I can, so does Henry. James fix shed. I am thankful and happy for one thing and that is Henry and Sarah know and realize I have done all in my power to help them & they are welcome to stay in my home so long as I have one. my prayer is that I may live and have a home for them to come, and help them as long as they may need my assistance. Henry says his hip is sore to night. I fear he hurt it skating last Sunday and he gets his feet too cold. May the Lord guide us aright, may he direct us what is best to do, be it his will I pray it may get well. best wishes & good night to Sarah & all. cold & windy some last night & to day has been 10 below zero. Snow.

Wednesday
9

I done the work with Henry's help. James do chores, churn &c. Henry went to Town, he is anxious to get something to do. I *know* it is unpleasant for him when I am so nervous and weak. I try to be pleasant and do all I can to make it pleasant for him. Sarah is away—best wishes & good night to her. *deep* Snow

Thursday
10

John has been here this evening. Henry help me do the work. James went to town I went with him. get few groceries. when we came home I was getting *real* cold. I asked him to tuck the robe down as I felt the wind on my feet. he did not like it, though he did, and said in a terrible sarcastic jeering tone *"you are the most helpless woman I ever saw for anyone that pretends to know as much as you do*, you *know every* thing but cant do *any* thing." I made no reply—Henry had a fire & I got supper. he (James) sat down—after awhile he said I would get about 70 or 75 dollars for my turkeys, that would be enough to pay the taxes. I told him I did not think I could pay the taxes this year that I must pay Henry & Sarah what I borrowed of them and I needed clothes—as in truth I *do*. I have not a single winter dress   all I have is my velvet, 2 calico ones and this old suiting one. *poor* shoes & only 2 prs of stockings. he said "the turkeys *will* pay the taxes. if *I* have to foot all the bills Ill have all that is raised on the place." I did feel grieved and mad too—to think I almost worked on my hands & knees to raise my poultry & then have no right to use the money I get for them. I shall not raise any next year, I can *not* be such a slave any more. Henry told him he ought to be ashamed of himself great stout healthy man and then ask ma as weak and sick as she is for her turkey money. alas! I sometimes hardly know what to do. I will trust the Lord to direct me aright. Cold. [In margin:] Henry to see George Brook this evening. he is sick.

Friday
11

I do all I can, Henry help. he went after Sarah. she is well & doing well, has 30 pupils. James ~~mended~~ do chores etc as usual. I have the blues I guess and must banish all worry and try to be happy. I patch & sew a little. Cold. sleighing

Saturday
12

We all work. Sarah and Henry went to town, brought home his chest of tools & got pair of over-shoes for Sarah. All at home & all is well—I feel nervous, my heart beat is too rapid—blood rushes to my head most all of the time. I trust I will get well again. I do feel as if it is not right that I should be *obliged* to pay the taxes. yet I am *perfectly* willing to do it for their feed. Sarah and Henry feel real bad about it and so do I. fear not but trust. *Cold*

Sunday
13.

All at home all day, and a beautiful day it is. *Harry* was here—he intends to go to *Cleveland* next Wednesday, has his patent at last. Zero. *Cold* [In margin:] gave a handkerchief to Henry.

**Monday
14**

Mr *Jernegan* of *Boston* came to buy my turkeys. he is to pay 8 cents. they go Wednesday, Henry help work in doors and out. he took Sarah to school this morning. James tried to smoothe over what he said the other day about taxes &c, but at last he said he must have help either physically or mentaly. I did not reply to what he said for I certainly do feel abused. him and Henry mended socks. I do all I can. Henry and I went to Uncles this evening, he covered me up head & all in the robe so I came home warm. Cold.

**Tuesday
15**

I work & sew, Henry help & feed turkeys. James go to Mill, he brought home a rooster & said he would have brought a turkey, he seems to think he has taken away from me the last of any thing I could have any claim on as my own to use as I thought best. he felt so elated about it. it was more than I could bear. I told him I thought it was darn mean that he should try to take my poultry away from me in the way he was, that the turkeys were mine—I should have what I raised too, that I could not be crowded intirely out of existance. that I had rights as well as he and they had got to be respected too. I am indeed sorry and thought I would try to give up my all and let it go, rather than say a word, for I *do* dislike to have trouble and think it is so very *bad* in a family. too much—too much. though I hope all to be right at last, one thing is sure. I have never yet spent a dollar, but I tried to make it count the most I possible could for the benefit of us all. May the Lord give us Wisdom and health. a good night to Sarah & all is well   Pleasant
Mr. Premble call for wood.

**Wednesday
16**

James wash and do other chores. Henry went to Manchester to see Harry as he intends to go away this evening   he gave a "General Grant book to Henry." James had a regular splurge talking against educations being of use to people,

advocating that those who were not educated were the best
off etc. I proved to him that education done no harm to any
one & that it helped they who were inteligent & ambitious,
while those that were lazy &c received benefit by it for it
was all they ever were that was worthy of notice. I was very
tired and nervous all day. wish I knew how Sarah is. Harry
went to bid her his adieu yesterday. pleasant.

Thursday
17

Sold 100 of my turkeys to day to Mr Jerigan or rather James
carried them to Manchester for him, he received for it
$2.00. They weighed 1097 lbs *$87.76.* they said they were
the *best* they had received this year. I have kept 29 hens &
must buy 2 nice goblers. will sell 4 of the hens. the 31 at
present time are worth $18.56   also keep about 25 domes-
tic hens & a rooster worth $4.00. the feed through Novem-
ber & 20 days in Dec has cost about $8.00   feed for re-
mainder of year is about $6.00   have made for profit or
rather for my work about $88.17. sell also hens & roosters
worth $3.28   James kept it & did not mention it until I
asked him—he only said $3.28   raised 1 peacock worth
2.50—I am quite satisfied, have made enough clear to get
my carriage. James tells me how I ought to do to raise poultry. Henry *is* tired, he feels as if he were not doing much,
but he can when winter is gone. I feel better than I did last
night, hope Sarah is well Henry says she will have Dobson
to contend with next—& has a hearty laugh of it. he works
on shed & *chores.* Warmer [In margin:] Make a plush cap
for Henry. It looks well.

Friday
18

Henry has gone after Sarah. James churned & takes butter
to market. I do not feel very well to day, have done too much
& helped sort poultry & got cold. Thawing   James churned
& carry butter to market, get few groceries, have them for
Children to bring home, they forget them. Dobson went with
Henry to visit Sarahs school, she gets real tired, says it is
perfect *hurly-burly* all the time.

how good it seems to me to all be at home. Warm [In

margin:] Mr Segar came just as Children did, supper ready. he stayed & paid me $.25   thinks of building again.

Saturday 19

Work is just the same whether sick or well. I get *very very tired*. James chore &c. Henry and Sarah attend the Teachers association at Masonville, report a general good time. Sarah on programme for an *Essay* at next meeting. they are tired & *were* hungry. Maud Brook call for eggs. *George is sick*   Thaw.

Sunday 20

Henry went to visit at John Andersons (Hattie Beals') they are going to Kansas. Albert Dobson & Henry (a clerk for Catron) were here most all day Sarah says "she scarcely gets rid of one beau before another comes." I *do* cincerely thank Henry and Sarah for being so kind. pray the Lord give them wisdom & health and happiness. when Henry had gone to bed last night—he said "Good night Sarah. Good night Ma. now ma you must try to sleep good." Oh! that I may get well for his sake. what would he do without Ma & Sarah too just the same. May Gods will be done. we will trust in Him that all be well. Henry had a *good* visit and *good* dinner. I *am* glad. we are all at home to night & happier for having pleasant visits. it enlivens our souls when friends come to see us and makes us feel better. there is so seldom a lady comes into the house. not that they are enemies, but because I owe them all visits. I have had to stay at home so long, and *work work work* that I make no calculations to go visiting. [In margin:] James has always been so opposed and managed so I could not, that he has nearly accomplished his threats to break up my going any place, it seems as if it may be all right some time. I have my Carriage—now if I can have a horse to use it will seem nice.

Monday 21

James churn & chores & work on farm timber. he kept Henry helping him every minute after he came home from taking Sarah to her school. I try to do all I can for I do not like to ask Henry to help so much, he needs more rest and some time to study too. this morning before he started he said "Ma I think we will get along all right after this—dont you." yes Henry, I said, we will we always have. *he is very tired to night*, he said "his hip—he did not know about it, it was no better than it was a month ago." I know it worries him—and fear it is worse, though he does not complain, he has rode over the rough ground too much and done to much all the week. he gets his feet damp. I will help him get better shoes, for he must keep his feet dry & warm. a good night & best wishes for Sarah—and cincere wish if it be Gods will for Henry to get well, pray he keep up good courage and never despair. I must now go to bed too. (first lamb yesterday) Thaw. [In margin:] I will try to not be so discouraged any more, be contented to do the best I can. may be Henry will feel better for it, he seems to feel bad because I do not ask him to help me more. it seems wrong to ask him to do so much yet I will if it makes him any happier for it. I surely will not do wrong if I know it.

Tuesday
22

James & Henry work on shed etc. Henry help me too. I feel sorry that he has to help me so much, he does not like to wash dishes & cook and do various chores about the house. I do not think it good for a yound [*sic*] man to do *such* kind of work, too puttering—as Henry says—it gets one in a habit of being careless, in a dont-care-way. he helps me because I can not do the work. if we can manage to get along for a couple of months, then we must try to have some one to do the work. a good night to Sarah & all. Warm like spring. pleasant.

Wednesday
23

Henry work on shed. James churn clean yard etc. I try to see & do all I can. Henry & I go to Town. I buy a Lamp for Sarah to give to Albert for Christmas present & a Glass Cube for Henry to give to him: a boot [?] of perfumery for Henry to give to Sarah. bought a *cube* for myself too. they

are 2-1/2 inches square (8 cubic inches solid glass) & used
for paper-weight while writing. it seems so much bother for
me to get out & in a wagon that I almost rather stay at home,
& would, but Henry is so kind & careful to help me that it
makes bad seem *not* so bad as *might* be. mr Blake says my
Turkeys were the *best* he ever saw. well I *am* proud of it.
mr. Jernegan paid me 12.97 more than he could get in Boston when they arrived there. he will not lose though, for he
keeps them for next Thanksgiving. *good* roads & warm.
Sarah good night   [In margin:] a letter from Mr. Gilleas
claims that the R.R. to *not* be liable for the killing of my
turkeys & that they *flushed* & *flew* upon the track ahead of
the train. *that is not the nature of a turkey*

Thursday
24

Finish plush Caps for Henry & Sarah. they *are really* nice
& good. Willie Mead brought Sarah home this evening, she
saw hers first thing, wanted to know who that's for—put it
on & wore it. she wants me to come to her school tomorrow.
We all work & are tired. Sarah is to have a Christmas tree,
speaking and anticipates a general good time. all is well.
damp & Chilly.

Friday
25

Fill 40 Cornicopias with candy and pack up presents. sew
buttons on my dress. James chore &c. Henry does too.
Henry & I are about ready to go to Christmas-tree-gift-party.
wish James could go too. Henry came in this morning &
said "Ma I have got something for you." What is it?—"A
Merry Christmas." and his eyes sparkled with joy that he
had thought of it first. when James came in I wished him
Merry Christmas. [In margin:] James mopped & done up the
work real nice.

Saturday
26

We got home late last night, all pleased with our presents.
was pretty cold though. when we went we stopped in Town.
I bought a teacup of Oysters a pickle and *two crackers for my*
dinner. it seemed as if I never ate any thing that tasted better

in my life. Albert went with us. his present to Sarah Autograph Album $1.50—and a pocket-book-toilet for Henry $. Sarahs Lamp to Albert $.40—Henrys Cube $.28 to him. Sarah gave Henry a beautiful hand mirror $.75 & perfumery boot $.25   she gave me a beautiful pair of Vases cost $1.25—Henry gave her a perfumery boot. he wanted to make her a nice present but feels as if he could not. I gave them each a *Ten dollar gold piece*. Sarah gave each of her scholars a copia of candy. she received some *real nice* stationary a toilet set &c. we ate Supper at Mrs Wilcox's. pleasant   [In margin:] Sarah went to town, we had oysters for supper, we all work. James washed Henry went this afternoon to skate. Sarah has a bad cold, and is tired out.

Sunday 27

It is half past five, James has gone to take Sarah to her school. her cold is not quite so bad. I do hope she may be over it soon & get rested. Henry went to meeting about half past nine, he has not come home yet—I *do* worry about him staying so for he intended to come home early. I am so afraid of the ice giving way, he did not take his skates but might fall through some rotten place in trying to cross. O may he not, may him & Sarah & James too have a safe return. has rained all day and is icy. freezes some but not *very* hard. *O how* lonesome when Henry and Sarah are both gone, it is all right however and when I know they are doing well it makes me happy. James came back half past six. Henry came about five minutes later, he has been at Mrs Bates. snow about gone. Rain

Monday 28

James and Henry work on shed, & help me. James draw manure, & some timber around for shed & chores. he took me to see George Brook, & came after me just as supper was ready. Emma gave me a piece of pie (mince) so rich I could not eat it, & a piece of Sausage. George is sick sore throat & pain in his bowels. he is poor, can not eat much. seems quite like quick consumption and he is *perfectly in-*

disposed, lies in bed all the time. a good night to Sarah, hope she is well of her cold & rested. *Rain*   [In margin:] I do all I can & sew on overalls. I almost feel as if drunk when I walk, as if I would pitch over, & have no strength at all.

Tuesday 29

Sew & do what I can about cooking. James churn & chore & sleep. he says "if we can not get a girl he will hire aman [*sic*] to drive the team. he can do the house work, tend to the cows and work in the garden." what an horid idea. a *man* whose work is to be done, able to do it himself, think of puttering away his time. why he could work by the day & earn more. a man would cost $20. cash: board $6 for board; 7 waste etc. waiting upon him would be at least a total cost of $30. per month—while a girl would cost only $12. pr month. Henry work on shed &c. he is *real* tired, we are having a genuine thaw. rain hard all day. how *glad I am* that Sarah does not have so far to go to school   Rain. [In margin:] would like to know how Goerge is—he will be apt to never get well. too bad for Emma, 3 children, no home. such is life.

Wednesday 30

Thats to day—a new year will soon be here. James & Henry at work in the barn. I am about ready to sew. *is Colder & snows*. Evening again. wish I knew how Sarah is: I wish her better of cold & good night. Henry is tired, James says he is too. I—well I do not feel much rested any time, yet I think I am not as bad as I was last winter. how thankful I am. *Snow all day*

It is not pleasant to sit in a dirty place, but when one has worked out what else can they do. have patience, trust in providence. pray for Wisdom & do right are our only friends and our consolation that all is well. Snowing

Thursday 31

Good-bye old year, farewel to thee
Our sorrows have been almost too much to bear

Yet—greater are the blessings of Mercy
Of Wisdom and health that have been bestowed,
We are thankful for our lives to be spared
And pray that all years may be no worse.
Asking Gods blessing, again good-bye old year.

James went to Auction, I went as far as Mrs Schmidts, Henry stayed at home, he done up the work *real nice*   he has gone to see how George Brook is, the doctors were to hold counsel to day. George was thought to be dying this morning—roads are terrible rough   Chilly.

[This is the end of the full month's transcription.]

JANUARY 1886

Sunday
3

* * * I welcome the New Year and hope it to bring blessings to all. I do hope to never have to experience such a year of trouble as I have since I went to Michigan, all is well to night. *I will try to never complain of any thing   Rain*

Saturday
9

Sarah does up most all the work & washed her collars & things, and do all our big ironing. James do chores, he brought a turkey in the house that is so cold she will not eat. I said I knew they were about starving that I intended to buy some corn first chance. "well then you must exert every nerve to help me next spring when I want to plant corn," he said. . . . no use to write more here, he is very unreasonable, he said considerable to the effect that I never done anything to help. I told him to shut up I would not hear that lingo anymore—he said "you are the bigest fool of a woman I ever knew." my reply was—*it is nice to be a man* if one *is* a man—. yet for all, I feel that all will be well. * * *

Thursday
14

It is bedtime. James has chores done   he was at Georges [Brook] funeral (pallbearer) * * * I feel sorry for Emma— she will be lonely—I wish her & her family to rise above their present situation in financial circumstances. they are left worse off than nothing, owe several hundred dollars, with a mortgage covering more than she has. such is life. death meets bad calculations with an untimely settlement. James was not very pleasant last evening. he wants me to sleep with him, and said "if he had to sleep alone he would have it so he could sleep warm or he would build himself a house and live alone & done with it." I do not feel as I once did for such talk but let it pass. then this morning he came to my bed & said 'are you awake?' I asked what did he want? he said he was going to get into bed with me. No! I told him I could not lie back in the cold—he would not speak all morning. * * *

Monday
18

Late. James done chores &c., has gone to bed. he gave me $5.00 to give to Henry—that makes $8.00 he will have left when he gets to Kansas City. * * * he [Henry] is so kind and careful of me, it seems when he is gone there is no one to care for me only Sarah and she can not take me as Henry does, though she is just the same. I thank God for them. . . .

Tuesday
19

Fifteen minutes past 10 A.M. am writing. James has gone to take Henry to the cars—I put up a half Valise full of lunch, 1/2 cranberry pie—2 mince pies, 1/2 Cocoanut cake, and a lot of sandwitches (Mutton & Beef between Rye & Graham gems) meant to put in apples but forgot them. he started in good shape only I wish he had more money. he shook hands and kissed me good-bye Ma, told me to take care of my health, and not to feel bad. I did try not to cry but I could not help it. . . . James is doing the chores. he has been more kind this afternoon, helped more & more sociable. he said he *dreaded* to *part with Henry* the *worst of anyone in his life*. . . . now he is going to make everything as comfortable as possible for him and me, he is not going to be in such a worry about his work. Ah! I have heard such talk too many times to believe it will last until time shall tell. in two or three days he generally forgets. he said it made him think of when La Fayette [James's deceased brother] left home, indeed he tries to make himself believe he is all right. I say not one word, I hope he *may* be more pleasant. I have fully determined to never, let him do or say what he will, to never let it so affect me as in years gone by. it seemed I could hardly eat supper to night—alone; alone; the bright stars of my life are not here. . . . * * *

Wednesday 20

Near eight. evening. have had a dull headache all day. I do not know but it is weak that I should have shed tears. ah yes they ran over my flushed cheeks, hot and fast. they seemed a relief to my full and grieved heart—and my head feels better. grief at parting with my Children is almost unbearable. . . . *Belva Lockwood* lectures in Manchester this evening. *O how much* I would like to hear and see her, but it is not mine to ever go to any place since the children do not go to school. hope on hope ever, I may sometime have an oportunity. we must be thankful for our good home. my Children have thus far amply repaid me for all troubles & sorrows. May they be happy to night[20]

Monday 25

No letter from Henry yet. * * * if Henry finds a home, a place where he can do well I will try to go and help him if I am able to. perhaps we might rent our place here & all go. Sarah is doing *well* here, but like myself when a girl, she has so many admirers that she will be obliged to be very careful to avoid the gossip of illdisposed people. I must go to bed to night without knowing where Henry is. . . .

FEBRUARY 1886.

Wednesday 3

* * * Too well I know why I felt so sad yesterday and thought of Henry all day as if something was wrong. I received a card from him to day it was written Jan 26—mailed the 29th. he was very much worried, said this was his last card or stamp, and he had not yet received any money & only one letter. . . . Dear boy—he says "if you will send me only a little for present needs, you may feel sure I will be able to pay it back to you if you send me any money" . . . James doing chores. he does not seem to realize what a bad trouble Henry has to endure. he says "if he's well Ill risk him it'll be the best lesson he ever had." . . .

Thursday 4

Noon. have been scraping a couple of [musk?] Rat skins that were dry, just like dry beef. Oh how I hope Henry is well and has received his Money. . . . At half past 10 this morning there was a *ringing in my left ear*, omen of death. I was facing the west. My head feels full and bad at the top of my brain most of the time. will be glad when I can get out of doors in fresh air & Sunshine. Cold to day too 24 below zero at 8. * * * James has done chores &c, has a hard time to keep up three fires & help but little around house. . . .

Saturday 6

This would have been Mothers 70th birth day, but *she is gone*. It is now evening. James carried Sarah and me to the Teachers Association. Sarah read a very nice Essay "Theory." it *was splendid*. * * * he [James] *has one of his fits again* to night. he shook his fist in my face and said "Emily you treat me worse than I treat my cows in the stable." *my* how he looks, he has been working himself up to it for a week or more, ever since Henry went away. . . . I hope James will feel all right in the morning, I shall not sleep much. I lie awake most of the time every night untill after twelve. why fear him.

Sunday
7

This was to have been the 50th aniversary of Mothers wed-ing day, and father lives but 40 rods from here. he will not speak. Edna & Henry never even write one word to me, they are in Michigan. Harriet within 40 rods too, alas! can I ever feel but she has done me an everlasting wrong by talking and writing such untruths. I must let it pass. they *must* some day know their error & then—have they any con-science remorse will be as great a punishment as they can bear. . . . * * *

Saturday
13

Sarah worked all day. I did too made mince pies & fry cakes. I promised Mr Saterlee that Sarah and I would come to their house to day, but James went after corn & we could not. *am sorry*—for when I look for company I do not like to be disappointed. * * * *coppied* a *lot* of examples for Sarah, and help her learn her declamations &c. she thinks it would be hard work to get along without Ma, as indeed it *would.* . . . Sarah is such a girl to sit up late. I can not blame her, for *she is myself living over again.* * * *

Thursday
18

Am getting Supper, we have been to Uncles. he is going to come here to dinner tomorrow, I will kill a turkey for him. he is to be 72 Saturday the neighbors are going to buy a *chair* for him cook etc & go there tomorrow evening to Sur-prise him. * * *

Below is a list of Sarah, Henry & my new things. [A list of gowns and accessories follows. Sarah's goods total $42.84, Emily's $33.34.] Sarahs & my clothes have cost a *small* amount beside the cost of Cora Brooks Brocade Silk. *it* was $60, while Sarah can have for $40.09 a dozen nice dresses. . . .

Wednesday
24

Evening again, alone—Henry and Sarah gone. were it not for my journal, I feel so lonely that I could not endure the quietude. no cheery words are spoken. I so weak as not to be able to get in or out of a carriage alone & must use a cane to walk with. . . . We *did* go to Blanchards. Emma Cora & the two boys. James seemed to enjoy the visit, & they did but I can not say I did. . . . Old Mr Nelson was there, he did not recollect me for some time, then he said it was because my hair was so gray. * * *

Thursday
25

James do most of the work, he is doing the chores, has been in the house most all day. He said if he was like other men he would have been up gassing with Emma, under the circumstances. I told him must be he thought of it—well I wouldnt but you talked to me so. *Indeed* never *one half* what I *ought*. I cleaned some more furs and *am* tired, so nervously tired that tears must give relief. * * *

Sunday
27.

All alone, am writing. it seems by the tone of Henrys letter he is doing well and enjoys himself, but he loves to stay at home. he thinks of Ma—yes I know he misses the care, and the little helps I always done for him, his collars, cuffs & jewelry, every thing he always asked "how does it look Ma?" it is hard for him to give up home. * * *

MARCH 1886.

Monday
1

This is James' birth day. 50 years old. I would he might be happy all the rest of his days. O! dear! I *am* tired. . . . There is one singular thing that appears to act upon my brain, or has done so at times when I am tired or need to sleep. a sensation—not of pain but like a flash, of some unseen object passing through or rather over the very top of head beneath the skull. it must be an electric curant of an immortal hope; or a helper for invariably when such flashes occur my thoughts are active in extreme. my pen will go faster and faster untill a story founded upon facts is completed in romance. I believe I will write a novel & get it published. will found it upon truth upon facts which have come under my observation. I only wish I had never burned my stories. * * *

Friday
5

We went to visit Sarahs school this afternoon, the people in the district were most all there. . . . she was reading an Essay—a poem—a farewell to each one (20) when about half done reading, the scholars, and men & women all began to cry. it upset Sarahs feelings so she broke down and let Eddie Wilcox finish—he too could finish it scarcely. It *was really affecting*. Then after school closed they had a regular commotion, to settle who should have Sarah teach. . . . [Two districts wanted Sarah to teach the next term.]

Monday
8

Sarah pick up things & sleek up the house. I help all I can. James do chores &c. he went after *Lizze Beardslie*. she is going to work awhile for me. think she is a good little girl, but I do not know whether she will be strong enough to do the work. * * * Well I finished our furs,—tanning them— they are nice too. now if I can find a good patron [cloak pattern], can make them. * * * James said Harriet told him *Aunt Nancy Baker* died about two weeks ago. She is another one to die a slave to work and the will of man to rule. she *was* a good woman. how vivid to memory is the day she came to Uncle Bens. he was there waiting for her to be introduced to him. he then intended to get her for a *wife to work*, and she *did work*. * * *

Tuesday
9

I have cut a patron for cloak &c. * * * James says he felt real sad to see Emma & them go [to the Dakotas]—orphans and nothing, that he felt the worst he had any time. I think *it* true—the men of the neighborhood all were very much taken to sadness at her sorrow, while those of their own could suffer unnoticed   ah! truth is stranger than fiction. They but perhaps go along to Dakota and see that the young widow has so much sympathy shown her that she need not work. . . . he [James] says Mrs Blanchard was about as I am and she took a patent medicine, that he did not see why I did not do something—I would if I could. I would ride out every day & have oysters & fish and other healthy diet & happiness for my brain & let patent medicine go into the turkey feed. Sunshiny & Chilly.

Sunday
14

We are at home only Henry. May he be well & all right. *am thankful* I am better, will be *very* glad when I can walk. Cora Brook came to stay all night, gave her picture to Sarah. she is almost without home or friends, poor girl, but she would not work. *Vanity*. my—she is made up of bustles, pads, corsets and tight high heeled shoes. am sorry for her. * * *

Friday
19

* * * Mr Bailey paid me $57.00 to apply on note, he gave me a new one of $50.00—Let James have $20, to pay Taxes—gave Sarah $15.00. Now her & Henry have each that I let them have $25.00 and I paid Sarah $10.00 to apply on note of $32.64   I have $12.00 left for myself. I do not think it right that I have to pay the taxes, and now he wants me to buy a harness, *then* he says he will get a mate to Gipsey and then we will have a nice rig. *we* sounds nice, never mind it will be right some time. . . .

APRIL 1886.

Thursday
1

Sew on Cloak, write letter to Henry, Sarah write too. Jas saw wood & chore. he will not answer me when I ask him a question unless he sees fit. so I told Sarah to ask him how much he rec'd for Butter & Eggs yesterday & how much he paid for groceries. she was indignant & I was too, for he would not tell her, said he didnt know. I told him *he would find out when he had to pay it over* This the last of my keeping Book for him, for I have tried long enough. I can *not* beg him to tell me how much he pays out or receives any more. am sorry it is so, for I *know he will be the loser.* Alas! The old Chip over. he is no worse than he was, only I can not get around to do the trading very well. how *can* I like him. *warmer*

Am 48 to day. I had hoped at this period of life to have good health. This morning Sarah said "Ma reach under your pillow and see what you will find." I found this pen with which I am writing. it is a *very fine Gold Pen* with a Pearl handle and Gold base containing a slide to draw the Pen inside when not in use. Very fine indeed. it is my first birth day present of any value. I was so glad of it, that I must cry. Sarah is so kind. . . . *I am thankful* I am no worse, but feel better at heart, though I fear my disease is paralysis from over-work physically and mental trouble for the past ten years has been more than I could endure, especially the last five years, but I have tried with all my might to overcome the great strain imposed upon me by him who promised to protect and support through life. but my nerves broke down, my strength failed & now I scarce can walk. however I can not be too thankful I have been permitted to retain my mind. And still pray & hope to get better. * * *

* * * I told Sarah . . . all must surely die sooner or later that I would make my will if possible that justice should be done them when at last it was left to them. . . . It is my place, for had it not have been for me it would have not been given in the first place for his (James) wages, & then I kept him from signing a note the first year we were married, & alas he so got in debt he was likely to lose it and he gave me the Deed, saying I knew I could keep it for our home & that he could not. I *did* keep it & worked myself almost to death to save all I could so as not to get in debt, and Suffered his abuse, suffered & taught the children to be careful to not displease him—for time & again he pretended to be

crazy & threatened to kill himself. finaly I told him if he wanted to cut such a miserable caper he could, the sooner the better & that he need never look for any sympathy from Children or me again. I know he made it all [up] for he has not tried it since. *Can I*, oh, how can I forgive him. I can—& wish him no harm—but he is almost loathsome in my presence. . . .

Sunday
18

Near night, am all alone. James gone to take Sarah to Mrs Wilcox'. she commences another term (her 5th) of school, in same place as last winter, is to get $24.00 permonth. she sent $25.00 to Henry yesterday, she has sent him total $105.00. I let him have 30.00. * * * James wanted me to go too but I can not ride comfortable nor enjoy going in that old rickety wagon, especially, when I have just such an easy Phaeton as I need, & I worked so hard for it too. we have three horses & it would not cost any more to keep one that I could drive, than to run in the pasture. . . . I have not been any place this spring only once to Uncles & then I rather have stayed at home, he takes up nearly the whole of the seat & leans his leg over upon me so that I can *not* endure it. I can drive yet as well as ever, but I would need a more gentle horse. once I was not afraid to drive any horse that any one else could, & ride them as fearlesly well. My strength is gone. * * *

MAY 1886.

Tuesday
4

Noon—have not done much to day. Believe I will write to Dr Chappell, tell him how I am and ask him how much it would cost to tell me what to do & send me something to take, for I do need something. . . .

Wednesday
5

Am sitting on the East porch in the sunshine. last night I could not walk in from the barn & asked James to let me take hold of his hand. "he thought it would be easier for him

and insisted on my riding on the wheelbarrow. I tried, but
it made me sick & I could not, so he said I could take hold
of the back & get on, on my knees." Eronious idea when I
could hardly hold my head up—had to use harts-horn to
keep from fainting away. Well he led me in, Lizzie helped
me lie on the couch, but for all I had to vomit & have a real
sick time. I feel better but as if I had been sick a long time.
* * *

[There are no entries from May 11 to May 15. The May 16
entry is almost unreadable due to Emily Gillespie's deteriorating handwriting. The first part of the next entry is written
on the top margin of the journal page, indicating it was written as a later commentary.]

Sunday
16.

September 5, 1886. O how sick I was that Sunday & for
weeks my life was hopeless, but God heard & answered our
prayers to let me yet live. To day is Sunday 16. have not
been very well for a week, so have to copy it. * * * Albert
[Dobson] wrote to Henry to come home, and Sarah resigned
her school, I do feel sorry that they have to be at such a
loss. * * *

[After a May 21 entry, the next is for May 26th and is in
Sarah's handwriting.]

Wednesday.
26.

Ma cant write in her journal & wants me to. She is feeling
some better is able to sit up awhile. She came very near
dying. It seems almost impossible to keep her alive every
night.

Aunt Hattie sat up last night—The night before I sat up
alone—Had to call Pa up once but he won't do a thing. Ma
almost died that night. . . . All the neighbors call to see
Ma. . . .

[The next entry is in June, in Emily Gillespie's hand.]

JUNE 1886

Thursday
3

Tis the first I could write for near two weeks. Henry & Sarah *are so kind to me.* . . . The neighbors have all been in & I thank them. Albert & Dr Fuller have been up too. Not one had any hope of my life: but I do not give up—for it seems I must live for my Childrens' sake. *James has rubbed my feet three times. All is well.* . . .

[The diary then skips to the following entry in Emily's handwriting.]

AUGUST 4, 1886.

Wednesday
4

It has been a long time since I have written in my Journal. * * * The dropsy is about gone, I think it left me so poor that I only weighed about 50 lbs. nothing but a perfect wreck of humanity. the joints & bones—O! how they hurt when I was moved. Ah, me. . . . Sarah is attending the Normal. I take her & go after her part of the time. I ride most every day in my new *Carriage*, drive Dr Hines' horse. . . . I wish Henry might go to Normal too, but he will not leave me alone. (not one could be more true.) he sent to N.Y. City & got some *"health food".* it is Cerials & *excelent.* And James—what can I say of him, but twice has he manifested any care or the least anxiety. and now he says He is going to break up keeping house this fall, wants me to go with him to [cousin] Elisha Hawleys with my Carriage or for Sarah & me to go. says I cant do any thing here that I am of no use & might as well go and stay among my relation next winter as not. Alas! what can he think, as weak & helpless as I am. I do believe more than ever that he is crazy. . . . he got one of his *raving mad fits* to make Henry draw & work in hay, & Sarah to drive to unload. he shook the pitch-fork & threatened to ———— Henry (he meant to pound him). . . .

[The diary is kept sporadically until August 27.]

Sunday
28

We are all at home to day. all seems pleasant. * * * Orson Adams has been here two weeks. we hire him to stay here on account of James having grown so much worse & having such fits of insanity. Three weeks tomorrow he tried to choke Henry to death and declared he would kill him; chased him with the pitch-fork—& a club too; he declared he would be the means of him & of all the rest of us. . . . Lizze *was frightened* too, her & Henry came where I was soon as they could, they put me in the Carriage & drew me to Harriets. *horrible!* . . . Henry left me at Mrs Provens after we saw a lawyer. he took the horse & Carriage back home & got John to go with him—nothing could pacify James, he was like a *raving Maniac.* Mrs Proven said we could stay there, so we did untill the next friday night we went & stayed at Johns. (Mr Bronson, Lawyer, had been to see James. said he found him in a *deplorable* condition in the house—windows & doors all closed, that he—himself really feared him, but he finally pacified him so he promised to come to town & try to make some arrangements what to do.) so he did—and proposed to rent the place to Henry for a year to commence next Wednesday Sept 1, & he would go to work for Uncle or go on a journey somewhere.[21] . . .

SEPTEMBER 5, 1886.

Sunday
5.

Once more I try to write, am sorry indeed to have so neglected my journal & could have written many things I would like to have remembered, but each time when I felt like writing no one was near to ask for pen & ink & Book, or were busy. It seems to me a *deep, sorrowful & bad afflic-tion* that I can *not* wait upon myself. * * *

Monday
20

It is a beautiful morning, I have had to wait so long to write. Sarah is doing up the work. I *do* feel sorry she has so much to do, & Henry too. he is trying to plow. he is not strong enough to do very hard work. James is at Uncles, he went away Saturday (18) afternoon or evening just as supper was ready, went with Mrs Vanalstines. he goes and comes at leisure, we only know where as we hear. he does not say where he is going, but usually mentions where he has been. * * *

Saturday
25

* * * cannot walk yet. it is indeed a trial to bear. The heart sometimes is broken by trouble & its possor [*sic*] dies a martyr. I tried so hard to live through it without it being known by the outside world, suffered untold sorrow by hear-ing his abusive language, yet I did not dare to displease him. I have written *many* things in my journal, but the worst is a secret to be burried when I shall cease to be. God alone knows I have prayed every day that I might have Wisdom, that I might know the right way, & *do* right in all my words and doings. *I can say with all my heart my conscience is clear.* * * *

NOVEMBER 1886

Sunday.
Nov. 14

It is Evening—Henry doing chores, he took Sarah to Mr Underwoods. (9 miles.) she is to board there, commence teaching in their district tomorrow, 16 weeks. . . . We had the good fortune to get a hired girl. (Mrs Day came to see if she could work for us, yesterday. . . .) * * * Johns folks all gone to Nebraska. they went Nov. 3—Father went back to Mich. *Harriet made me a visit* before she went away. I think she took *My Beauro.* Ah! *Stolen* from My dead Mother. I am sure I do not know what father will do . . . . *joy with them & peace to my soul, may their untruthful tongues cease their evil words.* * * *

**Friday
19**

* * * Mrs Day do work, *have to keep drawers locked,* otherwise she does very well only wastes. Henry *is* tired. I sit here all the day. . . . hired girl runs off to put on clean dress when men come in & lets two tins of nice victuals burn to a crisp. silly old widow.

**Sunday
21**

* * * *James came* home & stayed to supper & all night. he brought me some sausage & Sweet potatoes, seemed glad to see us &c. but he went to the barn & looked (or felt) all round to see if things was all right. I could see he was not pleased. *he went away this morning* just as breakfast was ready to Uncles. *he looked* as if he was *awful angry.* . . . Sad it seems, yet we almost, yes quite fear to eat what James brings us. . . .

**Monday
22**

Mrs Day has her chores done. I have been winding zephyr [worsted yarn]. *am tired.* Henry has had a bad time with the turkeys. . . . he plowed too & done the chores. . . . Ah I know not what we will do another year. Henry says write in your Journal, "that he commenced to keep horses in stable nights one week ago Saturday."

DECEMBER 1886.

[There are only seven entries for December. They are primarily about Emily Gillespie's deteriorating state of health.]

**Sunday
26**

Am cold. fire down. Henry forgot to shut the door & is doing chores; he is just comeing to fix fire etc. O what a trial it is for him, he is so kind & patient; him and I were here alone yesterday for our Christmas until last evening Oscar [Un-

derwood] brought Sarah home. now we are to have supper.
Snows.

JANUARY 1887.

Wednesday
5

Here it is, another New Year has been ushered in upon us.
* * * The last year has been the most sorrowful & sad of
my life. it has not been as we could have wished. we will
let it pass as a thing of the unhappy past, and begin the New
in hopes that All our future may be more happy, & be it
Gods will I pray as ever that I may walk again. * * *

Sunday
23

Henry doing chores. Katie [Pheyton, girl hired to replace
Mrs. Day] doing up work. I am writing. * * * I *try* to be
pleasant and happy all the time, though I am so poor in flesh
that the hip-joints are so sore I can scarcely lie on them at
night. yet I have a good appetite & good digestion. I really
crave oysters & lobsters, and Beef & pork, but I suppose it
is *not* healthy to eat too much and Henry does not like for
me to eat it, thinks it not fit to eat, so I do not often ask for
it—

FEBRUARY 1887.

Thursday
3

* * * Henry does the chores and all the work, best it has
been done in a long time. Katie sometimes helps him when
she has the time. they have jolly times playing. it is strange,
yet true that all must spend a portion of their lives indulging
themselves in what old-folks call silly folly. aye *we* were
once young ourselves, we ankored safely through *our* girl-
hood, and though not quite escaped the vile tongue of slander, we know we passed or rather came out victorious. Pure
and undefiled virtue. We pray for our children to never do
worse. * * *

Here I sit & think all the day long,
The wind is whistling her doleful song; . . . * * *

Sarah is gone, the wide world is her home.

**Monday
14**

Am feeling quite well to day. may be I can walk some time.
Kate is out to the barn with Henry, has been for an hour.
fire all out & late. Beautiful

**Saturday
19**

* * * I can not write very well on my lap and my cords are
contracting or jerking which feels disagreeable enough, if I
only can keep as well as I am now untill warm weather I
hope to be able to walk. James *wanted* to get a *counsil* of
doctors; I think more for a public show than to cure me, he
is fat & weighs about *180 lbs*. I almost dread spring—for
from appearances & talk he intends to come and stay
here—if so, the children could not get along with him at
all. * * *

MARCH 1887.

**Monday
14**

Have been splitting zephyr—commence pr cuffs for
Henry. . . . Henry took Katie home yesterday (8 miles): she
has been a little offended because I did not approve her
going and staying so long at the barn. *not* that I thought it
wrong but did not look well. . . . Sarah has done more to
day than has many times been done in three. . . .* * *

APRIL 1887

**Saturday
9**

It is a beautiful day—as none but April can give—Dr
Munson of Maquoketa a magnetic Dr. came yesterday. Sarah met him at the train or in town. he rubs and spats. it
seems as if he may make me better so I can walk[22]. . . .

Tuesday
12

What can I say? take alltogether I think I am improve-ing. can use my feet to rock my chair—which I believe I could not do since last summer. Dr M.——says "I will be healthier and stronger than I ever was, like a girl of six-teen." I can hardly comprehend that it is so, for all my life has been so frail. it seems too that my hair is not as white. it is like bringing the dead back to earthly life. . . . *One thing is certain—my hope is the belief that when we cease to live here, our life in imortality will be happiness supreme.* Yesterday was my birth day *49.* * * *

Friday
22

Am feeling real well to day. *Dr Munson* is here yet. he gives me two treatments every day; (rubbing, patting and a gen-eral magnetic drawing of his hands over me, of fanning (which feels as a soft breeze), and shakes his hands over me (as of drops of something invisible)   In the evening when he draws his hand over me, one can plainly see an electric light follow his fingers upon my flesh. he says he thinks I will get well & be healthier than I ever was before. . . . * * *

Monday
25

Am I better permanently or only for a short time? is a ques-tion we ask; and no answer comes. . . . *Dr Munson* went home to day, he said he would be back in about a month & treat me again. It costs so much for them to pay for me that I can not express my feelings of gratitude. . . . * * * Sarah has, it seems decided to think of Joseph Hutchinson as her beau-ideal   I hope she may never be disappointed in mak-ing a choice should she sometime be offered his approval. I think he is a very fine looking, and to all appearances a gentleman. his father is an English Banker. I will not judge now at least. I only do hope she may not see the trouble I have. Ah; *marriage is a lottery.* how full of Deceit do they come with their false tongues and *"there is no one as dear as thee"* until after one is married *then "you are mine now we have something else to do besides silly kissing"*

MAY 1887.

Monday
2

* * * James came home, yesterday. he seems to be more sorry about me sometimes, but is very anxious that I get well, so I can work "& see if we can do something to make up what we have lost," he says. his eyes look bad. . . . * * * Mr Huftenlen came up for a ride, told Sarah "if she would ride with him he would take her to school"   she went. it saves Henry 18 miles drive this morning but she rather it be the Banker instead. 'indeed it *was* a perfect sell.'[23] * * *

Wednesday
11

Mr Huftenlen came up Sunday, & stayed to dinner. * * * Sarah helped Henry plant corn—saturday—they were both real tired. it is too hard work for her. . . . I rode with Henry to Town *Monday* & also to day too, it seems nice to go away & see something diferent, yet the riding is not very comfortable because I am obliged to tie a scarf in front of me to keep from falling out of the seat. . . .

Sunday
22

All alone. Sarah asleep. Henry gone to catch me a fish. James came and stayed a few minutes. . . . Dr Munson came friday to give me more treatments. we feel it almost impossible to pay him. . . .

JUNE 1887.

Wednesday
8

Half past two P.M. am all alone. Sarah went to her school monday morning. Silas Underwood came to supper Sunday, he stayed all night so as to take her. *he is a queer fellow.* Frank Mead came to take her Sunday evening late. I was real glad she had she had [*sic*] another chance, for he seems to think to much of her, for her to be too friendly or sociable unless she returns his friendship. I do not believe in trifling with love or friendship, nor does Sarah. . . . but Sarah has her real affections given to one that is more suited to her, though he perhaps does not know it. yet he shows a very friendly regard for her, and should he fail to realize the fact, it would for a time make her unhappy. may it be all right & end well. I do firmly believe it a lady's right, in honor & law, to propose marriage to one she loves, just as much as the old custom of the man only to be granted that sacred right. by it many happier families would be. *Many* a girl is married to those they can scarcely respect, much less love, but there seemed to be no oportunity of ever winning their secretly loved choice, always living a life of sorrow in the memory of those whose society they could never realize. O that equal rights maybe gained, and man & woman get out of the old ruts, centuries old. * * *

**Monday
13.**

Sarah has worked real hard since she came home, she walked to town and will get a horse to go to her school. * * * Sarah looked for Frank Mead last evening to take her to her school, and he was to visit in afternoon. he did *not* come. Were I to have known of the hypocricy of which people are possessed, and the cunning used to dupe one's reason untill they get one lured from happiness to the cares and sorrows of married life, I most surely would never again be more than once disappointed by a young man's not being punctual to meet their promises, for they grow worse and *worse*, & *worse*, untill all confidence is lost, heartbroken and then dispair   Ah Sarah, Frank is too much like Pa about some things, had any one brave advised me, to beware of where I was going to to seal my future life, before it was too late. All those seemingly good excuses would be but idle talk.

JULY 1887.

**Monday
25.**

* * * Mr Huftenlen came up Friday evening—brought a crate of peaches, 6 pears & a dozen tomattoes to me. he is

kind & may he be rewarded as also other friends. Uncle brought Box Sardines, & Mrs Schmidt a Bottle wine. James came yesterday . . . said "he loved his family etc. that he came near committing suicide last fall and that he would *have* to if things continued in this way." . . . * * * I dreamed last night of a great snake wrigling & twisting every way near me. it seemed between two person fairy like and in a sky of waves.—Omen to Jas coming. Warm

[There are no diary entries from July 30 until August 30.]

AUGUST 1887.

Tuesday
30

I *am Sorry* to so leave my Journal   To day I am about the same, *not* very well, have been sick in bed since the 10th of this month   a bed-sore came on the joint of my left hip from sitting upon it too much. *Dr Sherman* has dressed it 4 times, he cut out a piece of dead flesh larger than a walnut. it is better, has been O *so sore*. Mr Huftenlen came here the 10th to board & make his home, last *monday he asked Sarah to marry him   too old*, about 60, she 22. he pay us [to board] ever liberal. . . .

[There are no entries for September or October.]

NOVEMBER 1887.

Sunday
6

O! dear; I had to cry when I saw how long since I wrote in my Journal. we are so lonely when Henry is gone. he is at Ottawa at work building Depots & water-tanks for the Illinois R.R. Co. Pleasant.

Monday
7

The Children could not make a bargain with James to rent the place. they rented ahouse [*sic*] in Manchester   I came

Journal of Emily. E. H. Gillespie.

Commencing January 1. 1885.

In the past year trials and sorrows has been ours to bear. yet there were many pleasures intermingled. to day is clear with sunshine and our surroundings bid fair for a bright and happy NewYear. Henry's was indeed a very sad accident. his falling 74 feet from the Church Spire, on which he was at work, the 3rd of October. not a scratch, not a bone broken. but seemingly crushed. his left hip is lame yet it is slowly getting better however and the many black-and-blue places have resumed their natural color. words nor pen can express how thankful I am that he was saved from death Sarah and I watched over him night and day for weeks James was anxious about him too as were all who knew him for no one thought it possible for him to live. Sarah is away from home this winter teaching near Edgewood. 14 miles. she enjoys her school of 27 scholars and can come home Sundays. though it is lonesome without her. but it is all right that they can do well when gone, My earnest prayer is that they may possess wisdom and health and ever

Samples of Emily Gillespie's 1885 and 1888 diaries, showing her deteriorating handwriting.

Sunday 8   Henry is yet gone, how I would
like to see him, he says he is well & doing

letter to   well, that he made $38 the last month orders &c
Henry 8   & had to pay $16.50 for his board. I think
days ago &   that is better than losing. he intends
one from   to go to Cherokee & then to Ramova soon.
him.   25 minutes past 2. we had duck for dinner
letter to   yesterday. Pauline went on a spree Saturday
Henry as   noon. came back tuesday evening. she
one from   said she was sick & went away wednesday
him last   morning. Maggie Pringle came wednesday
Thursday.   noon. she is a real good. I have $.50
Card from   per week. I rec'd a package from some
Henry yesterday one of a big white Rabit. I believe
                Henry sent it. shot through the head.
Rabbit   guessing
                weighs 15 lbs. I guess I will now retire
my letter   and try to rest. I am lame all over just
had been   like inflamatory Rheumatism. when will
opened   it cease?   Cold
Wednesday 23   Well thereby:— & Thankfully
I rec'd   I received a Jack rabbit from Cherokee the
a letter   big Jack Rabbit. Henry did send it
from   for my Newyears present. Mr Hightalen
Henry   skinned it today stretched on a board
                it is 2½ ft long & 23 inches wide.

with them, so they could take care of me, Henry was to work
in the shop and store for Huftalen, but he (Huftalen) got the
idea into his head that Henry interfered with Sarahs marrying him—and treated him ever so mean that he could not
stay with him pleasantly, so he [Henry] went away the first
day of November (Tuesday evening)   my hip-joints are both
sore, I am feeling better. James brought some Apples. . . .

November
16, Wed.
1887.

[This entry is in Sarah's hand.] Ma is tired & I am standing
over her trying to write a few lines for her. Have got the
beans & pudding in the oven for supper & she is trying to
write a lying here on the bed. * * * We are living in Lu.
Loomis house in Manchester   I came to live with the children that I might be taken care of—Henry is at present in
Smithland, Iowa working at his trade we are looking for a
letter every day. Mr Huftalen still boards with us and it
makes it very well for us. . . . * * * I sat up twice nearly 2
hrs. each time to day. Dr. Sherman was in to night and left
a rubber attachment for urinal purpose   it looks quite practical. I wish I could see Henry to night, I listen for his
footstep and to hear his gentle word still he does not
come. . . . * * *

[There are only two entries for December.]

DECEMBER 1887.

[Wed.]
28.

[In Sarah's hand.] Ma wishes me to write in her journal and
she is to tell me. It is so cold she can not write. Christmas
is past; Henry is gone; We have not heard from him for over
2 weeks and do not know where he is and I feel extremely
anxious about him. I worry for fear he will starve or freeze.

Sarah takes the best care of me she can. We have had such
cold weather & I am real cold & Sarah has drawn my bed
nearer the stove. James comes often and it seems bad to

have him up there all alone. We spent a very happy Christmas though if Henry had been here we would have enjoyed it much more. . . . * * *

JANUARY 1888. LEAP YEAR.

Thursday
12.

Blizzard of drifting snow. * * * Sarah is here and cares for me the best she can. Dear Daughter it is to Ma more than words or pen can tell   It is not always to last. Ma's work nearly finished   And all is well. Snow

FEBRUARY 1888

Thursday
2

Calamous day. Clowdy. Sarah cutting a vest for Henry, her & Mr Huftalan have taken care of me about two weeks I have two terible sores, hip joints came through the flesh *Oh how glad I was to see Henry. he came home yesterday morning* he has earned $ since he went away—in 3 months,   days work.

[A six-page will, dictated to Sarah, begins after the February 7 entry. Emily Gillespie willed all real and personal possessions to her children. She mentions many items, including hair flowers, but does not mention her multivolume diary. She bequeaths one-third a life estate to the farm to James, void if he remarries. Then follows a long explanation of how the deed she signed over to James was given by force in front of a lawyer and therefore invalid. The will ends:]

My dear Children: I sincerely feel that my physical work is finished. It seems, however, that my mental mission is yet needed in some unforeseen future. It is to me the brightest joy of my life to *know Thou art so true*; that we may enjoy one anothers society,—if not always together—our *let-*

ters.—O, how comforting and how we look for their coming. I can truly say with all my heart I am ready when God calls me; that I have no remorse nor regrets of ill doing. I believe my soul will leave this mass of helpless clay, and be clothed in immortality; that my spirit shall hover near thee, untill we shall meet where there is no more pain, nor sorrow but an eternity of happiness.

The following is Ma's last request: That my funeral sermon be from the words, "my mission here is finished   I have only gone before, all is well," in a church, by a Universalist Preacher is my preference. . . .

Sunday
19.

Sarah is lying down to rest. she is tired   it grieves my heart that she has had to get up to care for me every night, I coughed so hard am better now. . . . James was here every day this week, sawed wood   he went home very much offended that we do not want to go back there. he says "he can not earn any thing alone, that I must come and help him. that it is ended with him if I do not, that that [*sic*] he will support me no longer, if I have anything I must get it myself." he takes Laudanum   I hope he may not, but fear he might. Maggie [the hired girl] going to cook us Turkey, the last one perhaps I can ever have in raising. . . . it seems sad that we must give up all so young, yet truly happy that we leave this world with a clear concience, fully. truly trusting to go into the future in immortal glory all is well. Rains, and thaws.

MARCH 1888.

Friday
9

To day is very stormy. rain and snow. we have callers almost every day. . . . Mr Huftalen helps take care of me. James said he has rented our place to Joseph Hutchinson. he intends to work for Uncle. how I wish he was so we might all live together. I have not been very well the last two weeks.

a Blue Bird has come to visit and cheer me. she roosts scarce six feet away on a grape vine near my window[24]

Sunday
11

'Tis a *beautiful* day. * * * I hope we may hear from Henry soon. he said, not write untill he did, that he would tell us when he *left the Dakotas.* Mr H. wants us to go south. I am willing to go any place where the children can do best and to promote them more happiness. It seems sometimes unbearable to endure such pain, that my work is nearly done, yet there is presentiment to stay yet longer.

[The above is the last entry in Emily Gillespie's diary. She died on March 24, 1888, of "paralysis," according to the county death records. Sarah recorded in her own diary her mother's last moments:]

. . . She could not cry, for the muscles of her face were paralyzed. She would say 'who are these?' 'when will they come?' 'How long, how long' 'O! I can't tell you' & 'write' & 'paper' I got her pencil & paper, but she could not use her right arm.[25]. . .

CHAPTER EIGHT

Emily Hawley Gillespie, Woman

During the last decade of Emily Gillespie's life, numerous comments in her journal about woman's lot show her growing awareness of gender structures and her emerging political sense of sex role identity: "woman is but a mere tool" (February 3, 1878); "woman is always lovely—until her strength & beauty fails" (August 16, 1881); "a slave to man's will" (August 15, 1883). The journal develops from a diary of a young woman's vague unease ("why am I sad?"), into a confidential book of complaints about her husband's behavior and her unappreciated household work, and ultimately into a personal documentary record of what made Emily Gillespie and other women she knew co-sufferers. Despite her immersion in typical female life patterns during her early years, the mature Emily Gillespie was able to sometimes gain a larger perspective on sexual politics. Perhaps the atypical events that troubled her in the 1880s—alienation from kin, strife over property, threats of divorce, family violence—compelled Gillespie to look beyond her personal situation in order to make some sense out of her extraordinary later life.

In the public realm, Emily Gillespie continued her interest in women's suffrage and temperance, gender-linked causes she had supported for years. Women's rights issues were brought home in the turmoil over her inheritance of a bureau from her mother when Gillespie realized, "father took it just because he could" (January 8, 1885). This step from a personal sense of injustice to a broader political one was not common in the women's correspondence studied by Marilyn Ferris Motz: "While many women discussed the unfortunate situations of women of their acquaintance, they seldom connected the misfortunes of individual women with legal constraints or suggested that women's suffrage might alter women's position in society."[1]

Emily Gillespie inductively arrived at feminist rationales for equal pay and comparable worth through her personal experiences in the family farm economy. On several occasions she calculated the cash value of homemade goods, noting in her diary that her production time was worth money. For example, on October 11, 1882, she wrote that store-bought cans of grapes were cheaper than those put up at home when one added in the "three or four hard days work" of woman's time required. Gillespie's argument, a rather radical departure from the popular image of women canning to economize, would probably have met with the approval of Iowa newspaper columnist Nellie M. Rich, a contemporary. In the *Vinton Eagle* Rich sometimes argued for gender role reform and lamented the expenditure of female labor on homemade items that could be commercially produced. "An industrious woman in Marshall County has immortalized herself by making a Centennial bed-quilt containing 14,100 pieces. We would not in the least detract from the praise due her industry and perseverance but must confess that such immortality is dearly purchased. What is a bed-quilt after it is done that a smart, capable woman should stitch her life, both soul and body, into it? . . . you have only a piece for the outside of a quilt which is equivalent to seven and a half yards of calico at eight cents per yard. Sixty cents! And days, weeks, even months spent in putting together bits of cloth that when pieced are only worth that."[2]

Emily Gillespie, on the other hand, *did* count her time as worth money when she produced handwork. The value of her labor made an item far more valuable than the price of its materials: "Finish my Sopha cushion Cover. tis indeed beautiful, there are 96256 stitches on it. could broider at the rate of 100 stitches per seven minutes, which would take   days, providing it was all plain. it is worth at least 15 or 20 dollars to make it. the cost of material was one and one half dollars" (March 2, 1877).

Emily Gillespie's lifelong interest in the cash value of her work is attested to by her extensive account records of profits from home production of everything from clothes to canaries. Her practice of independently spending most of her earnings began when she was an unmarried dependent in Michigan and continued throughout her married years. There are several reasons why, according to the diary, this became increasingly irritating to James—and vehemently defended by Emily. First, the amount of money Emily Gillespie earned grew in significance; for example, her 1880 net income from sales of poultry was $142.78. She wrote in her diary on May 28, 1879: "James help me, about an hour fix turkey pens, (he *does not like* to do *any* thing with the poultry, but *never refuses all* the *money* they bring!)." Male disdain for poultry raising and a begrudging recognition of its economic value were part of the discussion at an 1897 Iowa Farm Institute, according to historian Deborah Fink: "Another Institute speaker who advised on poultry housing and feeding noted that although chickens were below the dignity of a (male) farmer, they did bring in cash. According to him, two hundred hens would pay the store bills of a farm family." At the same institute, Henry Wallace, Sr., supported women's rights to this hard-earned money, arguing, "He [the farmer] . . . must give the wife a chance by providing poultry comforts and must give her the poultry money, and if he borrows money from her to pay the taxes or interest let him give her his note and pay interest on the same. The wife's chickens and the man's money . . . discouraged many a good wife, and has marked a smallness which no farmer in Iowa should be guilty of for a single moment." Thus Emily Gillespie's tears over James's use of her money to pay taxes, expressed in her diary on May 29, 1885 (and a practice in past years, according to her ledgers), was an experience shared with other farm women.[3]

A second issue underlying the dispute over Emily Gillespie's right to her income was her choice of expenditures and what this choice symbolized. By helping to pay for her children's private educations, fine clothes, and books, Emily Gillespie was buying them a route to freedom from farm drudgery. Her critical comments about her sister Edna's farmer sons, her sentiments about the sorry lot of farm wives, and her own son's belated and brief exposure to chores like milking and plowing must have seemed a constant rebuke to James Gillespie. Thus his wife's independent income was educating his children away from the farm. (Emily Gillespie's words must have also cut James. On May 20, 1882, their daughter, Sarah, wrote in her diary, "At home help Ma. Pa is mad & has & is all the time. at noon we were speaking about the millinery trade and Ma said if she had not ever been hindered from doing any-thing she might have been rich. That fired Pa's fury."[4]

Emily Gillespie also used her earnings to purchase goods that symbolized her higher class aspirations. Her choice of home furnishings caused marital strife over what was "too nice" for the Gillespies. When Emily purchased a carriage with $65 of her poultry money (advanced from Sarah at 10 percent interest), she wrote in her diary, "*it* is *splendid*, but James is *too harsh* for anything *so fine*" (September 27, 1885). The clothes and accessories Emily Gillespie purchased or made for herself and the children represented substantial expenditures, especially when compared to clothing allocated for James. Her 1884 accounts show purchases of velvet, silk, gossamer, and cashmere fabric plus trimmings, kid gloves, and hoods for Sarah's and Emily's dresses. The diary records the hours of home sewing that went into creating elaborate women's clothing. That year, Emily Gillespie made Henry two suits (one fine), compared to a modestly priced suit made for James. His only other clothing expenditures were for two pairs of boots, overshoes, and "overhauls." The Gillespies, then, were dressing to play their parts: gentlefolk versus the antisocial farmer. Emily Gillespie's sense of financial independence even enabled her to envision a house of her own. On November 17, 1885, she wrote of buying a house in town—"and after I buy it then I will mention it to James."

Offsetting Emily Gillespie's sense of financial agency were legal realities that harshly demonstrated the limits of women's rights in the 1880s. Her father, Hial Hawley, retained legal ownership of the bureau Emily thought she was morally entitled to inherit. The bureau symbolized the gender inequities in the Hawley family. The only son, an unreliable farmer and husband, was given the Michigan homeplace only to lose it, while the three daughters each received a box of clothing and personal items. It must have doubly stung Emily Gillespie that the only valuable memento of her mother—the bureau—had after legal consultation to be returned to the other male Hawley, her father. The same male prerogative to enforce ownership arose several times concerning the Gillespie horses. Emily would become attached to a horse that James allowed her to call her own, only to be reminded of its true ownership when he sold or traded it without her consultation.

The ultimate demonstration of male legal power came when circumstances combined the rights of her father and husband to force Emily Gillespie to relinquish the deed to the farm. In order to protect her assets (the farm) from her father's claim for filial support, Emily Gillespie had to hide legally behind her husband by deeding back the farm to James. Ironically, her financial success became her burden, as she was the only one of the Hawley children with property enough to support her penniless father. And her sense of honor in receiving the deed to the Gillespie farm, described in the opening diary passages of 1874, became disgrace when she was compelled to sign away the deed in front of a lawyer eleven years later. It is difficult to ascertain how typical female farm ownership in Iowa was at this period. The 1880 agricultural census, for example, names James Gillespie as the property owner, even though Emily Gillespie held the deed. A state suffrage newspaper, *Woman's Standard*, reported in 1886 that 673 women owned and directed farms. In Emily Gillespie's case, however, ownership was ephemeral and more symbolic than real. While her name was on the deed in the county courthouse for eleven years, she did not control the farm operation or income. During her ownership, nothing changed in the family dynamics in which James ran the farm and Emily was responsible for the home.[5]

Emily Gillespie's growing influence over the house through expenditures of her money on furnishings and appliances and use of her time in decorative arts codified her defense of woman's domain in her separate sphere. In moments of conflict, the language in the diary reveals tension over this division. In June 1876, James was loath to go into debt to complete a new larger house while Emily argued, "Fortune favors the Brave." After purchasing construction materials in town she wrote, "*rather* James would get such things but he says I must, if I build a house, do it my self" (June 7, 1876).

"Emily's" house was counterbalanced by "James's" farm, where she again used gender to define and defend limitations on her chores. The classic nineteenth-century concept of separate spheres both protected her from heavy farm labor and emotionally distanced her from the farm that she could never really call her own. While she labored diligently in the family garden, grew marketable produce like berries, and raised her poultry, Emily Gillespie's criticism of her sister Harriet's tasks indicates what farm chores she found unfeminine: "she is a perfect slave to work, feeds hogs & calves, *milks eight cows night and morning.* poor foolish girl. I too once was no wiser" (June 7, 1883). Two months later she wrote of Harriet, "she looks more like a beggar than any thing else. a perfect Slave to mans will & hard-work. indeed I am sorry. I do think woman ought to retain enough of their pride to keep themselves in a shape proper to their sex. no woman need to get so low as to do such filthy work" (August 15, 1883).

Emily Gillespie's definition of milking as a man's chore was atypical, according to three midwestern farming histories cited by John Faragher. Milking *and* feeding of cows were traditionally women's work and "the western people of the early days entertained a supreme contempt for a man who attended to the milking." Faragher says women delegated this chore as early as possible to their children, but according to the Gillespie diary, Henry and Sarah did not milk a cow (and then unsuccessfully) until in their twenties. It is clear that Emily saw milking as below her dignity and the dignity of her children; therefore, James did this filthy work, reinforcing his low status within the family. James complained of this chore to the empathetic McGees, according to the diary, and lamented of it to Hulda Lewis when she visited (May 25, 1885) but got no sympathy from her. The issue of which sex should do this onerous chore was obviously open to debate.[6]

The larger issue symbolized by these arguments over milking and other farm chores was about who worked hardest in the Gillespie family. While this rift was not over the task-oriented versus time-disciplined work patterns that characterized urban couples, each spouse perceived the other's lot as easier. Emily Gillespie saw James's workload vary with the seasons. He was exhausted and short-tempered during spring and fall, yet could spend all day in town during the winter and sleep away Sunday afternoons while she sewed. James, on the other hand, plowed fields while Emily entertained female visitors for the afternoon, busily sewing while she socialized. Content analysis of the diary for July 1884 shows Emily Gillespie's own perception of her days. Her descriptions of tasks predominate, including the catch-all term "usual work." She mentions gardening twenty-three times; "usual work" thirteen; sewing nine; poultry eight; food preparation four; and field work once. In contrast, she mentions visitors twelve times and visiting twice. She notes being tired nine times during July 1884. Emily Gillespie's assessment of herself as a hard worker is verified by the 1880 census account of the farm. While Gillespie cared for fewer children than most women, she did earn more per bird from her poultry than did the average farm wife.

The struggle underlying this debate was over who earned family authority by working the hardest and contributing the most. By emphasizing her workload, Emily Gillespie was seeking recognition for her contribution— and right to power—in family affairs. Her record of James's belittling remarks shows no such recognition, which was typical, according to Faragher's study of midwestern farm families in the 1850s: "The question of power is not only a question of what people do but also of the recognition they are granted for what they do and the authority that recognition confers. There is little evidence to suggest that men, for their part, gave women's work a second thought. That it was a woman's lot to work that hard was simply taken for granted." [7]

If Emily Gillespie could neither own the farm property nor gain equal authority over it through hard work, she could at least control the moral and emotional world within the home. There, Emily Gillespie's children were the fertile ground for maternal influence. Numerous studies of middle-class family ideology show that at this time there was much emphasis on the mother as moral shaper of her offspring. Emily Gillespie's Universalist belief reinforced this approbation. Its doctrinal rejection of the natural depravity of the soul and stress on the mother's role in the rational guidance of children perfectly tapped Emily Gillespie's emotional and intellectual talents. Her belief in discipline via persuasion rather than punishment is shown in the early diary when she admonishes herself for losing her patience with her young children and later in her ongoing involvement in the community debate about how children should be corrected in school (significantly abridged in this edition of the diary). By following the trend in nineteenth-century child-rearing philosophy that increasingly stressed maternal affection over patriarchal authority, Emily Gillespie truly made Henry and Sarah her own. The children became the models of "man & womanhood, virtuous and pure," as she had planned. Their increasing alienation from James, who resorted to physical force for authority in his frustration, was a testament to Emily Gillespie's power on her domestic terrain. [8]

Emily Gillespie's change to a critical perception of James reinforced the moral and class gulf between husband and wife. While James did not have the classic male failing of drunkenness, as attested to by the diary and by family correspondence, he was criticized by Emily for cruelty to animals. His growing propensity toward violent and suicidal "spells" (or is it only that Emily Gillespie now openly documented them in her diary?) fit her image of herself as rational, intellectual, even spiritual and her husband as depraved and carnal.

Thus Emily Gillespie sought the last resort of powerless women and built a sentimentalized home, to use Ann Douglas's paradigm, where moral children and mother existed on a higher plane than father. In this little realm women could have power, as made explicit in books by professional domesticians like Catharine Beecher and her sister-in-law Eunice (Mrs. Henry Ward) Beecher: "What honor can be greater than to found such a home? What dignity higher than to reign its undisputed, honored mistress? . . . To be the guiding star, the ruling spirit, in such a position is higher honor than to rule an empire." Gillespie's belief in such a home, combined with her support of women's rights, matches the "seemingly contradictory visions" of domesticity and feminism that form the theoretical framework of Nancy Cott's *The Bonds of Womanhood.* As Emily had written in her two stories twenty-five years earlier, she wanted power within her private home *and* opportunities in the public world. To twentieth-century readers, these desires do not seem contradictory—nor yet fully realized.[9]

Emily Gillespie's comments about woman's sorrowful lot increase in her diary as her personal situation deteriorated and her larger gender identity grew. When Gillespie wrote, "seems just as if I burned up twenty years of my life by the heat off that stove," she joined a large chorus of women's lamentations available from a wide range of literary sources. As one folksong said of women, "Always controlled, they're always confined. Controlled by their family until they are wives, then slaves to their husbands the rest of their lives." What follows is a sampling of the literature contemporaneous with Emily Gillespie's life. Close to home were "The Household" columns by Iowan Nellie Rich in the *Vinton Eagle.* Embedded in Rich's advice columns on good mothering and household management were critiques of gender arrangements that strikingly parallel Emily Gillespie's private observations. On courtship and marriage, Rich wrote, "for until she is married the sweet Dulcina has all the attention a maiden's heart could crave: she is taken to all public entertainments, is fed to excess on candies and sweetmeats, is called a dear little duck, and the sweetest creature in all the world—presto! When married and the settling-down process begins she is wonderfully transformed." Emily Gillespie wrote in her diary on April 25, 1887, "Ah; *marriage is a lottery.* how full of Deceit do they come with their false tongues and '*there is no one as dear as thee*' until after one is married *then 'you are mine now we have something else to do besides silly kissing.*'" In a column encouraging women to look beyond drudgery to their greater domestic influence, Rich said, "We often wonder if other women sometimes feel that they are mere machines, destined to revolve so many times per day! destined to accomplish a certain round of work, and in time become useless and worn." This echoes Gillespie's comments about woman being a "mere tool" and her question, "I sometimes wonder what *was* destined for woman to do." Aging and removal to institutions was a common enough specter facing women for Rich to generalize from a local divorce case: "The husband, generous soul! will give her twenty-seven hundred dollars to go and leave him free! He has no conscience to haunt him—free to marry again and send, ere long, another victim to the Insane Asylum, to be supported by the State. But the woman—oh girls, think of it! What has she in all the world now? No home, no friend, no reason! Poor Victim!" When Emily Gillespie learned that her friend Mrs. Brook had been institutionalized, she too saw a pattern: "I only wonder that more women do not have to be taken to that asylum, especially farmers wives. No society except hired men to eat their meals. Hard work from the beginning to the end of the year." [10]

A large body of literature sympathetic to the particular lot of farmers' wives and daughters existed on both popular and professional levels. An article in the 1884 *American Farmer* noted: "The records show that, of the whole number of females admitted to the Connecticut Hospital for the Insane from the beginning, which is 558, 215 are housewives, and of course for the most part the wives of farmers. When one considers the method of life of this class of persons, it does not seem so surprising. . . . The average farmer's wife is one of the most patient and overworked women of the time." The first annual report from the U.S. Department of Agriculture, published in 1862, warned about the life young newlywed Emily Gillespie was just entering: "In plain language, in the civilization of the latter half of the nineteenth century, a farmer's wife, as a general rule, is a laboring drudge. . . . It is safe to say, that on three farms out of four the wife works harder, endures more, than any other on the place; more than the husband, more than the 'farm hand,' more than the 'hired help' of the kitchen." [11]

Another topic close to Emily Gillespie's heart and prevalent in nineteenth-century women's lament literature was the theme of frustrated talents. In her diary of June 8, 1885, Gillespie summarized a phrenologist's report about her, underlining every word: "Said *it was the most remarkable head he ever examined. that it was almost impossible for a person to reach as high a position as I was capable of doing. . . . That I could be one of the finest poets, one of the best authors & in the finest arts I could have reached the very highest.*" This lament is similar to a passage in a book by Eunice Beecher which historian Altina Waller says is a thinly disguised account of her early years of marriage to Henry Ward Beecher: "Her youthful aspirations were brought vividly back to her mind. . . . To spend a lifetime in this wearisome, unchanging routine—caring only for bodily wants—to cook—to wash and mend—that was all woman was born for?" [12]

The epigram "marriage is a lottery" appeared in the Gillespies' home medical book by Edward B. Foote and was elaborated on in another marriage manual in *The People's Home Library*: "Marriage is a lottery. You may draw a prize, or your life may be made miserable. It is so much better to remain single than to make an unfortunate marriage." Gillespie drew on the lottery image when writing in her diary about her daughter's suitors (April 25, 1887). Given Emily Gillespie's bitter situation at the time, this image drawn from popular literature linked the "bad luck" of the mother to the prospects of the daughter in a man-made world. The rather cool evaluations of Sarah's beaus in the diary are reminiscent of young Emily Hawley's judgments of suitors during her own courtship. [13]

Perhaps closest to Emily Gillespie's innermost fear was the literature that dealt with the "seasons of a woman's life"—aging. Gillespie at age forty wrote in her diary, "I do wish I may not be so nervous. . . . I too well know my mind sometimes fails in strength to what it used to do. My hope & prayer, that I may never lose my reason as many have done at my age of life" (May 6, 1878). The sympathetic Dr. Hall of the Department of Agriculture put it this way: "There are 'seasons' in the life of women which, as to some of them, so affect the general system, and the mind also, as to commend them to our warmest sympathies. . . . Some women, at such times, are literally insane." While Hall may have been referring to the menstrual cycle or stresses of pregnancy, the issue of woman's emotional vulnerability played on Gillespie's mind as she approached menopause. Her comment about what she termed her increasing "nervousness" was accurate, for content analysis shows that the number of strong opinions— negative and positive judgments—increased in Gillespie's diary as she aged. For example, there were only two such comments in July 1863 and 1873, Gillespie's placid middle years, compared to five in July 1858, when she began keeping a diary during her unsettled youth. But in 1878, at age forty, she recorded eight such opinions and in 1881 there were fourteen, half of them critical. By 1884, the last full July of the diary, the number rose to seventeen. The increasing vociferousness and "irrational" behavior that Gillespie had witnessed in other women and feared in herself was attributed by many professionals simply to female biology rather than to the gender inequities that generated women's complaints. Gillespie inhabited a world in which the laments of women's literature were enacted in the lives of her own growing network of institutionalized, divorced, and overworked female friends. Her increasing critical comments during the last decade of her life, then, resulted in part from her observations and personalization of injustices. [14]

Another opinionated diarist, Mary Chesnut, observed southern slavery and saw parallels with women's situation that prompted similar criticisms. After watching a slave auction, Chesnut noted that women also sold themselves in marriage and continued, "You know what the Bible says about slavery—and marriage. Poor women. Poor slaves." She was constantly critical of her father-in-law and generalized from his actions: "How men can go blustering around—making everybody uncomfortable simply to show they are masters—and we only women and children at their mercy." Chesnut described feeling "like a beggar—utterly humiliated" when compelled to ask her husband for spending money, a financial struggle that also plagued the Gillespies. Mary Chesnut bitterly observed, "There is no slave, after all, like a wife." [15] Gillespie's private generalizations about woman's lot, like Chesnut's, grew out of personal experience but found reinforcement in a chorus of women's literature of the time.

In Emily Gillespie's case, we know from events recorded in her journal that some of her feminist opinions and criticisms were not kept private, especially when she grew angry with James. As historian Charles Bowden puts it, the nineteenth century turned any truly alive woman into a shrew. Nonetheless, Gillespie was resilient and often ended her narrative of her own woes and those of her female friends with the paradoxical refrain, "All is well." Perhaps, as Elizabeth Hampsten observed of women's fixation on bad things in their private writings, noting other people's griefs reinforces one's own sense of survival. As Emily Gillespie wrote her daily narrative of troubles shared with other women, she gained at least a sense of sorority.[16]

While Gillespie developed a loyalty to sisterhood in theory, there is little evidence in her diary of the "loving friendship" with other women that Carroll Smith-Rosenberg illuminated in her ground-breaking study "The Female World of Love and Ritual." Because the emotional centrality of female networks has been documented in numerous and diverse feminist studies by scholars such as Nancy Cott, Elizabeth Hampsten, and Blanche Wiesen Cook and presents a positive view of women's lives, the ways in which Emily Gillespie's experience differs from this model are informative. It is clear from her diary that Gillespie had social contact with women through visiting exchanges and church and community gatherings. But the emotional component of the special relationship between women friends exemplified in Smith-Rosenberg's work and Hampsten's North Dakota study is missing. While Gillespie *at times* inhabited a homosocial world, she does not fit Hampsten's conclusion: "The writings we have been looking at show that women . . . seek out other women, and that these relationships have tenaciously been cherished and nurtured through time, sometimes at great cost."[17]

The main difference between Gillespie's minimal emotionalism when writing about female friendships and women in other studies is, I believe, determined by the genre of the primary sources. The major document of Gillespie's inner life is her diary, while studies of women's emotional networks rely heavily on their letters. The difference between what one writes in correspondence versus one's actual behavior has been succinctly argued by psychologist Gordon Allport and historian John Faragher. This "genre gap" is strikingly demonstrated by Virginia Walcott Beauchamp's comparative study of persona in Madge Preston's nineteenth-century letters and diary. In fact, letters of Mary Hallock Foote quoted by Smith-Rosenberg suggest that affection-by-mail was more acceptable than emotion in person. Foote wrote to Helena Gilder, "Imagine yourself kissed a dozen times my darling. Perhaps it is well for you that we are far apart. You might find my thanks so expressed rather overpowering." Earlier correspondence from Foote to Gilder shows their actual contact was quite restrained and was only expressed with emotional intensity *after* Foote was again safely a continent away: "I have not said to you in so many or so few words that I was happy with you during those few so incredibly short weeks but surely you do not need words to tell you what you must know." [18] If indeed distance between female friends and kin provided the emotional space necessary to reveal one's heart, then one would expect Gillespie's diary to describe less effusive encounters with nearby women. In fact, Gillespie's emotional sentiments about her dear mother in her diary stop during visits between the two women, indicating that distance was indeed a fuel to Gillespie's nostalgia.

In all fairness, even Gillespie's surviving letters are not as demonstrative as those found by other historians, with the exception of one youthful line home to her sister Harriet: "dear would I not like to be there to night we would have one good visit—Ill bet—dont you." Adult letters to her mother and son Henry, objects of great affection in Gillespie's diary, deal with health, the weather, and banal topics like how to mail a pumpkin. Beyond the differences between women's letters and diaries, then, are personal and structural factors in Gillespie's life that explain why some women might not fit the model of intimate female friendship. [19]

On the personal level, the same critical eye that Emily Gillespie focused on gender inequities was sometimes aimed at her female acquaintances. While she empathized with friends raising large families and with her sister's workload, it is clear from her disparaging comments about other women's appearance and behavior that Gillespie did not live in the female world described by Smith-Rosenberg in which "hostility and criticism of other women were so rare as to seem almost tabooed." Passages in the diary indicate that Gillespie in turn was the target of women's gossip and criticism. Her critical bent, exacerbated by Hawley family economic straits, also eventually alienated all of Emily's siblings, eliminating the "inner core of kin" Smith-Rosenberg found supporting most women. The end of affectionate relations with Harriet, sister and dear friend, was a double loss to Emily Gillespie. Underlying her critical nature were the high class and cultural aspirations the young Emily Hawley showed when judging suitors and the older Emily Gillespie used when choosing elevated companions for her children. If even some of her critical comments about her neighbors were permitted outside the "safe distance" of the private diary, Gillespie would suffer the social isolation other intelligent pioneer women like Caroline Kirkland reported when her neighbors suspected "that we held ourselves above them." [20]

The structural barrier of rural isolation mentioned many times in the diary surely made maintenance of close ties with women difficult. Gillespie's diminished mobility during the first years of marriage compared to her single days (see analysis in chapter 5) continued throughout her life. From 1874 to 1884 content analysis shows she received an average of 6.6 visitors a month, went visiting 3.4 times, and went to Manchester 3 times. The narrowing constriction of such isolation was blamed for women's oppression in articles on farm life and has been sympathetically portrayed in the fictional work of midwestern writers Willa Cather, Hamlin Garland, Ruth Suckow, Bess Streeter Aldrich, and Susan Glaspell. Garland depicted farm women's lives with shocking realism in both his fiction and autobiographies. He said in *A Son of the Middle Border*, "the majesty of the colorful sunsets which ended many of our days could not conceal from me the starved lives and lonely days of my little sister and my aging mother." While some of the "wasted and worn" women he portrayed in *Main-Travelled Roads* seem mercifully unaware of their slow decline, others have horrible knowledge of their future as farmers' wives: "I was a fool for ever marrying. I made a decent living teaching, I was free to come and go, my money was my own. Now I'm tied right down to a churn or a dishpan, I never have a cent of my own. He's growlin' round half the time, and there's no chance of his ever being different." Willa Cather summed up the cost of rural life on a thinking woman: Alexandra, the successful farmer of *O Pioneers!*, says, "We grow hard and heavy here. We don't move lightly and easily as you do, and our minds get stiff. If the world were no wider than my cornfields, if there were not something beside this, I wouldn't feel that it was much worth while to work."[21] Emily Gillespie had the sensitivity to perceive and resent the narrowness of her life on the farm. She dreamed of leaving it for life in town, a house of her own, a career as a writer. While she had poor luck creating fiction based on sentimental memories of her girlhood past, she was writing the far better and more bitter story of her lonely life in the diary.

Despite her social isolation, Emily Gillespie did hold close to her heart three emotional relationships during the last decade of her life. One was with her mother, Sarah Hawley, although the depth of feeling was only clear after Hawley's death. While Gillespie wrote of her parents nostalgically, her expression of affection after the loss of her mother makes the bond more explicit. Again it seems only the ultimate distance imposed by death on the mother-daughter relationship released impassioned feelings not previously evident in the diary or correspondence. By the time death severed this tie in 1882, the next Sarah—Emily Gillespie's daughter—was seventeen and already a kindred spirit. In this relationship, affections like those Smith-Rosenberg documented are expressed, as Gillespie took pleasure in Sarah's development and felt lonely pain during Sarah's absences. One could argue that Emily Gillespie so molded her son, Henry, in accord with feminized values that he, too, fit into her world of confidential love. Her children offset some of the rural isolation. She wrote of them, "Still we enjoy visiting together, perhaps better than with others—it is a bright & happy thought" (April 22, 1885).

The most constant relationship was of course with the diary, as Gillespie wrote many times to her "dearest friend" late at night after all were asleep or upon rising first. As Florence Nightingale put it, "Women never have an half-hour in all their lives (excepting before and after anybody is up in the house) that they can call their own, without fear of offending or of hurting someone. Why do people sit up so late, or, more rarely get up so early? Not because the day is not long enough, but because they have 'no time in the day to themselves.' "[22] Gillespie's lack of empathy for women outside the tight circle of her family is not a sign of "lack of ego development," as Susan Arpad characterized a similar pattern of aloofness in the diary of Samuella Curd. Rather, Gillespie's closest friends were rather egotistical: herself via her diary and her reflected self in her children-companions.

If Emily Gillespie was limited in the role of friend due to physical isolation and personality traits of criticism and reticence, how did she fit other role expectations as a daughter, wife, and mother near the end of her life? By examining the relationships of individual women and comparing them with other women's, we can refine and enlarge our view of nineteenth-century families. In writing of the sordid Beecher-Tilton testimony that fascinated readers like Emily Gillespie, historian Altina Waller sums up what insights we can now gain from re-viewing such unpleasantness. "On the shadowed stage of Victorian family history, the Beecher trial shines a bright spotlight on one family—thereby illuminating the contours of nineteenth-century family dynamics."[23]

As a daughter, Emily Gillespie was attentive, even though she could visit both parents only once during her married life. Comments in her diary show a regular exchange of (unexpressive) letters and parcels between Emily Gillespie and Sarah Hawley. Throughout the diary from 1861 when she left home to her mother's death in 1882, Gillespie when sad mentioned her parents and childhood's home. It is unclear from these entries whether memories of home caused unhappiness or if, when sad, Emily turned to thoughts of simpler days in Michigan for solace. At any rate, the "little family circle" was forever broken by Sarah Hawley's death in July 1882.

As a mourning daughter, Emily Gillespie was atypically intense, according to a study of the grieving process by Paul C. Rosenblatt, *Bitter, Bitter Tears*. Only 2.5 percent of the over two thousand nineteenth-century diaries Rosenblatt and assistants read met criteria for inclusion in his study, and Emily Gillespie's was one of them. Diarists had to mention the loss of a close relative within three years or mention the loss of another person more than three times. Gillespie did both, noting in her diary two deaths and twelve separations, according to Rosenblatt. (The actual number mentioned in the diary is far higher.) Emily Gillespie also remembered her mother after death more often than other mourners in Rosenblatt's study. While 33 percent mentioned a loved one's death within a month of the event, only 7 percent (Gillespie among them) recalled the loss a year later. Gillespie again mentioned her mother two years after the loss, as only 3 percent of the mourners did. At three years, only 0.7 percent remembered the dead, and Gillespie was not among them. Her diary for that month, July 1885, focused on Sarah and Henry, her deteriorating relationship with James, and her health. But Gillespie mentioned her deceased mother far more often than on the anniversaries of her death, although for brevity's sake these repeated comments have been edited from this version of the diary. She remembered her mother's birthday, her parents' wedding anniversary, and events associated with items like fabric long ago received from Michigan.[24]

Why was Emily Gillespie so intensely focused on her lost mother? Rosenblatt notes that "most diarists, in a first entry reporting a loss or in the early entries after it, wrote that 'we will meet in heaven.' " Gillespie, on the other hand, wrote far more about the separation and loss than about anticipation of a reunion in heaven. While she had composed poetic eulogies upon the death of her father-in-law, friends, and even the suicide James VanAlstyne, for her own mother Gillespie copied over a poem composed for another friend's death two years earlier. This poem, with its reunion hope in stanza three, seems the epitome of "sentimentalism," that mouthing of ideas in which there is little emotional investment. Perhaps Sarah Hawley's death was so traumatic to Emily that her only response was employment of pat imagery from an earlier poem. By 1882 Gillespie no longer attended religious services, the Universalist church having disbanded and none other suiting her. Comments throughout the later diary about people's responsibility to help themselves and her anticipation of earthly punishment for her detractors may indicate a growing secularism on Gillespie's part. Turning to God only in moments of great crisis, Gillespie most often relied on her own resources. If she no longer truly believed in the final heavenly reunion with her mother, Gillespie would naturally focus on the earthly separation which was forever. A similar pattern appears in the nineteenth-century diary of agnostic Corwin Snow, who was obsessed with the death of his wife, Amanda, and wrote movingly of his secular grieving process, which took three painful years.[25]

Two years after Sarah Hawley's death, memories of her were reawakened by the arrival in Iowa of Emily's father, Hial Hawley. He brought with him the heirloom bureau that proved what dutiful daughter Emily had always hoped. After she discovered an inscription by her mother on a drawer of the bureau, Gillespie wrote, "I always felt that Mother loved me above all others, but could not know it until today. it seemed almost when I read her gift to me that she came to tell me, that I might have proof that it *is* surely mine and *not* Harriets as she claims it to be. *it is well*" (May 27, 1884). Gillespie's changing relationship with her father is an example of the pattern of emotional intensity that characterized her life. At age twenty-three, as Emily Hawley prepared to leave home for the Far West, she wrote longingly in her diary, "ah, that I cannot always have a home at Fathers, why, because my Father will not live always" (May 12, 1861). Twenty-three years later when Hial Hawley appeared on her doorstep, she wrote, "I can scarcely believe that Father would have come here, but he *did* come last night about eleven o'clock. . . . I think a great deal of him and respect him though I feel it an imposition upon us all" (May 15, 1884). When separation was imminent in 1861, Emily was emotional; when her father was present, however, she was pragmatic and eventually hostile.

Initially Sarah Hawley's death drew father and daughter closer. Emily went home to Michigan to visit for six weeks in 1884. Did she extend an invitation to her father at that time to come stay with her, thinking that the distance to Iowa made her "safe" from his acceptance? One cannot tell from the diary or existing letters; nevertheless, Hial Hawley arrived in Iowa a month after Emily's visit. Her diary makes it clear that the popular cherished image of happy extended families all sharing a home together a century ago may be inaccurate. By the mid-nineteenth century, such a family configuration was rare; Mary Ryan's study of New York census records shows that in 1864 only 5.9 percent of households contained extended families. The degree of acrimony within the Gillespie household during Hial Hawley's abbreviated stay was unusual, however, compared to Marilyn Ferris Motz's findings. In the correspondence of over one hundred Michigan families, she found only one instance of a dependent adult complaining of mistreatment by a daughter. The differences between letters and diaries throw this conclusion into question, however, for few parents would probably write of such an embarrassing situation, or descendants might purge such correspondence from collections of family papers sent to archives.[26]

The arguments between Emily and her father, with the children and James taking their respective sides, eventually led to Hial Hawley's furious exit and allegiance with Emily's sister Harriet McGee. Rather than define herself as an awful daughter, Emily Gillespie chose to redefine her kin, excluding them from her increasingly narrow definition of the family circle. She wrote on July 16, 1885: "father, I can not feel he *is* a father, & Harriet is no sister, & James what is he—as to what a husband should be." (Hial Hawley went on to so alienate Harriet that he became dependent on the county and lived with Harriet's in-laws, who received payment to board him. He eventually returned to Michigan, where he died in 1889.) Gillespie's diary, then, documents a situation perhaps suppressed in family correspondence and avoided by the vast majority of families that stayed tightly nuclear. It is a record that hints at complexities of nineteenth-century family life scholars have long suspected. Lillian Rubin put it this way: "So much of what we think about the family of the past is a fable. . . . The dream of that earlier time seemed a simpler one. . . . The old dream didn't work so well for most people most of the time even then; marriages staggered under the burden of these role definitions and the dream began to look like a nightmare."[27]

By the mid-1880s, the relationship between James and Emily Gillespie had indeed turned into a nightmare for the entire family. Emily, who had so aspired to be a good wife in her 1860s journal, was not critical of herself by 1880. It was James who had descended in Emily's eyes from being her "best friend" in 1861 to an enemy and threat. "I am sorry my love or friendship for him is broken," she wrote (July 2, 1885). The diary relentlessly records the bitter quarrels between husband and wife over myriad topics, leading to a separation in 1886. The Gillespies' disagreements over their economic and domestic roles in the family have been described and the causes analyzed. These disputes became increasingly vehement, occasionally breaking into violence or threats of suicide by James, as Emily became more nervous and he more inclined toward "fits."

There are several possible explanations for James Gillespie's loss of control over his behavior. Perhaps his "spells" were symptoms of a psychological disorder such as manic depression or dyscontrol syndrome. Or James simply may have had more than he could bear and found release in rage, just as Emily found hers in tears. Another explanation for James's fits that matches indirect evidence in the diary is that they were caused by sexual frustration. This explanation is suggested by the case of Calvin Stowe, who suffered mercurial emotional swings which he attributed to desire for his wife, Harriet Beecher Stowe, according to Mary Kelley. Calvin called his moodiness "hypochondriac morbid instability" and found release through sexual relations with Harriet, who tried a variety of strategies to regulate his demands.[28] Passages in Emily Gillespie's diary indicate that by the mid-1880s the couple had separate bedrooms and Emily refused "to lie back in the cold" with her husband, eventually blocking her doorway with a chair. James's remark that Emily should take her new carriage to bed with her indicates this abstinence was not to his liking. Another indication of possible celibacy on Emily Gillespie's part is a break in her regular pattern of marks (!!!) that recorded her menstrual periods. These marks, resumed in November 1866 after Emily finished nursing Sarah, continue with regularity until January 1884, when they stop for almost a year. They begin again in December 1884, but are sporadic until they end completely in May 1887. This broken pattern may of course signal the gaps in the menstrual cycle that some women experience with the onset of menopause. But the combination of interrupted marks, twitting over sexual issues documented in the diary, and Emily Gillespie's growing interest in "social purity" point to a possible cause of James Gillespie's moods: the loss of intimate relations with his wife.

Since sexuality was a topic Emily Gillespie circumnavigated in her journal, the causes for this break in conjugal relations are unclear. The most frustratingly evasive passage in the diary hints that some action of James's was too heinous to record: "I . . . suffered untold sorrow by hearing his abusive language, yet I did not dare to displease him. I have written *many* things in my journal, but the worst is a secret to be burried when I shall cease to be" (September 5, 1886). Since Emily had documented elsewhere in her diary James's violence toward the farm animals and the children, physical abuse of his wife surely could have been recorded. Did James sexually demand of Emily something that caused her to withdraw from him and think him a brute? In other areas of their marriage, Emily found her tastes "too nice" for "harsh" James. By April 1886 she wrote, "he is almost loathsome in my presence." Perhaps she now included her most private sexual self as too nice for the demands of her husband.

Other women's explicit narratives about their husbands' demands for sexual frequency or practices appeared in feminist publications that promoted "social purity." The purity literature argued for "voluntary motherhood" through birth control practices such as abstinence and withdrawal rather than through contraceptive devices. The movement was often linked with the free love philosophy of free association between women and men without taint of sexual interest. Emily Gillespie's defense of Sarah's and her own friendship with Mr. Segar echoes this philosophy. Certain terms that recur in the diary—purity, nobility, human spirit—were commonplace in purity literature, as were themes favoring "the triumph of Reason, Knowledge, and Continence" for regulating sexual desire. Woman's agency in the voluntary motherhood movement was crucial, according to Linda Gordon. In the dichotomous view of woman as spiritual and man as brutishly carnal, passionlessness became woman's superior defense. While forced abstinence would understandably incense James Gillespie, Gordon argues the woman's point of view: "'Sex-hating' women were not just misinformed, or priggish, or neurotic. They were often responding rationally to their material reality. Denied the possibility of recognizing and expressing their own sexual needs, denied even the knowledge of sexual possibilities other than those dictated by the rhythms of male orgasm, they had only two choices: passive and usually pleasureless submission, with high risk of undesirable consequences, or rebellious refusal."[29]

In her mature years, then, Emily Gillespie attempted to control the four structures of her life that Juliet Mitchell argues are crucial to a transformation of woman's condition: production, reproduction, sexuality, and the socialization of children. By claiming moral superiority to James, she linked herself to the history of American feminist thought, from Seneca Falls to twentieth-century suffrage. The bitterness of the debate with James over her empowerment, however, also shows the limitations of change possible within the "complex unity" of one family.[30]

The diary is also the record of a couple attempting to make the transition to a new life stage. They had completed their early adulthood tasks, he successfully farming, she rearing two fine children. Now that the farm had weathered the recession and the children were more independent, the Gillespies were faced with choosing what new tasks to undertake. To use an apt phrase from Willa Cather, both Emily and James Gillespie had "grown to be more and more like themselves." She resumed her artistic pursuits and development of her inner life, while he adamantly focused on the farm, the monument to his life's work. In an era which increasingly stressed the desirability of a "companionate" marriage, the Gillespies entrenched themselves in separate, irreconcilable spheres. Separate spheres by definition need not be so destructive to marriage, according to Robert L. Griswold's study of couples' expectations: "People in the nineteenth century witnessed the arrival of family relations grounded in a partnership between husbands and wives who, although working in different spheres, owed each other mutual deference, respect, kindness, and love."[31] Griswold found in divorce testimony that the prescriptive ideal of the husband-companion indeed affected the lives of rural women and men. But the ideal was in conflict with nineteenth-century realities: "Consensus and mutual respect did not come easily when the law, the economy, custom and nature still conspired to make husbands vastly more powerful than their wives. . . . Once the wife was allowed to voice opinions, the opportunities for overt conflict multiplied. The companionate ideal, in short, raised the emotional stakes in marriage," says Suzanne Lebsock. James Gillespie, in his wife's view, certainly was not the genteel man she had loved as a suitor. He did not fit the model Griswold found described in *Godeys*: "A good husband always regards his wife as his equal . . . and never addresses her with an air of authority, as if she were, as some husbands appear to regard their wives, a mere housekeeper." James, in contrast, fit the patriarchal model of marriage rather than the modern companionate one, just as he was an authoritarian father rather than a progressive one. [32]

Emily Gillespie's diary became her dearest companion, displacing James. When she called the diary her only "confident," did she choose the masculine form of the word on purpose, perceiving the diary as her lover as well as friend? Ellen Rothman found that Victorian couples stressed communication in the most intimate sense between those in different spheres. As one woman wrote to her lover, "My heart is a castle with most obstinate doors. . . . *you* have a right to enter in, explore and know all the recesses of my heart." When the Gillespies were first married, James played this role and Emily termed him her "best friend." The lack of personal details in the diary during these early married years suggests Emily was confiding in James. But by 1885, it was James who was shut out from intimacy and the diary that received long confidences. If James were cut off from both physical and emotional intimacy with Emily, the crisis in the Gillespie relationship is understandable. [33]

It is harder to understand, given the details of the deteriorating marriage, why James and Emily Gillespie did not divorce. By the 1880s 1 in every 481 couples were divorcing, according to U.S. government statistics. In Iowa, 5,603 divorces were granted between 1882 and 1886. There was a fourfold increase in the U.S. divorce rate between 1860 and 1900, due to a variety of factors such as changing marriage ideals and women's greater rights to education and separate incomes. Emily Gillespie wrote of at least ten other area couples who had separated or divorced, and James pressed for a divorce several times. Once in the diary Emily did mention having considered leaving James as an option: "I only regret that I did not go away and leave him when I first knew and found out what a terrible despondent disposition he had. then I was well. I could have taken my children & taken care of them" (August 17, 1885). By the late nineteenth century, two-thirds of divorces were obtained by women, a figure reflected in Iowa divorce courts. In the "cruelty" category of divorce petitions, the proportion of women filing was 88 percent. Iowa law reflected the national trend toward higher expectations for happiness in marriage, expanding the definition of cruelty to include "mental suffering" in 1886. The incidents recorded in Emily Gillespie's diary surely would have enabled her to successfully sue for a divorce. She perceived herself as capable of earning a living and by the mid-1880s her children were also employed. What factors mitigated against divorce? [34]

Comments throughout the diary show Emily Gillespie's disapproval of divorce and the public scandal involved. Even Elizabeth Cady Stanton, who deplored "man-made" marriage and was separated from her husband for the last twenty years of her life, did not seek a divorce. The complex relationship between one's ideals and personal exigencies Elizabeth Griffith analyzed in the case of Stanton may have operated for Emily Gillespie. [35] But by August 1886 James's rage drove the family into town for safety and a lawyer had to arbitrate a settlement. The family's buried secret of strife was now public. Emily wrote in her diary, "I tried so hard to live through it without it being known by the outside world, suffered untold sorrow" (September 25, 1886). Even after the legal ban on James kept him from living with the family, Emily did not pursue a divorce, perhaps still hoping to reconstruct her ideal of Home.

What is even more striking in the unfolding Gillespie family drama is a comment in the diary that suggests this experience was not atypical. In the midst of her troubles Emily wrote, "I wish we might ever lived happily together, and we have when compared with many that I know" (November 8, 1885). The rapidly rising divorce rate in the nineteenth century, then, only documents the worst cases of domestic unhappiness. Lebsock found in Virginia women's letters and diaries that one-third were miserably married; another third "wrote as though their husbands lived on some other planet." [36] It is paradoxical that Emily Gillespie, who abhorred public scandal during her life, left such a graphic account of her deteriorating marriage and a hint that what she recorded was being experienced within other Victorian homes.

The most successful female role in Emily Gillespie's life was that of mother. In the diary one can trace her methods for raising educated, thoughtful children. Sarah became much like Emily Gillespie, eventually keeping a diary with language and viewpoint that paralleled her mother's (see the Conclusion for a comparison of the texts). In numerous passages recounting her trials, Emily Gillespie expressed gratitude for having such pleasing children. In the "account" of her life's work, the children offset the deficit of Emily's unhappy marriage: "My children have thus far amply repaid me for all troubles and sorrows" (January 20, 1886). As her strength waned, she received vicarious pleasure from their accomplishments, saying of Sarah, "*she is myself living again.*" As the children, living monuments to her sacrifices, went out into the world of work and college, Emily Gillespie lamented the loss of her companions in the emotional language she had used twenty years earlier for James.

Then in May 1886, her final role—invalid—sadly brought the family circle together again as the children returned home to care for Emily and to attempt to run the farm. For almost two years one or both of the children nursed their mother, first at the homeplace rented from James and finally in a rented Manchester house. The children's devotion to their mother reflected her earlier sacrifices to them. Gillespie perfectly fulfilled the role of Victorian mother that Henry James worshiped: "To bring her children into the world—to expend herself, for years, for their happiness and welfare—then, when they had reached a full maturity and were absorbed in the world and their own interests—to lay herself down in her ebbing strength and yield up her pure soul to the celestial power that had given her this divine commission." [37]

Women's reports of ill health were commonplace in the nineteenth century. Robert Griswold found that 27 percent of the women in divorce documents described their health as poor. Bad health was interpreted according to the world view of the observer. In Emily Gillespie's mind, the organic causes of her edema were secondary to the deeper source: years of overwork. Sarah Gillespie felt her mother's life was unnaturally shortened, as it indeed was. According to life expectancy statistics, Emily Gillespie should have lived to be seventy. [38] While Emily saw her growing paralysis as the symptom of long misuse, James saw it as female complaining and was infuriated by his wife's invalidism. This gulf in interpretation reflected the gendered view of illness. When Catharine Beecher heard repeated stories of women's illness during her travels, she concluded that these were symptoms of woman's unfair domestic role and called for reform. S. Weir Mitchell, on the other hand, encountered hysteria in upper-middle-class women and attacked the patient's motives as passive aggression rather than criticizing gender roles that sent some women to bed. Modern historians

Henry Gillespie as a young man.

Sarah Gillespie Huftalen at fifty-nine, M.A. graduation photo.

have continued the debate about the motives of women's physicians and the unconscious motives of bedridden women whose illness became a means through which they could control their families and nurses. [39]

In the Gillespie family, it was Sarah upon whom most of the nursing burden fell. By the time of her mother's death, Sarah was twenty-three, unmarried, and in financial straits from caring for an invalid. In the last months of Gillespie's life, Emily and Sarah paradoxically changed roles. Catharine Beecher and Harriet Beecher Stowe idealized the nurse Sarah had become: "God himself made and commissioned one set of nurses. . . . He made them to bend tenderly over the disturbed and irritated, and fold them to quiet assurance in arms made soft with love; in a word, he made *mothers!*" [40] At the very end, then, Emily Gillespie had drawn her children back to her side and suffered as a metaphor for woman's oppression from hard labor. Her death was an allegory for her life. She had struggled to fulfill the roles of daughter, sister, wife, and mother, and ultimately was a bedridden symbol of suffering womanhood. Toward the end Gillespie called herself a martyr and saw her life's accomplishment as serving others and sacrificing for her children.

Gillespie's characterization of her life as selfless, especially given the talents and insights she demonstrated in her diary, may strike modern readers as frustratingly narrow. But as Mary Kelley has argued, "A selfless life is not . . . 'a life that has no story.' It is a life that has many different stories." Emily Gillespie's selfless life was not easily achieved, nor was it a silent one. She bound together her many roles in her diary, her own Golden Notebook. She then preserved this part of herself by giving her diaries to her daughter in a matrilineal act of faith. When we read the diary over a century later, Emily Gillespie is indeed herself living again. [41]

Emily Hawley Gillespie's children did achieve much to fulfill her wish that they "might do what I might have done and be what I might have been." For several years Henry Lafayette Gillespie pursued itinerant work such as cabinetmaking and running a ferris wheel at the 1893 Columbian Exposition. In 1894 he earned a Bachelor of Divinity degree and became a Universalist minister. After James Gillespie's death in 1909, Henry returned to the family farm. He was known in Manchester as a progressive farmer interested in new methods to reduce drudgery. Sarah Gillespie married William Huftalen in 1892. She continued teaching and became superintendent of schools for Page County, Iowa. She was president of the Delaware County WCTU for nine years and president of the Iowa State Teacher's Association for fifteen years. She earned her Master of Arts from Iowa State University at age fifty-nine. After her retirement from teaching Sarah, then a widow, moved back to the family farm to keep house for her brother, "thinking it my duty as he never had a home of his own." She wrote historical articles, researched her family genealogy, and collected family materials for preservation. Sarah Gillespie Huftalen also wrote extensive diaries, which she preserved with her mother's. They chronicle her life of achievement and the growing bitterness between Sarah and Henry after her return to the homeplace. Suzanne Bunkers has traced gender dynamics in Sarah's diaries that mirror those between Emily and James Gillespie.[42]

Conclusion:
The Diary as Female
Autobiography

Writing books is too good an idea to be left to authors.

Thomas Mallon[1]

D iaries like Emily Hawley Gillespie's contain compelling new American voices that challenge the current intellectual boundaries of history, literature, and American studies. It is clear that Gillespie's journal is not an objective personal history. Rather, it contains an intricate story that opens up in suggestive ways when examined as autobiography.

The study of autobiography as literature emerged as a respected field of inquiry approximately a generation ago. Employing interdisciplinary methodology, scholars analyzed personal texts to expand the elitist boundaries of thinking about American culture. Such diverse autobiographies as *The Education of Henry Adams* and *Black Boy* were read anew as both intellectual history and literature. In recent years, a few American women's autobiographies have entered the boundaries of the curricular canon, particularly in women's studies courses. The life stories of notables like Elizabeth Cady Stanton and autobiographically grounded texts like "Silences" by Tillie Olsen and Adrienne Rich's *Of Woman Born* have become classics. But along with hard-won acceptance by the academy has come limitations: autobiography is subjected, like a stepchild, to traditional literary criteria.

The current study of autobiography has moved steadily away from readings of what James Olney calls "the simplest and commonest of writing propositions" to increasingly literary forms of the genre such as Vladimir Nabokov's *Speak, Memory* and Maxine Hong Kingston's pastiche of myth and memory *The Woman Warrior*.[2] The autobiographies of ordinary people like Lucy Larcom and "plain" Anne Ellis are defined as historical/social documents rather than as literature from distinctive American voices. Autobiography scholarship has become established, complete with high-ranking theoretical scholars, classic essays, a canon of heavily studied texts, and boundaries.

The diary, that form of written personal narrative least colored by artifice, closest to the American life, truly "the story of a distinctive culture from within" that autobiography was once touted to be, is outside the interest of most scholars. A few diaries are included in the historical canon due to their content rather than their innovative literary form. For it is a notion of significance—important periods in military/political history, famous people encountered—that permits a few "important" diaries inside academic boundaries. The only woman's diary extensively studied for its form is the atypically literate one written by Anaïs Nin. Thus the diary is acknowledged as a legitimate autobiographical text only when either the times recorded are extraordinary—William Byrd's, Mary Chesnut's—or the writer is extraordinarily established in literature—Henry Thoreau, Anaïs Nin.

Why are the estimated 100,000 publicly available American diaries, which record that dynamic interaction of the ordinary individual and society we seek in American studies and women's studies, virtually ignored as both literary and cultural texts by the very scholars who once expanded the critical boundaries of history and literature to encompass autobiography? Partially it is because we have yet to establish the critical tools that will make an unwieldy extensive diary like Emily Gillespie's accessible. It is also because we were trained as scholars to see ordinary people's stories as inherently less interesting than those told by Henry James, Henry Thoreau, or Henry Adams.

But on a deeper level, I would argue, the diary is resisted because in both form and content it comes closest to a *female* version of autobiography. The diary given to an adolescent girl symbolizes the type of life she is expected to record. "The little girl is being trained to appreciate dailiness, and ordinariness: her lot in life is the quotidian; her brother will do whatever transcending there is to be done," observes Thomas Mallon.[3] Mary Jane Moffat in her collection of women's diaries ironically links the terms that both woman and diary engender: "emotional, fragmentary, interrupted, modest, not to be taken seriously, private, restricted, daily, trivial, formless, concerned with self . . . endless."[4] The narrative of an American life that is both female *and* ordinary, the diary remains marginal in the eyes of most literary scholars. But feminist literary theory has shown that being on the margins gives women a great amount of freedom. Because diaries "lay safely within the province of the personal," according to Jean Strouse, they were permissible buried outlets for the voices of talented women like Alice James.[5] And as more about women's psychology, language, and historical experience is illuminated by theorists such as Nancy Chodorow, Carol Gilligan, Suzanne Juhasz, and Carroll Smith-Rosenberg, the diary is emerging as a text that reflects female patterns of experience.[6]

How can we as scholars, brought up on the canon, trained by the academy's fathers, learn to read these designs? We can invert the critique of diaries that excludes them as too problematic for literary study and find that the insistence upon an obvious literary Design in autobiography obstructs our reading of a separate Truth as told by female diarists.[7] We can examine anew the diary's characteristic language, perspective, and narrative structure, then reassess it sui generis, as itself, rather than as "deficient" autobiography. By crossing many of the formalist boundaries of published autobiography, I would argue, diarists both tell their truth *and* create female design—a supersubtle design, similar to a quilt's, made up of incremental stitches that define a pattern.

The language of ordinary people's diaries is considered tedious because it is often literal and repetitive. As one can see from a one-month full transcription of Emily Gillespie's diary for December 1885 (chapter 7) and as Elizabeth Hampsten noted in her study of North Dakota diaries, intensity of experience is usually signaled by quantity of language rather than by metaphor.[8] But if the public literary language of metaphor is indeed a male tongue, as Hélène Cixous argues, then the private, plain-speaking voice within a woman's diary may be close to her true tongue.[9] Using a both/and strategy, we can look at diary language both as a truer rendering of "real life" via real speech and as design.

If quantity of concrete language is characteristic of the prose, content analysis is one way to find out, literally, what "counted" in women's diaries. Note that I said diaries and not lives, for there is not always a correlation between what a diarist writes about and what really matters. In fact, topics upon which most diarists were virtually silent—sexuality, birth control—were probably so important that they were taboo. Therefore we need to read between the lines as well as count sentences. While content analysis such as that done by John Faragher on overland trail diaries is still vulnerable to the scholar's interpretation, it is one way to move beyond the limitations of infinite individual texts to conclusions based on the growing body of diary literature.[10] Thus Paul Rosenblatt has been able to define nineteenth-century grief patterns through analysis of a collection of diaries.[11] My earlier comparison of themes in Emily Gillespie's diary with the small number of published women's diaries available shows numerous common links between women.

When the language within a diary is excessively metaphoric, on the other hand, it may obscure rather than inscribe true emotion, just as it does so fetchingly in public autobiography. Ann Douglas has argued that lush metaphor in nineteenth-century women's prose about death and children, for example, is obfuscation, a camouflage of pat imagery provided by a culture that no longer values the very things it sentimentalizes in language. The sanctioned images that diarists use to cope with death, for example, perhaps employ metaphor to stop raw emotion from pouring out onto the page.[12]

Finally, a diarist's language may form a design through the imagery of unconscious metaphor. For example, in almost every middle-class nineteenth-century woman's diary I have read, the image of Home recurs. This icon, a unifying metaphor in Gillespie's diary and life, will be traced below. The deceptively simple language of the diary, then, can be denotative, consciously literary, or tell the truth "slant" through its unselfconscious use of imagery chosen from daily life.

In traditional critical literature on the autobiographer's perspective, certain criteria recur: coherence, systematic retrospection, a sense of one's personal and historical significance. This orderly view of the self and life, transposed to the writing of autobiography, is an androcentric one not always characteristic of women's autobiographies, according to critics Estelle Jelinek, Patricia Meyer Spacks, and Suzanne Juhasz.[13] Women autobiographers such as Elizabeth Cady Stanton and Charlotte Perkins Gilman wrote from a different perspective, emphasizing their personal lives rather than their public accomplishments.

When the "uncertainties, false starts and momentariness" Pascal found characteristic of diaries are cleaned up and edited out to create traditional autobiography, the reader is presented with a falsely coherent story supported by an infrastructure of artifice. Art in autobiography obscures life, while the diary allows the reader to vicariously live it. "More than any other form of literature, it allows a reader to step, as it were, into the very boots of a character and to watch his real development, not his remembered growth, here glossed over, there emphasized," says Daniel Aaron.[14] Diarists are less attached to traditional literary concerns and yet create cohesive autobiographies, as I will show.

The initial sense of incoherence one gets when reading an ordinary woman's diary—comments on the weather, health, tomato canning, followed by a stanza of sentimental poetry—occurs because we are accustomed to constructed books rather than those that "happened," as Thomas Mallon defines diaries. Anaïs Nin called them organic texts, in contrast to the imposed texts that result from a controlling intelligence. It is informative that women writers adept in several conventional literary genres—Nin, Virginia Woolf, May Sarton—have kept journals in parallel with their public writing. Diaries offer a freedom inviting to the creative, noncategorical mind. Woolf wrote, "What sort of diary should I like mine to be? Something loose knit and yet not slovenly, so elastic that it will embrace anything, solemn, slight or beautiful that comes into my mind. I should like it to resemble some deep dark old desk, or capacious hold-all, in which one flings a mass of odds and ends without looking them through."[15]

On the other hand, the diary is obviously not a literal transcription of a day in the life. The diarist too selects what to describe and creates what I call "diary time," giving a full page to thoughts surrounding a lover's single sentence, while describing fourteen hours of the day with the single telling phrase, "did usual work." Or the diarist will remind the reader of her power to withhold and control information. For example, Emily Gillespie probably planned her 1866 trip home to Michigan for weeks but only mentioned it in her diary on the first day of the journey. In fact, diary writing is one way in which women have controlled and made coherent their experiential lives. Paul Rosenblatt observes, "As one writes about what has happened and how one feels, one is defining the situation and one's reactions. The act of defining may be seen as an act of controlling, delineating, and shaping."[16] Within the text of the diary, then, a coherent world formed by the writer's perceptions does exist: populated by reappearing characters; mappable, even if only the size of a household.

The changes that occur across time form the natural plot of the diary rather than the imposed plot of autobiography. Women's life stories generally do not fit the individualistic, linear narrative pattern of most men's autobiographies. Diaries suggest that some men's lives are also fraught with vicissitude. James Boswell was honest enough to record the inconsistencies of his life in his diary: "I am vexed at such a distempered suggestion's being inserted in my journal, which I wished to contain a consistent picture of a young fellow eagerly pushing through life. But it serves to humble me, and it presents a strange and curious view of the unaccountable nature of the human mind."[17] Feminist scholars have noted that women's lives also move forward but within a more subtle sequence of relational cycles. Henry Adams portrayed himself as a "mannikin" who arrived at multiplicity from chaos; a woman may see *herself* as multiplicity—daughter, wife, mother, teacher, widow. This lack of closure, of denouement, gives the diary a form similar to life itself and by comparison renders autobiography the more lifeless form. Anaïs Nin described why she preferred the diary form: "The diary made me aware of organic and perpetual motion, perpetual change in character. When you write a novel or a short story [or an autobiography?] you are arresting motion for a period of that story, a span of time. There is something static about that. . . . And so in many cases, reading novels, I had the feeling of still life rather than a perpetual motion."[18]

In the classic autobiography, the author attempts, as Yeats did, "to stand apart" from his life in order to "judge." The diary, by contrast, demands everyday immersion in the text that parallels one's immersion in life. The significance demanded by Goethe, who avoided in his autobiography "the incoherent realia strewn about [that] must necessarily disturb the good effect," is the antithesis of the contextual diary, rich with realia, that reflects a different view of life. The question of whether distancing oneself from a subject enables the knower to see the "truth" has been a central concern of recent feminist theory. The desirability—or possibility—of having "an objective relationship to oneself," in Pascal's term, or "aperspectivity," as Catharine MacKinnon calls it, is undermined by the diarist's profound knowledge of the self gained through proximity, not distance.[19]

Reading *from* the diary, rather than discarding it or editing it to show some externally applied concept of significance, we might discover a different bios, a life lived by women, as did psychologist Carol Gilligan when she listened to women's words rather than to men's theories: "When one begins with the study of women and derives developmental constructs from their lives, the outline of a moral conception . . . begins to emerge and informs a different description of development. In this conception, the moral problem arises from conflicting responsibilities rather than from competing rights and requires for its resolution a mode of thinking that is contextual and narrative rather than formal and abstract."[20] Likewise, the diarist, less concerned with "significance," writes a more vital reflection of her life, what Germaine Bree calls an "autogynography." She creates her life story in situ, rather than pulling one out of context with some intellectualizing forceps to be examined "objectively" in the light of significance. The diary, then, is the ultimate reflexive female life text.

The critics' insistence on "the retrospective stance" is still considered essential to truth in personal history, laments Albert Stone.[21] For example, Lillian Smith wrote in "On Women's Autobiographies": "What a courageous and almost demiurgic task to set out on the quest for the meaning of one's life, what stoical honesty is required in order to write it down! No wonder most of us settle for smaller matters. No wonder women for the most part have settled for notebooks and diaries and journals."[22] Yet this criterion must soon crumble, as some of our best autobiographers like Maya Angelou and Maxine Hong Kingston write perceptively about their childhoods and young adult lives with white-hot immediacy. Angelou's multivolume life story, told by a still-evolving persona, forms a "serial autobiography" not unlike that formed by the diary.[23]

After we reassess our ideas of what constitutes legitimate autobiographical design, we can appreciate the nearer truth that exists in diaries. I liken reading a diary to watching a young child at play. If you can catch her in a private moment, you come close to hearing her real voice; once she knows you are listening, however, that voice becomes adulterated. It becomes even more modified for a larger audience. It still poses as a child's, but the private voice was much better. A study of diaries may reformulate our ideas of how ordinary women spoke, thought, and perceived their worlds. Once diaries are considered texts (no longer subtexts), we can use them to read women's culture, no longer seen as a subculture.

"My Only Confident":
The Diary of Emily Hawley Gillespie

While Emily Gillespie's diary is an invaluable historical document that traces at great length an ordinary woman's experiences, I believe it is also autobiography, with thematic purpose, persona, and imagery. When read intertextually with other women's narratives, this type of diary will help us rewrite nineteenth-century women's history through their own serial autobiographies.

The purpose of the diary, as stated on its opening page, is to give "reminiscences of the life, from day to day, of Miss Emmie E. Hawley." The use of the word *reminiscences* at the start of a diary can alert us to as many meanings as Henry Adams's use of the word *mannikin*. It could signal a conscious selectivity operative in the diary, a sign at the outset that this writer will record what she wishes to remember rather than the whole story. We can expect to find and do find flattering suitors, personal triumphs, and incidents that vindicate the diarist. In a later volume opened with a poem, the diarist/autobiographer is again signaling the theme and positive bias of her text:

Another book is added to my journal of life
May it not be filled with sorrow and strife.
Let pure & undefiled Virtue, its pages unfold
May our hearts be as pure & bright as fine Gold.

The rather literary term *reminiscences* might also indicate Emily Hawley's lofty plans to start a book. And, indeed, the diary progresses from loose sheets of foolscap, to ribbon-tied "booklets," to account notebooks, and ultimately to fine leather-bound journals. Many writers of long diaries transcribe earlier volumes in order to leave a more permanent "Book of my Life," according to Robert Fothergill. "It is particularly common to find a diarist discovering in retrospect the book he has been creating, almost unwittingly; the diary so to speak becomes conscious of itself, and the writer grows to appreciate the shape that his own image and likeness have taken."[24] It seems even youthful diarist Emily Hawley intended her journal to be a bona fide book, as chapter headings like "Home" and "Virtue" show at one point. If so, then questions of audience should arise, as they do in her very first volume. In one incident she asks "dear reader" if she should not be pitied, a form of authorial address straight out of sentimental fiction. Literate diarists like Dorothy Wordsworth and Alice James, while not bold enough to publish, secretly wished for readers, suggests Fothergill. Thomas Mallon concludes from his long study of diaries that "no one ever kept a diary just for himself."[25]

Regardless of her ultimate literary plans, Emily Hawley early shows a strong sense of privacy, as well she should, for her sister Edna read some of the diary and wrote in it. Even when Emily Gillespie was in her forties, her father opened her diary to write a cryptic message, perhaps to counter her depiction of him: "Pride unconserved leads to shame and disgrace many times." While Emily Hawley elliptically refers to an event as a memory aid, she keeps details away from the public realm of language. She writes, "George . . . and I went to take a walk; we went perhaps forty rods from the house and sat on a log beneath a beautiful shade tree and talked,—well never mind what about."

This explicit show of the "author-ity" to omit perhaps the most important events of her life (which may have been sexual, since she was also coding her menstrual cycle in the diary's margins with exclamation marks) shows both the strength of diaries—their refreshing honesty about their own construction—and their ultimate limitation, like all autobiography, as documents about "reality." Later in her life, when her tale of romance has become instead a painful chronicle of a wronged woman, Gillespie still withholds the most unpleasant aspects of her story from the eyes of whatever audience she anticipates. After detailing her husband's cruelties, she declares, "I have written *many* things in my journal. but the *worst* is a secret to be burried when I shall cease to be." This reluctance shows what a powerful entity the diary has become. Rather than bury the book because it tells all, she will take her agony to her grave so that the diary itself will never "cease to be."

In Gillespie's diary, the goal to reminisce increasingly wars with her desire to have an "undefiled" book as her personal unhappiness increases. She insists on remembering, however, drawing small Victorian-style hands in the book's margins to point to entries for quick reference: death dates, proud moments in her children's lives. She also threads together her life by intratextual reference, noting on a certain date where she was ten years earlier, according to her diary. This leads to a type of internal closure which this diarist seems to have desired, as she links together thematically significant events far apart in time: comets observed, the history of a piece of fabric, her teaching salary of two decades ago compared to her daughter's. And while she never stands apart from herself to judge, as did the formal autobiographers of her era, she does rather ruthlessly objectify others, as does everyone who portrays others via language.

Another, more cynical reading of the term *reminiscences* would alert the scholar to the possibility that the title was applied after the moment of the diary's origin, perhaps years later when the writer reread her journals, as Gillespie noted doing. Almost no century-old personal document remains unaltered by either an author with second thoughts, a nervous relative, or the elements. Indeed, practically every published diary I have encountered, from Mary Chesnut's to the more obscure Samuella Curd's, contains the editor's explanation of alterations detected in the manuscript.[26] This inability to leave well enough alone again suggests that an autobiographical impulse to potentially go public exists within those who persist in keeping a diary.

While Gillespie's need to remember stays consistent throughout the composition of her book, the narrative's purpose—and therefore her choice of literary form—changes across three decades. Her book, definitely not a still life, could be called a meta-autobiography. To recapitulate, it opens in a sentimental vein, as Emily quotes her many suitors on the same pages in which she refers to sentimental fiction like *Tempest and Sunshine*, wishing perhaps in her diary's pages to mirror the trysts of novels. She describes the courtship methods and failings of men with drinking habits, fiery tempers, and speech defects, saving herself for "*the* one" who will honor her ideal of a husband and lover. As she moves to Iowa to live and work in her uncle's inn, the diary briefly lapses into the form and language of a travel account, for which there were many published models. After her arrival in Iowa, the diary returns to the sentimental mode, with Emily playing the orphan alone in the wide, wide world of the Far West.

Early in her marriage to wealthy James Gillespie, the romance disappears from Emily's diary: "do my wash,—finish shirt—my cow has a calf this morning. James chop wood & kill the calf." Had her daily routine really changed that much from her tasks as a hired girl at her uncle's inn, or had Emily Gillespie decided that as a wife she should record less frivolous memories? The diary soon becomes the couple's book; Emily mentions several times asking her husband at day's end what she should write for him. The young wife emphasizes financial accounts, a constant element in her diary. This literal "accounting" for Gillespie's time fits her belief that those who work hard will see their wealth—and happinesss—accumulate.

When the two Gillespie children become old enough to appreciate Emily's life plan for them as "young folks" (academy educations, minimal farm chores, fancy dress clothes), her diary becomes a record of their mother's deeds and beliefs. Again, the diary follows a tradition, that of the memento book. Anne Bradstreet dedicated her seventeenth-century autobiography "To My Dear Children":

This Book by Any yet unread
I leave for you when I am dead,
That being gone, here you may find
What was yr liveing mothers mind.[27]

As the children mature and go out into the world in activities Emily admires, she gives them more and more space in the diary, her own activities less, and James only a line. The egotism necessary to write a diary, at war with the altruism Gillespie feels for her children, is resolved in the act of dedicating the books and much of their contents (as she did her life) to her offspring.

As Emily Gillespie's mind becomes more embittered by strife with James, her late diary increasingly resembles the accounts of "injured females" like Elizabeth Ashbridge's, which were popular in England during the eighteenth century. In this genre, drama and religious messages were combined in tales wherein a woman played the Christian and her husband the lion, according to Daniel Shea.[28] James, Emily now reveals in a narrative of much different tone, had never been an ideal husband; now she records his unnatural failure as a father in the diary kept to burn memories into her children's minds as well as her own. The diary becomes so vital a "confident" and family member that when she is ill the children take dictation for it. Obsessive diarist Arthur Inman likened his intimate diary to a thrashing snake that demanded to be constantly fed. "The diarist is symbiotically attached to it, and the Diary can exist only on a diet of words," says Inman's editor Daniel Aaron.[29] Emily Gillespie's final words— "write, paper"—show how deeply attached she was to her diary until death parted them.

Despite the grotesque mutation that domestic dreams took in Gillespie's life and the changing form of her diary, her narrator's voice remained almost rigidly consistent, as did Franklin's in his autobiography. Thomas Mallon has described this type of older diary persona as "horizontal," in that one's personality is perceived as staying consistent across time. Like the Puritans, Gillespie asks in her diary, "How well was I myself today?" (Modern diarists of the psychoanalytic age usually envision themselves as mutable, moving vertically through time. They ask, "Who am I today, compared to myself two years ago?") Gillespie's diary, however, does not completely follow the earlier religious model of daily self-criticism. She is quite well pleased with herself, increasingly defending her viewpoint in her book. Her diary, then, is a transitional one, as reflected in its persona.

Because Gillespie views her life through the female lens of relationships, her persistent persona—the striving sufferer—is often portrayed relationally. At the diary's start, she is an under-esteemed daughter who obeys her mother's warning about going to New York for art training and agrees to stay home. As a betrothed young woman, she describes a nightmare in which she finds it impossible to please James's parents. Then she strives to be the perfect mother, making herself suffer in her diary for chastising her children, writing prayers that ask for more patience. Later she describes herself as the unappreciated wife of a farmer, the misunderstood daughter of her elderly resident father, the maligned sister of jealous siblings. Only near the end of her diary does she begin to look beyond relationships, to criticize the social structure that has predetermined the pattern of her life and book, rather than the individual antagonists. Ironically, most of this insight comes via personal relationships. When a dear neighbor woman is institutionalized, Gillespie writes, "I only wonder that more women do not have to be taken to that asylum. Especially farmer's wives. No society except hired men to eat their meals. Hard work from the beginning to the end of the year." Later, she worries when her daughter, Sarah, is courted by an attractive man and again goes from the specific relationship to the generalization: "Ah, marriage is a lottery." So while Gillespie's self-portraiture is consistent, her persona does develop an increasingly vigorous voice. Her ego emerges, reinforcing my earlier interpretation—that this never was intended to be a diary that recorded life. Rather, it was a book incrementally written to frame an author-ized version of life—selective, immutable as the self-image driving it, eventually vocal and judgmental.

Gillespie's creation of "characters" in the diary is clearest in her evolving depiction of James. In the early years, his activities are seen as heroic, his moods as merely fine temperament, his words as quite romantic. In the middle years, Emily uses the words "spell" and "blues" to vaguely describe

James as unpredictable. In the last years, he is described as subject to fits and insane; when Emily quotes him, she writes his words in the dialect of a rube. This changing "creation" of James—lover, hard-working companion, tyrant—is the evidence of Emily Gillespie's creative license at work in her diary. An intertextual comparison of her diary with that of her daughter reveals other choices Gillespie made when recording and creating the book of her life.

Emily Gillespie gave both of her children homemade journals early in their lives, along with Franklinesque sentiments on the useful economy of diary keeping. She wrote in Sarah's diary for May 30, 1880:

'A stitch in time saves nine'
Then write every day, for an incident lost
now and then, you might sorely repine.
A day once forgotten can be gained at no cost.

For the most part, Sarah's diary entries for the late 1870s and the 1880s tell a story similar to her mother's. Her word choices are uncannily like Emily's, and it is clear from some entries that Sarah recorded her mother's version of some events Sarah did not actually witness. (Emily Gillespie had access to her adult daughter's diary and would read a few entries and write encouraging words in Sarah's journal.) In several cases, Sarah Gillespie recorded criticisms of James that are absent from her mother's journal, particularly involving his mistreatment of farm animals. By age sixteen, Sarah's opinion of her father was set down: "He is too slick tongued to strangers and they *know* him *not*" (May 21, 1882). Sarah also notes incidents of her mother's sickness when Emily does not mention illness in her diary. In general, then, Sarah Gillespie's version of life in the family corroborates her mother's and shows that in some cases Emily downplayed negative events and emotions.

In the realm of characterization, however, Emily Gillespie seems to have omitted details from her diary that would undermine her persona. For example, Emily perceived herself as somewhat superior to her neighbors and took pride in the premiums she won at the county fairs. After the 1877 fair, she listed all her prizes. Sarah, however, mentioned that the judges said all Emily's entries were not worthy of their awards. This unmentioned incident may explain Emily's rather righteous comments of September 8,

1881 (see chapter 6) over another judging dispute. When her sense of justice was sufficiently outraged and when she won the argument, the disagreement entered her diary. Four years earlier, the judges' insults did not "occur"—in the diary.

Another textual comparison shows how a subtle difference in Emily's and Sarah's descriptions of a major quarrel is consistent with Emily's characterization of James as irrational. Emily's version:

James help the carpenters all day. Henry help too. Sarah help me. Mr Alcock here yesterday and to day—digging potatoes. we retire to sleep, our hearts filled with sorrow, yet with a prayer and trust that all will end well. James has one of his fits of—well I do hardly know what—whenever he has to pay out any money for any thing he seems to think, I ought to get every thing for myself & the Children without calling on him for it. (October 8, 1881)

Sarah's version of the same event:

At home, the Carpenters done all they could so Henry could finish. After they had all gone, Ma says "James what made you tell Mr Alcock (a man digging potatoes for pa & who owed Ma $2 for pickles) that you would pay him anyway & let it run any length of time," At which Pa said, "*Now* Emily, do for heavens sake dont bring up every little nasty thing, & commenced to tell Ma to pack up & leave" etc.

In this version, it is Emily who picks the quarrel and James who is reacting. While one cannot expect the diarist to record every word of a heated argument, Emily's version is consistent with her persona: she is the sufferer, James the "lion."

Emily Gillespie characterized her children as ideal models of young manhood and womanhood. This would explain why many of the children's quarrels and misdeeds that upset Emily are recorded only in Sarah's diary. One incident shows Emily's omission of a very hurtful wrong done her by Henry. Her diary entry of July 11, 1884, simply says she is sleeping that night on the floor in Sarah's room and offers no further explanation. In Sarah's diary we find the painful cause:

Got woke up by the turks at 3:15 a.m. and have not slept any since. Henry came home earlier to night and went up to Sellens' where Mr. Parkhurst is working and brought him down to stay all night. Ma & I came up to make the bed. Henry came up & said Ma would have to get up early or Mr. P—— would see her as he has to pass her bed. May says—"You ashamed of Ma"? And he said—yes in the morning—she did not look very handsome in the morning. And she cried & felt so bad about it. He did not mean any-thing wrong. But he and Mr. P—— think a good deal of each other and he wanted every-thing all right I suppose. So Ma put down some quilts at the foot of my bed in my room on the floor & has just retired—Will not sleep in her bed in the hall. I feel real sorry. Ma takes every-thing to heart so. Now I can't half sleep.

If James had insulted Emily, his words would surely be recorded. But to "protect" her son's gentle persona in the diary, Emily Gillespie omits his thoughtless words and her tearful reaction.

In sum, Emily Gillespie, like all writers to some extent, created selective portraits of individuals in her diary. Some are heroes, some villains. Misunderstood by her husband and the townspeople, Emily Gillespie recorded her victories and their irrationality in her book, leaving out uncharacteristic incidents. Her diary was a necessary element in her "psychic economy," to use Fothergill's term for certain types of journals: "The function of the diary is to provide a compensatory outlet for that valuation of [herself] which circumstances conspire to thwart."[30]

If we view this diary as constructed autobiography rather than as mere recorded narrative, certain images can be traced that serve as metaphors for Emily Gillespie. One such that I alluded to earlier, Home, informs her book, as it did dozens of other women's diaries and the prescriptive literature of the nineteenth century. Gillespie's book shows how difficult it was to enact this idealized image with real-life people.

For young Emily Hawley, home was called "father's" and it was clear that a dependent unmarried daughter must leave it. Never "at home" at her uncle's inn, forced then to live in a wing of her new father-in-law's house, Gillespie finally delights in a rented place of her own: "we are at home enjoying life finely." When adorable children are added to this home, she thanks the Lord for her "happy family circle." While neighbors succumb to the agricultural depression of the mid-1870s, the Gillespies build a large house and Emily receives a deed to the entire farm from James. (The autobiographer's depiction of this incident changes with her marriage. At the time of the event, the present of the deed is treated as a great honor from James. Only later, in the embittered years, does Gillespie write that James deeded over the farm to protect it from creditors.) Later, as a carpenter completes an addition to the home, the entire family argues over money. When a Brussels carpet and new furniture are put in the parlor, Emily excludes James from her image of the home, noting that the finery is too nice for him. Sarah writes with unintentional irony in her diary: "Im O so sorry. Have as much as we do. But its all an old & true saying. That 'the more any one has the more trouble it is to keep it.'"

Home also turns upon Emily Gillespie, who complains about the social isolation of the farm which causes her to "always be at home," a phrase she wrote with such pleasure ten years earlier. When the marriage explodes and she is forced to rent her own home from James, Gillespie sees the embodiment of her life's round of "usual work" slipping away. Moved as an invalid to a rented house in town, where she had always wanted to live for the society, she is ultimately confined to a bedroom. Having achieved the ideal home for only a few years of her life, Gillespie records through its imagery the diminishment of her dreams that could find no residence. Her diary, an unrelenting descriptive document, stands as a stark counterpoint to the home so touted by writers like the Beechers, balancing our view of women as seen through prescriptive literature.[31] By first reading within diaries and then conducting an intertextual analysis, we can begin to understand what really happened to Victorian women living among icons of children, church, and home.

Another image in the Gillespie diary, that of perpetual motion, connects stunningly with Anaïs Nin's use of the same conceit 117 years later for her own diary, that "novel of the future." It seems almost inevitable that a pioneer woman immersed in the "usual work" of daily routine might arrive at the image of perpetual motion in a complaint. But for Gillespie, the image appears in an unearthly dream that shows her desire to exist on a higher plane, to somehow profit from the "perpetual motion" that was her life:

Oh how grand it would be if one could live two hundred years, live to see the wonders wrought, to see the progress in art & science. *not* live for mere life alone. it almost enraptures us in reverie of thought to even have an idea of such a life. *There is one invention which I do believe can be made to be a perfect success*, & that is *perpetual-motion as I dreamed it about 15 or 18 years* ago. it must be done by weight and pressure by springs on an inclined plane, similar to a machine used by putting a horse into a sort of tread-mill—

The frame was silver and sparkling stones,
The horse was gold-tied with a golden chain,

Beneath his feet was an inclined plane
So bright, as it turned beneath his tread,
That it seemd too real to be only a dream.
Within this golden horses feet, cut in notched form
Were diamonds, to fit & drive the bars of gold
On which were notched plates of dazling brightness.
Standing near this wonder of art and skill
Was the inventor: his raiment—gold and silver thread,
A cloak embroidered with glistening diamonds.
Right proud he was, of his rare invention.
I too—for once—was dressed in gorgeous array
If *twere* in a *dream*. Aye three times this presentiment.
As I stood beside him I asked "What's the name of this?"
With uplifted hand he answered "Perpetual Motion."

(November 10, 1885)

The way that Emily Gillespie made sense of real-life perpetual motion
was to recount daily what her drudgery amounted to, both literally in her
financial records and emotionally in the record of her children's development. Gillespie's diary, then, is a self-kept tally of how she did indeed
account for something. Her long and emotional entries indicate that at this
stage in the writing of her multivolume journal Emily Gillespie could see
that she had created a serial autobiography. Fothergill explains how the
long diary bridges the gulf between traditional autobiography and the daily
record (I have substituted the female pronoun): "If she were suddenly to
die the diary would have the prime responsibility for declaring what she
was and what she did, so it had better contain whatever she may want to
say by way of explanation and commentary. Thus, from a moving vantage-
point, the serial autobiographer constantly mediates between a provisional
interpretation of her life's meaning and direction, and the fresh experience
which may modify that interpretation."[32] As Emily Gillespie sensed death
was near, she increasingly tried to explain the meaning of her life and its
repetitive patterns.

Her final persona, that of the invalid-sufferer, was her "perfect success."
Her martyrdom was recorded forever in her diary, kept privately and relentlessly while she endured life's hardships. When she was ultimately
silenced by death, her diary, passed through generations, would proclaim

her angelic sacrifice more movingly than any words on a headstone. For Gillespie created two forms of lasting art—her diary and her devoted daughter, who shared her sense of history—that combined to perpetuate her memory. Gillespie's diary, preserved and "published" by its placement in historical archives, was her ultimate life's artistry, far more lasting than the paintings and stories she consciously created and that are now lost. Emily Gillespie at last can speak and be appreciated through the narrative form that mirrors the perpetual pattern of her life.

Emily Gillespie's journal suggests that rich autobiographical texts reside in ordinary women's diaries. The genius of the stories is that they are embedded in a seemingly ingenuous form. If we can see the gender-blindness of the current literary criteria that disregard diaries and overcome our fear of new forms when faced with dusty, scribbled narratives, I predict that we can again expand the boundaries of our reading and thinking to include this literature from new American voices—voices no longer buried.

Notes

Introduction: The Diary as Living History

1. Walker, "Finding Celie's Voice," p. 72.
2. Adams, *Education of Henry Adams*, p. 353.
3. Ordinary women's diaries are central to several important historical studies, including Cott, *Bonds of Womanhood*; Faragher, *Women and Men on the Overland Trail*; and Jeffrey, *Frontier Women*. Edited diaries of ordinary nineteenth-century women that I have found useful include Nelson, ed., *Diary of Elizabeth Koren, 1853–1855*; Sanford, *Mollie*; Myres, ed., *Ho for California!*; Mohr, ed., *Cormany Diaries*; Schlissel, *Women's Diaries of the Westward Journey*; Arpad, ed., *Sam Curd's Diary*; Stanley, ed., *Diaries of Hannah Cullwick*; Farnsworth, *Plains Woman*; and French, *Emily*.
4. Smith-Rosenberg, *Disorderly Conduct*, p. 29.
5. An excellent history and survey of English diary writing is Fothergill, *Private Chronicles*.

   Throughout this study I use the terms *diary* and *journal* interchangeably, as do most diary scholars. Emily Gillespie called her books both diary and journal. Matthews in *American Diaries* distinguishes between terms: "A diary is written for personal reasons, . . . a journal, although otherwise similar to a diary, is kept as part of a job." He goes on to say, "In practice, there is often little or no distinction" (p. ix).

   John Adams to John Quincy Adams, May 14, 1783, in Allen et al., eds., *Diary of John Quincy Adams*, vol. 1, p. xxii. Adams's admonition to his son demonstrates how pleasurable as well as valuable diary keeping was perceived to be: "If you have omitted this Useful Exercise, let me advise you to recommence it, immediately. Let it be your Amusement, to minute every day, whatever you may have seen or heard worth Notice. One contracts a Fondness of Writing by Use."
6. Quoted in Cott, *Bonds of Womanhood*, p. 16.
7. Fothergill, *Private Chronicles*, p. 9.
8. Wilder, *Politics and History*, pp. 132–133.
9. Emily Hawley Gillespie, Diary, Book 1, March 26, 1876, Sarah Gillespie Huftalen Collection, Iowa State Historical Society, Iowa City, Iowa. Boswell quoted in Fothergill, *Private Chronicles*, p. 80.

10. Stone, ed., *American Autobiography*, p. 7.

11. Franz Boas quoted in Mandelbaum, "Study of Life History: Gandhi."

12. See chapter 4, "Motive and Manner," in Fothergill, *Private Chronicles*.

13. Emily Hawley, Diary, Book 1.

14. See Mandelbaum, "Study of Life History: Gandhi," for a history of this field of inquiry. A recent collection that addresses questions of the ethnographer's world view is Clifford and Marcus, eds., *Writing Culture*.

15. Smith-Rosenberg, *Disorderly Conduct*, introduction. Differences in psychosocial development are described in Chodorow, *Reproduction of Mothering*. Sociolinguistic difference is described by studies in Thorne and Henley, eds., *Language and Sex*, and in Philips, Steele, and Tanz, eds., *Language, Sex and Gender in Comparative Perspective*.

16. Faragher, *Women and Men on the Overland Trail*, pp. 130–133.

17. Fothergill, *Private Chronicles*, pp. 87–94.

18. Lensink, Pioneer Woman's Life."

19. Schlissel, *Women's Diaries*.

20. Geiger, "Women's Life Histories," p. 348.

21. Excellent reviews of women's history scholarship that provide the models which follow are Gerda Lerner, "New Approaches to the Study of Women in American History" (1969) and "Placing Women in History: A 1975 Perspective." Both are in Carroll, ed., *Liberating Women's History*. Another valuable review is Sicherman, "Review Essay: American History."

22. Kerber, "Separate Spheres," May 1987 draft, pp. 30–31.

23. Welter, "Cult of True Womanhood," pp. 151–57; Cott, *Bonds of Womanhood*; Kerber, "Separate Spheres," p. 26.

24. Smith-Rosenberg, "Female World of Love and Ritual"; Motz, *True Sisterhood*.

25. See Degler, *At Odds* and Lebsock, *Free Women of Petersburg* as excellent examples of the debate on women's domestic power. Smith-Rosenberg, *Disorderly Conduct*, p. 17.

26. Waller, *Reverend Beecher and Mrs. Tilton*, p. 14.

27. Among the works I have found useful and interesting because they focus on this tension are Sklar, *Catharine Beecher*; Cott, *Bonds of Womanhood*; Berkin, "Private Woman, Public Woman," Kelley, "At War with Herself" and other fine essays collected in Kelley, ed., *Woman's Being, Woman's Place*; and Hampsten, *Read This Only to Yourself*.

28. Sicherman, "Review Essay: American History," p. 474.

29. Chopin, *Awakening*.

30. Mallon, *A Book of One's Own*, p. 210.

31. Sarah L. Gillespie Huftalen, "Introductory," n.d., Sarah Gillespie Huftalen Collection, Iowa State Historical Society, Iowa City, Iowa.
32. See Woodward's introductory essays, "Diary in Fact—Diary in Form," pp. xv–xxix and "Editorial Problems and Policies," pp. liv–lvii in *Mary Chesnut's Civil War*. Johnson, "Mary Boykin Chesnut's Autobiography and Biography" provides a commentary on Woodward's editorial decisions. Aaron, ed., *Inman Diary*, introduction.
33. Geiger, "Women's Life Histories," p. 338.
34. Watson and Watson-Franke, *Interpreting Life Histories*, p. 43.
35. Lensink, Kirkham and Witzke, "'My Only Confidant.'"
36. Chevigny, "Daughters Writing."
37. Geertz, "Thick Description." This essay was central to the development of my methodology and perspective on Gillespie.
38. Rich, *Diving into the Wreck*, p. 22.

One. "A Home at Father's": 1858–1860

1. Biographical information about the Hawley family comes from the Sarah Gillespie Huftalen Papers in two archives: the Iowa State Historical Society in Iowa City and the Michigan History Division in Lansing. In subsequent references to the papers the provenience will be noted. In addition to the Emily Hawley Gillespie diaries, the Iowa collection contains genealogical studies, scrapbooks about family members, Huftalen's diaries, and miscellaneous materials. The Michigan collection contains some duplicate materials and a substantial number of family letters. Quoted comments about the family are from Sarah Huftalen's biographical sketches.
2. Immigrants like the Hawleys and Bakers from northeastern states, predominantly New York, made up over 90 percent of Michigan's residents in 1860, according to the U.S. Bureau of the Census, *Ninth Census, Volume I*. In 1860 8 percent of the southern Michigan population was native-born white like the Hawleys, compared to only 33 percent in the northern peninsula area noted for its minerals, according to Hawley, "Population of Michigan 1840 to 1960," Table 34, p. 64.
3. Census information about the Hawleys and their neighbors in the township comes from the U.S. Bureau of the Census, *Eighth Census of the United States, Lenawee Township*. Information about the location and size of the farms

in the area comes from Everts and Stewart, comps., *The Combination Atlas Map of Lenawee County.*

4. Benjamin Osborn, forty-two, was the husband of Emily's mother's younger sister Mary, thirty-five. The Osborns had five children and lived on a large farm about two and one-half miles southeast of the Hawleys.

5. The Horace and Rachael Culver family are listed in the 1860 census as living near the Hawleys but are not listed on the property plat maps, which suggests they may have been renters. Emily had some social contact with Rachael Culver and her sons Lester ("Let"), twenty-one, and John, eighteen.

6. Hiram Crane is listed in the 1860 census as thirty-six, although elsewhere in the diary Emily indicates that he is older. He lived about one mile south of the Hawleys on forty acres and declared for the census a real estate value of $1,000, the same as Hial Hawley's.

7. Canandaigua, three miles to the northeast, was the closest town. It had 139 residents, according to the ninth U.S. census.

8. Medina was a town of 212 residents, approximately three miles north of the Hawleys.

9. Fanny Brower was probably a daughter of George Brower, who owned a sawmill just south of the Hawley property.

10. The Richard and Susan Sims family lived in neighboring Seneca Township, two miles east of the Hawleys. Fred was two years older than Emily.

11. Emily Acker, twenty-five, was another of Sarah Baker Hawley's sisters. She and her husband, Jonas, lived three miles south of the Hawley farm.

12. Hairflowers were decorative miniature flowers created by winding human hair around thin wire shaped into rosettes. Clusters of these flowers, made with the hair from several members of a family, including the deceased, might be formed into a wreath and displayed in a frame.

13. Harvey Baker, thirty, a younger brother of Emily's mother, was married to Nancy Jeffers.

14. A "Bloomer costume" consisted of a knee-length skirt covered by a loose tunic and Turkish-style pantaloons. The outfit, advocated by Amelia Bloomer in her journal the *Lily*, became identified with feminist reform.

15. Morenci, population 458, was five and one-half miles southeast of the Hawleys in Seneca Township.

16. Nathaniel Horace Baker, thirty-two, a younger brother of Sarah Baker Hawley, lived just north of Morenci with his wife, Ann Sweeny. Their eighty-acre farm was four miles from the Hawleys.

17. Jacob Baker, another brother of Sarah Baker, was only two years older than Emily.

18. Cochineal is an imported red dye derived from the bodies of female cactus insects.

19. Hudson was approximately eight miles northwest of the Hawley farm in neighboring Hudson Township. It had 1,489 residents.

20. Lucina Hawley, sixteen, was a cousin who lived in Morenci with her parents Marquis and Sarah Hawley, and two brothers, Albert, thirteen, and Jerome, nineteen. Marquis (spelled Marcus in the diary) was probably Hial Hawley's brother.

    This was not Emily Hawley's first teaching certificate, for she had taught school seven months earlier during the winter term of 1857, according to her correspondence with an uncle (Emily E. Hawley, letter to Henry Baker, February 1, 1857, Huftalen Papers, Michigan History Division, Lansing).

21. Two Warne families lived just south of the Hawleys; each lived on a twenty-acre parcel.

22. Nelson Baldwin, fifteen, lived on his parents' sixty-acre farm a mile south of the Hawleys.

23. This is the first marginal coding of what appears to be Emily Hawley's menstrual cycle. The exclamation marks appear before entries of no apparent exceptional significance on the following dates in 1859: March 29, April 17, June 6, June 30, September 11, October 2, November 17, and December 16. In 1860 the marks appear on February 6, March 8, and April 4. The gaps between markings could be the result of Emily Hawley's omission, omission by her daughter when copying the diary, a very irregular cycle, or the lack of necessity for recording her cycle during certain months. The marks do not reappear in the diary until November 1866, fourteen months after the birth of her last child (see section on female sexuality in chapter 3).

24. Julia Blanchard, who was Emily's age, lived with her husband, Marshall, and two children on a farm valued at $1,500.

25. The Beaches lived one and one-half miles to the west of the Hawleys.

26. Lewis Baker was Emily's mother's youngest brother. He was twenty-eight and probably a widower.

27. Dr. Chappell (no first name given) had practiced medicine in Canandaigua since 1844, according to Hogaboam, *Bean Creek Valley*.

28. The Daws family lived one and one-quarter miles west of the Hawleys.

29. According to Sarah Huftalen's biography, the school was the Oak Grove Academy, founded in 1853 by Medina citizens through a joint stock company. It included a preparatory school, similar to a high school in curriculum.

30. John Fuller, seventeen, son of a painter, lived in Morenci and worked as a clerk in a store.

31. John Brown was hanged December 2, 1859, for treason against the state of Virginia after his raid on the Federal Arsenal at Harper's Ferry. The "Kansas matters" probably refer to Brown's raid of May 24, 1856, on proslavery forces at Pottawatomie Creek, Kansas. This is the first entry in the diary about the slavery issue.

32. Nathan Lowe taught school, probably at the schoolhouse adjoining his family's land two miles south of the Hawleys.

33. James C. Chappell, a peddler, stayed overnight with the Hawleys in August 1859, according to the diary. Chappell had written Emily in September and again in January. The latter correspondence, preserved in family papers, deals mostly with the weather and peddling. Chappell calls Emily "Dear" and writes, "Saw a good many Ladies But none to my Eye as much a [*sic*] yourself" (J. C. Chappell, letter to Emily Hawley, January 6, 1860, Huftalen Papers, Michigan History Division, Lansing).

34. Horace Garlick, fifty-two, was actually a great-uncle. He was Emily's mother's maternal uncle and lived in Morenci.

35. Carlo was the name of a dog in Charlotte Brontë's *Jane Eyre* (1847). Emily Dickinson also had a dog named Carlo.

36. Hamlin is listed as a carpenter living in Hudson in the 1860 census, which spells his name "Silvenus."

37. *The Angel of the Household* (1854) was written by Timothy Shay Arthur, the prolific author of such books as *Ten Nights in a Bar-room and What I saw there.* In *Angel*, a confused mother reclaims her deserted babe, who has proven a blessing on its adopted household as well. The biological mother redeems her child and herself, proclaiming, "As for me, I desire nothing beyond my own home, and an entire devotion of all I have and all I am to my child" (p. 175).

38. *Tempest and Sunshine* (1854) by Mary Jane Holmes was a great popular success. The novel depicts the fate of two sisters, one who epitomizes sunny good nature, the other a tempestuous schemer. The darling marries, while the "tempest" finally develops character and wins her father's love. The novel has been interpreted as championing domestic darlinghood by some critics and as a subtle indictment of manipulative goodness by others, according to Baym, *Women's Fiction.*

39. Lucy Ann Garlick, a second cousin to Emily, was married to Robert N. Sims, twenty-eight. The Sims family lived on a two hundred–acre farm about two and one-half miles south of the Hawleys.

40. Quilling was the winding of yarn around a reed or hollow stem.

41. Michigan was a solid Republican state and Lincoln was elected by a majority

of 20,000 votes. Republicans also captured every congressional seat in Michigan.

42. The Smiths lived on ten acres immediately east of the Hawleys.

43. *The Three Mrs. Judsons and Other Daughters of the Cross* (1855) by Rev. Daniel C. Eddy is the biography of the wives of Dr. Adoniram Judson, a missionary to India. The author exorts women "not called out to other lands to die amid strangers, [to] yet here at home develop those high virtues and those noble traits for which this cluster of Christians have become so widely and justly distinguished" (p. 270). Those traits in women that Eddy lauds are a sense of adventure linked to wifely Christian submission.

   Dora Deane, or the East India Girl (1859), the fifth novel by Mary Jane Holmes, follows a Cinderella pattern, according to Baym, *Women's Fiction*. The impoverished heroine is aided by a male benefactor who sends her to Boston, where education transforms her into a town belle.

44. Henry Baker, forty-seven, Sarah Baker Hawley's older brother, owned a large inn and farm in northeastern Iowa. His wife, Elizabeth (Coffin), had died in December 1859, leaving him a widower with a 16-year-old daughter, Susan. In March 1860 he had written to Sarah asking if one of her older girls would be willing to come to Iowa to work for him during the summer and offering to pay her well (Henry Baker, letter to Sarah Hawley, March 3, 1860, Huftalen Papers, Michigan History Division, Lansing).

45. Stephen A. Douglas had been the Democratic party candidate against Abraham Lincoln in the national election of 1860.

   This is the first mention of the Civil War in the diary. Fort Sumter was fired upon on April 12, 1861. On April 15, the day that President Lincoln called for 75,000 volunteer Union soldiers, there was a mass meeting of 1,000 people in Adrian, according to the Bonner history. Sixteen men enlisted the next day.

46. *Ida Norman, or Trials and Their Uses*, was written in serial form in 1846 by Almira Hart Phelps, a leader in women's education reform and sister of Emma Willard. Baym says, "Like other fictions of the thirties and forties, *Ida Norman* asserts that a woman can depend on nothing but her own moral character. In the 1855 edition of the novel, a female teacher who prefers to remain single says, 'I assert the right of every woman to marry, or not to marry; if she decides on the latter, I protest against her being considered as a victim to be commiserated'" (Baym, *Women's Fiction*, p. 83).

47. Colonel Elmer Ellsworth, twenty-four, leader of a group called the Zouaves, was shot by an innkeeper in Alexandria, Virginia, when he cut down a Confederate flag. His body lay in state at the White House, and he became for

many northern editorialists the first war hero, according to Catton, *Coming Fury*.

48. *The Lamp Lighter*, by Maria Susanna Cummins, was published in 1854. Baym, *Women's Fiction*, calls it a successful imitation of an earlier novel about an orphan by Susan Warner, *The Wide, Wide World*. Cummins's orphan eventually succeeds in becoming independent and finding a home.

Two. "We Cannot Always Live at Home": 1861–1862

1. Emily E. Hawley, letter to Henry Baker, February 1, 1857, Huftalen Papers, Michigan History Division, Lansing.
2. Henry Baker, letter to Sarah Hawley, October 27, 1861, in ibid.
3. Sage, *History of Iowa*. Sage's information comes from *Census of Iowa, 1836–1880* (Des Moines: State of Iowa, 1883).
4. Wall, *Iowa: A Bicentennial History*.
5. *History of Delaware County, Iowa*.
6. Emily E. Hawley, drawing, n.d., Huftalen Papers, Michigan History Division, Lansing.
7. Dunlieth, Illinois (now East Dubuque) was the terminus of the Illinois Central Railroad line. To continue west into Iowa, passengers took a boat across the Mississippi River (a bridge was not completed until after the Civil War) and boarded the Dubuque and Pacific Railroad (Sage, *History of Iowa*).
8. Susan Coffin, sixty-five, was Henry Baker's mother-in-law and the wife of Clement Coffin.
9. The Bailey farm of 320 acres adjoined the Baker property to the north. Mrs. Smith was probably Araminda Smith, twenty, wife of Francis Smith, a laborer, according to the 1860 census. She had a one-year-old child.
10. Delhi, seven miles southeast of Manchester, had a population of fewer than four hundred in 1860. It was founded as the county seat in 1841 because it was in the geographical center of Delaware County.
11. John E. Schmidt, thirty, a native of Germany, worked for Henry Baker and lived at the inn for five years. Catharine Nelson, fifty-seven, lived nearby with her husband, N.A., and three adult children, unnamed in the 1860 census. From the context of other diary entries, they were Emily, Henry, and Milton Nelson.
12. From information contained in other diary entries, it appears that Hathaway was an acquaintance Emily Hawley made during the train trip to Iowa.

13. *Peterson's Magazine* was the most popular women's magazine in America during this time, with a circulation of close to 140,000, according to Mott, *History of American Magazines. Vol. II: 1850–1865*, p. 309.

14. Emma Dorothy Eliza Nevitte (E. D. E. N.) Southworth, author of such novels as *Retribution* (1849) and *The Hidden Hand* (1859), was one of the most popular writers in America at this time. In 1857 Southworth began an exclusive contract with Richard Bonner, editor of the popular fiction magazine *New York Ledger*, for serialization of all her fiction. Southworth's published autobiographical sketches demonstrate that a separated woman with a young child to support could triumph as a writer through work and faith in herself (Baym, *Women's Fiction*, pps. 110–114).

15. A philopena is "a friendly or playful practice by which when two persons have by agreement shared a nut with two kernels, or the like, the person who fails subsequently to meet certain conditions is bound to pay the other a forfeit" (Barnhart, *American College Dictionary*).

16. Emily's homesickness, according to her Uncle Henry, was the result of receiving letters from her mother. He wrote to his sister in Michigan: "Sarah why do you go on so about Emilys being out here any one would think from the run of your letters that she had run away and that you was trying to reclaim her or that she had got among some verry bad or immoral folks, or among heathens . . . the main drift of your letters is Come home Emily ah Emily do come home" (Henry Baker to Sarah Hawley, October 27, 1861, Huftalen Papers, Michigan History Division, Lansing).

17. James Fawcett Gillespie, twenty-five, lived with his elderly parents, Lorinda, fifty-seven, and Hiram, sixty-two, and his younger brother Dennis on their two hundred–acre farm located three miles southeast of the Baker inn. The 1860 census lists the value of the Gillespie farm—owned by Lorinda—as $3,000, which made it the second most prosperous in the township after Baker's, which was valued at $9,000. However, the value of several large area farms is omitted in the census record.

18. Milton Nelson enlisted in Company 7, 12th Infantry, on October 15, 1861 (*History of Delaware County*, p. 443). Iowa troops went to Jefferson Barracks in St. Louis for processing. Iowans reacted enthusiastically to the call for Union volunteers, ultimately furnishing about 74,000 men—one-half the male population (Sage, *History of Iowa*). In Manchester, Union sympathies also ran high, as an anecdote from the county history illustrates: "In 1861, the lot on the northeast corner of Franklin and Main streets . . . was vacant. On this lot stood a 'Liberty pole' about fifty feet high. One bright morning, when the good citizens of the town began to be astir, they discovered the rebel flag flying

from the top of that pole. Immediately the whole town was ablaze with excitement and indignation. Who was the traitor who had dared to raise that flag? Nobody knew, but there floated the Confederate flag and it must come down. A boy was sent up to cut the ropes, but when he had climbed to within six or eight feet of the top he found the pole had been greased and he could get no further. Then they tried to cut the rope with bullets, but this was not successful, and after some time axes were brought and wielded by strong arms, the pole was cut down and the hated emblem of treason was cut in pieces by the loyal and indignant populace. It was discovered afterward that some young men for pure love of fun had, during the night, tied the flag to the pole. . . . The incident served to demonstrate the loyalty of the people. The young men who perpetrated this practical joke afterward entered the service of the United States and served three years" (*History of Delaware County*, p. 487).

19. This was the Rev. Joy Bishop, also known as Father Bishop.

20. Patrick and Julie Ann Trumblee lived on a farm directly south of the Baker inn.

21. Factory was unbleached muslin.

22. The Soldiers Relief Society originally comprised thirty-three members (eighteen women and fifteen men) and was formed, according to Secretary Emmie E. Hawley's notes, "for the purpose of making articles needed to make the wounded and sick Soldiers of our Army comfortable." The group resolved to hold weekly meetings and charge membership fees of $.50 for gentlemen, $.25 for ladies (Soldiers Relief Society notes, Huftalen Papers, Iowa State Historical Society, Iowa City).

23. Alfred Camp, thirty-five, is listed as a laborer in the 1860 census; Huldy Kamp, forty, and four children are also listed in the household. Their location on the census roll suggests they were inn boarders or nearest neighbors to Henry Baker.

24. At about this time, Emily Hawley described her feelings and philosophy of marriage in a letter to her parents: "Thought I would write and tell you something you will not expect to hear, yes tis that which I did not think I would when I came here—do you not know Mother what Emmie has so often said she would never do? (*she thought she wouldnt too*) but Mother I became acquainted with James about Christmas. he has been at Uncles a number of times the past winter: and—shall I tell you? yes I will; though I had thought to wait 'till I came home. Mother your Emmie has made a vow which never passed her lips 'till now. she has promised *to be a bride*: I have had long enough time to think what I was doing, and I *did* think too—of the many times I have heard you warn us against the deceitfulness of the world—and

not be hasty. O no use to write of all you have told me but I kindly thank you for the advice, and think I have profited by it. for you well know mother i have been with quite a number of different ones, and had it not have been for some preventing providence (your advice) perhaps eer this I should have made the same vow. . . . Mother I hope this will not be too unexpected for it can not be helped now, the whole responsibility rests on Emmie, for she has been influenced by no-one, but *herself*. . . . I have always thought and said I would never be married to *any one* untill they had first a home but I may however. you well know Father there are many wealthy people in the world who commenced the journey of life without any thing but their hands, *and a good big bump of calculation.* the two go well together if industry and health are with them. I do not know why they could not do as well for me as any one. . . . hope I may prove myself worthy the love of the only one Emmie ever thought she could share the happiness trials and troubles of the future" (Emmie Hawley to Mother and Father, March 2, 1862, Huftalen Papers, Michigan History Division, Lansing).

25. Milton Nelson died having never seen combat. Of the 13,001 Iowans who died in the Civil War, the vast majority (8,498) succumbed to disease, while 3,540 died from battle wounds (Sage, *History of Iowa*, p. 155).

26. Emily Hawley described attending Lyceum activities several times in the diary and in letters back to Michigan. She sent her family a copy of a poem she read at one Lyceum, "Home Friends," and asked her brother to put it in her letter box.

27. Masonville had no population listed in the 1860 census. It was a new community located on the Dubuque and Pacific Railroad line four miles southwest of Henry Baker's farm. Emily Hawley was the first teacher in Masonville's new schoolhouse.

28. A sacque is a loose-fitting coat or jacket.

29. Emily Hawley prepared a written closing address for her last day as a teacher. Her letter to her students thanks them for their obedience and admonishes them to enjoy their schooldays before life's duties descend. Part of the presentation seems autobiographical: "Some of you perhaps may be teachers: should you perchance be a teacher in a strange land among strangers—far from a fathers home you will *then* look back to these days when *you* were school children—and should your pupils, any of them disregard your interest for them, and not give due attention to their studies—you will then feel the need of some kind friend, and I hope you may never look back with regret then, that you have sometime disobeyed your teacher" ([Emmie Hawley], to Scholars, August 31, 1862, Huftalen Papers, Michigan History Division, Lansing).

THREE. Emily Hawley, Unmarried Woman

1. Jeffrey, *Frontier Women*, p. 28, says emigration west was a family affair. Faragher, *Women and Men on the Overland Trail*, p. 34, says that emigration by single females unaccompanied by families was statistically insignificant.

2. T'ien, "Demographic Aspect of Interstate Variations in American Fertility, 1800–1860," p. 129.

3. Faragher, *Women and Men on the Overland Trail*, p. 50. His estimate for the proportion of daily caloric sustenance provided by women comes from S. B. Nerlove, "Women's Workload and Infant Feeding Practices: A Relationship with Demographic Implications," *Ethnology* 13 (1974): 207–214.

4. Faragher, *Women and Men on the Overland Trail*, pp. 53–54.

5. Dublin, *Women at Work*, says that the correspondence of Lowell operatives suggests most women kept their earnings. In *Farm to Factory* he generalizes from two diary sources that most daughters living at home retained part of their income. Ryan, *Womanhood in America*, says that her study of Utica women supports the findings that factory girls kept their earnings while farmers' daughters' labor went to the family (p. 82). Cott, *Bonds of Womanhood*, in contrast says Lowell factory girls sent their wages home but cites no specific sources (pp. 55–56).

6. Smith, "Parental Power," Table 3, p. 425.

7. Cott, *Bonds of Womanhood*, p. 83, 77–78.

8. Rothman, *Hands and Hearts*. The marriage manual cited is William Alcott, *The Young Wife* (Boston, 1837), p. 29.

9. Gordon, "The Ideal Husband." The marriage manual cited is Michael Ryan, *The Philosophy of Marriage* (1873).

10. Smith, "Parental Power," p. 422.

11. Woodward, ed., *Mary Chesnut's Civil War*, p. 729.

12. Cott, *Bonds of Womanhood*, p. 17.

13. Letter received from Paul C. Rosenblatt, December 22, 1983, in response to a query about the coding he alluded to in *Bitter, Bitter Tears*. Personal communication with Polly Longsworth, author of *Austin and Mabel*, September 28, 1986.

14. Smith and Hindus, "Premarital Pregnancy in America"; Degler, *At Odds*, p. 218.

15. Dublin, *Farm to Factory*, p. 23.

16. Motz, *True Sisterhood*, p. 85.

17. Lebsock, *Free Women of Petersburg*, chapter 1.

18. Bernard and Vinovskis, "The Female School Teacher." Rothman, *Hands and*

Hearts, quotes the diaries of several young teachers who were very eager to accelerate their wedding days.

19. Rosenblatt, *Bitter, Bitter Tears*; Jeffrey, *Frontier Women*, p. 37.
20. According to Smith, "Family Limitation," only 7.3 percent of Emily Hawley's cohorts never married.
21. On the high end of the average age of marriage scale are two studies based on data from the northeast: Ryan, *Cradle of the Middle Class*, and Dublin, *Women at Work*. Nancy Cott, *Bonds of Womanhood*, estimates the age of marriage at the turn of the century to be 22–23. Faragher, *Women and Men on the Overland Trail*, found 20.5 to be the mean age of Overland Trail women when marrying.
22. Henry Baker to Mrs. Sarah Hawley, January 28, 1879(?), Huftalen Papers, Michigan History Division, Lansing.
23. Faragher, *Women and Men on the Overland Trail*, p. 147.
24. Hampsten, *Read This Only to Yourself*, p. 9.
25. Jeffrey, *Frontier Women*, p. 68.
26. Unruh, *The Plains Across*; Smith-Rosenberg, "Female World of Love and Ritual."
27. For a fuller discussion, see Ryan, *Cradle of the Middle Class*. She cites C. Wright Mills, *White Collar: The American Middle Classes* (New York, 1951).
28. Degler, *At Odds*, p. 372.
29. Riley, *Frontierswomen*, especially pp. 110–135.
30. Typed stories in biographical scrapbook on Emily Hawley Gillespie, 1948, by Sarah Gillespie Huftalen, Huftalen Papers, Iowa State Historical Society, Iowa City.
31. Emmie Hawley to Mother and Father, March 2, 1862, Huftalen Papers, Michigan History Division, Lansing.
32. Motz, *True Sisterhood*, p. 18.
33. Emmie Hawley to Mother and Father, March 2, 1862.
34. "Farming Life in New England," *Atlantic Monthly* (August 1858): 341, cited in Dublin, *Women at Work*.

Four. "Seems Good to Know We Live at Home": 1862–1874

1. Emily Hawley Gillespie, letter to Mother and Father, September 18, 1862, Huftalen Papers, Michigan History Division, Lansing.

2. Sarah Gillespie Huftalen, "Gillespie Family Line," Huftalen Papers, Iowa State Historical Society, Iowa City.

3. The closest midwestern farmers came to producing sugar from cane was sorghum molasses. During the Civil War, sugar prices rose dramatically (from $.09 per pound in 1861 to $.235 in 1864) and sorghum mills processed local farmers' cane for market. After the war, sorghum production was less profitable and many farmers grew only an acre of the crop for home consumption, according to Bogue, *From Prairie to Corn Belt*, pp. 139–140. The 1870 agricultural census, however, shows the Gillespies still producing 180 gallons of molasses. U.S. Department of Agriculture, *Agricultural Census, 1870*, August 15, 1870, pp. 1–2.

4. James Gillespie's sister Margaret, twenty-nine, was married to William Jerome Doolittle, thirty-six. They had four children and lived in Manchester, where Jerome was a partner in a wagon shop.

5. According to family deed records, Lorinda Gillespie purchased this two hundred–acre farm in Section 36 of Coffins Grove Township in 1859 for $3,500. While the Iowa constitution (1846) did not mention property rights for women, the state code of 1851 gave married women certain rights and privileges. The right of a married woman such as Lorinda to purchase property and hold it in her own right was upheld by an Iowa Supreme Court decision in 1860, according to Gallaher, *Legal and Political Status of Women in Iowa*, p. 87. Although the deed states that Lorinda "sold" one hundred acres of her property to her son James for $1,000, probably no cash was exchanged. Emily's diary entry of December 30, 1861, says James "received the deed in payment for his wages since he was of age."

6. Lydia Ann Zerphus, as her name is spelled in the 1860 census, was the twenty-year-old daughter of a family living near Henry Baker. John Schmidt probably was still living at the Baker Inn as a hired man, as he had when Emily lived there.

7. Gilbert Yeoman, a merchant, was the husband of James's sister Marcelia, twenty-four.

8. As Mrs. Lewis is not mentioned previously in the diary as a social acquaintance and Emily Gillespie notes paying her for her services, she was probably the local midwife.

9. If Mary Evans was one of the children of Henry Baker's neighbors John and Elizabeth Evans, she would be quite young—ten years old at most.

10. According to a township plat map, John Evans owned three parcels of land in the sections northeast of Henry Baker's property (Davis, *Township Plat Book of Delaware County, Iowa*).

11. LaFayette Gillespie was born in 1824, making him the Gillespies' firstborn son; he died in 1854 of consumption. The practice of naming children several months after their birth was commonplace (Saum, "Death in the Popular Mind"). Saum's study of census records showed children even a year old listed as "anonymous" and "unnamed." One argument for such a practice is that infant mortality rates of at least 10 percent compelled parents to distance themselves from vulnerable newborns by leaving them nameless. Saum found numerous diaries in which infants were simply called "the little stranger" for months. A contemporary of Emily Gillespie's, Samuella Curd, wrote in her diary, "The baby has a bad cold it distresses to hear her cough am afraid something will happen of it. I trust not to cling too much to her, for we are not permitted to make to ourselves idols & keep them" (Arpad, *Sam Curd's Diary*, p. 119).

12. According to historian Leland Sage (*History of Iowa*, p. 155), of the 7,548 men whose names were drawn in Iowa's only draft of September 1864, 16 percent avoided service by hiring substitutes. In total, only 25 percent of those drafted in Iowa actually served. Nationally, 10 percent of the draftees in 1864 hired substitutes, according to Morris, ed., *Encyclopedia of American History*, p. 239.

13. Paramatta is a light twilled dress fabric having a silk or cotton warp and a wool weft.

14. A firkin is a wooden tub roughly equivalent in size to one-fourth of a barrel.

15. This is the first reference in the diary to Emily Gillespie's plans to return to Michigan with her two young children to visit her family.

16. Lucy Ann Sims was the daughter of Horace Garlick, one of Emily's uncles. During Emily's recent visit to Michigan, she wrote in her diary that Lucy Ann acted "real strange" (July 25, 1866). According to a newspaper account called "The Medina Tragedy" (*Tecumseh Herald*, October 11, 1866, p. 1), Sims was described as "known to have been subject to attacks of insanity for a long time, but was never considered dangerous." Emily Gillespie learned about the murder/suicide in a letter from her sister Harriet written two weeks after the event. Harriet's account parallels the gruesome newspaper story. She wrote that two thousand people attended the funeral and that Lucy Ann Sims and her four children were buried in a mass grave. Harriet mentions that Lucy Ann wrote "a good [suicide] letter" to her husband, Robert Sims, but does not quote from it, saying it will no doubt be in the newspaper (Hattie Hawley, letter to sister and brother, October 14, 1866, Michigan History Division, Lansing). In a 1909 county history biographical sketch of Robert Sims, his first marriage to Lucy Ann Garlick is noted, but the number of children she

bore is inaccurate and the tragedy unmentioned (Bonner, *Memoirs of Lenawee County, Michigan*, p. 459).

17. This is the first !!! mark in the diary since April 1860; the marks recur with monthly regularity until 1884. If these marks do indicate Gillespie's menstrual periods, the onset of menstruation fifteen months after the birth of Sarah can be compared to the pattern of childbirth identified in Potter, "Birth Intervals," cited in Faragher, *Women and Men on the Overland Trail*, p. 197. There were twenty-two months between Emily Gillespie's two pregnancies; this interval is a full standard deviation shorter than the mean of twenty-nine months. This might indicate she nursed Henry for less than the standard one-year period and thus recovered from postpartum amenorrhea earlier. Gillespie's menstrual onset after the birth of Sarah is two months later than the mean, on the other hand. This suggests (1) the limited applicability of a study done on twentieth-century women to a nineteenth-century woman; (2) that Gillespie was anemic for a very long period after Sarah's birth, for she noted in the diary that she weaned the baby at ten months, and the menstrual cycle usually begins soon after the cessation of nursing; (3) that the !!! mark was indeed a means of birth control, which would explain its absence between the two births: Gillespie was not concerned with avoiding pregnancy after the birth of her first child, although she was after the birth of her second; (4) that if indeed the marks indicate a way to tell if she was pregnant, Gillespie would not need the system if she was not having sexual relations with her husband until fifteen months after Sarah's birth.

18. Albert J. Hersey, thirty-six, was fifteen years older than Susan Baker, who was now of age. She had inherited several thousand dollars from her grandfather Clement Coffin in 1867. Brief comments in the diary and letters to Michigan suggest Emily Gillespie did not approve of Hersey.

19. The Turkey River was about twenty-five miles northeast of Manchester and was surrounded by rich woodlands. James Gillespie drew wood from this area to town, where he sold or traded it for about $5.00 a load.

20. This was the third (according to the diary) or fourth (according to the 1878 county history) "great prairie chicken hunt" and picnic held at Henry Baker's. This event later became known as the Harvest Home picnic and was a local tradition until 1878.

21. In 1866 or 1867 John Schmidt left Henry Baker's employment and moved to sixteen acres just east of Baker's land. Here he ran a vineyard and orchard with his wife, Maggie, a native of Austria. In the 1870 census his name is Anglicized to John Smith.

22. According to the 1878 county history, the *Delaware County Union*, a Democratic paper, was published between March 1864 and 1872.

23. Jimmy McBride, thirty, was one of the sons of James and Betty McBride. Judging from the position of their name in the 1870 census list, both McBride families lived near the Gillespies.

24. E. H. (or E. O.) Sellens, a wealthy immigrant from England, lived directly west of James and Emily Gillespie on a one hundred–acre farm.

25. John McGee, twenty-nine, was one of seven children of Isaac and Sarah McGee, who lived just east of Henry Baker. The McGee farm was prosperous. In the 1870 census it was valued at $16,820, compared to Henry Baker's ($20,000) and James Gillespie's ($5,000) farms.

26. Two Scanlan families lived to the west of the Gillespies, according to the 1894 plat map. Clark M. Bronson is listed as a dealer in Singer sewing machines and musical instruments in the 1878 county history.

27. The Agricultural Society of Delaware County had sponsored a fair since 1855. The fairs were discontinued during the Civil War and restarted in 1869. About $1,000 a year was awarded to premium winners, according to the 1878 county history.

28. Emily Gillespie's observation of emigrant wagons going west and the departure of several of her neighbors indicate how mobile the population still was in the 1870s. Iowa was now a place to pass through instead of a place to homestead, and some Iowa families moved ever westward in search of a better life, as Hamlin Garland recorded in his autobiography. Mildred Throne ("Population Study") found that only 38 percent of the farmers who lived in Wapello County in 1850 were still there in 1860 (Bogue, *From Prairie to Corn Belt*, p. 25).

29. Local Universalists had been conducting services in the Congregational church building on alternate Sabbaths during 1864 and 1865 and again since 1868. Several leading citizens of Manchester—a bank director, several merchants, and an attorney—pledged $5,000 in 1869 to build a Universalist church. It was completed on May 7, 1871, at a total cost of $8,030.44, according to the 1878 county history. Rev. E. R. Wood became the regular minister in September 1871. Nationally, there were 54,957 Universalists in 1890. A 1926 census showed that two-thirds of the membership was female and half the parishes were rural (U.S. Bureau of the Census, "Universalist Church"). In Iowa, there were 132 Universalist Societies or preaching sites between 1830 and 1963, according to Quist, "Universalism and Unitarianism in Iowa."

30. The Chicago fire of October 1871 was interpreted by some clergy as God's punishment against a wicked city. In contrast, the radical feminist paper, *Woodhull and Claflin's Weekly* (December 30, 1871), argued that God was not vengeful—or interested—enough to destroy Chicago.

31. H. M. Congar & Co. was a dry goods store in Manchester; Congar was a member of the Universalist church.

32. Daniel, thirty-one, and Mary, twenty-nine, Ryan and their three children lived on a moderately properous farm in neighboring Delaware Township to the east of the Gillespies.

33. *Enceinte* is a word meaning "pregnant," from the French for "ungirted"; the Spanish term is *encinta*. Emily Gillespie used *encienta* when writing in her diary about other women but did not use it to refer to herself during her pregnancies.

34. *Woodhull and Claflin's Weekly* is called "the most spectacular advocate of suffrage in the period" in Mott, *History of American Magazines. Vol. III: 1865–1885*, p. 95. The magazine was published irregularly from May 14, 1870, to June 10, 1876. Mott says the irregularity was due to jail sentences for obscenity, bankruptcy, and the lecture tours of its editors/publishers, Victoria Woodhull and her sister Tennessee C. Claflin. The paper's banner read "Progress! Free Thought! Untrammeled Lives! Breaking the Way for Future Generations." Its circulation peaked in 1873 at 40,000, in part due to its exposure of the Beecher-Tilton scandal. Its coverage of the adultery scandal, however, also led to many of its problems with Anthony Comstock's Society for the Suppression of Vice (ibid., pp. 443–453). In comparison, Stanton and Anthony's equal rights paper the *Revolution* had a circulation of 3,000; the *Nation* had 12,000; the women's magazine *Peterson's* (similar to *Godeys*) had a circulation of 150,000.

35. There are sporadic x marks in the margins of the diary in both Sarah Huftalen's holograph copy and in Emily Gillespie's original. The significance of the marked entries to family history (e.g., the first day the children attend school, the day family portraits are made) indicates that a family member who read the diary (Emily, Sarah, or Henry Gillespie) may have used the marks as a finding aid.

36. Horace Greeley, founder of the *New York Tribune*, was the Democratic/Liberal Republican presidential candidate. Greeley, a Universalist, was a strong spokesman for the antislavery and antiliquor movements. He received 71,000 votes in Iowa, compared to the 131,000 votes cast for Republican Ulysses S. Grant. The Republican party had held a firm majority in Iowa since 1854, especially during the Civil War.

37. *Peterson's Magazine* was a popular women's publication similar to *Godeys* (see note 13, chapter 2). The *Western Rural* was a farm paper begun in 1862 by H. N. F. Lewis of Illinois; by 1877 it was a paper of the Farmers' Alliance, a political organization (Mott, *History of American Magazines. Vol. II: 1850–1865*, p. 90, and *Vol. III: 1865–1885*, p. 149). The *Inter-Ocean* was a Chicago newspaper edited by Frank Palmer and started March 25, 1872. Its

banner read, "Independent in nothing; Republican in everything." At its peak its circulation reached almost 100,000 and it had the second highest postage volume to subscribers in the United States in 1879 (Blanchard, *Discovery and Conquest*, p. 478).

38. George Toogood is listed in the 1870 census as a Manchester retail grocer. The Richard Brook family lived near Henry Baker, given the placement of their names in the 1870 census rolls. Marilla Brook was forty-five; the Brooks had two sons and two daughters.

39. Silas Estey and his family lived in neighboring Delaware Township. He is listed in census records as running a boarding house (1860) and being a milk dealer (1870).

40. This poem refers to a love of 1858 or 1859, which would place the event prior to the start of the diary. Stanza ten of the poem was not completed. In Sarah Huftalen's biography of her mother, she includes this poem as "'Valentines Lamentations,' composed in 1875 in memory of 1860, Supposed in memory of Dr. Chappell, her lover" (Huftalen Papers, Iowa State Historical Society, Iowa City). The discrepancy in dates of origin for the verse could be due to Emily Gillespie's habit of copying over poems to revise them or to send them to friends and family.

41. Agnes Josephine Smith, twenty-one, was ten years younger than Henry Hawley.

42. Willie Grey was an orphan who lived with a series of families and worked for his room and board.

43. Thorp Bros. & Co. was a general store, and Fred Glisendorf ran a meat market, according to the 1878 county history.

44. Seth Brown ran the oldest shoe business, founded in 1859, in Manchester.

45. Adams and Freelove was a hardware business in Manchester.

46. Isabelle McGee was Harriet Hawley McGee's sister-in-law.

47. Phrenologists related the mental and temperamental characteristics of an individual to the bumps and hollows of the skull. It was a very popular "science" up to the beginning of the twentieth century.

FIVE. Emily Gillespie, Wife and Mother

1. Fothergill, *Private Chronicles*, chapter 4; Lensink, "Pioneer Woman's Life"; Faragher, *Women and Men on the Overland Trail*, pp. 128–133.

2. U.S. Department of Agriculture, *Agricultural Census, 1870*.

3. See, for example, Bogue, *From Prairie to Corn Belt*, p. 256, and Riley, *Frontierswomen*, p. 86.

4. Suckow, *Country People*.

5. Ryan, *Womanhood in America*, p. 50; Faragher, *Women and Men on the Overland Trail*, p. 181.

6. Diary of Corwin Snow, December 14, 1894, Special Collections, University of Iowa, Iowa City.

7. Arpad, *Sam Curd's Diary*, pp. 149–150.

8. Rothman, *Hands and Hearts*, p. 113 (Mary Butterfield to Champion Chase, January 22, 1848, Champion S. Chase Papers, Yale University Library, New Haven). See also Cott, *Bonds of Womanhood*, p. 83.

9. Bernstein's studies, "Elaborated and Restricted Codes: Their Social Origins and Consequences," in Alfred G. Smith, ed., *Communications and Culture* (New York: Holt, Rinehart and Winston, 1966) and "A Socio-Linguistic Approach to Socialization: With Some Reference to Educability," in *Class, Codes and Control* (London: Routledge and Kegan Paul, 1971) are cited in Faragher, *Women and Men on the Overland Trail*, pp. 131–133.

10. Motz, *True Sisterhood*, p. 78. Motz also uses Bernstein's theory to examine the difference in language codes (restrictive for diaries, elaborated for correspondence) of Michigan women.

11. Genevieve, "Woman's Duties," *Godeys Lady's Book* (February 1873): 166, cited in Motz, *True Sisterhood*.

12. Dawes diary cited in Cott, *Bonds of Womanhood*, p. 75; Curd diary in Arpad, *Sam Curd's Diary*, p. 67; Stewart diary in Faragher, *Women and Men on the Overland Trail*, p. 176.

13. Diary of October 1, 1854, in Nelson, ed., *Diary of Elizabeth Koren*; diary of Eunice Wait Cobb cited in Cott, *Bonds of Womanhood*, p. 75.

14. Cott, *Bonds of Womanhood*, p. 74.

15. Smith-Rosenberg, "Female World of Love and Ritual," Cott, *Bonds of Womanhood*, pp. 160–196.

16. Demographic sources on fertility in the mid-nineteenth century are markedly similar. The 5.21 figure comes from Wilson H. Grahill et al., *The Fertility of American Women* (New York, 1958), pp. 14–15, cited in Ryan, *Womanhood in America*, and Rothman, *Hands and Hearts*. Daniel Scott Smith draws upon Ansley S. Coale et al., *New Estimates of Fertility and Population in the U.S.* (Princeton: Princeton University Press, 1963), p. 36, for the same 5.21 figure in his study "Family Limitation," pp. 119–136. Faragher, *Women and Men of the Overland Trail*, p. 57, uses the figure of 5.7 children per midwestern family in the 1850s from the *Compendium of the Eleventh Census, 1890, Part I—Population*, p. 866.

17. Arpad, *Sam Curd's Diary*, p. 22.

18. Fertility decline statistics are from Smith, "Family Limitation," p. 123, based on Yasukichi Yasuba, *Birth Rates of the White Population in the U.S., 1880–1860* (Baltimore: Johns Hopkins University Press, 1962).

19. Smith, "Family Limitation"; Lerner, "Placing Women in History"; Lebsock, *Free Women of Petersburg*, pp. 48–53.

20. The trends in rural birth rates are from Yasuba, *Birth Rates*. Fertility average during Sarah Hawley's childbearing decade (1830) of 6.5 is from Smith, "Family Limitation," p. 123. Hampsten, *Read This Only to Yourself*, pp. 102–111.

21. A summary of various nineteenth-century theories of the female reproductive cycle can be found in Haller and Haller, *Physician and Sexuality*. Rothman, *Hands and Hearts*, pp. 139–143.

22. Degler, *At Odds*, pp. 218–219, says Foote was the first to offer the diaphragm. Foote, *Medical Common Sense*, p. 380. The earliest edition of this book was published in Philadelphia in 1859. The Gillespie family copy of Foote's book is kept with the Huftalen Papers, Iowa State Historical Society, Iowa City.

23. Cassara, ed., *Universalism in America*, pp. 31–32, 2.

24. Quist, "Universalism and Unitarianism in Iowa."

25. A list and historical background of Universalist/Unitarian women can be found in Gitlin, *Roots of Our Strength*. Olympia Brown, "The Higher Education of Women," *Repository* 51 (February 1874): 85, cited in Cassara, ed., *Universalism in America*, pp. 212–213.

26. Judith Sargent Murray, *Gleaner* 1, no. 17 (1798), cited in Kerber, *Women of the Republic*, p. 205.

27. *Woodhull and Claflin's Weekly*, December 12, 1874.

28. Ibid., March 23, 1872, p. 12.

29. The basic history of the women's rights movement in Iowa is Noun, *Strong-Minded Women*; see also Riley, *Frontierswomen*, chapter 6.

Six. "Tis the Saddest . . . Merely to Be Always at Home": 1874–1883

1. U.S. Department of Agriculture, *Agricultural Census, 1870*.

2. U.S. Department of Agriculture, *Agricultural Census, 1880*, Schedule 2.

3. Land prices for this time period in two Iowa counties are described in Bogue, *From Prairie to Corn Belt*, pp. 53–56. Farm wholesale price index data are in Morris, ed., *Encyclopedia of American History*, p. 481. An analysis of state

census data that provides average farm size and productivity figures for Delaware County is Jackson, *Census of Iowa.*

4. James Gillespie's concern about the farm property "should he die first" may refer to the ambiguous interpretations of a wife's right to dower in the Iowa state code (Gallaher, *Legal and Political Status*, pp. 94–105). When the deed transfer to Emily Gillespie was recorded in Delaware County, a sale price of $500 was listed, which would prevent the farm from being considered a gift from husband to wife. Emily Gillespie's promise to keep the farm "free from incumbrance" may refer to an 1870 revision in state property laws that clearly held women liable for indebtedness of their property and no longer protected by coverture. An 1877 Iowa Supreme Court decision stated, "Coverture, in Iowa, ought to be no shelter to the wife against the enforcement of the rights of others growing out of her contracts. . . . In short, the statute, in bestowing upon her equal property rights with the husband, imposes upon her the same obligations he bears" (ibid., p. 121).

5. Temperance activity in Iowa reflected renewed national pressure for prohibition that characterized the 1870s and 1880s. In Manchester, the Ladies Temperance Society was organized in January 1874 with thirty-six members (*History of Delaware County*, p. 508). In February they held a mass meeting in the new city hall and attracted seven hundred people, according to Bailey, *Three-Volume History.* This was followed by the organization of the Band of Hope, a juvenile temperance group of sixty members, under the auspices of the Women's Christian Temperance Union, in April 1874. In March 1877 the Manchester Reform Club, comprised of forty habitual drinkers who pledged to abstain, was organized. In other communities, temperance fervor also ran high. In Marshalltown, for example, a Blue Ribbon Jubilee rally of the 1870s attracted 15,000 people (Smith, "A Martyr for Prohibition"). The Bailey County history reports that several lawsuits against saloons in Manchester on behalf of drunkards' families effectively closed all such establishments. The prohibition issue divided the Iowa Republican party throughout the 1870s. A state constitutional prohibition amendment passed the General Assembly in 1880 and 1882 and was ratified by a popular vote. Prohibition became the law of Iowa in July 1882 but was found unconstitutional in October of that year (Sage, *History of Iowa*, p. 203).

6. The polar opposite of rationalist Universalist belief, religious revivalism, according to Ryan, was characterized by "abject submission to the will of a superior God coupled with a commensurate distrust of the convert's self-efficacy" (*Womanhood in America*, p. 86). Ryan says in another study, "As early as the 1840s the raucous aspects of revivalism and reform produced

some appeals for retreat into familial and private spaces. The Universalists eschewed public and even family prayer in favor of 'moments of privacy and meditation'" (*Cradle of the Middle Class*, p. 142).

7. The Henry Ward Beecher–Elizabeth Tilton adultery scandal, first publicized in *Woodhull and Claflin's Weekly* in November 1872, was now the focus of a Congregationalist church investigation. This hearing was given heavy press coverage, and Emily Gillespie mentions in her diary several times reading about it. While Beecher's liberal theology, belief in phrenology, and acceptance of evolutionary theory paralleled Emily Gillespie's, her comments about the scandal indicate her disapproval of all three parties. The July 31, 1874, *Manchester Press* reprinted on its front page a column from the *Chicago Post and Mail* that called Theodore Tilton a "pale faced Othello" for his jealousy and went on to criticize "miscreant Tilton, the advocate of free love and the rhapsodist of Woodhull, and finally the accuser of his own wife and the destroyer of his own home." Beecher, on the other hand, was called "a true Christian, liberal, affable, eloquent and without reproach," a minister whose duty it was to hear unhappy wives. An intellectual history of the scandal from a feminist perspective is Waller, *Reverend Beecher and Mrs. Tilton*.

8. James VanAlstyne, thirty-four, was the son of Henry Baker's neighbors, the George VanAlstynes, a family Emily Gillespie had known since her arrival in Iowa. James VanAlystyne's property was listed as worth $10,000 in the 1870 agricultural census. He left a wife and at least three children.

9. George Brook, twenty-seven, was the husband of Emma Brook, a close friend of Emily Gillespie's. He was the son of a wealthy Coffins Grove Township farmer, Richard Brook, who owned a 120-acre farm, according to the 1870 agricultural census. George Brook's name does not appear on either the 1870 or 1880 agricultural census rolls of land ownership. For a discussion of farm tenancy in Iowa, see chapter 7, note 3.

10. The Patrons of Husbandry, known as the Grange, was an economic organization of farmers founded in 1867. By 1870 there were 1,999 local Granges in Iowa (Sage, *History of Iowa*, p. 189). In Delaware County there were 12 Granges in 1873, but only 5 left in 1878 (*History of Delaware County*, p. 426), which supports Sage's analysis that the 100,000-person Iowa membership figures during the troubled 1870s may be inflated or based on ephemeral local groups. While the Grange engaged in controversial political activities and contained elements of Masonic ritual and secrecy, it also sponsored educational meetings, such as the Delaware County Farmers' Institute, a yearly three-day event.

11. The *Western Rural* is the only publication mentioned in both Emily Gillespie's

1872 and 1876 lists of subscriptions. However, she occasionally notes in the later diary reading *Peterson's* and the *Inter-Ocean*, perhaps borrowed copies. The *Phrenological Journal* was a weekly publication of Fowlers and Wells, who printed several "improvement and progress" journals. One of the contributors to *Phrenological Journal* was Walt Whitman (Mott, *History of American Magazines, Vol. II, 1850–1865*, p. 42). The livestock journal Emily Gillespie refers to is probably the *National Live Stock Journal* (1870–1891), a publication from Chicago that contained articles on poultry raising (ibid., *Vol. III, 1865–1885*, p. 159). *Harper's Weekly* (1857 to 1910), with a circulation of over 100,000, was one of the most consistently popular magazines of the mid-nineteenth century. It featured a full pictorial record of the 1876 Centennial Exposition in Philadelphia for its readers. *Harper's Weekly* was pro-Democratic and much more political than its sister publication *Harper's Monthly*. Frank Luther Mott says, "It is as a vigorous political journal of conservative tendencies that it was most noteworthy" (ibid., pp. 486–487). *Youth's Companion*, originally a Congregationalist paper containing highly moral narratives and poems, had a circulation of almost 100,000 by the mid-1870s. It then featured stories by such writers as Harriet Beecher Stowe, Henry Ward Beecher, Elizabeth Stuart Phelps, Rudyard Kipling, and Rebecca Harding Davis. Mott says the magazine's popularity and longevity (1827 to 1929, then continued as *American Boy*) resulted from its family orientation and fiction attractive to adult readers (ibid., pp. 262–274). The *Champion* mentioned by Gillespie may be a precursor of the Chicago antiprohibition periodical, *Champion of Freedom & Right* (ibid., p. 311). Its position on temperance, the opposite of Emily Gillespie's, might explain why she says it was "sent by unknown." The *Delaware County Union*, which the Gillespies subscribed to in the 1860s, ceased publication in 1872. The *Manchester Press*, also Democratic, began publication in June 1871.

12. Gillespie is probably referring to the book *Wife No. 19 or The Story of a Life in Bondage* (1877) by Ann Eliza Webb Young, who had sued Morman leader Brigham Young for divorce in 1873. Ann Eliza Young went on a popular lecture tour to speak about the evils of polygamy; her tour included Washington, D.C., where she was considered influential in persuading Congress to pass antipolygamy legislation in 1874 (Brodie, "Young, Ann Elizabeth Webb," vol. 3, pp. 696–697).

13. Sarah Gillespie's 1877 diary is in the Huftalen Collection, Iowa State Historical Society, Iowa City. Sarah Gillespie Huftalen preserved seventeen volumes of her diaries irregularly spanning 1877 to 1952. See the Conclusion for a comparative discussion of these diaries with Emily Gillespie's.

14. This petition for the removal of teacher Miss Gill, signed by ten people, was

the result of several community meetings in which philosophies of teaching and discipline were heatedly debated.

15. On January 11, 1878, a nine-line announcement appeared in the *Manchester Press* for Susan B. Anthony's upcoming talk, "Women Want Bread, not the Ballot." Anthony was billed as "the most noted lecturer of her sex." The January 18 paper reported that Miss Anthony spoke for over two hours without notes to an audience that filled city hall and "she found here, many warm and earnest supporters." The article quoted Anthony as saying "not only will her sex continue to be comparatively degraded, so long as she is deprived of the suffrage, but that the great moral reforms of the time cannot be carried out without the aid her exercise of the right to vote would afford."

16. Congar Brothers' Banking House was founded in Manchester in 1875. Henry M. Congar and his brother had been supporters of the Universalist church. Henry Congar had been a director of Manchester's first bank, opened in 1868 (*History of Delaware County*, pp. 12–13).

17. The Manchester Academy and Normal School and Commercial Institute, a private school, was founded September 5, 1879, after a petition for a public course in higher learning failed before the school board. The academy offered a one-year normal course, a common school, and a preparatory school. Tuition was $8.00 a term and classes were held in the former Universalist church building. The first principal (1879) was A. S. Kissel, former state superintendent of public instruction. The second principal (1880 to 1882) was Walter Haben Butter, a lawyer who later (1891 to 1893) served as a Democratic congressman from Iowa. The Manchester Academy closed in 1882 due to low enrollment and a public high school was opened (Sarah Gillespie Huftalen, personal scrapbook on Manchester Academy, Huftalen Papers, Iowa State Historical Society, Iowa City).

18. Despite Hulda Lewis's loss of her pension by remarriage, she probably retained her widow's dower right to lifelong use of one-third of her first husband's property. In the late 1860s, Iowa court decisions held women responsible for alienation by agreement of their dower; for example, a woman could sign a contract agreeing to take a pension in lieu of dower rights. But by the 1880s, women's dower rights were more strictly protected from post-nuptial agreements and could be lost only through divorce (Gallaher, *Legal and Political Status*, pp. 105–114).

19. Emma Brooks, who was institutionalized in July 1877, stayed in the asylum only about a month, according to Emily Gillespie's diary.

20. According to the *History of Delaware County* (p. 407), Manchester had unsuccessfully petitioned to move the county seat from Delhi in 1869, 1874, and 1875. By 1880, the population of Manchester was 2,275, compared to Delhi's

524, and the petition was again put to a vote (U.S. Bureau of the Census, *Statistics of the Population*, pp. 163, 172). The *Manchester Press* of November 5, 1880, reported the election results as Manchester 228, Delhi 1,652.

21. James A. Garfield (Republican) was elected U.S. president November 2, 1880. Although Garfield was shot by Charles J. Guiteau on July 2, 1881, the president did not die until September 19. Guiteau was executed June 30, 1882.

22. Devils Backbone was a rugged and high limestone outcropping along the Maquoketa River approximately ten miles north of Manchester.

23. Mrs. Butter was the wife of Walter Haben Butter, a University of Wisconsin–trained lawyer who was principal of the Manchester Academy where the Gillespie children attended school.

24. It is unclear from the context of the diary whether Emily Gillespie means "intentional abortion" or is using the term more generally to mean "miscarriage," which James C. Mohr says was in use among rural people in reference to their livestock. On the other hand, according to Mohr, "by 1882, people were more likely to use the word abortion with some precision, and mean by it what we generally do: an intentional procedure" (letter received from James C. Mohr, February 27, 1987). Given the growth of antiabortion legislation at this time and the particularly harsh statutes against married women and their doctors undertaking abortion (an 1882 Iowa law increased potential prison terms for physicians from one year to five), it would be desperate indeed for Harriet McGee to purposefully terminate her eighth pregnancy. See Mohr, *Abortion in America*, particularly chapters 8 and 9.

25. Elisha Hawley, one of Emily Gillespie's cousins, lived 120 miles south of Manchester in Rose Hill, Iowa.

26. The Anamosa Prison, built in 1872–73, was located about thirty miles southeast of Manchester. According to the 1885 state census report, at this time the prison held 269 males and 12 females in confinement (Jackson, *Census of Iowa*).

Seven. "No Home Here": 1883–1888

1. Information on the size of the 1876 Gillespie house is from its current owner, Wilbur Kehrli (letter received from Wilma Kehrli, April 4, 1987). Information on the Brussels carpet is from the account book compiled in 1946 by Sarah Gillespie Huftalen from her mother's diaries and account records, entries for December 9, 11, and 16, 1880, p. 72 (Huftalen Papers, Iowa, State Historical Society, Iowa City).

2. The city of Manchester in 1885 had a population of 2,338 (Jackson, *Census of Iowa*), compared to 800 when Emily Hawley first came to Iowa. Many of the frame buildings had been replaced by substantial brick ones, and commerce in agricultural products boomed (*History of Delaware County*, pp. 512–514). The social gap between city and country people described in the works of Iowa writers such as Ruth Suckow and Hamlin Garland is re-flected in the pages of the local Manchester newspaper. In my attempts to find more information on major events in the Gillespies' lives, I read the *Man-chester Press* from 1871 to 1888. No notice was made in the "Local Jottings" column about Henry Gillespie's departure for Adrian College in Michigan, for example, while news of local trips "to the country" of prominent Manchester families like the Congars and Loomises appeared almost weekly.

3. Farm tenant John McGee was at the opposite end of the agricultural economic scale from the Gillespies, who rented out part of their land on shares. In 1880, 22.4 percent of the farms in Delaware County were rented for cash or on shares (Hull, *Census of Iowa for 1880*). The percentage of Iowans renting farms more than doubled between 1860 and 1880, partially in response to the economic recession of the 1870s (Bogue, *From Prairie to Corn Belt*, pp. 57, 65). Having lost his farm to foreclosure, John McGee was moving down the tenure ladder rather than upward in the traditional pattern. Only 12 percent of the men his age were still farm tenants (Cogswell, *Tenure, Nativity and Age*, Table 2.6, p. 35).

4. Adrian College was founded in 1859 by Methodist minister Asa Mahan. This small coeducational college was located in Adrian, Michigan, approximately twenty miles northeast of Emily Hawley's birthplace. According to the Len-awee County history, "The class of students are for the most part from better homes of the middle classes" (Bonner, ed., *Memoirs of Lenawee County*, vol. 1, p. 546).

5. The McGees, Cooks, and Tripps all had children in the school Sarah Gillespie taught, located on Issac McGee's land in section 23 of Coffins Grove Town-ship. Issac McGee was the father of John McGee (Emily's brother-in-law), and Ervin McGee, twenty-one, was one of John's brothers.

6. Robert Sims's first wife had been Lucy Ann Garlick, a cousin of Emily's. Lucy Ann Sims killed her four children and took her own life in 1866.

7. Edmond (? handwriting unclear) Seger, forty-nine, was listed as an insurance agent in the 1880 U.S. census. He lived in Manchester with his wife, Sylva; no children were listed in the household.

8. The Dubuque and Pacific Railroad (now the Illinois Central), which bisected the Gillespie farm, reached Manchester in 1859. James Gillespie's parents, Horace and Lorinda, jointly owned the property until January 1859, when it

was deeded solely to Lorinda. (There was also a brief period in 1858 when a Gilbert Yeoman owned the land.) A woman's rights in the conveyance of jointly held property were not covered in the Iowa code of 1851. Thus Emily Gillespie's hopes for recouping a financial settlement from the railroad at least twenty-five years after the fact were small (Gallaher, *Legal and Political Status*, pp. 86–88).

9. Charles E. Bronson, who studied law in Iowa City, had been an attorney in Manchester since 1866. He had served as state senator (Democratic) from 1877 to 1879 and was currently in law partnership with E. M. Carr (*History of Delaware County*, pp. 514, 569).

10. The accident was reported in the "Home News" section of the *Manchester Press* on October 10, 1884: "Last Friday, while Henry Gillespie, a young man of about eighteen, a son of J. F. Gillespie of Coffins Grove, was at work on the steeple of the new Methodist church, he lost his footing, and he fell from the scaffold on which he and another workman were standing. He first struck on the roof of the church, and went off that to the ground, fortunately striking on a pile of loose lath and rubbish, by which his fall was broken. This doubtless saved his life. He was severely injured on the hip and back of the head, but is doing well and is now thought to be in a fair way to get well. The height from the ground to the scaffold from which he fell, is about seventy-two feet, and he may congratulate himself on having a very fortunate escape."

11. Hial Hawley was referring to his right as husband to inherit the personal property of his wife—if she left no will. (Michigan law since 1855 had given a woman the right to bequeath her own property without her husband's permission. See Motz, *True Sisterhood*, p. 23.) Emily Gillespie, on the other hand, probably considered her mother's notations on the bureau a de facto will that showed her intent to give Emily the memento (see diary entry of May 27, 1884).

12. According to the 1894 Coffins Grove Township map and 1870 census, Benjamin Smith, sixty, lived on a large farm between Henry Baker and the Gillespies.

13. "The reason why I keep a deed of our place" may have been to protect it against James Gillespie's creditors. Historian Mary Ryan remarks, "A married woman's property rights . . . were often used simply as a device to avoid a husband's bankruptcy" (*Womanhood in America*, p. 103). Thus Emily Gillespie's desire when she received the farm deed in 1874 "to keep it free from incumbrance" may have meant James's economic encumbrances, not her own potential ones.

14. Michigan law held children responsible for the support of pauper parents, but

money was collected only from those of "sufficient ability," therefore exempt-
ing Henry Hawley (Motz, *True Sisterhood*, pp. 42–43). As the eldest (and
wealthiest) daughter, Emily Gillespie was the best candidate to support Hial
Hawley. According to Ruth Gallaher's study of Iowa law, "a married woman
is responsible for family expenses if she has property in her own name" (*Legal
and Political Status*, p. 136). If Emily Gillespie deeded back the farm to her
husband, she would have no assets for her father to sue in his quest for
support.

15. Iowa territorial law since 1840 attempted to protect women from involuntary
    alienation of their rights. Judges could order a private hearing with wives
    suspected to be under compulsion from their husbands (Gallaher, *Legal and
    Political Status*, pp. 106ff.). In this case, the lawyer and county officials must
    have felt, despite Emily Gillespie's comments, that she willingly gave her
    husband a deed to the farm. The deed was registered in the county courthouse
    on April 2, 1885. James "paid" Emily $500 for the farm, as she had paid him
    in 1873, a formality which prevented the deed transfer from being interpreted
    as a gift.

16. Frank Mead, twenty-one, who had shown an interest in Sarah for three years,
    lived on a farm with his parents in neighboring Delaware county. He is listed
    in the 1880 census as the eldest son at home.

17. Cora Brook, nineteen, was the sister-in-law of widow Emma Brook and lived
    with her in Manchester.

18. Emily Gillespie first used the term *dropsy* in her diary for her condition on
    May 8th of this year. Dropsy is an excessive accumulation of serum in body
    cavities or tissues.

19. Gillespie was inaccurately quoting lines from John Greenleaf Whittier's ballad
    "Maud Muller" (1854). It is the story of a young farm woman and a wealthy
    judge who have a brief encounter, then realize they must walk their life paths
    separately due to class differences. They each marry and secretly long for the
    other throughout their lives. The poem closes,

    God pity them both! and pity us all
    Who vainly the dreams of youth recall.
    For of all the words of tongue or pen,
    The saddest are these: "It might have been."

20. Belva Lockwood, fifty-five, was a noted feminist lawyer and speaker. She
    earned her law degree at age forty-three and was the first woman lawyer to
    practice before the Supreme Court. She successfully argued cases for equal
    rights to property and child guardianship for women in the District of Colum-

bia. She was also a U.S. presidential nominee of the National Equal Rights party of the Pacific Coast in 1884 and 1888 (Park, "Lockwood, Belva Ann Bennett").

21. There is no other record of the August 8 family violence described retrospectively in this entry. (The diaries of Sarah Gillespie in the family papers skip from August 1, 1886, to January 10, 1887.) However, the family strife did reach the public record. In the August 13, 1886, *Manchester Press* the following notice was printed in the "New Advertisements" section of p. 2:

PUBLIC NOTICE

Notice is hereby given, to all whom it may concern, not to trust any person whatever, on my account, without my written order, as I will pay no debts otherwise contracted in my name.

J. F. Gillespie
Coffin's Grove

Ruth Gallaher said of this practice, "Husbands whose wives left them, whether for good cause or not, frequently attempted to safeguard themselves and punish the wives by publishing notices." However, "if either husband or wife abandoned the other for a year without providing for the family, the other might obtain authority from the district court to administer the property" (*Legal and Political Status*, p. 130). By allowing his wife and children to remain on the property and by occasionally bringing them foodstuffs, James Gillespie probably avoided the charge of desertion. The Iowa Supreme Court still gave the wife common law agency to make contracts in the absence of her husband. Therefore, James's notice may have had no legal authority but did indeed bring the family quarrel into public scrutiny.

22. Magnetic physicians, also known as "magnopaths" and "electropaths," saw the human body as a receptacle and emitter of currents. They recommended application of mild electrical charges for correcting physiological imbalances that caused disease. The book *Medical Common Sense* by electropath Edward B. Foote had been in the Gillespie family library for probably twenty years and was preserved in the family papers by Sarah Gillespie Huftalen.

23. William Henry Huftalen, sixty, was a Manchester pawnbroker and twice a widower (record of ancestry form sent to New England Genealogy Society by Sarah Gillespie Huftalen, March 9, 1942, Huftalen Collection, Iowa State Historical Society, Iowa City).

24. An agreement dated October 13, 1888, between James Gillespie and Henry Hutchinson probably reflects an earlier arrangement between the two men. It gives Hutchinson rental of the farm and lower part of the Gillespie house,

allows James access to the second floor for one year, and is renewable. Henry Hutchinson was described in the 1880 census as a "capitalist" living in Manchester.

25. Sarah Gillespie, diary entry of March 27, 1888.

EIGHT. Emily Hawley Gillespie, Woman

1. Motz, *True Sisterhood*, p. 72.
2. Burchfield and Kerber, eds., *"The Household,"* pp. 44–45.
3. Fink, "'Mom, It's a Losing Proposition,'" p. 29. Fink's primary source for Farm Institute speeches was the *O'Brien County Bell* of February 18, 1897.
4. Diary of Sarah Gillespie.
5. *Woman's Standard* 1, no. 3 (November 1886), cited in Gallaher, *Legal and Political Status*, p. 92.
6. Faragher, *Women and Men on the Overland Trail*, p. 51, draws on several midwestern farming histories for his conclusion. (Sources are listed in ibid., note 46, p. 220.)
7. See Cott, *Bonds of Womanhood*, pp. 59–61, for a discussion of task-oriented versus time-disciplined work; Faragher, *Women and Men on the Overland Trail*, p. 63.
8. Studies of the literature and ideology of Victorian motherhood include classics such as Sklar, *Catharine Beecher* and Douglas, *Feminization of American Culture*. Universalist doctrine on motherhood is discussed in Cott, *Bonds of Womanhood*, p. 87. Ryan's *Cradle of the Middle Class* presents arguments and evidence for the shift from patriarchal to maternal influence philosophies of child socialization.
9. Mrs. H. W. Beecher, *Motherly Talks with Young Housekeepers* (1873), in Juster, *So Sweet to Labor*, pp. 259–260.
10. Alan Lomax, *The Folk Songs of North America in the English Language* (New York: Doubleday, 1960), p. 220, cited in Faragher, *Women and Men on the Overland Trail*, p. 181; Burchfield and Kerber, eds., *"The Household,"* pp. 46, 44, 47.
11. Juster, *So Sweet to Labor*, pp. 209–210; Dr. W. W. Hall, "Health of Farmer's Families," in *Report of the Commissioner of Agriculture for the Year 1862* (Washington, D.C.: U.S. Government Printing Office, 1863), pp. 462–463, in Faragher, *Women and Men on the Overland Trail*, pp. 59–60.

12. Eunice Beecher, *From Dawn to Daylight. The Simple Story of a Western Home*, in Waller, *Reverend Beecher and Mrs. Tilton*, p. 32.

13. Foote, *Medical Common Sense*, p. 303; R. C. Barnum, comp., *The People's Home Library* (Cleveland: R. C. Barnum Company, 1911), cited in Hampsten, *Read This Only to Yourself*, p. 110.

14. Hall, cited in Faragher, *Women and Men on the Overland Trail*, p. 60.

15. Woodward, ed., *Mary Chesnut's Civil War*, pp. 15, 261, 284, 59.

16. Personal interview with Charles Bowden, May 28, 1986; Hampsten, *Read This Only to Yourself*, p. 73.

17. Smith-Rosenberg, "Female World of Love and Ritual"; Hampsten, *Read This Only to Yourself*, pp. 225–226.

18. Allport, *Use of Personal Documents*, p. 109; Faragher, *Women and Men on the Overland Trail*, pp. 204–205; Beauchamp, ed., *A Private War*; Smith-Rosenberg, "Female World of Love and Ritual," pp. 6–7.

19. Emily Hawley letter fragment, n.d., Huftalen Papers, Michigan History Division, Lansing.

20. One other nineteenth-century diary I am aware of records such family alienation after divorce that a daughter cut off all ties with her mother: French, *Emily*. Since this diary only covers one year, the causes of the family situation are undeveloped. Kirkland, *A New Home*, p. 95. See also Tillson, *A Woman's Story*.

21. Garland, *A Son of the Middle Border*, p. 403 and *Main-Travelled Roads*, p. 80; Cather, *O Pioneers!*, p. 124.

22. Nightingale, *Household Prisoner*, p. 91.

23. Waller, *Reverend Beecher and Mrs. Tilton*, pp. 15–16.

24. Rosenblatt, *Bitter, Bitter Tears*, Table 6.2, p. 77.

25. Ibid., p. 133; Corwin R. Snow Diary, Special Collections, University of Iowa, Iowa City.

26. Ryan, *Cradle of the Middle Class*, Table A.5, p. 249; Motz, *True Sisterhood*, p. 117.

27. Rubin, "Midlife and the Changing Dream."

28. Kelley, "At War with Herself."

29. Haller and Haller, *Physician and Sexuality*, discuss purity literature on pp. 124–131. See also Cott, "Passionlessness." Gordon, "Voluntary Motherhood," p. 62.

30. Mitchell, "Four Structures," pp. 385–399.

31. Looking at the Gillespies from a life-stage perspective was suggested by Peter Filene, letter, March 7, 1982; Griswold, *Family and Divorce*, p. 5.

32. For a discussion of prescriptive literature and real-life expectations, see Gris-

wold, *Family and Divorce*, pp. 1–17; Lebsock, *Free Women of Petersburg*, p. 28; Griswold, *Family and Divorce*, p. 13.

33. Serena Ames to George Wright, August 26, 1859, George B. Wright and Family Papers, Minnesota Historical Society, St. Paul, cited in Rothman, *Hands and Hearts*, p. 114.

34. Griswold, *Family and Divorce*, Table 5, p. 28; Gallaher, *Legal and Political Status*, p. 78. The divorce count in the Gillespie diary was done by Dailey in "The Family Farm." U.S. divorce statistics are from O'Neill, "Divorce as a Moral Issue," p. 138; Iowa figures are from Gallaher, *Legal and Political Status*, pp. 77–80.

35. Griffith, "Elizabeth Cady Stanton."

36. Lebsock, *Free Women of Petersburg*, pp. 27–28.

37. Matthiessen, *The James Family*, p. 129.

38. Louis I. Dublin et al., *Length of Life* (New York: Ronald Press, 1949), p. 326, in U.S. Bureau of the Census, *Historical Statistics*, p. 56.

39. Griswold, *Family and Divorce*, Table 15, p. 54. Nineteenth-century writers concerned with health include Beecher, *Letters to the People*, and Mitchell, *Fat and Blood*. Smith-Rosenberg, "Hysterical Woman."

40. Catharine E. Beecher and Harriet Beecher Stowe, *The American Woman's Home* (1869; repr. Hartford, Conn.: Stowe-Day Foundation, 1975), pp. 342–343, cited in Motz, *True Sisterhood*, p. 107.

41. Kelley, *Private Woman, Public Stage*, p. 354.

42. Suzanne Bunkers, paper at session on women's private writings, Modern Languages Association, December 1987.

Conclusion: The Diary as Female Autobiography

1. Mallon, *A Book of One's Own*, p. xvi.

2. Olney, ed., *Autobiography*, p. 11.

3. Mallon, *A Book of One's Own*, p. 210.

4. Moffat and Painter, eds., *Revelations*, introduction.

5. Strouse, *Alice James*.

6. See, for example, Chodorow, *Reproduction of Mothering*; Gilligan, *In a Different Voice*, Juhasz, "Toward a Theory of Form"; Smith-Rosenberg, "Female World of Love and Ritual."

7. I refer here to the framework still powerful in autobiographical criticism set out by Pascal in *Design and Truth in Autobiography*.

8. Hampsten, *Read This Only to Yourself*, pp. 1–28.

9. Cixous, "The Laugh of the Medusa."

10. Faragher, *Women and Men on the Overland Trail*. For a primer on content analysis, see Gordon Allport, *Use of Personal Documents*.

11. Rosenblatt, *Bitter, Bitter Tears*.

12. Douglas, *Feminization of American Culture*.

13. Jelinek, ed. Introduction, *Women's Autobiography*; Spacks, "Reflecting Women" and "Selves in Hiding"; Juhasz, "'Some Deep Old Desk or Capacious Hold-All.'"

14. Aaron, *Inman Diary*, p. 9.

15. Virginia Woolf, *A Writer's Diary*, p. 13, cited in Juhasz, "'Some Deep Old Desk or Capacious Hold All.'"

16. Rosenblatt, *Bitter, Bitter Tears*, p. 107.

17. James Boswell, quoted in Fothergill, *Private Chronicles*, p. 45.

18. Nin, *Novel of the Future*, pp. 161–162.

19. MacKinnon, "Feminism, Marxism, Method and the State."

20. Gilligan, *In a Different Voice*, p. 19.

21. Stone, ed., *American Autobiography*, p. 7.

22. Smith, "On Women's Autobiographies."

23. "Serial autobiography" is Fothergill's term for an extensive diary. See his *Private Chronicles*, pp. 152–192.

24. Ibid., pp. 44–45.

25. Ibid., pp. 12, 33; Mallon, *A Book of One's Own*, p. xvi.

26. See editors' introductory essays in Woodward, ed., *Mary Chesnut's Civil War*, and Arpad, ed., *Sam Curd's Diary*.

27. Bradstreet, "To my dear children."

28. Shea, *Spiritual Autobiography*.

29. Aaron, *Inman Diary*, p. 9.

30. Fothergill, *Private Chronicles*, p. 82

31. See, for example, Catharine Beecher and Harriet Beecher Stowe's *Principles of Domestic Sciences; As Applied to the Duties and Pleasures of the Home* (1870), and Harriet Beecher Stowe's *Uncle Tom's Cabin* (1851).

32. Fothergill, *Private Chronicles*, p. 254

Bibliography

Aaron, Daniel, ed. *The Inman Diary: A Public and Private Confession.* Vol. 1. Cambridge: Harvard University Press, 1985.

Adams, Henry. *The Education of Henry Adams.* 1918; repr. Boston: Houghton Mifflin Company, 1961.

Allen, David Grayson, et al., eds. *Diary of John Quincy Adams.* Cambridge: Harvard University Press, 1981.

Allport, Gordon. *The Use of Personal Documents in Psychological Science.* New York: Social Science Research Council, 1942.

Arpad, Susan S., ed. *Sam Curd's Diary.* Athens: Ohio University Press, 1984.

Bailey, Belle. *A Three-Volume History of Delaware County, Iowa 1834–1934.* Manchester, Iowa: Manchester Press–Democrat–Radio, 1935.

Barnhart, C. L., ed. *The American College Dictionary.* New York: Random House, 1965.

Baym, Nina. *Women's Fiction: A Guide to Novels by and about Women in America, 1820–1870.* Ithaca: Cornell University Press, 1978.

Beauchamp, Virginia Walcott, ed. *A Private War: Letters and Diaries of Madge Preston 1862–67.* New Brunswick: Rutgers University Press, 1987.

Beecher, Catharine. *Letters to the People on Health and Happiness.* New York: Harper and Brothers, 1855.

Berkin, Carol Ruth. "Private Woman, Public Woman: The Contradictions of Charlotte Perkins Gilman." In *Women of America*, ed. Carol Ruth Berkin and Mary Beth Norton. Boston: Houghton Mifflin, 1979.

Bernard, Richard M., and Maris A. Vinovskis. "The Female School Teacher in Antebellum Massachusetts." *Journal of Social History* 10 (March 1977): 332–345.

Blanchard, Rufus. *Discovery and Conquest of the North-west, with the History of Chicago.* Wheaton: R. Blanchard and Company, 1881.

Bogue, Allan C. *From Prairie to Corn Belt: Farming on the Illinois and Iowa Prairies in the Nineteenth Century.* Chicago: University of Chicago Press, 1963.

Bonner, Richard I., ed. *Memoirs of Lenawee County, Michigan.* Madison: Western Historical Association, 1909.

Bowden, Charles. Personal interview. May 28, 1986.

Bradstreet, Anne. "To my dear children." In *The Complete Works of Anne Bradstreet*, ed. Joseph R. McElrath, Jr., and Allan P. Robb. Boston: Twayne Publishers, 1981.

Bree, Germaine. "Autogynography." In *The Southern Review*, ed. James Olney and Lewis P. Simpson. Baton Rouge: Louisiana State University Press, 1986.

Brodie, Fawn M. "Young, Ann Elizabeth Webb." In *Notable American Women*, ed. Edward T. James. Cambridge: Harvard University Press, 1971.

Bunkers, Suzanne L. "'Faithful Friend': Nineteenth-Century American Women's Unpublished Diaries." *Women's Studies International Forum* 10, no. 1 (1987): 7–17.

———. Untitled paper on women's private writings, Modern Language Association Meeting. December 1987.

Burchfield, Robert, and Linda K. Kerber, eds. "*The Household* Conducted by Mrs. Nellie M. Rich." *Palimpsest* 61, no. 2 (March–April 1980): 42–55.

Carroll, Berenice A., ed. *Liberating Women's History*. Urbana: University of Illinois Press, 1976.

Cassara, Ernest, ed. *Universalism in America. A Documentary History*. Boston: Beacon Press, 1971.

Cather, Willa. *O Pioneers!* New York: Houghton Mifflin, 1913.

Catton, Bruce. *The Coming Fury*. Garden City: Doubleday, 1960.

Chambers-Schiller, Lee Virginia. *Liberty, A Better Husband. Single Women in America: The Generations of 1780–1840*. New Haven: Yale University Press, 1984.

Chevigny, Bell Gale. "Daughters Writing: Toward a Theory of Women's Biography." In *Between Women*, ed. Carol Ascher, Louise DeSalvo, and Sara Ruddick. Boston: Beacon Press, 1984.

Chodorow, Nancy. *The Reproduction of Mothering*. Berkeley: University of California Press, 1978.

Chopin, Kate. *The Awakening*. 1899; repr. New York: W. W. Norton, 1976.

Cixous, Hélène. "The Laugh of the Medusa." In *The Signs Reader*, ed. Elizabeth Abel. Chicago: University of Chicago Press, 1982.

Clifford, James, and George E. Marcus, eds. *Writing Culture: The Poetics and Politics of Ethnography*. Berkeley: University of California Press, 1986.

Cogswell, Seddie, Jr. *Tenure, Nativity and Age as Factors in Iowa Agriculture 1850–1880*. Ames: Iowa State University Press, 1975.

Cott, Nancy F. *The Bonds of Womanhood: "Woman's Sphere" in New England, 1780–1835*. New Haven: Yale University Press, 1977.

———. "Passionlessness: An Interpretation of Victorian Sexual Ideology, 1790–1850." *Signs* 4, no. 2 (1978): 219–236.

Dailey, Christie. "The Family Farm: A Case Study of Rural Exchange Networks." Unpublished paper.

Davis, J. E. *Township Plat Book of Delaware County, Iowa*. Chicago: J. E. Davis, 1894.

Degler, Carl N. *At Odds: Women and the Family in America from the Revolution to the Present.* New York: Oxford University Press, 1980.

Douglas, Ann. *The Feminization of American Culture.* New York: Alfred A. Knopf, 1977.

Dublin, Thomas. *Farm to Factory: Women's Letters, 1830–1860.* New York: Columbia University Press, 1981.

————. *Women at Work: The Transformation of Work and Community in Lowell, Massachusetts, 1826–1860.* New York: Columbia University Press, 1979.

Eddy, Rev. Daniel C. *The Three Mrs. Judsons and Other Daughters of the Cross.* Boston: Wentworth, Hewes and Company, 1855.

Everts and Stewart, comps. *The Combination Atlas Map of Lenawee County.* Chicago: Everts and Stewart, 1874.

Faragher, John Mack. *Women and Men on the Overland Trail.* New Haven: Yale University Press, 1979.

Farnsworth, Martha. *Plains Woman,* ed. Marlene Springer and Haskell Springer. Bloomington: Indiana University Press, 1986.

Filene, Peter. Letter to author. March 7, 1982.

Fink, Deborah. "'Mom, It's a Losing Proposition': The Decline of Women's Subsistence Production on Iowa Farms." *North Dakota Quarterly* 52, no. 1 (Winter 1984): 26–33.

Foote, Edward B. *Medical Common Sense.* New York: E. B. Foote, Publisher, 1863.

Fothergill, Robert A. *Private Chronicles: A Study of English Diaries.* London: Oxford University Press, 1974.

French, Emily. *Emily: The Diary of a Hard-Worked Woman,* ed. Janet Lecompte. Lincoln: University of Nebraska Press, 1987.

Gallaher, Ruth A. *Legal and Political Status of Women in Iowa.* Iowa City: State Historical Society of Iowa, 1918.

Garland, Hamlin. *Main-Travelled Roads.* New York: Harper and Row, 1891.

————. *A Son of the Middle Border.* New York: Macmillan, 1917.

Geertz, Clifford. "Thick Description: Toward an Interpretive Theory of Culture." In *The Interpretation of Cultures.* London: Hutchinson and Company, 1975.

Geiger, Susan N. G. "Women's Life Histories: Method and Content." *Signs* 11, no. 2 (Winter 1986): 334–351.

Gillespie, Emily Elizabeth Hawley. Diaries and writings. Papers of Sarah Gillespie Huftalen, Iowa State Historical Society, Iowa City, Iowa.

Gilligan, Carol. *In a Different Voice: Psychological Theory and Women's Development.* Cambridge: Harvard University Press, 1982.

Gitlin, Susan. *Roots of Our Strength.* N.p.: Universalist/Unitarian Pacific Southwest District, 1980.

Gordon, Linda. "Voluntary Motherhood: The Beginnings of Feminist Birth Control Ideas in the United States." In *Clio's Consciousness Raised: New Perspectives on the History of Women*, ed. Mary Hartman and Lois W. Banner. New York: Harper Colophon Books, 1974.

Gordon, Michael. "The Ideal Husband as Depicted in the Nineteenth-Century Marriage Manual." In *The American Male*, ed. Elizabeth H. Pleck and Joseph H. Pleck. Englewood Cliffs, N. J.: Prentice-Hall, 1980.

Griffith, Elizabeth. "Elizabeth Cady Stanton on Marriage and Divorce: Feminist Theory and Domestic Experience." In *Woman's Being, Woman's Place*, ed. Mary Kelley. Boston: G. K. Hall, 1979.

Griswold, Robert L. *Family and Divorce in California, 1850–1890: Victorian Illusions and Everyday Realities*. Albany: SUNY Press, 1982.

Haller, John S., and Robin M. Haller. *The Physician and Sexuality in Victorian America*. New York: W. W. Norton, 1977.

Hampsten, Elizabeth. *Read This Only to Yourself: The Private Writings of Midwestern Women, 1880–1910*. Bloomington: Indiana University Press, 1982.

Hawley, Amos H. "The Population of Michigan 1840 to 1960: An Analysis of Growth, Distribution, and Composition." *Michigan Governmental Studies*, no. 19. Ann Arbor: University of Michigan Press, 1949.

A History of Delaware County, Iowa. Chicago: Western Historical Company, 1878.

Hoffman, Leonore, and Margo Culley, eds. *Women's Personal Narratives: Essays in Criticism and Pedagogy*. New York: Modern Language Association, 1985.

Hogaboam, James J. *The Bean Creek Valley*. Hudson, Mich.: Jas. M. Scarritt, Publisher, 1876.

Huftalen, Sarah Gillespie. Papers. Iowa State Historical Society, Iowa City, Iowa.

Huftalen, Mrs. Sarah. Papers. Michigan History Division, Lansing, Mich.

Hull, John A. T. *Census of Iowa for 1880*. Des Moines: Geo. E. Roberts, State Printer, 1883.

Jackson, Frank D. *Census of Iowa for the Year 1885*. Des Moines: George E. Roberts, State Printer, 1885.

Jeffrey, Julie Roy. *Frontier Women: The Trans-Mississippi West, 1840–1880*. New York: Hill and Wang, 1979.

Jelinek, Estelle, ed. *Women's Autobiography: Essays in Criticism*. Bloomington: Indiana University Press, 1980.

Johnson, Michael P. "Mary Boykin Chesnut's Autobiography and Biography: A Review Essay." *Journal of Southern History* 47, no. 4 (November 1981): 585–592.

Joyce, Rosemary O. *A Woman's Place: The Life History of a Rural Ohio Grandmother*. Columbus: Ohio State University Press, 1983.

Juhasz, Suzanne. "'Some Deep Old Desk or Capacious Hold-All': Form and Women's Autobiography." *College English* 6 (February 1978): 663–668.

———. "Toward a Theory of Form in Feminist Autobiography." In *Women's Autobiography*, ed. Estelle Jelinek. Bloomington: Indiana University Press, 1980.

Juster, Norman. *So Sweet to Labor: Rural Women in America 1865–1895.* New York: Viking Press, 1979.

Kehrli, Wilma. Letter to author. April 4, 1987.

Kelley, Mary. "At War with Herself: Harriet Beecher Stowe as Woman in Conflict within the Home." In *Woman's Being, Woman's Place*, ed. Mary Kelley. Boston: G. K. Hall, 1979.

———. *Private Woman, Public Stage: Literary Domesticity in Nineteenth-Century America.* New York: Oxford University Press, 1984.

Kerber, Linda K. "Separate Spheres, Female Worlds, Woman's Place: The Rhetoric of Women's History." *Journal of American History* 75, no. 1 (June 1988): 9–39.

———. *Women of the Republic: Intellect and Ideology in Revolutionary America.* Chapel Hill: University of North Carolina Press, 1980.

Kirkland, Caroline M. *A New Home—Who'll Follow?* 1839; repr. New Haven: College and University Press, 1965.

Langness, Lewis L., and Gelya Frank. *Lives: An Anthropological Approach to Biography.* Novato, Calif.: Chandler and Sharp Publishers, 1981.

Lebsock, Suzanne. *The Free Women of Petersburg: Status and Culture in a Southern Town 1784–1860.* New York: W. W. Norton, 1984.

Lensink, Judy Nolte. "The Pioneer Woman's Life: A Separate Reality." Missouri Valley Historical Association Meeting, Omaha. January 1979.

Lensink, Judy Nolte, Christine M. Kirkham and Karen Pauba Witzke. "'My Only Confidant'—The Life and Diary of Emily Hawley Gillespie," *Annals of Iowa,* 45, No. 4 (Spring 1980): 288–312.

Lerner, Gerda. "New Approaches to the Study of Women in American History" and "Placing Women in History: A 1975 Perspective." In *Liberating Women's History*, ed. Berenice A. Carroll. Urbana: University of Illinois Press, 1976.

Longsworth, Polly. *Austin and Mabel: The Amherst Affair and Love Letters of Austin Dickinson and Mabel Loomis Todd.* New York: Farrar, Straus and Giroux, 1984.

MacKinnon, Catharine. "Feminism, Marxism, Method and the State: An Agenda for Theory." *Signs* 8 (Summer 1983): 635–658.

Mallon, Thomas. *A Book of One's Own: People and Their Diaries.* New York: Ticknor and Fields, 1984.

Mandelbaum, David G. "The Study of Life History: Gandhi." *Current Anthropology* 14 (June 1973): 177–206.

Matthews, William. *American Diaries. An Annotated Bibliography of American Diaries Written prior to the Year 1861*. Boston: J. S. Canner and Company, 1959.

Matthiessen, F. O. *The James Family: A Group Biography*. New York: Alfred A. Knopf, 1961.

"The Medina Tragedy." *Tecumseh Herald*, October 11, 1866, p. 1.

Mitchell, Juliet. "Four Structures in a Complex Unity." In *Liberating Women's History*, ed. Berenice A. Carroll. Urbana: University of Illinois Press, 1976.

Mitchell, S. Weir. *Fat and Blood and How to Make Them*. Philadelphia: J. B. Lippincott, 1877.

Moffat, Mary Jane, and Charlotte Painter, eds. *Revelations: Diaries of Women*. New York: Random House, 1974.

Mohr, James C. *Abortion in America*. New York: Oxford University Press, 1978.

―――, ed. *The Cormany Diaries: A Northern Family in the Civil War*. Pittsburgh: University of Pittsburgh Press, 1982.

―――. Letter to the author. February 27, 1987.

Morris, Richard B., ed. *Encyclopedia of American History*. New York: Harper and Brothers, 1953.

Mott, Frank Luther. *A History of American Magazines. Vol. II: 1850–1865*. Cambridge: Harvard University Press, 1938.

―――. *A History of American Magazines. Vol. III: 1865–1885*. Cambridge: Harvard University Press, 1938.

Motz, Marilyn Ferris. *True Sisterhood: Michigan Women and Their Kin 1820–1920*. Albany: SUNY Press, 1983.

Myres, Sandra, ed. *Ho for California! Women's Overland Diaries from the Huntington Library*. San Marino: Huntington Library, 1980.

Nelson, David T., ed. *The Diary of Elizabeth Koren, 1853–1855*. Minneapolis: Norwegian-American Historical Association, 1955.

Nightingale, Florence, *The Household Prisoner*. In *Strong-Minded Women and Other Lost Voices from Nineteenth-Century England*, ed. Jane Horowitz Murray. New York: Pantheon Books, 1982.

Nin, Anaïs. *The Novel of the Future*. New York: Collier Books, 1968.

Noun, Louise. *Strong-Minded Women*. Ames: Iowa State University Press, 1969.

Olney, James, ed. *Autobiography: Essays Theoretical and Critical*. Princeton: Princeton University Press, 1980.

O'Neill, William L. "Divorce as a Moral Issue: A Hundred Years of Controversy." In *"Remember the Ladies": New Perspectives on Women in American History*, ed. Carol V. R. George. Syracuse: Syracuse University Press, 1975.

Park, Frances Fenton. "Lockwood, Belva Ann Bennett." *DAB* (1946).

Pascal, Roy. *Design and Truth in Autobiography*. Cambridge: Harvard University Press, 1960.

Philips, Susan, Susan Steele, and Christine Tanz, eds. *Language, Sex and Gender in Comparative Perspective.* Cambridge: Harvard University Press, 1987.

Potter, R. G. "Birth Intervals: Structure and Change." *Population Studies* 17 (1963): 155–166.

Quist, Oval. "Universalism and Unitarianism in Iowa, 1830–1970." Unpublished typescript. Iowa State Historical Society, Iowa City, Iowa.

Rich, Adrienne. *Diving into the Wreck.* New York: W. W. Norton, 1973.

Riley, Glenda. *Frontierswomen: The Iowa Experience.* Ames: Iowa State University Press, 1981.

Rosenblatt, Paul C. *Bitter, Bitter Tears: Nineteenth-Century Diarists and Twentieth-Century Grief Theories.* Minneapolis: University of Minnesota Press, 1983.

———. Letter to the author. December 22, 1983.

Rothman, Ellen. *Hands and Hearts: A History of Courtship in America.* New York: Basic Books, 1984.

Rubin, Lillian. "Midlife and the Changing Dream." Midlife-Crisis? Conference, University of Arizona, Tucson, May 9, 1983.

Ryan, Mary P. *Cradle of the Middle Class: The Family in Oneida County, New York, 1790–1865.* Cambridge: Cambridge University Press, 1981.

———. *Womanhood in America from Colonial Times to the Present.* 2nd ed. New York: New Viewpoints, 1979.

Sage, Leland. *A History of Iowa.* Ames: Iowa State University Press, 1974.

Sanford, Mollie Dorsey. *Mollie: The Journal of Mollie Dorsey Sanford in Nebraska and Colorado Territories, 1857–1866.* 1959; repr. Lincoln: Bison Press, 1976.

Saum, Lewis O. "Death in the Popular Mind of Pre–Civil War America." *American Quarterly* 26, no. 5 (December 1974): 477–495.

Schlissel, Lillian. *Women's Diaries of the Westward Journey.* New York: Schocken Books, 1982.

Sewell, Richard B. *The Life of Emily Dickinson.* New York: Farrar, Straus and Giroux, 1974.

Shea, Daniel B. *Spiritual Autobiography in Early America.* Princeton: Princeton University Press, 1968.

Sicherman, Barbara. "Review Essay: American History." *Signs* 1, no. 2 (Winter 1975): 461–485.

Sklar, Kathryn Kish. *Catharine Beecher: A Study in American Domesticity.* New York: W. W. Norton, 1973.

Smith, Daniel Scott. "Family Limitation, Sexual Control, and Domestic Feminism in Victorian America." In *Clio's Consciousness Raised: New Perspectives on the History of Women,* ed. Mary Hartman and Lois W. Banner. New York: Harper Colophon Books, 1974.

———. "Parental Power and Marriage Patterns: An Analysis of Historical Trends in Hingham, Massachusetts." *Journal of Marriage and the Family* 35 (1973): 419–428.

Smith, Daniel Scott, and Michael Hindus. "Premarital Pregnancy in America, 1640–1971: An Overview and Interpretation." *Journal of Interdisciplinary History* 5, no. 4 (Spring 1975): 537–570.

Smith, Lillian. "On Women's Autobiographies." *Southern Exposure* (1962): 48–49.

Smith, Thomas S. "A Martyr for Prohibition." *Palimpsest* 62 (November–December 1981): 186–193.

Smith-Rosenberg, Carroll. *Disorderly Conduct: Visions of Gender in Victorian America*. New York: Alfred A. Knopf, 1985.

———. "The Female World of Love and Ritual: Relations between Women in Nineteenth-Century America." *Signs* 1 (Autumn 1975): 1–29.

———. "The Hysterical Woman: Sex Roles and Role Conflict in Nineteenth-Century America." *Social Research* 39 (Winter 1972): 652–678.

Snow, Corwin. Diary. Special Collections, University of Iowa, Iowa City, Iowa.

Spacks, Patricia Meyer. "Reflecting Women." *Yale Review* 63 (1973): 26–42.

———. "Selves in Hiding." In *Women's Autobiography: Essays in Criticism*, ed. Estelle Jelinek. Bloomington: Indiana University Press, 1980.

Stanley, Liz, ed. *The Diaries of Hannah Cullwick*. London: Virago Press, 1984.

Stone, Albert E., ed. *The American Autobiography*. Englewood Cliffs, N. J.: Prentice-Hall, 1981.

Strouse, Jean. *Alice James: A Biography*. Boston: Houghton Mifflin, 1980.

Suckow, Ruth. *Country People*. New York: Alfred A. Knopf, 1924.

Thorne, Barrie, and Nancy Henley, eds. *Language and Sex*. Rowley, Mass.: Newbury House Press, 1975.

Throne, Mildred. "A Population Study of an Iowa County in 1850." *Iowa Journal of History* 57 (1959): 305–330.

T'ien, Yuan H. "A Demographic Aspect of Interstate Variations in American Fertility, 1800–1860." In *Birth Rates of the White Population in the United States, 1800–1860: An Economic Study*, ed. Yasuba Yasukichi. Baltimore: Johns Hopkins University Press, 1962.

Tillson, Mrs. Christiana. *A Woman's Story of Pioneer Illinois*. Chicago: Lakeside Classics, 1919.

Unruh, John D. *The Plains Across: The Overland Emigrants and the Trans-Mississippi West, 1840–1860*. Urbana: University of Illinois Press, 1979.

U.S. Bureau of the Census. *Eighth Census of the United States, Lenawee Township*. Microfilm M653, Reel 551.

———. *Historical Statistics of the United States, Colonial Times to 1970*. Part 1. Washington, D.C.: U. S. Government Printing Office, 1975.

————. *Ninth Census, Volume I: Statistics of the Population of the United States.* Washington, D.C.: U. S. Government Printing Office, 1872.

————. *Statistics of the Population of the United States at the Tenth Census.* Vol. 1. Washington, D.C.: U. S. Government Printing Office, 1883.

————. "Universalist Church. Unitarians. Statistics, Denominational History, Doctrine and Organization." In *Census of Religious Bodies.* Washington, D.C.: U. S. Government Printing Office, 1928.

U.S. Department of Agriculture. *Agricultural Census, 1870.* Schedule 2, Coffins Grove Township. Iowa State Historical Society, Iowa City, Iowa.

————. *Agricultural Census, 1880.* Schedule 3, Coffins Grove Township. Iowa State Historical Society, Iowa City, Iowa.

Walker, Alice. "Finding Celie's Voice." *Ms.* (December 1985): 72.

Wall, Joseph F. *Iowa: A Bicentennial History.* New York: W. W. Norton, 1978.

Waller, Altina L. *Reverend Beecher and Mrs. Tilton.* Amherst: University of Massachusetts Press, 1982.

Watson, Lawrence C., and Maria-Barbara Watson-Franke. *Interpreting Life Histories. An Anthropological Inquiry.* New Brunswick: Rutgers University Press, 1985.

Welter, Barbara. "The Cult of True Womanhood: 1820–1860." *American Quarterly* 18, no. 2 (Summer 1966): 151–174.

Whittier, John Greenleaf. *The Complete Poetical Works of John Greenleaf Whittier.* Boston: Houghton, Mifflin and Company, 1880.

Wilder, Joseph Carleton. "Politics and History: A Study of the Dialectical in Raymond Aron's Philosophy of History." Ph.D. dissertation, University of Notre Dame, 1986.

Woodhull and Claflin's Weekly. December 30, 1871; March 2, 1872; December 12, 1874.

Woodward, C. Vann, ed. *Mary Chesnut's Civil War.* New Haven: Yale University Press, 1981.

Index